Hold It Real Still

HOLD IT REAL STILL

Clint Eastwood, Race,
and the Cinema of the American West

Lawrence P. Jackson

Johns Hopkins University Press
Baltimore

© 2022 Johns Hopkins University Press
All rights reserved. Published 2022
Printed in the United States of America on acid-free paper
2 4 6 8 9 7 5 3 1

Johns Hopkins University Press
2715 North Charles Street
Baltimore, Maryland 21218-4363
www.press.jhu.edu

Library of Congress Cataloging-in-Publication Data

Names: Jackson, Lawrence Patrick, author.
Title: Hold it real still : Clint Eastwood, race, and the cinema of the American West / Lawrence P. Jackson.
Description: Baltimore : Johns Hopkins University Press, 2022. | Includes bibliographical references and index.
Identifiers: LCCN 2021045395 | ISBN 9781421444130 (hardcover) | ISBN 9781421444123 (ebook)
Subjects: LCSH: Eastwood, Clint, 1930– —Criticism and interpretation. | Western films—History and criticism. | Race in motion pictures. | Black people in motion pictures.
Classification: LCC PN1995.9.W4 J33 2022 | DDC 791.43/6278—dc23/eng/20220318
LC record available at https://lccn.loc.gov/2021045395

A catalog record for this book is available from the British Library.

Special discounts are available for bulk purchases of this book. For more information, please contact Special Sales at specialsales@jh.edu.

*To my Mom and Dad, my sons Nathaniel and Mitchell,
my friend Christian Allen, and the Saponi,
wherever they may be*

CONTENTS

INTRODUCTION 1

1
Black Representations in the Western 10

2
The Good, the Bad and the Ugly and Critique of the Colonial Aftermath 41

3
"That Damn War": *The Outlaw Josey Wales* and Reframing the Civil War 79

4
"Hold It Real Still": Black Containment and Structures of Inequality in *The Outlaw Josey Wales* 106

5
"Their Slaves, If Any They Have, Are Hereby Declared Free Men": *Ride with the Devil* and the Contraband as Decorative Adjunct 130

6
"I Am That One in Ten Thousand": *Django Unchained* and the Black Exceptional State 175

7
"Why Don't They Kill Us?" *Django Unchained* and the Politics of Deadly Force 207

CONCLUSION
The Return of the Native 227

Acknowledgments 245
Notes 249
Index 289

Hold It Real Still

Introduction

> We are a nation that worships the frontier tradition, and our heroes are those who champion justice through violent retaliation against injustice.
> —Martin Luther King Jr., *Why We Can't Wait* (1964)

> In the evening I went out to a movie, a picture of frontier life with heroic Indian fighting and struggles against flood, storm and forest fire, with the out-numbered settlers winning each engagement; an epic of wagon trains rolling ever westward. I forgot myself (although there was no one like me taking part in the adventures) and left the dark room in a lighter mood. But that night I dreamed of my grandfather and woke depressed.
> —Ralph Ellison, *Invisible Man* (1952)

In 2013, I lived in Bouaké, a central city in the West African nation Côte d'Ivoire. I worked as a professor in the Department of English at Alassane Outtara University. My job presented challenges different from those in the American universities where I had taught, challenges stemming particularly from colonialism and its aftermath. Before leaving the United States, I had grasped that it would be impossible to circulate English-language books and that students with their own personal computers and American-style internet access, let alone privileges at the exclusive internet service providers and academic platforms, would be a genuine rarity. But civil wars in 2004 and 2011 had destroyed portions of the campus; even in the library, there was no ready supply of books. In the cluster of student computers at a building funded by the US embassy, there was only intermittent internet access and about two hundred books I'd brought with me from the United States. The embassy-supplied volumes emphasized entrepreneurship and Euro-American contributions to the body of ideas behind democratic governance and individual liberty. To me, they seemed outdated and pedantic, like the American officials I met in country. The students' campus life, which in the past had been connected to political parties that were either banned or discouraged from organizing, did not have the carefree dimension of some of their American counterparts. Campus administrators kept the dormitories shuttered, and it was, in any case, far less expensive for students to take a room in town. Advanced students like the ones I taught, who had studied English for five or six years at the collegiate level, often traveled from remote parts of the country to attend classes, sometimes held over a long weekend. Half of the regular teachers lived in the coastal metropolis Abidjan, about five hours away by car. Ironically, while the classrooms were crowded and double-booked, the campus itself often seemed deserted.

I decided that a film course would be an effective way to surmount the hurdle of not being able to rely on books. I thought that films could offer students a vehicle for exploring their assumptions about Western power and their own ideals about upward mobility and their national future. I decided to confront the notion of America as a colonial innocent, an exception, a nation that was believed to have created itself outside of the raw brutality of European colonialism and imperialism. What were the overriding representations of a country that contemporary African people could imagine themselves and their children being favorably treated by?

With all this in mind, I designed a course on American western films as the centerpiece of my American Studies curriculum. The class got under way with D. W. Griffith's *The Birth of a Nation*, moving on to Gilberto "Gillo" Pontecorvo's *The Battle of Algiers*, and Sergio Leone's *The Good, the Bad and the Ugly*. The centerpiece was a close examination of Clint Eastwood's *The Outlaw Josey Wales*.

With a population of about a half a million, Bouaké was home to the university and its twenty thousand students, a train station, a large hospital, a water treatment plant, and an efficient electric grid. There were two football stadiums, several sprawling public markets, boulangeries, Moroccan- and Mauritanian-run electronics shops, and a bookstore owned and run by a French woman. Groups of men read the newspapers, mounted on tag boards, outside the bookshops in the afternoon, and other groups of men washed their hands and feet from plastic kettles and kneeled in prayer on the street corners. The city had been a headquarters of the rebellion during the 2004 civil war and had been bombed by Sukhoi jets, leaving a collapsed building in the center of downtown and a disabled French light tank. Near the Ivoirian homeland of the Baoulé people, Bouaké has been a long-standing commercial hub, much of the trade originating in the massive coastal metropolis of Abidjan and being redirected to the inland cities of Mali and Burkina Faso.

After colonialism officially ended in the 1950s, the country did not make brash strides toward independence, choosing to distinguish itself with the slave trading–era name "Ivory Coast" after it was no longer a part of the large configuration "French West Africa." In 1961, the radical West Indian psychiatrist Frantz Fanon ridiculed the lack of aggressiveness among Côte d'Ivoire's leaders with the one-liner, "They decolonize at such a pace that they force independence on Houphouët-Boigny."[1] Félix Houphouët-Boigny held the presidency and led the nation for more than thirty years (from 1960 to 1993), his crowning achievement the construction of the world's largest basilica in the capital, Yamoussoukro.

When socialist Ghanaian president Kwame Nkrumah was overthrown, his coup plotters planned and staged their assault in the more conservative and Western-friendly next-door neighbor Côte d'Ivoire. Like my colleagues at Howard University in Washington, DC, in the 1990s, uncomfortable with the world of our students such as Ta-Nehisi Coates, my peers in the Department of English only reluctantly discussed French colonialism and its radiant fissures that were shaping their lives. Though the most personally acute tensions seemed to collect around ethnic group struggles, which no one discussed openly, virtually everyone that I came across seemed deferential to Europeans.

The compatibility with neocolonial values spilled over into broadly antihumanist or authoritarian rhetoric. When I lived there, the national minister of education made public remarks to the effect that courses in literature were unwarranted at the college level. National traditions, culture, history, and values could be learned in the village. Our literature faculty attempted to conduct a forum to dispute this notion, but university officials refused to permit the use of classrooms to air the debate. It made obvious sense that colonial education and its aftermath had little to say about the slave trade or the lives of Africans in the Americas, even though Bouaké itself had been an entrepôt for the overland coffles that force-marched abducted Africans westward to ships that would carry them to slavery during the seventeenth, eighteenth, and nineteenth centuries.

The unspoken relation between a country like Côte d'Ivoire, ravaged during the slave trade and the colonial aftermath, and the United States was louder at some times than others. Alassane Outtara, the sitting president of Côte d'Ivoire, had studied for all of his degrees in Philadelphia and worked at the World Bank, and his ethnic group, the largely Muslim Senufo, was in power. Yet the American Western giant was different in important ways from the French colonial power that knotted groups of Ivoirians on the street felt had violently overthrown a democratically elected government headed by Laurent Gbagbo, Outtara's predecessor. Gbagbo, a history professor understood as something of a Pan-Africanist, had been replaced in a violent struggle by not only a traditional foe but specifically by an arch advocate of the neoliberal policies of the International Monetary Fund and World Bank (and also of conservative education ministers). As of this writing, Gbagbo is being held by the International Criminal Court at The Hague in the Netherlands for war crimes committed during 2011.

One fall afternoon before class began, I walked downtown from my neighborhood. Walking long distances is definitively considered the poor man's occupation. Working people share taxis or motorcycles to get around, and the upper classes have their own vehicles and security guards. On reaching the Place de Paix, a public field at a crossroads with an obligatory bronze statue of President Houphouët-Boigny, I encountered a man wearing stained but richly embroidered brocade. A new road was being installed in preparation for a visit from the nation's president, and as I walked to the center of the city, the man trod unsteadily beside me along the freshly torn-up route. Bantering loudly, the stranger introduced himself as Baoufelé. I have a light complexion and, unlike other Ivoirians I encountered at markets and restaurants and the maquis, the man on the road speedily adduced that I was an African American, in some way a sort of distant relative, returned to West Africa. Baoufelé talked about his origins in Guinea and his travels around West Africa.

I knew that Baoufelé wanted a few hundred CFA (the local currency), but I resisted being dunned. I offered to buy him food, since he seemed drunkenly loquacious, but he refused the customary meal from a street vendor, a plastic bag of ground cassava called *attiéké*. When we came in sight of some police officers, he dropped behind me and moved away. I stopped to see a friend, did some simple shopping, then took another route home, only to find my ungainly ambassador, an hour later, delighted to see me in the middle of a road parallel to the one where we had had our first encounter. I thought resignedly then that our fates were connected.

Proving himself to me, he dipped into his deep pockets and produced his identity card and other epistolary valuables, sealed in protective plastic, and continued to spill over about his life and travels. Such as I could in halting French, I engaged him in building out some of the dimensions of Pan-Africanism, a conversation that I inevitably pursued with men of my same age cohort. I understood that this was an ideological relation, based not on our shared lives as children of the 1960s or our gender or language. We had no shared relation out of wealth, education, or nationality. Instead, I groped forward into a place that we had both read about, had heard discussed, and might have sentimentally adored, and that also could be organized around our resistance to, or resentment of, colonialism. Even in the places where our sense of Pan-African futures might have been based on concrete acts, writing for newspapers or serving in rebel groups—whatever we might consider tangible resistance to the material practices of colonial forces—we still privileged an imaginary relation that transcended national borders and occupied the realm of the intangible. It was something that we had in common with Samory Touré, Bob Marley, and Ché Guevara, the most popular icons on the tee shirts worn by teenagers at the marketplace.

As I slipped him a 250 CFA coin, clandestinely so that I wouldn't be announced to the world as an easy mark, he delivered his final pronouncement: *"Clint Eastwood, c'est mon père* [that's my father]*!"*

During our conversation, we had obviously referred to such African notables as Guinean president Sekou Touré, Houphouët-Boigny, the nineteenth-century militant anticolonialist Samory Touré and Burkina Faso's revolutionary socialist president Thomas Sankara, but some unexpected force redirected my companion to another universal signifier of style and mythic power. At the same time, Baoufelé's notion of descent through Clint Eastwood was precisely the ribbon tying together a global conversation about race, ethnicity, slavery, colonialism, and commercial exploitation.[2]

What series of logics and constructs would fasten Eastwood's name to a phenomenon of kinship, a symbol of affinity in a transnational encounter in the middle of Côte d'Ivoire between a Guinean migrant living in the aftermath of colonialism and an African American traveler to Africa, who was more typically living in the aftermath of racial segregation? Obviously, I would know Eastwood as an actor, but I would also know him as the historical man who embodied the sum of his onscreen roles, specifically the films that feature him as a squinty-eyed, gun-slinging assassin. At the heart of Baoufelé's comment, I was expected to understand something about masculine survival tactics, intrepidness, and stylized displays of lethal force.

If Michael Jackson and Bob Marley are the global pop culture reference points tying many Africans to the Western Hemisphere, perhaps Eastwood has more than one way of getting to Africa as well. On the classic 1993 hip-hop album Dr. Dre's *The Chronic*, Dre's protégé Snoop Dogg (Calvin Broadus) raps, "I'm the maniac in black Mr. Snoop Eastwood." In the tough, politically relevant, and sometimes deadly competition of ranking musician in Jamaica, the dance-hall reggae performer Joseph Winston Sterling assumes the stage name "Josey Wales." That the rapper and dance-hall reggae star attest to the toughness of their fictional onstage badman by partly personifying the real-life actor and director Clint Eastwood, as well as one of his most famous fictional creations, shows that Eastwood's aura extends beyond the boundaries of his individual screen roles to encompass the totality of his real-life person. But more obviously, the popular cultural borrowing testifies to the unique strength of Eastwood as a symbol of power, even in hypermasculine Black culture (both Broadus and Sterling have been involved in high-profile shootings, which have seemingly enhanced their celebrity), and exactly at the pivot of hip-hop's dramatic vaulting in circulation from domestic to global arena.

Eastwood's name invoked a power that most men I spoke to in Africa openly sought. Embedded within this male symbol was a fundamental vision of Americanness, a unique power harnessed to the nation-state that men would claim shamelessly and seek connection to. Rather than resisting American might or risking a confrontation with its maneuverings—economically, militarily, or politically—it was always better to be on the side of anticipating and joining its force.

This book describes Eastwood and the western film's relation to discussions of race and imperial power during the era of Eastwood's consolidation of his stature as cultural icon. The book ponders how an actor closely associated with an avant-garde, anticolonialist discourse of "spaghetti" western cinema, which featured him prominently, reversed himself in the second half of the 1970s and created an important film that had at its heart the fantasy of Black erasure from the national life that was absent from more formidably racist films, like David Wark Griffith's 1915 feature *The Birth of a Nation*. This threat of removal and disappearance was always countered with the specious remedy of color-blind false equivalence that suited the emerging market state form of socioeconomic organization: neoliberalism.

Fascinatingly, no matter how narrowly Griffith's film was ideologically directed, Black people, played by white actors in blackface, and African American actors were integral to the film. Probably Griffith could not have imagined a film engaging centrally with the Civil War and its aftermath without Black people in it. Sixty years later, Eastwood's requiem vision of America in the era of the Civil War had become radically different. At the moment directly following the purported gains of the civil rights movement, Eastwood read a novel by a white supremacist and determined to create a Civil War tale removing the weighty decision to eliminate chattel slavery as a significant issue from his film, a maneuver reminiscent of the song "The Night They Drove Old Dixie Down," written by The Band's Canadian songwriter Robbie Robertson in 1969 and sung by Levon Helms, the group's Arkansan drummer.

Following the success of Eastwood's film, we see repeated gestures of erasure that, with minor exceptions, continue to be rigidly enforced at least through the election of Barack Obama and him and his all-Black family living in the White House.[3] Even Leone's western in Spain had included Blacks; legendary western director John Ford, a child of Irish immigrants, had, as early as 1939's *Stagecoach*, incorporated nonwhite characters and, by the 1960s, had created the Black western hero Woody Strode.

The Outlaw Josey Wales created more than just a mythology of the Civil War, sentimentalizing the Confederacy less than a decade after the murder of Martin Luther King Jr. When the film was released, it actually revived the western film genre, which had flagged with the lessening likelihood of war with the Soviet Union, and it was cannily used to harness the emerging domestic social antimonies created by the American civil rights movement.[4] On the domestic front, the election by 1975 of several hundred African American politicians signaled precisely such a transformative energy. The film collected the signs for a symbolic unity that helped to obscure class differences among whites and to unify them for a particularly ugly decade that followed, the 1980s. The erasure of Black Americans from the cinematic terrain helped to create in the American imaginary a pure space of the West that was untouched by the contemporary problems of injustice and inequality that would be dramatically exacerbated.

In the 1980s, it was key that the Welfare State of the Franklin D. Roosevelt era, which reached its peak as the Warfare state by the middle 1940s,[5] should not be merely dismantled but ideologically repudiated. Ronald Reagan was known for his attacks against unions and his adherence to a credo of deregulation and getting tough against his own target, the "welfare queen." By reinforcing in more and more potent forms—the genre of the western and its historic cold war ideological work, the lethal white male code hero who works from the pure Abrahamic moral code of vengeance, and the tactic of erasing the troubling signifiers of injustice—the film prepared an American public to imagine African Americans as unworthy of any state benefits at all, from the educational system to the police department to the municipal hospital emergency system. Eastwood's film, which rewrote the myths of America as it evolved from a coercively punitive labor state, is an emphatic mass culture product in this regard and, in its own way, as ambitious as *The Birth of a Nation*. In the immediate aftermath of the civil rights movement, Eastwood would redeem the Confederacy in general; more precisely, he would recuperate a group more horrific than the Ku Klux Klan. He would in fact create a normative role in the conscious of contemporary Americans for white supremacist terrorist groups.

Chapter One, "Black Representations in the Western," explains the rise of Clint Eastwood as a cultural icon. It traces the western film genre as an ideological vehicle back to its origins following the Civil War, spotlighting Eastwood's predecessor, John Wayne, whose movie roles crossed over into his life as a public hero-figure. How did Wayne perform complex liberal roles during the Cold War that Eastwood would alter and transform for Americans after the defeat in Vietnam?

Chapter Two, "*The Good, the Bad and the Ugly* and Critique of the Colonial Aftermath," examines the Sergio Leone film focusing on the dynamic interplay between Eastwood's hero "Blondie" and Eli Wallach's extraordinary portrait of the Native "Tuco." The chapter uses the ideas of social death and fungibility to investigate the two central characters' many shared scenes, especially the requisite understanding of African slavery as a critical circuit in their colonial relation.

Chapters Three and Four historicize Eastwood's classic film *The Outlaw Josey Wales*, especially the key canard that emerges during the transformative moment as Eastwood-the-western-film-star becomes an active director of American cultural values with his feature film: the total evacuation of Blacks from the slavescape and memoryscape of Missouri and Texas, key geographies of the Civil War. Eastwood's film delivers direct allegorical references to the budding "reverse racism" political philosophy, the implicit cornerstone of the *Bakke* decision by the US Supreme Court in 1978.[6]

Chapter Five, "'Their Slaves, If Any They Have, Are Hereby Declared Free Men': *Ride with the Devil* and the Contraband as Decorative Adjunct," explores the unique vision of immigrant director Ang Lee, who returns the western to Civil War–era Missouri and reinserts Black presence on the field of battle. Using the gifted Black actor Jeffrey Wright, Lee proposes a slaveholding aristocracy giving way to a West of immigrants and the formerly enslaved.[7] But Lee's film also revels nostalgically in the mid-twentieth-century racial liberalism of John Ford and John Wayne.

Chapters Six and Seven analyze *Django Unchained*, the most commercially successful western of all time, written and directed by Quentin Tarantino. The film emphasizes the repurposing of western discourse in the era of the "War on Terror" and the confluence between the anxiety connected to never-ending attack by a suicidal enemy and the exceptionalist narratives connected to the presidency of Barack Obama. Two moves are crucial. First, the filmmaker creates a movie ostensibly of a Black hero but one who is doubly surrogated, first by his name and then by a series of masters. Second, the explicitly ahistorical narrative introduces a Black hero who defeats his personal enslavement while leaving the regime of hyperexploitation fully intact.

The book concludes with "The Return of the Native," a brief discussion of two films that bring together the primary themes discussed in earlier chapters: Eastwood's *American Sniper* and the Coen brothers' *No Country for Old Men*. Here we can see the ongoing work of the Eastwood film archetypes, finely braiding the cowboy and military hero in the film *American Sniper*. The deadly jingoism displaced by the Eastwood archetype is resisted by the satirist filmmakers Joel and Ethan Coen, who reinvent the Indigenous villain as a nightmare (seemingly connected to a Cold War threat in the original Cormac McCarthy novel) that appropriates as his ontological mode the death relation or the sovereignty of death.

From D. W. Griffith and John Ford to Eastwood, and later (through Eastwood's cinematic influence) Ang Lee and Quentin Tarantino, the primary function of the western remains the same: the projection of American expansionism through the ideology of democratic liberalism with strong brackets of exception for nonwhites. The cinematic strategies discussed in this study—Manicheanism, occlusion, encasement, displacement, and erasure—finely delimit Black representation for coherent political aims. It is these tropes that have come to define not only the western but American perceptions of history and global geopolitics, as well.

CHAPTER ONE

Black Representations in the Western

> God meant for me to be white. God meant for me to be white. And it ain't easy. I got people with no lives. They're living through me. They're proud people, but they're people to worry about.
> —Buffalo Bill, *Buffalo Bill and the Indians, or Sitting Bull's History Lesson* (1976)

> The Western hasn't just declined and fallen, it's almost disappeared.... The awful truth seems to be that audiences are no longer interested. The Western having been dumped, motherhood and country could go next.
> —Vincent Canby, *New York Times*, Sept. 12, 1982

The US presidential election of 2012 was the first in history to be dominated by unregulated campaign contributions from millionaires and billionaires. Channeled through Super PACs, political advocacy groups, and organizations like Americans for Prosperity, the unlimited economic resources, some $2.5 billion, went to shape politicians' positions on issues like the science of climate change and the American tax code. About a quarter of that amount, $660 million, was directed at defeating the incumbent US president, Barack Obama.[1] Tea Party activists—a group directly connected to right-wing think tanks and billionaire funders and fueled by donations funneled through politically organized think tanks—sought to dismantle the federal government itself. Despite the power of financial backing, however, it remained uncertain whether fairly remote political issues could generate a mass movement among the American electorate, especially in key swing states like Ohio, Virginia, Pennsylvania, and North Carolina.

After a successful fundraiser in Iowa, Republican presidential nominee Mitt Romney invited an actor to address his party's convention, held at the end of August in Tampa, Florida. To energize a campaign known for its buttoned-down, corporate style, Romney selected a celebrity speaker with broad intergenerational appeal. He picked a person known to have regularly telephoned Ronald Reagan when he occupied the American presidency, and who had been considered a possible running mate by George H. W. Bush in 1988. He invited Clint Eastwood.[2]

Eastwood appeared onstage as network news coverage of the convention began, just minutes before Romney addressed the crowd. An eighty-two-year-

Clint Eastwood addressing the Republican National Convention, Tampa, Florida, 2012. NBC.

old, lean Eastwood walked toward the lectern, a collage of multistoried, electronic media screens behind him. The first image on the screens was a twenty-five-foot-high projection from the advertising poster of Eastwood's 1976 film *The Outlaw Josey Wales*. In the massive projection, the character Josey Wales holds two 1851 Colt Dragoon pistols, a graphic that event planners presumed would evoke Eastwood's mass appeal and steely resolve. The median age of 2012 Republican voters was fifty; they were encouraged to recall a connection to Eastwood from their early teen years.

The audience actually preferred another theatrical connection. Eastwood took to the microphone amid chants of "Make my day," an antiphonal request that attached another Eastwood cinema hero to the visible iconography of Josey Wales: an equally taciturn, truculent pistol shooter of lethal prowess, "Dirty Harry" Callahan. This congruity of film characters and public positions on the value of martial valor was perhaps more of what Baoufelé was really after with his salutation, "Clint Eastwood, c'est mon père."

With that kind of mandate, Eastwood, for twelve minutes—more than double the time he had been allotted—conducted an impromptu, unscripted, and palpably strained dialogue with an imaginary President Obama. The address was a critique of Obama's foreign and domestic policy, seasoned with an odd antiwar strain and edges of obscenity, tasteless banality, and Nixonian paranoia. When Eastwood concluded the dialogue, which attempted to prove to Obama the error of his ways in favor of Romney, the audience insisted that Eastwood mouth the movie line that arguably Ronald Reagan had made more famous than the film in which it was originally uttered.

In a March 1985 speech to the American Business Conference, Reagan had threatened to veto any congressional efforts to raise taxes. Pointing to his "veto" pen, he, too, had conjured an imaginary foe when he performed Eastwood's role for his supporters, ensuring them that he would fearlessly veto his opponents into oblivion: "Go ahead. Make my day"[3] (a line from Eastwood's 1983 film *Sudden Impact*, the third and perhaps least original installment in the "Dirty Harry" Callahan detective series, begun in 1971).

At the goading of the audience of Republican delegates in 2012, Eastwood agreed to perform the .44 caliber Magnum-wielding police inspector, collapsing the distance between the film line and Reagan's earlier reassurance to corporate executives. Eastwood's final words to the audience of Republican delegates was, "I'll start it and you finish it." "Go ahead," he called, to which the crowd shouted in delighted response, "Make my day!"

Eastwood's appearance represented far more than the simple endorsement of a candidate or a political party by a celebrity. His moment on the dais can be seen as the distillation of what he represents to American culture: the personification of a valiant, violent, righteous, and mythical national history, one that can be effectively glimpsed in the genre that launched him and that he has decisively helped to sustain since the 1970s: the cinema of the western.

Dirty Harry

Clint Eastwood's influence in reinforcing militant heroism in the western film genre is remarkably enduring, his work having codified an iconography of masculinist potency in need of resuscitation in the decades after the Vietnam War and leading up to the call for full-scale aggressive militarism in Iraq.[4] He has also skillfully performed the racialized dimension of that masculinity in an era that has seen the equivocation of white male dominance in professional athletics, increasingly rejected the specific language of racial bigotry, and searched for a new grammar of ethnic and national belonging. In the wake of public racial transformations in the United States on account of the civil rights movement and the loss of the war in Vietnam, Eastwood's films returned Americans to the western frontier in a complex renewal of the dimensions of white masculine identity. In the context of the United States, this is, of course, to engage squarely with the creation and reproduction of white supremacy.[5]

Eastwood's most important western and heroic portrait, *The Outlaw Josey Wales* (1976), offers a key to understanding the decisive reformation in attitudes and values that started in the United States in the late 1970s, like the non–Ku Klux Klan Christian vigilante and militia strain among the New Right, frequently mobilizing around a terroristic crusade against abortion clinics, taxation, gun ownership, and federal government encroachment. (I believe that the mass shootings in schools and public venues, committed by teen and young adult "loners," are strongly related phenomena, connected to the post-Vietnam crisis in white Christian masculine values.) Following the debacle in Vietnam, profound regroupings of ideological consensus occurred in the way that Americans, especially white men living in the homeland's interior, imagined their capacity to use force and occupy space as individuals, in relation to other citizens in the US and peoples across the globe.[6]

The presidential victories of Richard Nixon in 1968 and 1972 had called for new images of white masculinity, especially in terms of the public language used to mask discussions of racial groups and their legitimate right to national resources. Nixon, a candidate who strove to dismantle the federal government's social welfare apparatus, especially as it addressed African Americans (a group he referred to in private as inclined to live "like dogs"), expertly used public language stripped of obvious racial bias—like "forced busing," "states' rights," "law and order," and "security from unrest"—but carried strong racial connotations that might easily be grasped by his audience.[7] The strategy of coded racism in language has been likened to a dog whistle, which organizes the group by appealing to its hatred or bigotry through high frequency codes imperceptible on the surface. Nixon's attorney John Ehrlichman described their choice of language as a "subliminal appeal to the anti-black voter."[8]

The shift in public speech by elected officials coincided with new cinematic registers projecting the Black experience in America, which by 1970 was no longer dominated by references to the South, the rural or agricultural economy, or enslavement. By 1970, the majority of African Americans lived in industrial cities, generally in the North, making possible a society interacting in mixed-race public spaces in a manner that had been impossible in the 1960s. Legal victories of the 1960s in voting rights, public accommodations, and housing had brought an end to racial apartheid laws in America and were followed by a militant Black pride movement. Coincidentally, only three years into the 1970s, several films—like *Cotton Comes to Harlem* (1970), *Shaft* (1971), and *Superfly* (1972)—showed the economic strength of films starring Blacks in urban tales that arced thematically and ethically from portraits of law enforcement officers to private detectives to completely unrepentant criminal masterminds. Public images of African Americans transformed rapidly, and young Black radicals swiftly decried cinematic portraits of Black helplessness and subservience.

Eastwood opened up a new direction with a series of crime dramas, making a pivotal career choice in 1971 when he decided to take on the film role of the Nixon-era law enforcement maverick Harry Callahan. The role coincided with his performance of the diabolical wounded Union sharpshooter, convalescing at a Mississippi girls' school, in the film *The Beguiled* (1971). The Dirty Harry films are understood widely as "a conservative remobilization of traditional values in the Nixon era" and "a purposefully reactionary response to the contemporary fears over violent crime on the streets of America."[9] Following the 1968 riots, the television and film industry in the US made an abrupt shift to the production of images of policemen and detectives as dramatic heroes. By 1973, twenty-one of the sixty-three weekly prime-time slots were claimed by police dramas.[10] Eastwood's roles strongly reinforced the use of deadly violence by the police in upholding the spirit of the law hobbled by bureaucratic loopholes, the cornerstone of Nixon's 1968 and 1972 campaigns. The shift from the Johnson administration's Great Society social welfare programs to Richard Nixon's law-and-order regime and his cultivation of the "Moral Majority" may have been the most decided shift in public policy in twentieth-century American history, closely akin to the difference in national policy between 1876 and 1877. As Katherine Beckett argues in *Making Crime Pay*, the Nixon years saw the nation-state transformed from a polity with a vast public agenda of social welfare to one with a vast public project of social control.[11] Later films *Magnum Force* (1973) and *The Gauntlet* (1977) complicated the representations of law enforcement as the principal solution to social ills, suggesting the possibility at least of fascist control emerging through a corrupt, corporate-financed, privatized police state that functioned by extralegal force and public execution. But while these latter films militate against the threat from cabals and corporate militarization, they target, with equal vehemence, the bureaucracy of the welfare state, particularly its web of protections to guarantee citizens' rights and freedoms, like the Miranda Rights regulation. At the conclusion of *Dirty Harry*, Inspector Callahan throws away his police badge, ridding himself of his subordination to the mayor's office and its attendant human rights regulations.

While Eastwood avoided the public conflation of his film persona with political stands in favor of the Second Amendment later associated with the actor Charlton Heston, he developed a trope in *Dirty Harry* that seemed to connect the value of ultra-armed citizens and the conduct of rule of law in the US. While "Dirty Harry" is an officer of the law, he regularly finds himself needing to conduct his most important and valuable police work in his private life as an armed citizen. In essence, his role is hygienic: he cleans the city of crime with his handgun, which becomes a broom, a mop, an alcohol sponge eradicating disease. The logic of the stylishly wielded handgun and not the fist or irrevocable language as the arbiter of the ethical system emanated from Eastwood's work with Leone in the 1960s *Dollars* trilogy. But the starkly urban, antiallegorical format of the Nixon-era crime shows inserted a strongly Hobbesian, Malthusian logic into Eastwood's cinematic universe. While the complex social politics engaged by the film (the police helicopter prevents the sociopath from targeting a Black gay man, diverting him, instead, to kill a Black child) are not absolutely reducible to propagandistic slogans, the film offers extractable digestible scenes with their own segmented, discrete internal logic.

Dirty Harry, directed by Eastwood collaborator Don Siegel, however, created one of the most potent transmitted cinematic tropes of desire for vigilantism and lethal force directed against Blacks, linking it to the most famous film articulating the theme of Black hygiene, *The Birth of a Nation*. The film opens with police inspector Harry Callahan becoming "dirty" in his work to rid the city of crime. Three Black men are robbing a San Francisco bank in broad daylight while the detective casually eats lunch. (Harry's nickname stems from the fact that he, having grown up in Potrero Hill, a Black-majority neighborhood, hates "everybody" impartially: "Dagoes, wops, Hebes, Spics, niggers." He is "dirty" because he has "every dirty job that comes along.") Part of the hero's allure is his work as a racial hygienist, using the pistol to clean the city of debris. The operation is shown along a binary axis of right and wrong, good and evil. When the bank alarm sounds, Callahan interrupts his meal to foil the robbery by shooting dead two men, who expire in spectacular, violent somersaults, mimicking the style of death characterizing victims and villains alike in the openly satirical and absurdist film by Ossie Davis and Chester Himes, *Cotton Comes to Harlem*, released a year earlier. Callahan grievously wounds a third robber.

Instead of simply having the character wait for the arrival of uniformed police officers to finish the cleanup from the robbery, Siegel and Eastwood make a complex philosophical point at this early moment in the film. The downed robber—whom the film audience is encouraged to believe might be linked to a pararevolutionary group like the Black Panthers (whose members were convicted in 1971 of killing and wounding police officers in New York), Revolutionary Action Movement, Republic of New Africa, or Symbionese Liberation Army—thinks that perhaps he can grab his shotgun and shoot Harry. The robber cannot escape; he is badly wounded and doomed, but if he is an actual revolutionary, he might have the satisfaction of blotting out a symbolic sign of his torment and the actual man who has ruined his plan for liberation. The robber's thoughts are transparent to the detective, who informs him that he doesn't even remember if the weapon he is using to force him into submission is loaded. What follows is an exchange that has retained strong residual power for more than fifty years. Callahan casually approaches the wounded man, aims the pistol at him, and taunts him:

> CALLAHAN. Uh-uh. I know what you're thinking. Did he fire six shots or only five? Well to tell you the truth, in all of this excitement I kind of lost track myself. But being as this is a .44 Magnum, the most powerful handgun in the world, and would blow your head clean off, you've got to ask yourself one question: "Do I feel lucky?" Well do ya, punk?

The detective smirks, picks up the criminal's shotgun, and turns to walk away. The robber, played by Albert Popwell, an Eastwood company actor, then mouths plaintively in Black dialect: "Hey. I gots to know."[12]

Slightly surprised that the robber has enough courage to risk his life, Callahan points the gun at the wounded man and pulls the trigger, which he already knows is empty. As the trigger is being pulled, the robber moans with his mouth open, an allusion to the orgasm at the moment the death-wish is fulfilled.[13] Callahan smirks at the erotic experience, at his own immense phallic power kept in reserve and the submissiveness of the robber, who accepts the subordinate position in the symbolic exchange and fails absolutely in his pursuit of recognition and in orgasm.

The film's plot arc is nominally undergirded by racial liberalism: Dirty Harry guards and protects San Francisco against Scorpio, a sociopathic white murderer who, after assassinating an attractive female swimmer, threatens "Catholics and niggers." At the midpoint of the film, Scorpio is caught by Detective Callahan but must be freed because in the process of catching him, Callahan violates his Fourteenth Amendment rights. When Harry eliminates his nemesis at the conclusion of the film, he repeats the same patter from the early scene at the bank: "Do you feel lucky? Well do ya, punk?" In Eastwood's next film Callahan will have a likable, two-dimensional Black partner. But the vehicle of racial liberalism never divests itself fully from the fragmented series of arrangements that mark the emergence of postindustrial American life. Scorpio wins public sympathy by paying $200 to a dangerous Black man, who seems to resemble guitarist Curtis Mayfield (which would suggest the opportunity to conflate the position of Black male as musical celebrant and villain for hire), to beat him to a pulp, solidifying the association of Black men with the most extreme, professional depths of villainy.

Dirty Harry—whom the mayor censures at the opening of the film, blaming him for "trouble in the Filmore," San Francisco's most historic Black neighborhood—begins with the gravely symbolic act of putting to order feral Black men in urban America. After he shoots three men dead and wounds a fourth, Segal cuts to four Black house painters on scaffolding. The symbolism is quite heavy and obvious between the dirty Black robbers and the hygienic Black servicemen in coveralls swabbing white paint; they clean themselves as they clean the nation. Whether the Black men are turned villains by individual moral failing, greed, mental instability, or historic political injustice is not a concern. By using ultimate lethal violence, contempt, and then a joke, Harry renders them prone, libidinally unsatisfied in their simulated encounter with erotic death.

Like the persona enticing his Republican audience in 2012, Eastwood's genre hero, whether in western or detective film, insists on the subordination of the nonwhite character. Popwell's badman is permanently a ward of the state, either indiscriminately killed, wounded and permanently incarcerated, or cast as a painter washed in a white jumper, whitewashing the structure of Western race relations and inequities itself.

In the midst of increasingly successful urban crime dramas, Eastwood remained committed to making western films. Westerns provide a grammar for the imaginary relation between pioneers and the state, for settlers and the Indigenous, and for rebels, vigilantes, and sworn upholders of the law. Within the genre there are resolutions of apparent social conflicts and crises. Westerns have marshaled, over and over again, language and images to create a network of symbol, style, and value for making modern American subjects. In addition, film heroes and the aura that they generate play formidable, consequential roles in the maintenance of national character and values that enable nation-building and nation-expanding projects. Alternatively, westerns also contribute cues to help eliminate or silence areas of national attention or concern. If, as sociologist Loic Wacquant argues, the contemporary prison with its million Black people inside is the "main machine for 'race-making'" of our time, the mechanism that marks Blackness and maleness, the western and Eastwood's anchoring performance of cinematic vigilantism are a virtual equivalent, a "machine for race-making" for contemporary whiteness.[14]

Such a dynamic of reciprocity has long existed between mass culture and the communication of political identities. In Richard Slotkin's *Gunfighter Nation*, an important work showing the relation between the western film genre and American national politics, Slotkin reminds readers that "politics shape the concerns and imagery of movies," and movies, in turn, "transmit their shapely formulations of those concerns back to political discourse, where they function as devices for clarifying values and imagining policy scenarios."[15] Arguably there is also another dynamic, as films are designed to satisfy youthful audiences. They call out a sphere of object relations. Writer Rebecca Wanzo proposes that cinematically experienced "para-social interactions" "become doubles of real situations." Following Melanie Klein, Wanzo proposes cognitive conflation of the images occurs, which "cannot be verified by the means of perception which are available in connection with the tangible and palpable object world." As Western discourse shifted in the Nixon and post-Nixon eras, white male protagonists and audiences were confronted with a new problem, the "ability to hold on to flawed love objects."[16] Manifest Destiny, the Confederate States of America, the Ku Klux Klan, patriarchal violence, the Great White Hope, American Exceptionalism, castigated histories and emblems of nostalgia—all qualified as the forlorn preoccupation.

But while the personal identification between viewer and character aura in the consumption of cinema is key, the larger field of ideological relation corresponding to the needs of the Cold War structured more basic assumptions of the western genre. The moving-picture mythology of the western frontier was premised essentially on an imaginary conflict, its dramas of deadly force posing American expectations of democracy against the needs of winning an undeclared war. Or, as Slotkin put it, ideologically, it was "a period of continual conflict between the claims of democratic procedure and Cold War policies that required the use of armed force."[17] The gunfighter hero, often operating alone or only indirectly connected to democratic governmental power, was a specific cultural artifact generated to address this dilemma. When using scenarios set in Mexico and showing how white American cowboys contributed to the Mexican civil war and independence movement, the films of the 1950s used the history of the Southwest Territory to allegorize international dynamics of decolonization, communism, and anticommunism. Often they offered solutions to the problem of despotic regimes by creating covertly operating gunfighters, such as Eastwood would reprise in the 1970 film *Two Mules for Sister Sarah*. Eastwood's work in the western film genre in the 1970s carried over the political purposes that the genre had proved so useful in conveying to a set of new ideological challenges.

Such antagonism between democratic protections and the sacrifice of individual rights in the name of combating an unseen enemy echoes loudly in the contemporary, post–September 11, 2001, US-declared "War on Terror." Consider such Orwellian phrases as "enemy combatant," "preventative detention," "targeted assassination list," and other forms of language used in the USA Patriot Act to sanction extraconstitutional procedures and to reduce questions of sovereignty to what has been described by Achille Mbembe as necropolitics, the ability of a nation-state "to kill or to allow to live . . . to exercise control over mortality."[18] This impulse to consolidate and wield deadly force, a power firmly beyond the US Constitution, bears a strong resemblance to the demands made on citizens to forgo or accept the usurpation of rights during the Cold War era. State demands to defeat communism required a broad range of unilateral imperial actions, including the removal of elected heads of state and the subversion of democracies in Latin America, the Caribbean, Asia, and Africa, sometimes mainly for conflicts with US natural resources, industries, agribusinesses, and multinational corporations.[19] The western wrestled immediately with these double conflicts—the specter of enemy ideologies and the problem of opponents to the designs of empire.

But an examination of the role that films play in shaping the attitudes, beliefs, responses, and ethical values of Americans calls for a definition of *ideology* that is at once more precise and more broad. To mention Eastwood in terms of ideology implies that he endorses or responds to an "ideology" of his own choosing, that he advocates or rejects some organized body of thought, like conservative politics. The conversation also invites the notion that his body of work, or his work in specific genres, like the western, represents a "false consciousness," an ideological blanket and belief system where conscious reason is deceived. His ideological work is also supposed to project a network of beliefs that he himself would explicitly reject, such as the recent idea that his works convey masculine sentimentality in spite of their more obvious investments in chauvinist racial liberalism.[20] But it is more necessary to understand his film work, most explicitly the western films of 1976 and after, as contributing to the ideological in another way.

One of the very special achievements of cinematic narrative is its capacity to provide a compelling simulation of lived experience in real time, complete with an attendant visual memory. Rather than being removed from the realm of the ideological, actors and their contribution to the work of art or, in Eastwood's case, the fusion of his character portraits with the genre of the western, supply the conceptual space that makes imaginary relations possible. That is the fundamental ideological dimension of his work and its unfolding inevitability, which makes resistance by the viewer so difficult. These relations can be between people or between people and ideas or concepts, like the past, but they take on particular force when they construct relationships between people who have not met and whose ways of knowing each other are limited to the imaginary.[21]

The films crash across boundaries of shared group economic interests in a complex society, producing, at their most influential, cultural touchstones that help to create a worldview that enables the creation of broad blocs of shared human consensus bound by time and space. The images, language, and dramatized resolutions of films by actors like John Wayne and Clint Eastwood are harnessed in the formation of historical blocs that turn cultural influence into political power, like at the convention of 2012. By 1976, Eastwood was committed to a revision of the history of nineteenth-century America and a fictional reimagining of the Old West that would attain resounding popular appeal in the United States.

John Wayne and Racial Liberalism

Eastwood's significance as a cultural icon for the western genre since roughly 1976 has now fully replaced the western hero-figure who preceded him: John Wayne. Perhaps most easily harnessed in the opening scenes of Howard Hawkes's 1948 film *Red River*, Wayne's body of work would come to delineate the rough contours of settler colonialism in the territories of the West, more fully identifying him with the era of the 1950s and the most direct allegorical film references to questions of desegregation and decolonization. Wayne's film mythology and celebrity aura also coincided with the sharpest era of Cold War hostility, between 1946 and 1975.

However much John Wayne's relevance might have faded by the 1980s (Wayne died in 1979), there is no denying his role by the late 1960s as the American cultural lightning rod for a nation reconsidering questions of state-sanctioned violence, racial inequity, and imperial reckoning. Wayne rose to fame in the 1940s, performing roles as a man morally principled, fearless, and skilled at using typically defensive, though sometimes prophylactic, deadly violence in western movies like *Stagecoach* (1939) and *Red River*, and with military films like *The Fighting Seabees* (1944) and *Back to Bataan* (1945). By 1950 he had become the most financially successful Hollywood actor, and by 1968 his films had grossed more than $400 million, making him the most bankable Hollywood star for the studios. He had emerged from B-movie genre conventions of the 1930s that prized the marriage between the western movie hero with the real-life person of the actor. As his career evolved, the association between Wayne's onscreen roles and his personal politics would only increase. Though he never served in the military, Wayne was presented the Medal of Honor in 1979.

Around 1960, the "Golden Age of the Western," Wayne evolved from being simply a major Hollywood star to becoming a powerful cultural icon who occupied a higher plane of symbolic meaning. Wayne's cinematic portraits offered "an idealized and mythic presentation of national character and destiny, a vision that apparently transcends historically specific circumstances."[22] The laconic, spare acting style that Wayne cultivated in a string of films with director John Ford seemed to complement the right-wing politics that the Cold War western hero came to embody, particularly when Wayne began directing films like *The Alamo* (1960) and the equally hawkish 1968 pro-Vietnam War film *The Green Berets* (1968). Excelling in paternal or avuncular roles like sheriff, putative deputy, rancher, foreman, military officer, or veteran, Wayne represented the onscreen ideal of law on the frontier, a utopian space where the law and ethics of "fair play" come into existence after the empire no longer operates by raw military force. In this capacity, the chauvinistic (and typically chaste) Wayne hero transmitted the values of benevolent imperialism, the colonist as pacifier, citizen, reproducer, and manager.

Wayne's contribution to modern American racial attitudes is complex. He starred in several important films—*Fort Apache* (1948), *The Searchers* (1956), *The Alamo*, and *The Man Who Shot Liberty Valance* (1962)—that explained to audiences in a popular medium what has come to be known as *racial liberalism*. Legal scholar Lani Guinier explains the term's rise after World War II. Racial liberalism emphasized "the corrosive effect of individual prejudice and the importance of interracial contact in promoting tolerance. Racial liberals stressed the damaging effects of segregation on black personality development to secure legal victory as well as white middle class sympathy."[23] While "racial liberalism" was well capable of promoting itself as a discourse of modernity and of remediation, it also operated to suppress "political economic critiques of racism as . . . an index for the inequalities of capitalist modernity." Furthermore, the discourse of official antiracism was marshaled to develop explanatory codes and motifs that justify as its primary benefit "new forms of capitalist development" and "the health and security of the U.S. state." Critic Jodi Melamed explains finally that "state-sanctioned antiracisms have repressed counternationalisms and deflected criticisms of U.S. global power."[24]

Wayne's best effort to assert the values of American racial tolerance, the John Ford film *The Searchers*, dramatizes the agonizing internal odyssey of an unbowed Confederate soldier who eventually accepts the fact that the culture and bodily fluids of the Native American are not permanent pollutions to whites and that, indeed, exceptional Native Americans might become either relatives or whites themselves. Importantly, in that film, a captivity narrative, the two key Native American characters are portrayed by whites.

While the practice of white imitation does silence and erase Native Americans from the screen, it also opens the door to connection and shared intimacy. Often the white paternalism performed by Wayne included demonstrations of explicit cross-cultural expertise. Typically, Wayne's character, in contrast to other white settlers on the frontier, "knows the Indians" and is an expert in the language and culture of his adversary. In *Hondo* (1953), Wayne's character is part Native American. *The Searchers* comes quite close to showing the pernicious effects of strong racism on Wayne's hero, Ethan Edwards, and the other films emphasize his easy relations with enslaved Black men and freedmen, a sign of his project of showing some paternal or avuncular devotion to the properly powerless and subordinate.

Wayne and directors like John Ford did not have to take risks to produce these cinematic concerns after 1949, a benchmark year in the history of US film, and following the downfall of the censorship of racial content by the Motion Picture Association of America. Liberal racial ideals in US films—specifically, opposition to overt prejudice and the portrayal of Black characters as obsequious servants or shuffling entertainers—owe their genesis to the work of the NAACP during the World War II era. The civil rights lobbying group influenced the Office of War Information board, which governed film production during the war.

The board, after the conflagrations in Harlem and Detroit during the summer of 1943, hoped to avoid any more-widespread racial rioting and its threat to war material production. The board took steps to ensure that movies included patriotic portraits of Black men and women and did away with the degrading stereotypes ubiquitous in earlier films. Thus, important characters like Pinkie (Ernest Whitman) in Henry King's 1939 *Jesse James*, starring Tyrone Power, were deemed obsequious and emasculated and would disappear. The work of the NAACP and the censors peaked in 1949 with a group of transformative movies that far surpassed the limitations of Black cinematic portraiture in Hollywood films up to that time: *Home of the Brave*, *Pinky*, *Lost Boundaries*, and *Intruder in the Dust*.[25]

The Alamo and *The Man Who Shot Liberty Valance*, set respectively in Texas and Oklahoma, complicated notions of a frontier that needed to be protected from savagery and despotism by reflecting on the conditions of the lands the settlers were leaving behind, where slavery existed or had thrived. In *The Alamo*, which he directed and in which he acted, Wayne had resolved the problem of slavery and racial injustice by pairing Jester Hairston and Richard Widmark as enslaved Jethro and "Mr." Sam Bowie. In the 1960 film's trademark gesture of racial liberalism, Jethro is freed and encouraged to escape before Santa Anna's attack on the Texas outpost. The loyal Jethro decides to accept liberation from slavery but to remain with his former master in the suicidal defense of the Alamo, perishing in the futile attempt to protect a wounded Bowie. (The irony of the film's Black martyred manservant lay in the historical fact that enslaved Blacks were the only known survivors of the Alamo.)

Wayne's sometime collaborator and revered director John Ford's most famous expression of racial liberalism was the western *Sergeant Rutledge* (1960). The film featured the Hollywood western's only bona fide matinee idol, character actor Woody Strode, a former UCLA football star.[26] Sergeant Rutledge, a Black trooper in the Ninth Cavalry, is charged with rape and murder, and during his trial he defends himself against a persnickety judge advocate and a courtroom of drunken officers whose ethical conduct is doubly satirized when, during the course of the trial, they are repeatedly exposed as plunderers of Atlanta during Sherman's March of 1864. The Atlanta victory in the summer of 1864 is commonly credited with saving the election for Abraham Lincoln and ensuring the continuation of the Emancipation Proclamation.

But *Sergeant Rutledge* was historically exceptional for predicating itself on the fact that the War Department had, indeed, sent thousands of Black troops in the Ninth, Tenth, Twenty-Fourth, and Twenty-Fifth Cavalry Regiments to the American West after the Civil War. And although the plot was a melodrama of race and sex, once putting a shirtless Strode alone in a room with Constance Towers (playing Mary Beecher), the overriding theme of national belonging emerged as the title character revealed his highest motivation.

When the prosecuting attorney attempts to reduce the Black sergeant's valor in a battle against Native Americans to the savage passion of a barbarian suffering the loss of reason, "slave-born" Rutledge (who carries his manumission papers on his person) explains his eagerness to defend the flag and ultimately submit to baseless racist charges: "It was because the Ninth Cavalry was my home. My real freedom. And my self-respect. And the way I was deserting it, I wasn't nothing worse than a swamp-running nigger. And I ain't that. Do you hear me! I'm a man!"

Rutledge extols self-sacrificial martyrdom against the possibility of escape and self-definition as a rebellious "swamp-running nigger." The character makes clear his disapproval of the maroon society and its self-derived Black nationalist belief systems; he seeks the possibility of Black identity and resistance exclusively within the confines of the white order.[27]

Two years later, and again under Ford's direction, Woody Strode played John Wayne's morally irreproachable and dutiful sidekick, the ranch hand Pompey, foil and majordomo to Wayne's gunfighter rancher Tom Doniphon, in *The Man Who Shot Liberty Valance*. In one scene, Wayne roughly pulls Strode, who seems only recently become a freedman, out of a schoolhouse. Pompey has been trying to recite the US Constitution, but at the words "all men are created equal," he stumbles, admitting to his teacher, played by James Stewart, "I just plum forgot it." No matter, Wayne's character Doniphon sharply rebukes his employee for his ambitions: "What've you been wasting your time around here for? Get on back to work. Your schoolin's over." Strode's performance of masculinity diverged from his contemporary, the actor Sidney Poitier, who evoked a wincing, moaning vulnerability in dramas like *The Defiant Ones* (1958) and *A Raisin in the Sun* (1960). Strode was an obedient one-dimensional role-player (and, in the 1959 Korean War film *Pork Chop Hill*, a malingering malcontent), but he emphasized character traits that matched certain characteristics given to white cinematic heroes, like taciturn stoicism and straight-backed commitment to duty.

Residues of these performances of fidelity emerge in more contemporary western films, particularly in Clint Eastwood's *Unforgiven* (1992), a film coinciding with the reemergence of full-blown US imperial might after the invasion of Kuwait and Iraq in 1991. Eastwood was understood as extraordinary for naturalizing a friendship between his lead character, William Munny,

Edmond O'Brien, John Wayne, and Woody Strode in *The Man Who Shot Liberty Valance*, dir. John Ford (Paramount Pictures, 1962).

and Morgan Freeman's character, Ned Logan, without any reference to Ned's racial background or slavery at all. Nonetheless, Eastwood's direction of Freeman's performance repeatedly signals Ned's great affection and desire to nurture Munny. Ned is ultimately whipped to death by Gene Hackman's character and his cadaver displayed on the main street of Big Whiskey, Wyoming, as little more than an attempt to intimidate Munny.

As Cedric Robinson reminds us when he analyzes scholarship on Black Hollywood characters, it is a mistake to imagine all Black actors performing across time as menial subalterns whose stereotyped characters are essentially defined by antebellum caricatures.[28] In the 1954 Gary Cooper western *Vera Cruz*, Black actor Archie Savage played the role of Corporal Ballard in a cutting-edge role that showcased his artistic talents. Savage doesn't merely carry bags and drive for whites. Instead, his character rescues a Mexican woman from rape at the hands of Charles Bronson's character, Pittsburgh, and then fights, dying near the film's finale, and is avenged by the protagonist, paternalist ex-Confederate Ben Trane, played by Cooper.

The record-breaking athlete Jim Brown became an actor in the mid-1960s, immediately revising the standard of Black male portraiture. In his most important western, *100 Rifles* (1968), his character both represents the law and achieves an onscreen romance with Raquel Welch, who portrays a Latina character. Brown's dynamic success, albeit artistically limited, bears strong relation to Strode's earlier roles; he can broach the taboo of interracial romance and occupy the role of archmasculinity but only on account of his unwavering loyalty to the juridical principle and defining power of the state. The author Toni Morrison identified this tradition fundamentally in 1992 as one determined to produce the "serviceable lives of Africanist others": "an American brand of Africanism emerged: strongly urged, thoroughly serviceable, companionably ego-reinforcing, and pervasive. For excellent reasons of state—because European sources of cultural hegemony were dispersed but not yet valorized in the new country—the process of organizing American coherence through a distancing Africanism became the operative mode of a new cultural hegemony."[29] In 1949 Ralph Ellison hoped to disclose the cultural needs that demanded these Black "serviceable" cinematic portraits just as Wayne was reaching his iconic power.

> Actually, the anti-Negro images of the films were (and are) accepted because of the existence throughout the United States of an audience obsessed with an inner psychological need to view Negroes as less than men. Thus, psychologically and ethically, these negative images constitute justifications for all those acts—legal, emotional, economic, and political—that we label Jim Crow. The anti-Negro image is thus a ritual object of which Hollywood is not the creator but the manipulator. Its role has been that of justifying the widely held myth of Negro nonhumanness and inferiority by offering entertaining rituals through which that myth could be reaffirmed.[30]

The typical Black character finds some useful way to serve and thereby confirms the white hero's natural-born superiority, morally crowned by the white hero's racial inclusiveness as proved by his relationship with his Black sidekick. Several Black characters in later films would echo Woody Strode's enduring role. Remarkably enough, it is quite possible to glimpse these relations conjugated through 2015 with Samuel L. Jackson in the Quentin Tarantino film *The Hateful Eight*.

Vietnam and After

In part, events concluding the 1960s seemed to overwhelm Wayne's devotion to racial liberalism itself, after his 1968 *Green Berets* gave a crucial role, within bounds, to Black actor Raymond St. Jacques. The Black actor James McEachin would provide a perfunctory Black presence in Wayne films like *The Undefeated* (1969) and *True Grit* (1969), rounding out the decade. This absence within presence corresponded to Wayne's understanding of Black political evolution by 1971. In a *Playboy* magazine interview, he declared that "with a lot of blacks, there's quite a bit of resentment along with their dissent and possibly rightfully so. But we can't all of a sudden get down on our knees and turn everything over to the leadership of the blacks. I believe in white supremacy until the blacks are educated to a point of responsibility."[31]

Concerned about the possibility of college faculty like Angela Davis teaching his children the merits of communism, Wayne insisted on the necessity of white stewardship, a position fully complicit with the tenets of racial liberalism. He quickly recovered and qualified his remarks—"I'm not condoning slavery"—a point that certainly seemed reinforced by his multiple previous onscreen roles as a Union soldier. But while Wayne refused to condone slavery, which he associated with an era "five or 10 generations ago" (and a condition that he analogized to infantile paralysis), the event itself seemed of only minor consequence. As for Blacks who protested the conditions of US racism, he recoiled: "I wish they'd tell me where in the world they have it better than right here in America."[32]

Wayne was firmly invested in the genre by then, not only because of what the loss of its prestige might mean to his own career but for what it had to say about the collapse of a particular white American masculine ideal, a condition signaled for him by the unwillingness of middle-class whites to participate in the war in Vietnam. During the concluding episodes of that conflict, Americans fled the embassy in Saigon and pushed helicopters off the decks of naval warships into the South China Sea, a shameful embarrassment to people who connected themselves to the presidency of Theodore Roosevelt or the military exploits of George S. Patton, Curtis LeMay, and Douglas MacArthur.

He revealed his grave disappointment with the lack of the territorial and imperial ambitions of the contemporary generation of American men to *Life* magazine journalist Richard Kluge in 1972, an inadequacy that had deliberate racial connotations: "Your generation's frontier should have been Tanganyika.... It could have been a new frontier for any American or English or French kid with a little gumption! Another Israel! But the do-gooders had to give it back to the Indians!"[33]

Wayne's outbursts to journalists were different from his artworks, which bore only slight resemblance to his occasionally stinging public rebukes. Yet, racially liberal though it was, never did Wayne's work question the proprietary right of white settlers to the spatial territories of the American West.

Despite these early 1970s moments of crisis for Wayne's values, the obvious tenets of racial liberalism continued to be pronounced in Wayne's representations of the West. Wayne's production company, Batjac, released the film *The Cowboys* in 1971, and it included the most fully nuanced Black character to appear alongside Wayne. Veteran dramatist Roscoe Lee Browne's memorable performance in the role of Nightlinger, the chuck-wagon driver (in a sense, the most technically accurate representation of Black westerners of all Wayne's films),[34] showed particularly skillful handling of the tensions between Wayne's commitment to "white supremacy" and the sharpened Black consciousness of the era. Browne combined understated force, irony, and formal elegance, enabling him to contrast Wayne's iconic portraits of rugged masculinity, while leaving intact Wayne's aura of supremacy, Christian martyrdom, and omnipotence.

The Rise of Clint Eastwood

A generation younger than John Wayne, but groomed by the social uprisings at the end of the 1960s and early 1970s, Clint Eastwood might have been expected to advance positions theoretically beyond the principle of racial liberalism and its strong residue of Euro-American imperialism. Based on his starring in the 1964–66 trilogy *A Fistful of Dollars*, *A Few Dollars More*, and *The Good, the Bad and the Ugly*, directed by Italian filmmaker Sergio Leone, and later films like *Hang 'Em High* (1968), and especially *High Plains Drifter* (1971), Eastwood appeared to have a general disregard for specific moralizing projects ennobling western ideals.

In fact, as a film performer using as a primary ethic the necessity of violence, Eastwood is commonly understood as diverging sharply from John Wayne. Wayne's body of films often presented the difficulties and sacrifices necessary to bring or sustain law, domesticity, and order to the frontier. Typically, a massive image in the center of the screen, Wayne conveyed the morally righteous interests of the embattled minority, the cavalry outpost in hostile "Indian" territory, the sheriff struggling against well-organized sociopathic killers, the rancher facing off against the despots or greedy bankers. Eastwood, in contrast, seemed to insist that there was little possibility for the heroism of his characters and that absurdist irony, chaos, and entropy were the real forces to reckon with on the frontier. This is the orthodox narrative of contemporary film critics regarding Eastwood's divergent value system from Wayne's.

Eastwood arrived in Hollywood during this wholesale dismantling of prosocial heroism, armed with the knowledge (gained with Leone) of how to present heroic power in the total absence of any kind of social project. Leone's decadent European skepticism totally incinerates all idealist social beliefs and leaves the gunfighting hero—whose constitutional function hitherto has been to enable the good community—stranded in a literal and figurative wasteland with no interests to uphold but his own. The hero's mastery, no longer connected with a grand ideological project and denuded of classical camouflage, takes the form of a mysterious transcendent power.[35]

Eastwood is considered to have adapted to the political commitments of his early westerns with Leone and abandoned "prosocial," "ideological" investments. John Wayne lobbied to shift Eastwood's western portraits and to harness them to a more deliberate project of American nation building and righteous militancy. Rejecting a proposed collaboration from Eastwood, Wayne corresponded in 1973 to criticize the fabulist, ultraviolent, and gratingly brutal film *High Plains Drifter*.[36] Wayne thought that "the townspeople did not represent the true spirit of the American pioneer."[37] That Eastwood vehicle, putatively working to expand the anonymous gunfighter role he had created with Leone, struck a hard blow against the ideal of there being *any* ethical (or what the critics might have deemed an "ideological") project) resources in the Old West. Wayne apparently feared that Eastwood's hyperbolic violence would implode the genre. His communiqué acknowledged the obvious symbolic power of Eastwood by 1973, a walking synecdoche for the western. Wayne's riposte at least chronologically stands in place among the influences that caused the actor/director Eastwood to warm to a more traditional role of image-maker for white American men and women.[38]

Backward to *The Birth of a Nation*

The western film genre's interest in history and politics grows directly from the way these essential concerns were depicted in the earliest moments of American cinema, particularly in D. W. Griffith's epic *The Birth of a Nation*. Based on the novel *The Clansman: An Historical Romance of the Ku Klux Klan*, by Thomas Dixon Jr., Griffith's film broached a related series of imperial concerns but, crucially, racial subjugation, western expansion, and the frontier. There is considerable thematic overlap between Dixon's 1905 novel and Owen Wister's 1902 novel *The Virginian* (called "a colonial romance" by Wister), the book that launched the romantic narrative adventures of "the western."[39]

The Virginian introduced the anonymous cowboy as hero and has long been considered the forerunner of the western genre in books and film.[40] Although *The Birth of a Nation* takes place in the American South, the western narrative would shift those dramatizations of captivity and rescue to the other side of the Mississippi River. *The Birth of a Nation* enlarged the sphere of western antagonisms beyond the world of white settlers and dark-skinned Natives to include formally enslaved people of African descent. Within a few years of *The Birth of a Nation*'s release in 1915, purportedly five million Americans had seen the three-hour silent epic. With its emphatic repudiation of Black enfranchisement during the Reconstruction era and its sanctimonious portrait of the origins of the Ku Klux Klan (an organization founded in 1866 in Tennessee by a professional slave trader and cavalry general, Nathan Bedford Forrest), the film guided millions of Americans, especially recently arrived immigrants, into the attitudes and beliefs of white supremacy and hemispheric Manifest Destiny, or Anglo-European settlement and hegemony.

Cedric Robinson argues that *The Birth of a Nation* was an important device for controlling social and political thought among the laboring classes following the emancipation of enslaved workers, as America was economically coming of age at the peak of the Industrial Revolution. "At the beginning of the twentieth century, American capital was no longer a middling mercantile player in a global economy commanded by imperial European powers. Now it was a robust industrial society voraciously appropriating a vast but disparate labor force that required cultural discipline, social habituation, and political regulation."[41] *The Birth of a Nation*, as a dramatic celebration of these attributes, is powerfully extended two generations later by Eastwood's oeuvre, which made significant use of the rebel horseman as an avenging Christ, most decisively with the 1976 film he starred in and directed, *The Outlaw Josey Wales*. As we will see in chapter 3, one of the key moves in that film is its erasure of Black Americans from Missouri and Texas.

It is important to identify the extirpationist, eugenicist tenor of Griffith's work, advocating white racial expansion, settlement, and domination of nonwhite racial groups. In this goal of westward expansion and European-American continental hegemony (Manifest Destiny), permanent African subordination, and Native elimination, the western film and its tropes were critical tools to explain the violence of conquest. Before embarking on the definitive *Birth of a Nation*, Griffith had directed about thirty films with Native American characters and plots set in the West. Two films are quite significant. In 1912 he directed *The Massacre*, a film that shows the westward migration of a Southern couple after the debacle of the Civil War. The film is famous because it depicts a "Surprise Attack on the Indian Village," establishing US military intervention as the catalyst for the militant Native response and concludes with "the massacre" of white settlers and soldiers, as well as a cavalry ride-to-the-rescue as the film's finale. Griffith carefully depicts two parallel domestic scenes—one white, one Native. The white American family leaving the South and attracted by "The Lure of the West" will survive the bloodletting, with the husband pulling his wife and child from the corpses and leading "to the restoration of the lost object and the reconstitution of the patriarchal family."[42] The Native family—a father, mother, and infant (carried in a papoose)—are captured close-up in panic as they learn of the pending attack. The next frames show the woman and child dead on the ground. Griffith's camera definitely mourns the Native woman and child but nonetheless secures the "passing" of the Native race and the resurrection of the white.

The film that came a year later revealed far less ambiguity than the earlier portrait of dead Natives and redeemed settler families. The 1913 film *The Battle of Elderbush Gulch* provides the saga of white settlers overtaking Native Americans on the frontier. Griffith depicts Native Americans as indolent dog-eaters who attack a white homestead, symbolized by two white girls, described as waifs, whose two puppies are the source of conflict. Griffith deployed these same cinematic tropes—the outpost, the swarm of nonwhite combatants, and the cavalry rescue—to garner the audience's sympathy in *The Birth of a Nation*. He thus linked the emotional animus directed at African Americans for southern progressive age backwardness to the ancient resentment at the estimated five million Natives, largely farmers living in towns and who had artfully shaped paths and fields along coastlines and riverways and whose very (often dense) existence repudiated the idyllic fantasy of a virgin North American wilderness.[43] The cavalry would be replaced by the gunman on horseback arriving to rescue the white settlers on the frontier. For villains, westerns replaced armed, enfranchised Black freedmen with Native Americans, white outlaws, eastern corporate monopolies, and Mexican nationalists.

The Birth of a Nation validated the cinematic image of the violent white male mythic hero on horseback as the pivotal figure in restoring social order. Like the captivity narratives at the foundation of American literature, in *Birth*, the heroes, armed ex-Confederate horsemen, rescue white women from African American soldiers, their savage captors. Griffith himself described his vision of translating *The Clansman* to film: "I could just see these Klansmen in a movie with their white robes flying. . . . I could see a chance to do this ride-to-the-rescue on a grand scale. Instead of saving one poor little Nell of the Plains, this ride would be to save a nation."[44]

Unique decisions that Griffith made with his screenplay and film departed from Dixon's novel. Two shifts, in particular, positioned the film as a principal advocate of the "Lost Cause ideology." The first, which historian David Blight refers to as the "reconciliationist vision," is a tendency to forge unifying myths between North and South and to celebrate the memory of the antebellum era.[45] The second shift was Griffith's appropriation of minstrel conventions. *The Birth of a Nation* was elastic, exploiting newly circulating images borrowed from blackface minstrel shows and vaudeville performances to inform its Black characters far more than it borrowed from Dixon's *The Clansman*. Griffith was particularly interested in reducing the prominence of Black men, so he shifted Dixon's portraits of Black male faithful servants into an enlarged Aunt Cindy character, a bona fide "Mammy" caricature who singlehandedly defeats a squad of Union soldiers to enable the escape of Southern aristocrat Dr. Cameron. One of the most remarkable dimensions of the film is the manner in which the minstrel convention and Mammy stereotypes do not end in slapstick comedy.

Griffith resisted allowing Black actors to play the major Black characters, who were performed by whites in blackface. Part of the value for the decision, from Griffith's point of view, was clearly the unlikelihood of irony during the major scenes involving Black characters, including South Carolina lieutenant governor Silas Lynch, army officer Gus, housekeeper and mistress Lillian, and Mammy. (The ironic performance of Black stereotypes was one for which minstrel Bert Williams was especially noted.) In fact, the ideological tension of Griffith's racist narrative stumbles in the places featuring "real" Black people: the dances at the quarters; Madame Sul Te Wan and other women cheering the laws enabling them finally to marry white men and inherit property; and Silas Lynch's governor's party, revealing a "mulatto" standard of beauty that threatens to displace the attractiveness of the film's white heroine, played by Lillian Gish, and the ideal of European beauty. All of these elements—Black art, Black aesthetics, and the contradiction of white law—are bona fide threats to multiple surface narratives designed to restore and sustain white rule.

The Lost Cause Narrative

The Lost Cause had been a crucial wing of white southern memory, enshrined and vigorously ennobled by the end of the nineteenth century and the vanquishing of Reconstruction-era political realities, such as Black enfranchisement. The Lost Cause was "a public memory, a cult of the fallen soldier, a righteous political cause defeated only by superior industrial might, a heritage community awaiting its exodus, and a people forming a collective identity as victims."[46] *The Birth of a Nation* used a budding popular art form to reconcile North and South by vigorously extolling a shared union of white supremacy.

The concluding scenes of *The Birth of a Nation*, two of them drawn from the book of Revelation, imagine the "golden day" of violent judgment followed by paradise, and they emphasize the high moral purpose associated with Griffith's film. The creation of a white supremacist warrior group, the Ku Klux Klan, and the expulsion of Blacks, especially Blacks of mixed race, from the national body of citizens and political actors are linked to an eschatological vision and the appearance of archangel Michael and heavenly ordained retribution. In one concluding scene, an all-white multitude of the damned are slain by an avenging sword-wielding satyr. In another, the robed faithful are looked over by a gentle messianic European figure, an image actually superimposed over the group (a Griffith technical innovation). This redemption resolves the crisis introduced by the film's opening intertitle, "The bringing of the African to America planted the first seed of disunion." But before Christ can take his culled flock to salvation, his chosen representatives, mounted Klansmen, must disarm and disenfranchise the Black freedmen. *Birth* suggests that, like the eschatology from the New Testament book of Revelation, without strong violence, the exceptional destiny of American "union" is impossible to approach.[47]

Vietnam and the Civil War: "The Night They Drove Old Dixie Down"

The changed representations of Black people in America occurred alongside the end of the role of US combat forces in Vietnam in 1973, followed by the fall of the US embassy in 1975. American northern cities, the centers of severe rioting throughout the 1960s, experienced huge financial shortfalls in the 1970s, lost federal government investment in their social welfare and educational apparatus, and were deemed lost lands or poorly managed frontiers, teeming with Black and brown citizens.[48] The changed complexion of the cities, the military defeat, and reluctance to articulate the most obvious of the law-and-order solutions resulted in a crisis in American patriotism and chauvinism. During the last year of his life the civil rights leader Martin Luther King Jr. had spoken out against the involvement of the American military in Vietnam, calling the war "unjust" and "immoral," extending his domestic crusade against poverty and injustice to the international field of American economic and military expansion.[49] After King's assassination in 1968, his antiwar viewpoint went on to be adopted by millions of Americans who protested the conflict, turning the "police action" in Vietnam into America's least-popular military foray of all time.

The outspoken resistance to what some understood as a war of imperialism was also connected to an economic transformation in the United States, dramatically lowering the financial might of the American dollar. Globally, countries throughout the world were nationalizing their natural resources, eliminating the right of ownership to US (and British and French) corporate and industrial interests, whose footholds in Western, Central, and Eastern Asia and Africa were directly connected to the era of colonial conquest. This reclamation of resources abroad caused economic instability in the US, as the cost of consumer goods increased exponentially, which could be understood by the public as the unjust response of Asian, African, Central American, and South American states forming a "Third World project" of the underdeveloped and recently decolonized world.[50] Connected to this upheaval, little rebuilding occurred in major sectors of US cities after the arson and looting following King's death. In a sense, the large antimilitarist movement and the end of racial segregation were experienced by the public as a sharp decline in the quality of life at schools, parks, libraries, swimming pools, and on public transportation, the essence of shared urban life.

While these tragedies were localized to specific parts of the nation—sharply declining Black business corridors or heavily white ethnic manufacturing and extractive resource centers—a broader attitude of melancholy and diffidence became apparent in popular culture, often using historical allegory. Three touchstone songs for the youth rock music audience, the same cinema audience pursued by Eastwood, precede and set a context for the Eastwood film line powerfully conflating the Civil War and Vietnam.[51] In 1969 The Band released "The Night They Drove Old Dixie Down," the song made even more popular by folk singer Joan Baez in 1971, when she took a cover version of the song to number twenty on the annual Billboard singles charts. The song is a dirge, a slow tempo lament that bemoans the loss of a possible pro-South postwar industrial future by the protagonist, Virgil Caine, whose ideal of future success is destroyed by the invading Yankee army. The protagonist, who "served on the Danville train," pines for his past security, putatively assured, "Till Stoneman's cavalry came and tore up the tracks again." Caine, however, is a reluctant supporter of Southern aristocrats like Robert E. Lee and the ideology of the Lost Cause. He seems sentimentally connected to the antebellum nostalgia mainly when he invokes the combat death of a brother, "put in his grave" by a "Yankee." Additionally, despite his work as a railroad man, the real tradition that Caine longs for is that of his father, the humble, yeoman farmer, without any investment in slavery. Thus, he croons with a mixture of sadness and relief at "the night they drove old Dixie down."

When Baez took the song over, her stature as an antiwar and civil rights activist added another dimension of loss and mourning and, ultimately, a rejection of violent conflict to the song. "The Night They Drove Old Dixie Down" became a respectful lament, but the gesture signaled the decline of "Dixie" ideology. Even so, one extraordinary element of the song was its capacity to make a weighty articulation on the South an all-white affair; the song evacuates nearly half of the population of "Dixie." In other words, its achievement is the creation of a song of Southern loss Americans could enjoy without having to confront the fact that the Southern antebellum social world operated on a basis of rank injustice.[52] There were no Black people, slave or free, to consider.

Since the "Great Migration" of African Americans from the South to the American metropolises, often of the North, reached its fulfillment in 1970, the elimination of Blacks from the Southland also had a vivid contemporary salience. In the state of Virginia, for example, an 1860 total population of 1,219,630 included 527,763 people of African descent. In 1900, 1,854,184 Virginians included 660,722 Blacks. By 1970, the total population of 4,648,494 included 861,368 Blacks.[53] In 110 years, the Black proportion of the state had declined from 43 percent in 1860 to 35 percent in 1900 to 18 percent in 1970. A late-1960s song describing Virginia that eliminated Blacks made uncomplicated sense to the popular culture audiences living there, in the arc of the grand repositioning of the American racial landscape.

But silences and erasures in popular discourse were improvements of a sort, because they did not traffic in the ludicrous and pathological conceptual and plastic network of Black images deployed by the national entertainments of minstrelsy and vaudeville and later to the market of industrial-scale consumer goods.[54] The erasures were also a significant but underevaluated outcome of the first two-thirds of the twentieth century and the legal practices of racial segregation, the obverse of nineteenth-century practices of racial intimacy, presence, and cohabitation. Later, twentieth-century Americans, especially those exposed to racial liberalism and made uncomfortable when popular media broadcast racist terms like *nigger* and *darky*, were being groomed to find preferable a hygienic logic of exclusion and erasure that would have seemed odd to filmmakers like D. W. Griffith or even Cecil B. DeMille.

Finally, "The Night They Drove Old Dixie Down" had obvious allegorical dimensions, spending its lyrical energies in the mid-nineteenth century, but with obvious parallels to the transformed world at the demise of racial segregation. Dixie driven down in 1969 and 1970 was not the end of slavery but the challenge to racially exclusive resources in education, housing, employment, and healthcare, as well as legally enforced white social prestige. But without any images of southern Blacks, the song allowed the audience to obtain a sympathetic identification with a protagonist who does not have to be morally tainted by the problem of slavery, racism, racial bias, and discrimination.

A more deliberately reflective popular culture song, if crucially polemicized, was the Canadian songwriter Neil Young's "Southern Man" of 1971. "Southern Man" insists on a sharply Manichean ethical framework, forcefully orchestrating a binary system of Black and white that corresponds to poverty and wealth, and identifying brutality and hidden sexual desire. Young fashioned choruses in his polemic of heavy reparative and Christian ethical duty: "Southern man when will you pay them back" and "Don't forget what your good book says." Young subsequently joined the group Crosby, Stills, and Nash and took further anti–Vietnam War and anti–martial law positions in the early 1970s. In sharp contrast, the classic songs produced by African Americans with regard to the political issues of the 1960s and early 1970s—Sam Cooke's "Change Is Gonna Come," Marvin Gaye's "Mercy, Mercy Me," or Stevie Wonder's "Living for the City"—leave nineteenth-century history alone.

The reflexiveness and sensitivity of popular culture's "folk" genre was correlated with the final decision to abandon Vietnam and to end the selective service draft, as well as concerns centering on the Arab-Israeli War and the OPEC oil embargo. Internal shifts within the US media markets also eliminated and sharply reduced a joint public American culture prefaced on obvious Black participation. In 1969, AM music stations cut 40 percent of their Black music from their playlists, typically the Motown hitmakers, in response to the rioting following the assassination of Martin Luther King Jr. The cultural politics and format of the radio stations themselves were shifting. FM, or frequency modulation, air waves opened, and a new genre called "Urban Contemporary" was unveiled that included "soul" music, added white pop musicians, and eliminated Black cultural and political programs. Most decisive in transforming American popular tastes in the post–civil rights era were the "rock"-format FM radio stations and the elevation of the sonic aesthetics and worldviews of British and ultimately Australian rock groups. Some of the racial antagonisms lively during the era are captured by the "Disco sucks" rallying cry of 1976.[55] Perhaps the key reversal that symbolized the turmoil of the twenty years since the 1954 *Brown* decision and the enduring difficulty of school desegregation was the 1974 "busing" crisis. White mobs in Boston defied the courts and rioted in the streets, assaulting Black passersby.

In 1974 the band Lynyrd Skynyrd released "Sweet Home Alabama," a response polemic to "Southern Man," and, somewhat unusual for a rock band, a specific engagement with contemporary politics. (It's worthwhile to note that of the three songs, "Sweet Home Alabama" has retained the strongest core constituency, as well as widespread, anthem-like, popular appeal.) Lynyrd Skynyrd went so far as to cite "Mr. [Neil] Young" by name and, albeit with mock politeness, to dismiss him: "A southern man don't need him around anyhow." The gesture places their work generically in the realm of response polemic. But, fascinatingly enough, the song revealed the operation of the discourse of racial affinity in the US that overrode or bisected so easily other shared points of view. Evincing the long shadow of the Civil War on contemporary American culture, the song was particularly interested in redeeming the public myths connected to several historical events. It recuperated the city of Birmingham, Alabama, known to Blacks throughout the 1950s and 1960s as "Bombingham" for its white supremacist terrorist violence and defiance of federal law. George Wallace, Alabama's staunch white supremacist governor, ran for president in 1968 on a white supremacist political platform, and Lynyrd Skynyrd sings, "In Birmingham they love the Governor" and "Now we all did what we could do." But what is most extraordinary is the suture that is made between the aggressive claims to an unfashionable white supremacy and call for murder by Wallace and white supremacist terrorists and Nixon's scandal at Watergate. "Now Watergate does not bother me / Does your conscience bother you?" the vocalist continues. Here the subtext of Nixon's rhetoric of opposition to civil rights and promotion of law-and-order become connected to the practice of internal surveillance and the deployment of the police state, the crime for which Nixon was forced to resign to avoid the scandal of impeachment. (A similar case of surveillance is revealed by journalist Jim Risen in the account of the 2004 government scandal surveying telephone and internet records of American citizens, to be discussed in chapter 7.) Of the three songs, "Sweet Home Alabama" defiantly emanates from the gospel musical tradition pioneered by Black Americans, trumpeting its piety with the religious refrain, "Lord I'm coming home to you." It rings with a Black-sounding arrangement of choral voices, though it, like The Band's 1969 song, eliminates African Americans, slavery, and segregation from the lyrics.

Western Hero as Confederate

Thus, Eastwood's films and the aura connected to his gunfighter heroes would join the "commonsense" narratives that helped white Americans justify their massive resistance to integrated schools and neighborhoods, their nostalgic memories of the legacy of US imperial actions, and their antagonisms to the Black global freedom struggle and the Black Power movement. As Stanley Corkin writes, "the repressed dimension of the western is imperialism," and the revitalization of the genre during the same era that saw the demise of the Soviet Union calls for an analysis of its obvious commentary on American domestic life.[56]

Eastwood's work to unite the mythology connected to the outlaw gunfighter with the historic downfall of the Confederacy and the Lost Cause reflected the organization of this new historical bloc. The same Americans responding to his films were making sense of Black migration to the North, the radical shift of Black portraiture in the American national media, and the threat to the sanctity of white neighborhoods and new pressures on suburban America's spatial configurations. In particular, *The Outlaw Josey Wales*, like the *Star Wars* film released the following year, generates and revitalizes allegories for pure white, hygienic spaces in the US imaginary and establishes an important "color-blind" cultural grammar that has naturalized the massive resource redistribution within the United States, from cities to suburbs, from the Rust Belt to the Sun Belt. Sociologist Patricia Fernandez-Kelley refers to the shift that redrew major sections of American cities and state relations to a significant percentage of Americans as *capital regression*, or the curtain of effects systematically strangling Black American urban communities and most fully connected to the policies inaugurated by Richard Nixon.[57] These films participate in multiple optical fantasies of deliberate Black historical erasure (a Hollywood convention, in and of itself) that condition the white American imaginary perception of shared national space.[58]

Eastwood revived the guerilla-Confederate-as-American-patriot in the midst of this profound political economic realignment, a realignment that comprised two fundamental electoral shifts: the movement of Black voters away from the Republican Party in the 1930s to Franklin Roosevelt's Democratic New Deal reforms and, thirty years later, the abandonment by working-class whites of the Democratic Party in favor of the Republican. During the Nixon era, whites in the South and industrial North would forsake the Democratic Party, previously a solid bedrock of Lost Cause mythology. By the time of Richard Nixon's 1968 election, a new political tendency was under way, what pundit Kevin Phillips called "the Emerging Republican Majority with its bastions in the South and in the 'heartland' of the Plains and the Rocky Mountains."[59] Cultural works bundling the Lost Cause ideology, militarist nostalgia, and idyllic portraits of the nineteenth century appealed strongly to this group. (The extremist strands went on to constitute the militia movement of the 1980s and 1990s, which metamorphose into the "Alt Right" or "Three Percenters," "Proud Boys," and "Boogaloo Bois.") The Lost Cause also, of course, referred allegorically to the Vietnam War and the project of expanding American borders abroad, what Richard Immerman calls the "Empire for Liberty."[60]

Eastwood's later westerns offered an important series of resolutions to profound and new cultural anxieties, the "struggles of the 1970s [that] seemed to undermine their status and power as white men."[61] Additionally, Eastwood's dramatic portraits offered white Americans the proper affective disposition toward nonwhites. His films coached not simply behavior and attitudes but also the reasonable depth of emotive ties, the surface area of empathetic identification to ethnic America after the customs of segregation were banished, as well as men toward women in the era of equal rights. The conservative movement throughout the 1970s consolidated its political gains not on account of any shared economic programs but largely by referring to strict moral and ethical values that, often enough, had as their binding glue anti-Black animus. It would be the swerve of 55 percent of the nation's white men to the Republican Party in 1980 that formed the groundswell bringing Ronald Reagan into office. In an era of politically conscious and vocal American Blacks, independent African nations, and resource nationalism, Eastwood helped to provide a newly revised system of tropes and images set in a racially exclusive western tableau, reorganizing prowhite male American patriotism. Eastwood's vision in *The Outlaw Josey Wales* would be crucial because, even more important, he would show the South winning the war—something impossible to articulate during Wayne's era of the 1950s. By 1976, the Lost Cause would be rewon, as it had been in 1915 with Griffith's film.

CHAPTER TWO

The Good, the Bad and the Ugly
and Critique of the Colonial Aftermath

> It was a Western movie, packed, as they say, with action. In the Legislative Assembly the Africans had made believe that they believed in Western values; here, in this dark movie, they didn't have to pretend. Psychologically distant, they mocked at a world that was not their own, had their say about a world in which they had no say.
> —Richard Wright, *Black Power* (1954)

> I thought to myself they must be taking all of us who were involved in any sort of black political struggle and putting us into the Army as soon as they could so we wouldn't be a problem anymore.
> —Robert E. Holcomb, *Bloods* (1984)

Sergio Leone's 1966 film *The Good, the Bad and the Ugly* is recognized today as a masterpiece and pivot point in the life of the western film genre. Released in the US in December 1967, the film, the finale of a trilogy, shocked critics and titillated audiences with its exhaustive treatment of onscreen death and its putative refusal to substantiate a definable ethical or moral code of conduct. The *New York Times* called it "an entire supermarket" "of sadism" and suggested a new title: "The Burn, the Gouge, and the Mangle."[1]

American western film audiences were accustomed to cinematic presentations featuring stable, if complex, antipodes between good and evil and the righteous use of deadly violence, a network of effects formidably connected to box-office icons like John Wayne, Alan Ladd, and Gary Cooper. Now, three films released in the same year departed sharply from the mythic ideal of good battling evil. *The Good, the Bad and the Ugly* was preceded in release by the first two films in the trilogy, *A Fistful of Dollars* (1964; US release January 1967) and *For a Few Dollars More* (1965; US release May 1967), both of which were already phenomenally successful in Italy and Europe. As well as eschewing ethical codes, Leone's westerns seemed uninterested in cold war political ideology, the serial accounts in their predecessors of free-speaking individuals from the solid yeomanry who confront heavy odds of unrestrained lethal malice. On the surface, Leone's epic three-hour film offered a myopic concentration on the panache of the gunman and his method and technique of lethal dispatch. When asked about the political message underlying his western films, he famously responded with an evasiveness that took into account the tumult of postwar Italy, with its Far Left Communist Party and Far Right Monarchists and Neofascists. "We are not directors of conscience," he said in an interview. "The audience should be allowed to draw their own conclusions."[2]

The project starred three actors strongly associated with westerns: Lee Van Cleef as Sentenza, Eli Wallach as Tuco, and Clint Eastwood as Blondie. They combined to play the Bad, the Ugly, and the Good, respectively. Although Clint Eastwood had the least impressive screen credits of the three, he reached a new level of stardom because of the film. Throughout 1967, American audiences were being groomed to accept a new sort of western star, "a selfish and vicious nonconformist towards the inviolable moral code."[3] Produced in Italian and English and dubbed in English when it was released in the United States, *The Good, the Bad and the Ugly* launched Eastwood as a western antihero who would overlap with and eventually replace without precisely superseding the cultural significance of John Wayne.

Leone emerged from an Italian film studio system grappling with the political readjustments of postwar Europe. In Italy, two contests were under way: the challenge to the American-backed, private market state presented by the Italian Communist Party (legendary for its opposition to fascism) and the ongoing problem of unifying the white North with the less economically developed, less racially European South of Italy, a century-long project called *Risorgimento*.[4] The April 1948 victory of the Christian Democrat Party, made possible by "substantial financial assistance" from the US State Department, resulted in Italy's accepting the Marshall Plan economic funding, joining the North Atlantic Treaty Organization, and assuming a position as a bulwark against the Soviet Union.[5] No longer a first-tier global power, Italy joined the new configuration of Atlantic states. Italian diplomat Sergio Romano later noted that the unpopular alibi of European solidarity was necessary to "defend our economic sovereignty and to pay the price of the loss of our military sovereignty."[6] By the 1950s the US State Department preferred nationalist, authoritarian, Far Right Italian political parties to communists.[7] Politically centrist and left-wing Italian filmmakers issued stirring responses to the extraordinary level of direct US intervention in the Italian political scene and commercial economy.

A "sword-and-sandals" filmmaker who adored *Shane*, Sergio Leone turned to westerns in 1964. Within three years of his dynamic commercial success, a politically radical shift would revise the so-called "spaghetti westerns." The new subfield was named the "Zapata Westerns" because they recreated the revolution in Mexico and the land reform efforts of the southern commander Emiliano Zapata. The genre cohered in 1966 with the film *The Big Gundown*, followed a year later by *A Bullet for the General*. Both films were written by Sardinian Marxist Franco Solinas, who collaborated with Gillo Pontecorvo on *The Battle of Algiers* (1966), the key neorealist European film depicting the violent anticolonial struggle between European NATO countries and Africa and Asia in the 1950s. With *The Battle of Algiers* Pontecorvo, a former Communist Party member who had already completed the concentration camp film *Kapo* (1959), became the doyen of serious docudrama cinema. His celebrated film created new terms for radicalism by expanding the left-wing European gaze to include colonial resistance. Italian directors were notably meshing their concerns with radical politics and provocative reconsiderations of different film genres. While Pontecorvo and Solinas worked jointly with successful African revolutionaries, other Italian filmmakers, like Gualtierro Jacopetti and Franco Prosperi, used cinema to rage against the places in Africa and America where colonialism was more firmly in place. The *Mondo* docudrama series explicitly inserted satire and absurdism into the epic political docudrama film, depicting the gross exploitation of Africa in *Goodbye Africa* (*Africa Addio* [1966]) and following up in 1971 with *Goodbye Uncle Tom* (*Addio Zio Tom*), a feature investigating internal colonialism.[8]

In comparison to such peers, Leone's stylistic point of departure within the western genre was epic and mythic. But his films' putatively apolitical and anarchic archetypes also remained able to sustain interpretations purporting a fluidly radical political consciousness and critique of western imperialism. He considered Italy's film tradition overburdened by political messages but admitted, "If you want to look for it [political arguments] you can."[9]

Leone makes an older point about the work of art having no fundamental or permanent ideological valence, artistic value, or political meaning. Pontecorvo's deliberately neutral film was banned in France until the 1970s; the *Mondo* films were confused with the historic racist tracts they dutifully inserted to expose for their absurdity; and Leone's films were considered mere exclamations of gory violence. The ambiguous reception and deployment of the genre of realist docudrama, surrealist absurdist docudrama, or epic is not exclusively an academic problem. A film that purportedly served as a template for the militant plans of New York City Black Panthers in 1971,[10] Pontecorvo's film found its way to the Pentagon in 2003 as nearly an informative guide to assist in the management of local publics when conducting mass-scale interrogations and detentions in Afghanistan and Iraq.[11] The cinematic work of art was becoming renditioned into another data loop, a point of obvious incorporation into the surveillance and punishment mechanism of the state.[12]

The daring, edgy, and still today controversial neorealist and absurdist realist responses of the Italian cineastes Pontecorvo, Jacopetti, and Prosperi shaped the milieu of Leone's cinematic efforts, his attempt to produce genre films that were artistically robust and that might have a symbolic impact in Italy and abroad. Leone had pioneered his work in the western genre in the early 1960s when only a handful of Italian-directed and -produced films, typically shot in Spain, were made until the breakthrough year 1966, when seventy-three of the films were released.[13] The filmmakers shared a network of contacts including actors and film professionals. The German film star Klaus Kinski appeared in Leone's *A Few Dollars More* before going on to work with Damiano Damiani in *A Bullet for the General* and Sergio Corbucci in *The Great Silence*. Leone, Pontecorvo, and Damiani all shared the musician Ennio Morricone, who created original, haunting scores for the trilogy with Leone and for Pontecorvo, among many subsequent films. Morricone's work on *The Good, the Bad and the Ugly* is considered by some critics to have "redefined the relationship between music and moving image."[14] Solinas regarded the successful appeal to audiences made by Leone's westerns and swiftly bent the genre to a more direct vehicle for Marxist political struggle with the dramas *A Bullet for the General, The Big Gundown*, and *A Professional Gun*.

Leone's subsequent films paid close attention to the escalating radicalism during the peak era of the violent opposition to colonialism. After the 1966–67 breakthrough with American audiences and access to Hollywood financiers, Leone followed *The Good, the Bad and the Ugly* with a more unguarded representation of colonial violence in the 1968 film *Once upon a Time in the West*. In that film, which opens with a moment unprecedented for the genre—an extended close-up of veteran African American western star Woody Strode—Leone makes more explicit the symbolic architecture that similarly looms in *GBU*. He also features legitimate box-office stars in Henry Fonda and Charles Bronson. Leone unquestionably produced more stark representations of historical power relations in his films as the global reckoning with the legacy of European colonialism intensified at the end of the 1960s.

Leone continued the evolution in anticolonial politics, grown vastly more complex after the eruption of American and European military responses to the global drama of resource nationalism in parts of the world that had been colonial possessions. The western was an imaginative genre for narrative and film that owed its origins to the engagement of the real-world politics ideologically catalyzed by the credo of Manifest Destiny and the practical enactment of Anglo-imperial expansion and then by the territorial consolidation of lands that were controlled by Mexico and Indigenous Americans. Leone concluded his western films with his most direct political intervention in 1973's *Duck, You Sucker*, in which "his political discourse becomes more explicit and less mediated by metaphor or mythical transfiguration."[15] The film is original in its specific articulation of the shared anti-imperial projects and imbricated positions of Irish nationalists, terrorists, Zapatistas, and bandits. Also in Leone's finale to the western genre, he lodges a riposte to the more deterministic tastes of his peers in the overtly political Italian film, Corbucci, Sollima, and Damiani.[16]

The Good, the Bad and the Ugly

Leone secured funding, wrote, directed, and produced three films between 1964 and 1966 using Clint Eastwood as their main character. That trilogy culminates in scope and complexity with *The Good, the Bad and the Ugly*. By setting the western film in the temporal and geospatial realm of American national crisis, the Civil War, and addressing the dynamic conflictual relation between Native and settler, the film insisted on a historical reckoning rare for westerns. It also presented Eastwood in his most ethically indefinable role of the trilogy.

Though an experienced gunfighter in all the films, Eastwood played the role of Christ avenger and beneficent partisan in *A Fistful of Dollars*. Leone lifted the plot of the film from Akira Kurosawa's 1961 samurai classic *Yojimbo* and placed it in a western. The skilled gunman played by Eastwood rides into town and orchestrates the killing of fifty or so rival bandits, saving the peasants from the deadly conflict between two rapacious bands of settlers—one led by an Anglo named Baxter, the other a cruel outfit of Mexican thieves led by a man named Rojo. In the process he saves the kidnapped woman of the village, restoring her to her husband and son.

In the second film, *For a Few Dollars More*, Eastwood costarred alongside screen veteran Lee Van Cleef, noted for his appearance in the classics *High Noon* (1952) and *The Man Who Shot Liberty Valance* (1962). The men are introduced as competing bounty hunters, traversing the Texas, Mexico, and New Mexico landscape in search of outlaws with high bounties on their heads. The plot features a triangle of competing interests: the two bounty hunters vs. a rapacious Mexican border villain called "El Indio," played by the popular Italian film star Gian Maria Volontè. El Indio seeks a bonanza in US banknotes from a heavily guarded El Paso, Texas, bank. Douglas Mortimer, Van Cleef's portrait of a nearly fifty-year-old Confederate colonel from North Carolina, and Monco (Eastwood) are both in pursuit. The violent professionals compare wanted posters to saloon toughs and shoot them down. El Indio, recently broken out of prison, has a bounty of $10,000, and the men decide to work together to collect the reward for El Indio and his entire gang.

Leone's second western film featuring two American stars returned to the most fundamental of racist colonial tropes: the captivity narrative.[17] In a series of flashbacks laced throughout the film, the viewer learns that El Indio has murdered a newlywed husband and raped the bride. Because of shared key-chain music boxes with photographic portraits, the audience knows there is a connection to Mortimer. As Indio listens to the melody of the music box, he performs moments of psychic unease, derangement, catatonia, fury, and incapacity to recognize danger or his own interests. As the film concludes in a duel between Indio and Mortimer—symbolic characterizations of the Native and the original violent settler—the viewer learns that Indio has, in fact, raped Mortimer's sister, who then killed herself rather than endure the consequences of insemination and subjugation, the biracial product of the white European and the mestizo. There is an important explanation for the haunting: Indio had achieved the union with the objective of immaculate whiteness, but he is discomfited because of the awareness of his incapacity as a suitor and his rejection. When the colonial project has troubled itself with justification, it has returned precisely to this civilizationist narrative of reform: European colonialism exists to either reform or eliminate the Native inhabitant of the colony, the "quintessence of evil," "impervious to ethics" and "the enemy of values."[18]

Leone associated the moral project of righteous avenger with Van Cleef's Mortimer, who abandons the monetary bounty at the finale. At first, the Eastwood hero's principle is financial accountability, and the main tropes developed are Monco's skillful gunfighting and swift violence, a putative departure from the nuclear family reunion he had made possible in *A Fistful of Dollars*. But the concluding gunfight that avenges the rape and death of a southern white woman unites Mortimer and Monco. The film actually ends with Eastwood's Monco, already identified as "my boy," becoming the "son" of the "old man" from North Carolina and invested in his concerns. If the first film dutifully transposed the Kurosawa 1961 classic onto the western genre, *For a Few Dollars More* could accommodate an allegorical reading of *Risorgimento* northern and southern unity, with a cold war repudiation of an encroaching militant rogue band.

In *The Good, the Bad and the Ugly*, Leone enlarges the radical dimension of the anonymous bounty hunter. The cinematic ideal of the heroic bounty hunter, his embodiment of the useful collage of legal service and private gain, is linked to the noir genre of the private detective.[19] In an American context, the bounty hunter also invokes the slave patrol, the origin of the southern police force.[20] Eastwood's Blondie operates fully beyond the law; he is the bounty hunter who uses real and symbolic violence to capture and set free, habitually, the heinous criminal. And in this manner, Leone introduced certain archetypal positions of settler and Native. The Good character embodied the qualities of the traditional Anglo western expert marksman who searches for the bounty; his main rival is the Ugly, a mestizo bandit, whose passion for vengeance always interferes with his pursuit of lucre.

The film's gesture toward imperial politics lay in its identifiably non-Manichean character, "the ugly" mestizo, the Mexican bandit Tuco (Eli Wallach). Tuco represents the encounter between the Amerindian (the vast Southwest region along the river separating post-1846 Texas from Mexico hosted Comanche, Apache, Diné, Kikapoo, Ute, Pueblo, and others) and Spanish colonial conquest. He speaks English and Spanish and carries the biological heritage of the ancient Aztec and Mayan civilizations, the southwestern Indigenous, and the peninsular and creole Spanish (who would also carry African heritage from the Al-Andalus era).[21] Leone had already established in *A Few Dollars More* the position of El Indio as the D. W. Griffith–style villain, the barbaric Native who rapes, and now he poses the possibility that the mixed-race mestizo presents a problem of sexual violence.

Mahmood Mamdani supplies an important observation that moves a reading of the film beyond a confrontation between the settler colonist and Native. Blondie, who will confess later to being from Illinois, is a European-descended American. Equally at home on either side of the Rio Grande, Tuco is a Mexican whose borders are being successively displaced by the colonial war for Mexican independence, the arrival of more Anglo-American settlers (mainly from the South and with their enslaved Africans in tow), the war for the Anglo state of Texas, and the post-Appomattox hope of General Shelby to relocate a viable portion of the Confederacy to Mexico. A birthright border dweller and refugee, Tuco embodies the racial heritage of mestizo, a combination of Amerindian and Spanish. The European settlers are constructed as citizens with rights in the law. Non-European Mexicans are neither landed aristocrats of a sovereign nation nor persons able to claim a new citizenship after a war or treaty has redefined national borders. The 1848 Treaty of Guadalupe Hidalgo, which ended the Mexican-American War (a conflict fought, at least partially, to extend slavery westward), distinguished between property-holding Mexicans who were offered United States citizenship and those described in Article 9, "on an equality with that of the inhabitants of the other territories of the United States."[22] The territorial subjects, whose lands and lives became increasingly rigidly governed, are symbolized by Tuco, who is also defined less by law than by custom. European settlers and nonwhite Mexicans are forcefully distinguished by race, a vertical relation, unlike ethnicity, a horizontal one.[23] In *The Good, the Bad and the Ugly*, Leone emphasizes the isolation within the social world of nativity that defines Tuco, a member literally of a subject ethnicity and a subject race. If Van Cleef's character's ethnic name, "Sentenza" (a man intimately familiar with both Confederate and Union troops), signals his belonging in the Southwest on the basis of the post-Hidalgo-incorporated Mexican Americans, Tuco's condemnation as ugly stems from the fact that his racial ancestry perpetually makes him repulsive.

Leone's film title exploits the fissure presented by the twin problems of ideological Manicheanism and aesthetics. The western, with its determined culmination in multiple or climactic acts of violence, requires the development of viewers' discrimination so that they are compelled and aligned with the dramatic resolution, the desired execution of the villain. This adequacy, fulfilling the desire of the viewer in the onscreen death, relies on the application of taste.

These elements are, of course, all in the realm of aesthetics. By using his title to call direct attention to the beautiful as a category by pronouncing its absence, Leone also invites an account of the ways that the problem of style and taste exist along a subterranean layer that constitutes the foundation of ethical virtue. If viewers are unclear about what is beautiful, they are also unable to decide the difference between good and bad: the idealization of the beautiful can qualify and even anticipate the moral consideration of virtue, a field for political engagements. Jacques Rancière considers this problem of aesthetics shaping sensory perception, noting the givenness of an aesthetic foundation prior to judgment:

> Aesthetics can be understood in a Kantian sense ... as the system of *a priori* forms determining what presents itself to sense experience. It is a delimitation of spaces and times, of the visible and the invisible, of speech and noise, that simultaneously determines the place and the stakes of politics as a form of experience. Politics revolves around what is seen and what can be said about it, around who has the ability to see and the talent to speak, around the properties of spaces and the possibilities of time.[24]

By nominally privileging Tuco through the aesthetic and not the ethical, Leone directs the viewer to the "delimitation of spaces and times" that lay the groundwork for a statement about right and wrong, good and bad.

Of course, the film's other principals are constructed with an emphasis on appearance constituting ethical value instead of the inviolability of pure ethical judgment. The physical ideal of "beauty" is typically associated with Eastwood's character, "the good," crucially named "Blondie" by Tuco. Blondie provides comfort to a youthful, dying Confederate soldier, also blond, an Adonis figure who personifies beauty. Leone critic Christopher Frayling explains the ubiquity and narrative power of stylistic signifiers in the film:

> The heroes and villains of Spaghetti Westerns are almost invariably obsessed by "style," "image," "ritual," and their confrontations or interactions are, typically, symbolic ones: one of the trademarks of the Spaghetti (especially after *A Fistful of Dollars*) was to become the extended face-off, or duel, or settling of accounts; and the hero-figures are usually identifiable by a collection of external gestures, mannerisms, "stylish" articles of clothing, or even motifs on the soundtrack, rather than by anything remotely to do with the "inner man." ... This [is] obsession with style, ritual or external gesture.[25]

The relationship between style and performance in contrast to historical event and transhistorical ethics was of keen interest to Frantz Fanon, who advanced the Manichean, absolute, irreconcilable positions of the settler and Native, the white and the nonwhite in the 1950s. Fanon dedicated his thesis, which became the book *Black Skin, White Masks*, to his brother Felix, writing "the greatness of a man is to be found not in his acts but in his style."[26] Leone's emphasis on the catalog of surface symbolism suggests a similarly telling commitment to the aesthetic category as the a priori on which ethical acts might exist. In the creation of the relationship between Wallach's mestizo Tuco and Eastwood's Anglo Blondie, Leone depicted the colonial condition and its postimperial border as spaces managed by economies of style that guided economies of individual ethics. If the "ethical value of literature lies in the felt encounter with alterity that it brings with the reader," as argued by Dorothy Hale, and, by extension, film and the viewer, Leone seems to layer racial and ethnic archetypes to complicate cinematic meaning and ethical decision-making.[27]

The archetypes of good and bad, beauty and ugliness are most effectively eroded with the director's choice to cast Jewish American performer Eli Wallach as Tuco, an actor with principal roles in two of the most complex Hollywood westerns of the period. Wallach had played in *How the West Was Won* (1962), the film with Civil War battle scenes shot by director John Ford and that inspired Leone's own efforts; he had also acted in a larger role as the Mexican villain Calvera in *The Magnificent Seven* (1960), directed by John Sturges. *The Magnificent Seven* asserts a dramatic antiracist liberal ethic in its opening minutes, when stars Yul Brynner and Steve McQueen valiantly oppose racially segregated cemeteries. Wallach, sought after as an actor for his complex onscreen portraits of nonwhites during an era when Native American and Mexican actors rarely held lead roles,[28] provides the foil for the plot that joins antiracist liberalism to an endorsement of counterinsurgency that enabled neocolonialism. His performance surpassed the work of Volontè (*A Few Dollars More*; *A Bullet for the General*), Charles Bronson (*The Magnificent Seven*; *Once upon a Time in the West*), and Rod Steiger (*Duck, You Sucker*), performers whose appearance invokes both Native indigeneity and the colonial conquest creating the conditions of *mestizaje* of Leone's other westerns.[29] For Leone, the fundamental oppositional quality of Tuco was his explicit unattractiveness. This concern with aesthetics as a means of outlasting ethical determinism connects back to the filmmaker's evasion of a direct partisan intervention. "We have no right to prick the political conscience of our contemporaries. We are not magisters. The films we make ought to make people think. We are professional 'exciters.'"[30] The film insists that ethical questions are subordinate to aesthetic principles.

Fungibility and Race

The Good, the Bad and the Ugly opens with an establishing shot of a desolate mountain escarpment and arid plain. The presentation of the expansive terrain is abruptly interrupted by an extreme close-up of a gaunt-faced, light-

Eli Wallach in *The Good, the Bad and the Ugly*, dir. Sergio Leone (MGM, 1966).

brown-haired, blue-eyed man with an open wound on his cheek. Although he is obviously Anglo, he is also conspicuously and sordidly disfigured. The next shot is of an equally desolate town of abandoned prairie schooners, ramshackle wooden buildings, and mangy dogs. Crows seem to twitter in the background of this abandoned, desolate western town. Two more men ride into town and, together with the ugly Anglo, walk down the main street and converge on a saloon, identifiable on account of its swing doors. The trio push through the doors, the viewer hears five shots, the camera tightens on a wide triple-sill window, and a man crashes through the glass. He is bareheaded and dressed in peasant's cotton clothes, which in the economy of western films of the era signals Native American or mestizo ethnicity but not European. Tuco clutches an enormous turkey leg and a bottle wrapped in rope in one hand, a pistol on a leather string in the other. Leone freezes the frame and in cursive red lowercase letters appear the words "the ugly." As the words materialize, the audience hears a human imitation of a crowing bird and a flute playing five tones. These are the notes of Ennio Morricone's famous telltale soundtrack to the film, which borrows its staccato sonic cues from Dmitiri Tiomkin's score for *High Noon*. Shooting his enemies in response, the famished battling peasant (who, ironically, eats well in this place of famine and destitution for the Anglo), Tuco Ramirez leaps onto a horse and gallops out of town.

Tuco, identified as the antithesis to the film's missing fourth term, "the beautiful," bears the film's complex mediating weight between good and bad moral imperatives, which will be shown to be false equivalents. Another formal element of the narration suggests that Tuco occupies the film's center of gravity: he names the other principals, locked into their archetypal positions, with physical traits that reinforce their aesthetic claims to whiteness. Eastwood's "good" character bears the name "Blondie," after his Nordic hair, and Van Cleef's "bad" is named "Angel Eyes," a reference to the remorseless killer's blue eyes. The film thus places its hopeful possibility on this antimoral, anti-Anglo figure, the first principal introduced and the one who will also conclude the drama.

The Good, the Bad and the Ugly reprised key plot nuggets from *For a Few Dollars More*, such as the roles of Eastwood and Van Cleef as experienced bounty hunters. But here the father-and-son duo from the second film are enemies, simply competing skilled white gunfighters in a relentless pursuit of a fortune in gold. Leone introduces Van Cleef as a horseman riding from the arid plain and onto an Edenic, well-irrigated farm. The important second sequence opens with the camera revealing a brown young boy, the son of Confederate soldier Stevens and played by Antonito Ruiz, who had previously appeared in *For a Few Dollars More* as an El Paso street gamin. Now the camera lingers to capture the boy's innocent good looks, as well as the beauty of Stevens's dark-skinned wife (Cuban Chelo Alonso), who has prepared an ample dinner of bread and stew. The ex-Rebel Stevens (Antonio Casas) prospers as the chief of a dark family tilling the land. Van Cleef obtains information and smirkingly destroys the pastoral idyll not with malevolence but the studied logic of fungibility, of perfect species and commodity substitution: killing is a task like any other, and there is no ethical or moral threshold against death that seals off categories or disallows the transmogrification of forms of work. After shooting father and eldest son, Van Cleef returns to the man who has hired him, a Confederate sergeant named Baker, to whom he delivers information and then also kills. "You know the pity is, whenever I am paid, I always follow my job through, you know that," says Van Cleef, and laughs, before smothering the infirm soldier (who seems suffering from a gunshot wound and perhaps tuberculosis) with a pillow and shooting him in the head through the pillow. As Angel Eyes laughs at the deed, the words "the bad" appear on the screen. There are no human relations that outweigh the fetish for specie that motivates Van Cleef's character.

Leone spends ten minutes of screen time here, lingering in Angel Eyes's destruction of the snug nuclear, mestizo family and the homestead, before he provides a competing violent episode with the tubercular Confederate cavalryman Baker. While we are not confident about the precise historical time,

Leone rests the camera on a pristine Confederate uniform with the yellow piping of the cavalry, an important temporal clue enabling us to conclude that we are somewhere within the rough orbit of the Civil War, perhaps two years on either side of 1865. Here is also an allusion to John Wayne's Ethan Edwards of *The Searchers*. In the paired scene of men who have taken off from the cause of the war to pursue their own interests, "the bad" reveals the key plot element: the quest for El Dorado, the bonanza in gold. Then "the bad" murders the man who has paid him, proving not simply the lure of specie but the consubstantiation between gold and death. The crisis here is one of mythic proportion in that the lucre is deadly in itself, destroying everyone who encounters it.

Clint Eastwood's Blondie is not introduced until the eighteenth minute of the film. Although the director seduces the audience with the character— the witty, semicomic, Achilles hero—Blondie is tightly bound within the dimensions of the warrior's professional excellence, balanced by an ethos that involves self-preservation, stylish compassion, and equally stylish sadism. Leone creates a mystic aura around this crack-shot hero, teasing the viewer with the absence and presence of "the good" and reinforcing the concept that he is otherworldly. Eastwood walks into his first frame with his back to the camera, the surprised faces of three Mexican bounty hunters in front of him. Like all the film's bad men, he is a trickster figure and uses ironic tropes in his speech. When, for example, one of the Mexican bounty hunters taunts Tuco—"Hey amigo, you know you've got a face beautiful enough to be worth $2,000?"—Eastwood (at this point offscreen) interjects, "Yeah, but you don't look like the one who'll collect it." Blondie strikes a match, lighting the trademark cigarillo from the other films, then challenges the three non-Anglo bounty hunters to a duel. Leone gives a tight close-up to feature the faces of each of the three men at high noon. Two of the men appear to be Natives, and one wears a sombrero. These men are piquant, unattractive, and indigenous to the Southwest, like Tuco: when the gunfight begins, the audience is enlisted to delight in a contest between Anglo beauty and Native ugliness.

With only the rear of the hat, shoulders, and waist of duster-wearing Blondie in the center of the frame, Leone shows the quick battle and demise of the bounty hunters. During the shoot-out, the camera shifts to explore Eastwood frontally, synecdochically reducing him to a hand firing a pistol, with three tight shots of his waist and partly hidden gun belt, and then his right hand holding the pistol and trigger with the left hand prepared to fan the hammer. Instead of revealing the face of the fast gunman, Leone then shifts to a wary Tuco, whose eyes are cast down but then lift upward hesitantly and expectantly, a move swiftly joined to a close-up of Blondie's lethal killing hands and pistol.

After showing the hands, Leone returns to a close-up shot of the grizzled Eli Wallach, who then slowly seems to express admiration, gratitude, a glimmer of respect, and hope. Blondie holsters the Colt Navy revolver and strides forward. Tuco grins sheepishly in a practiced performance of obsequiousness, reaching toward his pistol in the dust in front of him. But the expert pistolero, his face still obscured, has closed the distance and steps on the gun. Tuco's hand, with two large silver rings and a leather band circling the palm of his left (with which to fan the pistol hammer) recoils. To the viewer's surprise, the stranger addresses him in a tone of familiarity: "How much are you worth now?"

Tuco considers the question of his reduction from subject to fungible object and adopts another register of recognition: he now addresses an intimate. "How much? Two thousand," he begins, and then the camera shifts to reveal for the first time Eastwood's face, shielded by a white wide-brimmed hat, a planter's hat. The viewer sees the actor's complete image when Eastwood looks up, smiles, and says in deadpan, confirming the estimate, "That's right. Two thousand dollars." The duo chuckle in a joined frame, and the viewer recognizes that they are coconspirators. Blondie's face is revealed, an apparition uncovered, the word and the death function made flesh, when the logic of fungibility is articulated: the Indigenous, nonmigrant Tuco can be successfully exchanged. With this dialogue Leone references the slave trade, the systematized exchange of bonds for human beings, the transformation of a category of human beings into bounties.[31]

Here the viewing of *GBU* benefits from an important insight generally provided us by the writings of Saidiya Hartman, Jared Sexton, and Frank Wilderson III. In their work, fungibility is the key relational complication produced by the event of the transatlantic slave system—to turn African people into equivalent commodified units of exchange. It is precisely this phenomenon, "a violence-effect that marks the difference between Black positionality and White positionality . . . a difference between capacities of speech," that also enables white psyches to appropriate Black representations through enjoyment and empathy. The point of the theorists of Blackness as fungibility is a permanent positional antagonism. "No web of analogy can be spun between, on the one hand, the free body that mounts fungible flesh on an emancipatory journey toward self-cancellation and, on the other, the fungible being that has just been mounted. The two positions are structurally irreconcilable, which is to say they are not 'contemporaries.' "[32]

Here we can grasp the continuation of bondage after the slave form of exchange has transformed, giving credence to the notion of "slavery and its aftermath."[33] For these critics, the problem of slavery is not trauma, a provisionally commuted death sentence, natal alienation, or dishonor but rather the "gratuitous violence" transforming the human being into a series of joined parts and affects exchangeable for a ready equivalent on a market. And while critics like Wilderson reject the similarity between nonwhite mestizos, Native Americans, and formerly enslaved Blacks, it is useful to recall that the plantation slavery project of human reduction to fungible object began with Spanish enslavement of Native Americans in the Western Hemisphere.[34] The attempt by the Anglos of the West, at the precise moment of the exhaustion of the plantation slave system in the East, to cement Tuco's fungibility, frequently in direct opposition to his partner and nemesis Blondie's irrevocable humanity, creates the key tension of the film.

Tuco is, in fact, a product of a racial fusion that is difficult to calculate, a joining of mainly Spanish Europeans and Amerindians (but not exclusive of Africans) that is called *mestizaje* and resides in a field dictated by three pressures.[35] One is the reduction to the category of the fungible. The other two are the eliminationist tendency of assimilation, as a preferred response to the third colonial encounter (1| New Spain, 2| Mexican-American War and creation of Texas, 3| post–Civil War settlement), and the final node is genocidal extirpation. But what is fascinating about the Tuco character is the collapse of the position of the fungible and the eliminated. The research of critic Patrick Wolfe suggests the polarity: "As opposed to enslaved people, whose reproduction augmented their owners' wealth, Indigenous people obstructed settlers' access to land, so their increase was counterproductive."[36] The film emphasizes Tuco's standing in both categories, as an element of bounty increase and encumbrance to development and Anglo hegemony.

The suggestion of collusion between Tuco and Blondie is a new path for the Leone films that had imagined and rationalized separate acts of Western colonialism to reflect a world and power relational dynamic joining the settler and the Native in commerce. In both *A Fistful of Dollars* and *For a Few Dollars More*, Eastwood's Anglo hero masquerades briefly as a member of the Native gang to expertly enact his revenge or destruction of the gang. His collusion is always a short-lived, insincere collaboration. But this is not the case in *GBU*. The Native goes from having to be saved by white expertise and power, to the settler defending himself from the barbarism of the Native, to a nexus of shared interests and partnership with the Anglo.

The apparent collusion between Blondie and Tuco is presented as temporary. After Tuco articulates his price, Blondie forces a dead cigarillo into Tuco's back teeth, and Leone quickly cuts to a shot of Tuco bound, trussed over the back of a horse, going through the muddy street of a town, yelling curses at Blondie: "I hope you end up in a graveyard with the cholera and the plague. Cut me loose, you filthy bastard!" Tuco cries out. The partnership seems to have collapsed in the face of fungibility. The indecision here is a crucial feature of the audience's relation to the evolving characters based on the bedrock of Western racist epistemology. The audience comfortably secures a logic of law through force to Blondie, but what about the hungry Latino? Is Tuco a comic captive? Collaborator and business partner? Bandit? Revolutionary? Escaped slave?

Leone brings to the screen the visage of "the good" hero at the precise moment of the conflation of "the ugly" with specie, the effort to reduce him to a fungible commodity whose value can always find an easy equivalence in commercial exchange. Furthermore, Tuco, we learn quickly, has an accumulative value exclusively anchored to his illegality, his immorality, his incorrigibility, his embodiment of the sin that was imagined to rationalize multiple generations of colonial conquest. He is taken swiftly and repeatedly to the regulated town marketplace for exchange, where what is presumably Anglo justice readily levies the punishment of execution for his crime. His sheepish response to the act of being rescued belies what appears at first beneficence, then a working relationship, then a relationship based exclusively on exploitation that constitutes the overriding dynamic of the partnership between "the ugly" and "the good."

One of Tuco's profane accusations against Blondie is that the Anglo is a bastard, a Judas, and the "son of a thousand fathers," reversing the logic of the patriarchal Western law on which his condemnation stands and to which the audience secures its earliest allegiance to Eastwood's character. The audience then finds Tuco astride a horse, the executioner's rope around his neck, while an Anglo male authority reads in monotone a litany of the crimes on which his conviction and sentence are based. Tuco is guilty of having committed specific violations of Abrahamic law, beginning with murder, theft, and habitual adultery. But the remarks soon encompass more significant nodes that fix him on the plane of an encounter in the New World. Instead of just a violator of Abrahamic law, Tuco is the specific anarchist against Western Enlightenment. He is the thief of "sacred objects" and has committed acts "contrary to the laws of this state." He has violated games of chance with "marked cards and loaded dice," special crimes that take Tuco beyond the pale of Abrahamic code and into the realm of violating the foundational epistemes of white settlers. Tuco exists not merely outside the law and moral order but in violation of the symbolic codes that designate sacrosanct theoretical positions, signaled by his attempts to rig the idea of chance and the suspended reality implicit in the concept of a game.

But what is more explicit is the conjunction with Shakespeare's Caliban, the figure identified in *The Tempest* by Miranda, Prospero's daughter, as the vessel for the litany of crimes justifying colonial inhabitation and sovereignty: "Abhorred slave," "goodness wilt not take," "capable of all ill," "savage," "A thing most brutish," "vile race," "good natures Could not abide to be with," and "Deservedly confined into this rock" (act 1, scene 2).[37] This catalog of ineluctable depravity properly defines the monstrous indigenous dweller of the colony.

At precisely the moment of irredeemableness, Leone returns the audience to Blondie, signified by the whistling tones of the trademark score and his ethereal symbol, smoke, as the spirit force that nominally frees Tuco, shooting the rope and enabling his escape from certain death. The condemned man—fully named by the would-be executioner as "Tuco Benedito Pacifico Juan Maria Ramirez"—escapes from the town, his hands yet tied, on the back of a horse, his noose shot away by the gunman, whom we identify now as a criminal partner of the condemned. The moment of partnership between the two, condemned and savior, is carefully articulated.

After Tuco's escape, the viewer understands that this is a well-worn ruse, a gimmick adopted to exploit a capital bonanza. Tuco, as the violating entity without peer, carries a bounty in newly stated Texas that matches the price of a very able enslaved craftsman or young concubine. The collision of the two positions, Tuco's value as a corpse with the African slave logic of fungibility, is explicitly reinforced at this cinematic moment with a strong associational symbol. After the pair flees the town, they split the reward money, which Blondie has collected. Significantly, Tuco receives from Blondie five one-hundred-dollar bills of Confederate scrip, Southern money issued during the Civil War, which features on bills images of enslaved Africans picking cotton. To recount, the Africans are enslaved by way of a sign—a conditionally commuted death sentence, gratuitous violence. Tuco is exchanged in dollars like the Africans on the bills, though putatively his difference is that

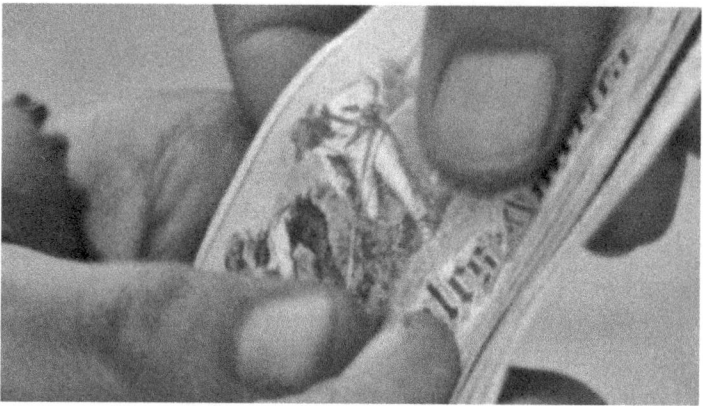

Eli Wallach and Clint Eastwood divvy up the spoils in *The Good, the Bad and the Ugly*, dir. Sergio Leone (MGM, 1966).

he is not condemned at birth to fungibility. He, however, is an impediment to territorial acquisition, a person whose main value is in death.

Nonequivalent Properties

Emancipated and paid, Tuco attempts to distinguish his position from the Africans with whom he is linked in slavery. He seeks to qualify his relation to people who have the sentence of death standing over them and who are commodified. He ventures to restore his value and reorder the nature of his relationship with Blondie and, at this moment, commits the prime violation in the film for which he will be perpetually punished. The viewer has been fooled. Instead of his violation of Western legal codes and contracts as the rationale for his death, Tuco is guilty of a deeper crime, a crime of questioning contracts, scales, and accounts.

Tuco, who has seemed bored by the likelihood of physical death, recognizes his value as negative property, and he concludes that this weight of possible death—his inexorable mortal vulnerability within the rituals of condemnation and execution—is heavier than the technological skill necessary for the art of shooting. The "risk" is inordinately his, he now understands, and the accumulation of incorrigibility necessary for his death value to increase should indicate that he earn greater levels of compensation. He presents Blondie with an argument: "There are two kinds of people in the world, my friend. Those with a rope around their neck and the people who have the job of doing the cutting. Listen, the neck at the end of the rope is mine. I run the risks. So, the next time I want more than half." Tuco objects to a basic principle of Western order: raw animal life is more valuable than the skillful applications of technology or "the job of doing the cutting." The proposition that the two criminals split the reward is founded on an inadequate equivalency: the idea that they occupy equal rights of property as subjects before the law and as indigenized Westerners.

Tuco's insistence on revisiting the terms of the financial relation with his partner-in-crime seems brash but actually invites us to revisit the terms of the original imagination of the encounter between Europe and the unknown, Thomas More's *Utopia*. When describing the case for a just war, and the subsequent basis for the possibility of slavery, More fantasized that it was legitimate to attack "a people which does not use its soil but keeps it idle and waste nevertheless forbids the use and possession of it." John Locke, the key English writer on social justice, liberty, and the state, took More's observation into the Western Hemisphere. A shareholder in the Royal African Company, the monopoly company trading in "Gold, Silver, Negroes, Slaves," an investor in the "Adventurers to Bahamas," the second-in-command of the Carolinas (modern-day Georgia, South Carolina, and North Carolina), and secretary to the Council of Trade and Plantations, Locke laid the deep groundwork for colonization and territorial dispossession. He wrote in the second of his "Two Treatises": "There are still great Tracts of Ground to be found, which ... lie waste, and are more than the People, who dwell on it, do, or can make use of."[38] Native Americans had neither a plantation system nor monetary transactions, and Locke deemed the lands common property suitable for claims.

This attempt at reordering seems one of Leone's ironic stiletto cuts against the stigma of Native "ugliness": ugly Tuco is unwilling to submit to the sign of degradation and stigma, the mark of the perpetually condemned. The film will sharply encounter the problem of aesthetics, the problem of separating the affective or precognitive apprehension of the beautiful and distinguishing it from ugliness. Leone concerns himself with style as a broadly empathetic project to perceive that which is desirable from that which is repulsive. The broader canvas is yet the problem of righteous Western moral law, instantiated through colonialism and imperialism, and the setting is a tableau of western symbolic iconography, ever envisioning spatial geographies where resistance can occur.

Blondie's response to Tuco's attempt to redraw the commercial arrangement is wry but completely automatic: the only basis for their contract, he insists, is equal shares. The insistence demands a false reduction of the two men to a position of equivalents and contemporaries, a reduction that is only possible if context and history are removed. In the course of the eighteenth century, the Native American was reduced from a landholder with rights to a savage without rights or land. "By the early nineteenth century, the theory of property that defined indigenous people as incapable of owning land and the grand narrative of savagery and civilization that contained it provided the means of redefining indigenous people as hunter-savages with no claim to ownership of land," asserts Maureen Konkle.[39] The principle of such an elision is fundamental in the US tradition of jurisprudence. As Chief Justice of the US Supreme Court John Marshall wrote to conclude his opinion in *Johnson v. M'Intosh*, "the North American Indians could have acquired no proprietary interest in the vast tracts of territory which they wandered over; and their rights to the lands on which they hunted could not be considered as superior to that which is acquired to the sea by fishing in it."[40] In fact, in considering Blondie and Tuco, we have a foreshadowing of the dilemma of preemption, a monopoly right to buy land from Natives, which in practice was transformed into another sort of covenant: "The American right to buy always superseded the Indian right not to sell."[41] Blondie's inclination toward equivalency relies on a similar exclusive contract, which then slips over into a privilege to insist on forms of work and exchange. In a sense, Blondie's confident recourse is to market primacy, as the "discovery" right moved seamlessly from the English sovereign to the federal US government.

Blondie solidifies his position with another myth, insisting that the technological apparatus—the rifle, the ability to use it, and the willingness to kill—is fully equivalent to the body, the land, the natural resource of the Native. Eastwood's entire body of work actually, and without the possibility of irony, becomes associated with this argument of equivalency, as the nature of racial history shifted from stigma to debt obligation. "If we cut down my percentage, it's liable to interfere with my aim," he tells Tuco, while making a mock gesture of politeness. He doesn't address the question of unequal risk. Instead, he indicates his willingness to allow Tuco's execution to be carried out, which is also to say that, like the credentialed representatives of Western law, he has the power to kill Tuco and his kind at will. To emphasize his meaning, the tenacity of his implied threat, he offers his trademark cigarillo to Tuco, the symbol he has used at the introduction of their relation to signify his willingness to exchange Tuco for money.

Tuco is a deliberate conflation of a series of increasingly abject positions with the conclusion of the Civil War and the post–Guadalupe-Hidalgo territorial consolidation of the Southwest. He is already the stateless Mexican peasant, on the borderlands between hegemons; the refugee Native American, outside of language and culture; the mixed-race offspring of an asymmetrical encounter between conquistador and southwestern Native. He returns the threat of death with the counterthreat implying vengeance but articulating the vacuum of knowledge—epistemic and ontological—between the West and "The Rest."[42] But Tuco's response emphasizes the broader global opposition to the colonial civilizationist imperative: "Whoever misses and leaves me alive, he understands nothing of Tuco. Nothing." Then in an important transformation of Blondie's proffer of empathetic identification—the tobacco—Tuco eats the cigar. Cured tobacco (*tobacco* is a Carib Indian word), the key commodity in the formation of English settlements and plantations in Virginia and a weed known for making people nauseous, is a meal for Tuco. He is a man about whom, at a visceral, digestive, internal level, we understand "Nothing." Tuco having an Afro-mestizo identity, like his digestion and consecration of the tobacco, along with the bills of enslaved Africans for which his life has been exchanged, would definitely be something that the audience, and Blondie, would not understand.

Tuco is effectively "negating the negation," the process of subject-making and freedom-taking described by Abdul Jan Mohammed:

> The hegemonic formation of minorities is itself based on an attempt to negate them—to prevent them from realizing their full potential as human beings and to exclude them from full and equal participation in civil and political society—and because minorities cannot take part in the dominant culture until this

negation is itself negated. The most crucial aspect of resisting hegemony consists in struggling against its attempt to form one's subjectivity, for it is through the construction of the minority subject that the dominant culture can elicit the individual's own help in his/her oppression.[43]

A few moments later Leone deepens the asymmetrical relation between the two principals. Tuco has been justly condemned for multiple violations of Western law, including the sale of fugitive slaves and violation of Sioux treaties, but also an especially repellant list of brutalities: "raping a virgin of the white race" and "statutory rape of a minor of the Black race." Leone reminds us of the species differentiation operating on multiple levels, not just that courts did not convict for the crime of Black women's rape but specifically that a Black minor can never be a virgin.

Racial designations undergird and construct categories of innocence and purity as much as they do criminality and illegality. "Black minor" and "white virgin" are fully exclusive categories. Leone reinforces the hierarchical dimensions by having the crimes read aloud, and he accents his point with a close-up of a middle-aged female white witness who moans perceptibly at the rape of the "virgin of the white race," juxtaposed to a silence that acknowledges the same violation against the Black minor. Slowly and almost imperceptibly, Leone turns the convention of the western, which had demanded African erasure, in the direction of a possibility. That missing possibility is the unvisualized African presence, which is the key to my reading of the film.

After the rescue, Leone returns to the principal tension: Tuco's major motive of vengeance, his consistent attempt to capture the complete fortune, and that narrative's conflation with Angel Eyes and Blondie's pursuit of bonanza capitalism. Tuco complains that, despite Blondie's promise, even premise, of expertise, he bungled the shot in the last town (one of only three moments that bring the three principals together). "When the rope starts to pull tight, you can feel the devil bite your ass," Tuco grates. Blondie's response is exclusively managerial: "There's really not much future in a sawed-off runt like you ... 'cause I don't think you'll ever be worth more than $3,000." He abandons the still-roped Tuco in the desert without water or horse. Tuco responds in the language of the savage cannibal: "If I ever catch you, Blondie, I'll cut your heart out and eat it! I'll skin you alive!" Blondie's response is in the classic language of Christian colonialism, rationalizing its exploitation as a mission of salvation: "Such ingratitude for all the times I've saved your life."

Here, at the twenty-ninth minute, Leone gives us the formal sign over Eastwood's Blondie, "the good."

The director cues the formal sign of "the good" to coincide ironically with a specific colonial and conquistador imperative: the saving of the savage from himself. Tuco, "the ugly," is not the noble savage uncorrupted by Western society and with resources of innate merit; he is designed as the opposite, the impure "half-breed," feral and immoral, lacking title to lands, a danger to others and to himself. This capacity of the displaced Mexican to require management from "the good" (which in American popular culture reached a point of significance in the early twentieth-century print culture advertisements with cartoons of Black children devoured by animals or in the act of being dismembered) also empowers the humor connected to his misfortune. By this frame, Eastwood's character is deliberately connected with the civilizing Western imperative, which leaves condemned the Indigenous source of wealth in the desert—tied and without resources. The sequence is structured to reinforce the idea that paternalism is what keeps the Indigenous Tuco alive. For his part, though, Tuco both begs Blondie for his life and curses him as a man unworthy of being called a man.

Closing the Colonial Door

The vengeance of Tuco, which takes over the middle portion of the film, has two remarkable scenes. The first is perhaps the film's genuine signature moment of nonviolent drama, when a severely dehydrated Tuco reaches town, having survived without water for perhaps three days, long enough to have traveled seventy miles. Tuco, before fully refreshing himself even, reaches a hardware store, a vendor featuring pistols. The store owner is a short, rotund, bald man, a stutterer, and polite. "I'm very sorry, but the store is closing," he tells the weary Native.

Tuco ignores the proprietor and forces a foot through the door, until, after angrily sweeping a dozen pistols off a counter onto the floor, he says with evident dissatisfaction, "Revolvers." The vendor keeps the "best ones" under glass, the Remingtons, Smith-Wessons, and Colts, especially the Colt Navy revolver of heavy caliber. Tuco picks up the 1851 Colt Navy revolver and removes the barrel and cylinder. Then he picks up the Roat—apparently an allusion to the Le Mat, the first cartridge pistol and used by the Confederacy—removes the cylinder, judges it for balance, and then takes another Colt for the barrel, perhaps the 1860 model, until he creates the proper action. Ignoring the ancient flask of black powder, which is the first object placed on the glass case by the proprietor, Tuco creates a phenomenally lethal weapon capable of accurately firing metal cartridges of a caliber large enough to split inch-thick wood. An adept craftsman whose capacity exceeds the imposed limits of the manufacturer, Tuco has become his own skilled machinist of metal tools.

At this point in the film the technology of Tuco's capability surpasses the audience's expectations. He is transformed into an inventor at the western edge of the Civil War as new technologies like the metal cartridge are transforming the nature of killing. The distance between the American Civil War, the deadliest war of its era, to World War I, the deadliest war of all time to its combatants, is a brief synapse. In the US Civil War, the majority of soldiers who died in the conflict died from diseases they acquired in the army camps; by World War I, the majority of men who died on the battlefield died on account of lethal machine technology, principally the machine gun and its belted metal cartridge. Leone does not give us a Tuco imitating whites but one who has mastered and created a new technological field. This sequence provides a formidable conjunction between Tuco and subsequent Leone film counterparts like Harmonica in *Once upon a Time in the West* and Anton Chigurh of *No Country for Old Men*, the nonwhite, non-Black person inseparable from lethal technologies and whose vengeance quest is not resolved by means of bloody bonanza accumulation or frontier conquest.

After inventing the weapon, Tuco practices shooting, illustrating his expertise to shop owner and film audience alike, and robs the merchant. The coercion of the robbery is conducted through a series of puns. "How much?" Tuco asks the storekeeper, who stands in front of a wall with hanging chains, and whose eagerness for the payday of mercantile capitalism is palpable. The diminutive clerk beams dreamily, considering how much he can overcharge for the weapon. Tuco laughs at the greed and the imaginary construct of himself as the obedient Native who adheres to the rules of colonial exploitation, who relies on contractual assumptions that guide market rationality. He waves the gun and pulls on the whisky bottle, and the audience, educated by the hangman's ruse, warily anticipates a painful reverse. Leone has established sympathetic conventions between the viewer and the camera's object, the bespectacled, shrunken store owner, who seems importuned upon by the rough, grizzled vulgarity of Tuco. Another affective impulse, one that rejects the slaughter of the weak and the innocent by the strong and experienced, also shapes the perception of the encounter between the Indigenous bandit and the Anglo bourgeois. Tuco's manipulation of the encounter is now becoming unpleasant. The irony of the lethal technology, the ambivalence of the tech-

Enzo Petito in *The Good, the Bad and the Ugly*, dir. Sergio Leone (MGM, 1966).

nologies of iron-age civilization, the Spanish horse changing the nature of western encounters and development even—all are evident.

When the store owner is asked the same question again, his glasses slip down his nose and he replies, "Fifty dollars?" Tuco turns the barrel of the gun on him, hardening in his language as the shop owner increases the price, begging, "Two hundred dollars, it's all I've got." Tuco walks to the door and locks it, seeming to consider killing the vendor. In the process, he notices the "closed" sign hanging on the back of the door. He forces the defeated shopkeeper forward and sticks the sign in his mouth.

This theater for the audience seems juvenile, an appeal to adolescent rebellion, and these moments of slapstick defiance are regular devices in the B-movie genre and also an important part of postwar Italian cinema. But the comic drama offers a more insurgently defiant sequence of events in the film, evinced in the subsequent scene when Tuco searches out his childhood friends, who live in a grotto and boil potatoes for sustenance. The shopkeeper selling weapons to settlers is making the territory "open" for business, and Tuco's symbolic forcing of the "closed" sign into the mouth of the white merchant briefly closes the commerce in lethal technology.

Tuco has assaulted a weapons dealer whose regular work is arming the settler population in the drive to overtake Texas, New Mexico, and then unacquired (or "free") Arizona, the next enclave for Anglo settler expansion. Leone specifically renders the settler population when Tuco's gang of Pedro, Ramon, and Chico track Blondie to General Sibley's Confederate outpost in a small Texas town. Here, on account of the historical reference, we learn

Henry Fonda in *Once upon a Time in the West*, dir. Sergio Leone (Paramount, 1968).

conclusively that the year is 1862. Leone provides a shot of four long-haired, heavily bearded men riding through town—bushwhackers from the border war in Missouri—who are joining this epic ride South to resist the narrative of slave emancipation.

The event of the Civil War itself announces the end of the Jeffersonian-era yeoman expansion. The New West is a place of railroad technology, repeating firearms, and industrial engineering punching through vast landscapes and dividing them into duchies and fiefdoms of landholders. Leone will dramatize the western territorialization of the monopoly capitalist in his next western, *Once upon a Time in the West*. In the finale to that film, he repeats the trope of silencing the rapacious bonanza capitalists, when the hero, Harmonica (Charles Bronson), stuffs his harmonica into the mouth of the villain Frank (Henry Fonda). In the moments before, the audience learns that Harmonica is actually a Native American who has been conducting a successful masquerade as a white. As a boy, he had been mockingly gifted the instrument as he unwillingly scaffolded his elder brother during a gruesome and sadistic hanging engineered by Frank. After 1966, virtuous retribution for the crime of Anglo western hegemony became a central feature of Leone's portraits of the indigenous and mixed-race.

Confederate Gold

The pivot plot point in the film reunites Tuco and Blondie as partners and seems to erase the vengeance motif. Initially, Tuco had tracked down and tortured Blondie by walking him across the desert, a scene introduced with

Eli Wallach and Clint Eastwood, *The Good, the Bad and the Ugly*, dir. Sergio Leone (MGM, 1966).

a striking orientalist trope. Tuco rides a horse into the desert with a lavender parasol, an image that recalls Eugene Delacroix's portrait from Algeria *The Sultan of Morocco and His Entourage* (1840). At the edge of the arid sea of land, Tuco chides Blondie about his color: "They say people with fair skin can't take too much." The patter reverses the apparently stable poles of beauty and ugliness regarding the Anglo aesthetic of beauty. The naming of "fair skin" (and the etymology of *fair* returns us to an Old Saxon word for "beautiful"),[44] a customary euphemism for white skin and, among nonwhite people light-complexioned skin, also evokes the opposite term, which begins with the Greek term "Aethiops,"[45] or burned skin, the original denotation of dark skin, black skin.

But the rivalry and the reduction of Blondie to a desiccated zombie is short-lived. After stopping a team of runaway horses and pillaging a carriage of Confederate corpses, Tuco uncovers the dying Confederate soldier Bill Carson, who offers to reveal the location of $200,000 in gold coins in exchange for water. In previous frames, Blondie's face blisters and peels as he slowly dies of thirst and exposure. The great fungible fortune is made the equivalent of the tiniest dose of the most abundant natural resource.

Carson's information, however, is incomplete. Tuco learns only that the fortune is at Sand Hill Cemetery but not the name of the grave where the money is located. Returning from his horse with his water bag, Tuco finds Blondie with his head next to a now dead Carson. Tuco threatens Blondie with death, demanding the secret. "If you do that you'll always be poor, just like the greasy rat you are," Blondie replies, the second time in the film that he explicitly refers to Tuco as vermin, reasserting a species distinction between the blond Nordic and the Native American and mestizo. Blondie has learned the name on the grave and barters his return to health in exchange for its revelation and, more important, the fifty-fifty split that had characterized the economic relationship earlier between himself and Tuco. They will, the audience knows, be in pursuit of Confederate gold, which is to say, they are in pursuit symbolically of slave profit.

But there is a crucial unexplained plot gap. On what basis does Carson share the name on the grave with the exhausted stranger? Blondie is barely alive and has nothing of value to exchange with Carson, except human companionship and recognition. Tuco has the "gold" of the desert, water, emphasizing his fundamental association with natural resources, the land, Indigenous people, and human physicality. Therefore, the agreement between Blondie and Carson can stem from only one plausible terrain: the Confederate soldier sees the blue-eyed man "Blondie" as a kind of spiritual avatar of the conflation of projects: the Confederate South, western expansion, the colonization of the Southwest, and the Anglo aesthetic project.

If Blondie is recognized by his spiritual brother, the dying Confederate bandit Bill Carson, Leone makes an exceptional parallel when Tuco encounters his own biological older brother while Blondie is recuperating at a San Antonio mission. If Blondie's natural brother is Carson, who shares the information necessary for the gold bonanza, then Leone makes a specific point by introducing Tuco's biological sibling, Pablo Ramirez, the head of the monastery where Confederate wounded are being treated. Tuco insists on an audience with his brother, who, he learns before the inevitable conflict breaks out, has just returned from their father's funeral. Father Pablo denounces his brother, Tuco, calling him a bandit and berating him: "Outside of evil what have you been up to?" Tuco's response inserts the significant historical dimension of colonialism and underdevelopment into the film:

> While I'm waiting for the Lord to remember me, I, Tuco Ramirez, brother of Brother Ramirez, will tell you something. You think you're better than I am. Where we came from, if one did not want to die of poverty, one became a priest or a bandit. You chose your way. I chose mine. Mine was harder! You talk of our mother and father. You remember when you left to become a priest, I stayed behind. I must have been ten, twelve, I don't remember which, but I stayed. I tried, but it was no good. Now let me tell you something. You became a priest because you were too much of a coward to do what I do.

Tuco's narrative (overheard by Blondie) establishes his middle position between the maternal-paternal ethical position of his brother, Pablo, who is aiding wounded Confederate soldiers (in the film world of Leone an ethically valuable act) but who at the same time stands as the chief agent of the Catholic Church, the hegemonic institution with the strongest relation to colonialism and manufacturing the subordination of Natives to colonial rule. Tuco's accusation that his brother is a nonviolent coward points to the dilemma of English-speaking settlers now overwhelming the region because of the new commercial and industrial circuits created by the political, military, and technological elements of the Civil War. But the discourse also overlays a historical context of the film (shot in Spain): Spanish invasions and the establishment of a creole landed aristocracy that forced Indian peasants into the oblivion of poverty and land dislocation.

At the other pole is Blondie, the representative of the most rapacious form of entrepreneurial capitalism—slave traders, robbers, and bounty hunters— an incarnation of historical figures connected to profit-seeking westward expansion during this era like trans-Mississippian Nathan Bedford Forrest, territory rangers from Texas to Minnesota like Frank and Jesse James, and New Mexico's Billy the Kid. Tuco's plaintive line to Blondie as the men share a wagon ride away from the monastery—"Even a tramp like me no matter what happens, I know there's a brother somewhere who will never refuse me a bowl of soup"—emphasizes Tuco's connection to social relations predicated on myths of family genealogy and ethnic heritage, not power lines of commerce, technological superiority, and the volitional capacity to perform lethal acts. The viewer learns that Blondie hails from Illinois, but Tuco, who leads them through Union lines, is the Native, the person reading the territorial landmarks as a map, who recognizes Apache Canyon and the desert, rocks, and rivers of the border. Even when he is transported by force several hours by train, Tuco can find his way on foot back over the landscape of modern-day New Mexico, Santa Fe, Fort Craig, southwestern Texas, El Paso, and northern Mexico. He is at home, the rabbit in the briar patch.

Blondie and Tuco are subsequently captured and taken to Batterville prison camp, where Van Cleef's character, Angel Eyes, has become a noncommissioned officer in order to screen Confederate prisoners in his search for the gold. Blondie and Tuco are accorded dramatically different treatment on account of their race. "Come on in, Tuco, don't be bashful. There's no formalities here," Angel Eyes says to Tuco, inviting him to a meal of stew and whisky. But when Tuco is not forthcoming when asked, "Why are you going under

Uncredited actors and Lee Van Cleef, *The Good, the Bad, and the Ugly*, dir. Sergio Leone (MGM, 1966);

the name of Bill Carson" ("One name is as good as another. Not wise to use your own name," he replies), he is marked for gruesome punishment. Tuco is about to suffer a second gratuitous violence, akin to the punishment he had endured in his survival walk through the desert. The peculiar emphasis on race operates in a sequence often commented on but whose constituent elements are incompletely understood.

To signal the commencement of the scene of torture, Angel Eyes ironically remarks, "Like a little music with your meal, Tuco?" He then motions to a noncommissioned officer in charge of an orchestra of imprisoned Rebel soldiers who play on command. The audience now learns that the music drowns out the sounds from the habitual torture of prisoners. As the camera pans the orchestra, Leone complicates the portrait of the smug and seated Union soldier, who lounges in the foreground. Brilliantly, oddly, and quickly, Leone's camera captures an utter anomaly for the film. The camera pans Black federal troops—stevedores and teamsters—seated immediately behind the smug corporal. The soldiers are seated in a circle, apart from anyone else. It turns out that these men had actually been in an earlier even swifter shot, more obscure, pushing a heavy wagon without any horses through the camp. In fact, the soldiers could also have been glimpsed marching past the window where Tuco was being interrogated, but their appearance and disappearance occur more quickly than can be registered—unless the viewer is prepared. Without the camera closing in on its subject, and without the proper context,

Uncredited actors in *The Good, the Bad and the Ugly*, dir. Sergio Leone (MGM, 1966).

neither foreknowledge that we bring to the film nor the capacity to read the filmmaker's cues, what we regard on the screen is opaque.

The principal consequence of having the only Blacks in the film appear at the prison camp at the moment of torture is to reverse the audience's affective orientation. At this key, split-second juxtaposition, Leone supplants the first irony of the music ("Very good for the digestion," Tuco had laughed in satisfaction) with a second irony that disables the moral economy the viewer brings to the film. The cruelty of the Batterville Union camp has been partially justified by Angel Eyes to the camp commandant because of the historic cruelty of the Confederates to Union soldiers at Andersonville, the notorious quasi–death camp in Georgia, where one-third of the forty thousand imprisoned federal soldiers perished.[46] Of the "dozen or more Negroes" at Andersonville, according to one inmate, "Nearly all are minus an arm or leg, and their wounds are yet unhealed. Many of them are gangrened and they all will surely die."[47]

Leone, however, seems neutral on the nature of the conflict. The prison orchestra playing during Tuco's beating in the guardhouse is a direct overture to the practice of the Nazis at Treblinka and Sobibor, death camps noted for musical ensembles and choral groups forced to play during murder and torture. At the Treblinka death camp, for example, after the roll call, former inmate Samuel Willenberg recalled being forced to sing Polish songs repeatedly because "the Germans were of the opinion that we did not infuse our singing with enough sentiment."[48] As the Confederate orchestra plays the dirge, a Union corporal, smoking a cigar and with his feet in the air, commands the prisoners to play with "more feeling," to invest more personal emotive spirit into the music, and subsequently mask the torture that occurs inside the guardhouse. The audience recoils at the horror.

But when we recognize the split-second insertion of Africans in the film—and Leone has gone to some trouble to include them—we begin to understand that we work from profoundly biased phenomenological and epistemological cues. The correspondence between our perception and affective response has been exposed as a capacity for being manipulated. As dutiful Westerners, the audience hastens to grasp the allusion to the death camps of World War II (heavily reported in the news in 1962 with the Adolf Eichmann hanging), but in the process, we are capable of eclipsing the imbricated horrors and genocides on which the edifice of the Western consciousness and Enlightenment project rest. Our sympathy toward the captured, badly treated Confederates is undercut by their war to continue the enslavement of the only (and thus strongly magnified) African presence in the film. The ethical system that we have in place does not prepare us to deal with what justice to Confederate soldiers looks like from the perspective of former slaves. The Confederate men are also wasting their sympathy on Tuco, who is not their comrade but a Native in masquerade, fighting for his own survival and indifferent if not hostile to them. The audience joins the circuit of wasted or misplaced empathy here as well, spending its sympathies on the screen selections of justice and injustice while having been cued to perceive them as manipulated. We are supposed to be enabled here to confront the problem of our judgment, that "culture involves practices in which the porosity of argument is inhabited by more noise, unstated habit, and differential intensities of affect than adamant rationalists acknowledge."[49] The correspondence between our perception and affective response has been exposed as tenuous, and it is this opportunity that the film offers us, a possibility of affective rupture that prepares the way for " 'regimes of feelings' which are bound to be constitutive of new political practices."[50]

We are viewing the Civil War conflict but with significant elements occluded from our historical understanding and perception. The brief segment demands that we recognize that the Confederate soldiers are being punished in turn for their crimes, which we as an audience are liable to forget or miss, in the same way that we are almost obligated to miss the African soldiers. The audience is, in fact, like the musicians, agents of distorted affective response based on ethical misperception. The same distortion shapes the audience's affinitive tie to "the good," on the basis of a series of hollow stylistic effects.

By giving us the Black men at the crucial middle of the film, Leone exchanges the implied racism of "the bad" and "the good," who are, rather than oppositional figures, mirrored figures. After the bloodied Tuco reveals the place of the fortune, Van Cleef delivers Eastwood to the torture chamber. But instead of cruelty, he asks Eastwood if torture would cause him to reveal his secrets. "No, probably not" is the response, to which "the bad" then assesses, "That's what I thought. Not that you're any tougher than Tuco. But you're smart enough to know that talking won't save you." Smart and rational and able to dominate speech, Blondie is freed by Angel Eyes.

The pronouncement regarding Blondie's mercenary intelligence and shared teleology with his purported nemesis demonstrates yet another united conference of white men who are principled and able rationally to control the body and working out of a joined, mutually legible worldview. The passion-driven, obsessed, and perpetually harnessed Tuco, the nonwhite Other now linked to the Black freedmen who have joined the Union army, of course, reveals the valuable information at the decisive moment of horrifying torture. Using English to hurl his curses, Tuco unwillingly participates in the discourse of Western rationalism that the Bad dominates and moves through, Union or Confederate, most fluidly. Thus, Leone unsettles Tuco's belonging with good or bad, as well as the death that is habitually forecast for him by his companions.

Ultimately, Eastwood's Blondie occupies the false position of the innocent, the position as the intelligent and aesthetically desirable, the one character not disfigured, not associated with Black soldiers, whose presence as the corporal evidence of the crimes of the regime against the enslaved demands a radical rereading of the surface sentimentality of the film. The viewer is also required to bring Tuco the ugly into alignment with the Black soldiers, whom Jeffersonian aesthetics had negatively ascribed the "immoveable veil of black" "which reigns in the countenances" and "foundation of a greater or less share of beauty in the two races."[51]

The Conclusion

Leone's conclusion reflects an effort to reverse the narrow political symbolism of his second western, *For a Few Dollars More*, and also begs for juxtaposition with the conclusion of his subsequent project, *Once upon a Time in the West*. In *For a Few Dollars More*, Leone produced the sheer colonialist fantasy, whereby the savage Amerindian and mestizo required subjugation by the technologically sophisticated white settler from the East. Eastwood's Monco participates in the finale, a "soft" triangulated gun battle, by rearming the colonel and regulating the duel with El Indio. Colonel Mortimer kills Indio and is so satisfied by the vengeance motif that he refuses any of the bounty money from the corpses, only claiming Monco as a new descendant:

MORTIMER. My boy you've become rich.
MONCO. You mean we've become rich, old man.
MORTIMER. No it's all for you. I think you deserve it.

The Good, the Bad and the Ugly offers its audience a more intellectually provocative series of concluding images in sketching out its terrain of colonial conflict. The finale gives us the three principals, "the ugly" Mexican Native, "the good" blond gunman, and "the bad" dark-haired professional killer. Blondie sets the terms of the event by stating to the group, "$200,000 is a lot of money. We're going to have to earn it." The gun battle that he proposes is a "Mexican Stand-Off," the unsatisfactory deadlock with the possibility that all of the men will be killed and that no one will "earn" the profit.[52] But in this concluding requiem, the audience is fully seduced in its crisis of style over ethics. The evocative theater of Leone's corrida-like warfare, a more complicated reprise of the finale duel from *A Few Dollars More*, prevents the audience from penetrating the essence of its masquerade: unbeknownst to us, Tuco has been disarmed earlier in the narrative, and the pistol contest, as in *A Few Dollars More*, is only occurring between two people—Blondie and Angel Eyes. Blondie, however, is the only person who has this crucial bit of information, in the same way that he was the only person who knew where the money was buried. There is only one difference between the professional killers Angel Eyes and Blondie. Angel Eyes in the sequence might be considered marked for doom in the false triangulation of the fight because he doesn't represent individualism but is a hired gun, the tool of managerial power and bureaucracy. Leone seems to make the point that what contemporary audiences will understand in a neocolonial relation as goodness is connected only to the unflappable panache and assertive smarts of the amoral hero, Blondie. He is shown as withholding affection in relations and insists on an inoperative relational circuit. Blondie shows empathy twice, to the Union captain and to the Confederate artillerymen, as the men are dying, a closed relation.

The film concludes with Blondie forcing Tuco at gunpoint to mount a Christian cross serving as a cenotaph, and, leaning over an open grave filled with gold, place his neck in a noose. Leone privileges the noose in its own frame, a decision that, alongside the brief image of the Black soldiers in the prison camp, amplifies its historical allusion to lynching and Black reenslavement following the Reconstruction era. The decision to pair the noose with the main symbol of Christianity, the crucifix, strongly conflates the martyrdom techniques of Roman civilization with those of the American West and South. Tuco teeters on execution, on having his commuted death sentence carried out, while he chokes and begs for release. We understand Tuco's cries as examples of his weakness, his incapacity to be an Anglo and silently and rationally accept his extermination. Tuco's cries further confirm his submission to technological power, and to embrace the aesthetics of style that set holster-wearing Blondie apart, so that he can at least become a man "wasted" well.

But Blondie's symbolic arc is not complete, the suspended death embedded in the Christian Western telos. He reenacts the ruse of turning Tuco over to the law and develops the theme of his apparent "good" qualities by making the most remarkable rifle shot of the film. He shoots the rope from such a great distance that he can't even be seen by Tuco. Added to the difficulty, he braces the Sharp's carbine on his forearm, while still holding the reins of his horse, and hits the rope just before Tuco loses his balance and would have fallen and hanged himself. Instead of being hanged, Tuco smashes headfirst into the gold bag, runs after Blondie, and delivers a final curse.

Blondie's seeming generosity doesn't make sense until the viewer grasps the terms of the paternalistic relationship at the core of the imperial relation. Blondie rewards and preserves Tuco. "The good" Blondie constantly reminds the Mexican peasant that he oversees the terms for his existence and, whenever Blondie decides, if the peasant should seek to rearrange the "deal" of imperialism or attempt to renegotiate the possibility of the bonanza, that Blondie might miss a shot, fire a howitzer, or rearrange the symbolism of the dominant religion to destroy his ward. In scene after scene, Tuco is required to understand the fact that he is utterly dominated by the force of arms and changing technology and to recognize Blondie as its single embodiment.

But Tuco permeates the boundaries in which American critics and viewers have encased him. Blondie engages only Angel Eyes in the final deadly competition for the gold. He has needed to disarm Tuco while the other has his rear in the air, prone and asleep, another apparent measure of Tuco's distasteful inadequacy. Tuco's unworthiness (and the practical moment of his being disarmed) has been symbolized by his odd position when the two men blow up the contested Branston Bridge, a deed necessary so that, according to Tuco, "these idiots will go somewhere else and fight." Tuco prepares for the explosion with his hind-parts in the air and sleeps thoroughly through the night in this prone position. The carnage of the war and the possibility of death are no greater than the other missing historical referent, the history of Spanish colonialism. He is participating in an epiphenomenon of violence that occurs without any meaning attached to it, a violence in a repetitive circuit, and thus does not merit his full attention. Instead of caution and vigilance, Tuco gives only his rear end to the most lethal combination of violence that horrifies and frightens the white actors.

Tuco's head-down, behind-up exposure, his "assuming the position," suggests a difference in the routine series of assumptions, both against the logic of the absurdity of war and the logic of the inevitability of colonialism and, especially, its afterlife. He is featured as exposed, and he will indeed be taken advantage of, but he is also empowered by what seems only his insouciant lack. In the words of Kevin Bell, Tuco emphasizes a "radical nonpositionality of [this kind of] figural irruptivity," a collection of moves, postures, gestures, and voice acts that "escape every symbolic coding and classification" and "break every contract of transparent meaning."[53] Significantly, too, Tuco had exposed himself after learning what he presumes to be the genuine location of the gold. When he has the bonanza in sight, he exposes himself fully and sleeps.

The multiple features of Tuco's character then become more compelling to Blondie. Tuco is the one person in the triangle of questers with whom Blondie can't satisfactorily bargain, the one person who already has a brother, a relation not predicated on either shared riches or shared commitments to exploitation, slavery, and violence. Tuco is the person whose bodily postures and vulnerabilities are incoherent to western aesthetics and western masculinity. Perhaps this explains Blondie's evolution from the duster to the serape at the conclusion, not simply an invocation of his other roles as gunfighter hero from the previous films but also as the Anglo savior who aggressively sutures himself to the Native to continue rewinding the terms for regenerative fortune.

In *The Good, the Bad and the Ugly*, the "ugly" Native, Tuco, ultimately overtakes the screen, and the antithetical aesthetic category "ugliness" operates at least as a splinter to the hegemony of shared consensus implicit in judgments of the good, or commonly held ethical positions based on reason, and the beautiful, the idea that inspires the play between understanding and imagination.⁵⁴ Ugly Tuco's usurpation violates the implicit "good" on which to base the fantasy of a well-governed social order. The shared consensus of the beautiful, in the words of Tobin Siebers, enables important possibilities in the political sphere:

> The vision of the beautiful object is also a vision of a beautiful "we" because it compels individuals to expose private feelings to judgment of other people while at the same time imagining them as members of an affective community that shares common goals and objects. Aesthetic judgment, then, provides the perfect analogy by which to imagine ideal forms of political judgment. It offers the experience of a free political space, a space of intersubjectivity, in which a multitude of thinking people are dedicated to open discussion. . . . Beauty is, in short, politics' idea of utopia.⁵⁵

Leone provides the analogy through his film, and the ugliness that he foregrounds in Tuco helps to destabilize our affect and turn us in the direction of a new basis for "common goals and objects."

Despite the fact that Eastwood's laconic, violent, nameless, and white supremacist-sentimental "Blondie" did not occupy Leone's *The Good, the Bad and the Ugly* as he had *A Fistful of Dollars*, the performance propelled his Hollywood career in the late 1960s and early 1970s. With ever more graphic violence reducing the distance between lived traumatic experience and imaginary trauma and enabling the widening of the "pathological public sphere," the zone that thrives off the spectatorship of wounds,⁵⁶ the western and its historic Cold War ideological work continued to assume heavy responsibilities in the 1970s. Eastwood remained in the genre most committed to proposing the lethal white male code hero who works from the pure Abrahamic moral code of vengeance. After two key historical events—the nationwide spring rioting in 1968 and the withdrawal of ground forces in defeat from Vietnam in 1973—Eastwood would reinvest the genre with an ideological purpose: the nostalgic reconciliation with the era preceding racial liberalism, a reconciliation that carried forward the equivalency debate between Tuco and Blondie from the early moments of *GBU*.

But Eastwood's works further counseled the American public to imagine African Americans as undeserving of any state sponsorship at all, from the educational system to the police department to a municipal hospital emergency system. Eastwood's film *The Outlaw Josey Wales*, which rewrote the myths of America as it evolved outward from a coercively punitive labor state, is an emphatic mass-culture product tailored to consumption in this regard and is, in its own way, as ambitious as Griffith's *Birth of a Nation*. In the aftermath of the Civil Rights Acts of 1964 and 1965, the 1968 riots, and the reaction against federal- and state-mandated racial integration of American schools, the suspicion from Peckinpah's gory *Wild Bunch* (1969) that body counts were unstable measures of political progress and military success, and that western heroes no longer mattered, Eastwood would redeem the Confederate Lost Cause. Even more, he would recuperate a group more horrific than the Ku Klux Klan, ushering into the conscience of contemporary Americans a normative role for the white supremacist vigilante.

CHAPTER THREE

"That Damn War"

The Outlaw Josey Wales and Reframing the Civil War

> The negro woman I send is to be retained. I would like for her to be returned to me as a cook whenever I rejoin the train. She says her master's name is, I think, Thompson. If he is a Federal, she will, of course, be confiscated.
> —Colonel Stand Watie C.S.A., Pheasant Bluff, Indian Territory, June 17, 1864

> You know . . . I'd like to know what the economics of that were. I mean freeing the slaves. I'd like to know what was behind it.
> —Clint Eastwood (1985)

A great deal has been written about Clint Eastwood's western *The Outlaw Josey Wales*. Much of it is high praise. The film "has some of the best gunplay, most poignant dialogue, most colorfully vile minor villains, and most fully developed Indian characters in the genre," explains David McNaron.[1] Although not a blockbuster, the film scored a respectable $13.5 million at the box office in 1976, and the iconography of Eastwood as the eponymous rebel gunfighter Josey Wales continues to define his career, as was obvious by the iconography at his 2012 speech at the Republican Party presidential convention.[2]

Eastwood, renowned for his skillful directing and acting, as well as for his work ethic and general productivity, regards the film highly in retrospect for its fascinating (if muted) political allegories. In the 2010 DVD rerelease of the film, the then eighty-year-old director embedded a permanent introduction onto the DVD. Eastwood's introduction, shot as a direct address to the viewer, can't be forwarded or skipped. In it, he explains his own position regarding the allegorical nature of the 1976 movie:

> I'd like to introduce *The Outlaw Josey Wales* because it is a film that is very, very close to me. I thought it was from a very appealing book. A story that needed to be told about the conditions of war on people at that particular time, especially in history, and the dissatisfaction that people were having with the war in Vietnam. Not that this was parallel, but just the basic illness of war and

what it could cause to people. I have been very lucky to have fit in in the western genre of filmmaking, and enjoyed that, but *Josey Wales* is certainly one of the high points of my career for that.[3]

A single, classic line from the film coincides with Eastwood's retrospective view, thirty-four years later, that *Outlaw* enabled an engagement with "the dissatisfaction that people were having with the war in Vietnam." The hero, Josey Wales, reconciles with the traitor who has been pursuing him by saying, "We all died a little in that damn war." Eastwood's claim that the film had wanted to explore the wounded memories and ignobility connected to Vietnam attests to cinema's capacity as a vehicle to both express political beliefs and reflect political dissatisfaction, aims that had become increasingly important to Sergio Leone's American-Mexican westerns after 1966.[4] The preamble implies that nation-state combat is "service," and wars have multiple, impure origins that cannot be causally isolated. War as synonymous with violent death is always unjustifiable from the victim's perspective. Individual soldiers should be judged first by their standard of loyalty to their immediate comrades and the obligations that military service requires, including inflicting and enduring violent death.

But the condemnation of "that damn war," uttered by the character Josey Wales to the man he had served under in the military, is the articulated summit of a mountain of false equivalents, a mendacious edifice of scale and detail set up and drawn out throughout the film. If we accept Eastwood's allegorical gesture from 2010, we understand that the film has actually narrowed the relative distance in meaning and value between the US Civil War and the undeclared war in Vietnam. The introduction asserts powerfully a philosophical logical fallacy, the flaw of "affirming the consequent," a failure in reason where a conditionally true premise is used to infer an invalid conclusion, derived from Aristotle's fallacy of accident.[5] In his introduction, Eastwood deliberately impresses a faulty analogy by proposing a similarity of properties—or possibility of substitution—between the two conflicts.[6] The analogy suggests that both Vietnam and the US Civil War were equal part wars of conquest and imperialism—wars that were unwinnable or should not have been waged—and a combat between sharply divergent ideological positions shaping the availability of the resources necessary for life.[7] Of course, since Josey Wales is un-uniformed (which eases his segue into the "western" gunfighter) combatant for the Confederacy, the suggestion of the analogy between Wales and the returning American servicemen and women from Vietnam engages sentimentally in a marriage of the defeated and supplies a tragic heroism. The edifice of insupportable analogy is actually the crux of the film's ideological claim.

More obviously in this analogy, the Civil War becomes an unfair war of "Northern aggression" against a resourceful and loosely allied "confederacy," allegorically similar for an American audience, in the way that violent civil conflicts in Vietnam and Korea were represented as aggressive acts by rapacious, fanatically ideological Northerners, invading the South (and with the help of powerful neighbors like China and the USSR). In a slightly longer historical view, however, the conflict represented a war of several heavily industrialized, arch-militarist invading Western nations (France, the UK, and the US) against an insurgency or peasant uprising, sometimes defending villages and countrysides. Part of the allegory with which Eastwood seems unconcerned, and that is eliminated from the film, is the genuine echo of American counterinsurgent military activity in Vietnam that closely paralleled the methods of the guerilla "bushwhackers" in Missouri and Kansas in the 1860s and beyond. The warfare of Missouri in the 1850s and 1860s, the first site of the film's horrifying violence, was declared by chroniclers during the 1860s as "an endless cycle of robbery, arson, torture, murder, mutilation, and an endless cycle of revenge."[8]

The stakes are quite high if the American Civil War, a watershed thought over and over again by professional historians to have created the defining transformative moment or epoch for the nation-state,[9] is collapsed with the Vietnam War. The latter was called a conflict, and one that formally involved the United States carrying out vestiges of a colonial war that had in fact been initiated by another Western power, France, for almost a decade beyond World War II. Eastwood's 2010 comments insist on a comparison between the American Civil War and the long colonial conflict in Southeast Asia as examples of a large foreign power attacking a smaller, racially different, independent country.

Furthermore, what does it mean to analogically collapse both moments together, as Eastwood specifically does, and to join a point of view about the abolition of slavery connected to the possibility of national reconciliation to a quite similar sectional and racial reconciliation and the abolition of the discriminatory legal apparatus that hobbled Black citizenship claims? The film framed by its director and star becomes a vehicle for conceiving the South as a territory unjustly invaded and roughly colonized, like Vietnam, and the center of guerilla war.

But there is also another turn. Eastwood's retrospective argues for a consideration of the film, and indeed his body of work from the 1970s through the 2010s, as a historical act of transmogrification, a transformation of shape and kind. Eastwood's political allegory is actually unconcerned with the "dissatisfaction that people were having with the war in Vietnam." Rather, the film centers on the righteous travails of Americans of "the South" who fought for the Lost Cause, aligning them with the US soldiers committed to the Vietnamese "South," the national government in Vietnam run from Saigon. Despite the film's popular appeal, connected to its graphic onscreen violence, Eastwood is actually suturing the Lost Cause of the Southern Rebels to the crisis of those dismayed by American military defeat and loss of prestige in Vietnam. This maneuver repairs the sinews between the Rebels and the hegemon, precisely the logic of D. W. Griffith's *The Birth of a Nation*.

While it might be an exaggeration to say that a single film can operate as a fulcrum for a cultural shift, a revision of a dominant mode of understanding social and material relations within overlapping fields of a national culture,[10] *The Outlaw Josey Wales* articulates and then deliberately reframes and silences central tensions and contradictions of post–civil rights America. Drawn in its context, the film enacts a political moment of "dissensus"—"a conflict between a sensory presentation and a way of making sense of it, . . . an activity that redraws the frame within which common objects are determined."[11] Eastwood's *The Outlaw Josey Wales* conducts the shift and in a key cinematic genre historically tasked with the circulation of the lexicon of cold war and imperial expansion and racialized national identity. *The Outlaw Josey Wales* radically revises and makes contemporary the historical terrain of the Civil War, a distant historical touchstone for 1970s Americans. Eastwood attached the imperatives of the gunfighter and outlaw to the Civil War, which, from an American perspective, had a much less obvious parallel to Vietnam than it did to the civil rights movement, the throbbing national conflict alluded to dramatically by multiple false equivalents in *Outlaw*. The film, like the *Star Wars* film following it the next year, were opportunities for the revision of national myth structures and deliberate public cultural reconciliations of formidable predicaments and contradictions of race and democracy.

From the distance of analyzing the failures of the civil rights movement of the 1960s,[12] the reduction of the Civil War to Vietnam is astounding. But ideological reduction by way of imprinting the faulty analogy, the insistence on narrowed fields of imagined social relations, is the spectacular achievement of the film. *The Outlaw Josey Wales* extends a relativizing logic that operates by stitching radical episodes of violence to radical episodes of presence and erasure and radical moments of illusory acts of speech.

The Post–Cold War Western

The crisis over racial integration, the politically ideological centrist movement in economic and military affairs, meshed with a crisis in patriarchy, as the women's liberation movement successfully galvanized support for the passage of the Equal Rights Amendment and the landmark 1973 abortion rights decision *Roe v. Wade*. Eastwood was formidably addressing the revolution in human rights in the 1960s—with judicial cases requiring Miranda Rights and search warrants and curtailing excessive police force—that conservatives linked to the rise in urban violence and crime. If the women's movement did not imperil the holders of white male privilege, the collateral organization of Native peoples and Chicana Aztlan movements vociferously called into question the righteousness of American settler colonialism. The environmental movement and the creation of a federal government bureau, the Environmental Protection Agency, added another level of abstraction to the national flurry of protest, as environmentalists, speaking forcefully for the preservation of undeveloped federal land and revealing the impact of environmental degradation on human beings, began arguing against pollution, industrial waste, and corporate might.

If the traditional civil rights movement had gravitated toward electoral party politics by the 1970s, additional radical engines of American public consciousness were flourishing. Film theorist Frank Wilderson has described the era in which Clint Eastwood emerged as an icon as "the paradigmatic zeitgeist of the Black Panthers, the American Indian Movement, and the Weather Underground." In this distinctly utopian epoch of "revolution" from the early 1970s, the antiwar, antipatriarchy, and antiracism activists adopted as their prime "ethic" the overturning of the American nation-state model.[13] Whether or not the model was robust, proponents like attorney and future Supreme Court Justice Louis F. Powell, author of the "Powell Manifesto," which favored enhanced corporate governance, understood the survival of white hegemony as a contest of American "hearts and minds," a problem where advertising and media would be crucial.

The western film genre had always been tasked with the most cutting of questions engaging American national life. In the 1940s and 1950s it had bent to translate into digestible myth two principal conflicts, the Cold War and the civil rights movement. But the removal of the segregation laws, the withdrawal from Vietnam, and the rapprochement signaled by Nixon and Kissinger's "détente" with the USSR and China signaled the sharp decline in the genre. Italian directors ultimately made hundreds of westerns, shot largely in Spain after director Sergio Leone's successes in 1964 and 1965. These films emphasized the amorality, surrealism, and absurdity of the frontier, and leading American directors and actors took note. They began to rethink the historical record and the cultural symbolism of the 1950s that had imagined white pioneers in vainglorious terms. Arthur Penn's *Little Big Man* (1970) and Robert Altman's *Butch Cassidy and the Sundance Kid* (1969) and *Buffalo Bill and the Indians, or Sitting Bull's History Lesson* (1976) debunked and demystified the enforcement of ritualistic ethical violence encoded in the western genre and rationalized through the mythic masculine swagger of Cold War–era western heroes. Like the Cold War it mirrored, after a seedtime during the 1940s, followed by a heyday during the 1950s and early 1960s, the western film genre seemed exhausted and possibly defunct by the early 1970s.[14] Hitting its stride alongside the Korean conflict, the western had achieved its maximum output and power under the "liberal counteroffensive" of US presidents Kennedy and Johnson but collapsed in the wake of America's withdrawal from Vietnam.

After 1973, the western's old racial politics of Native assimilation and Black serviceability were turned on their heads. Featuring Blacks and Native Americans on a bleak Canadian set meant to imitate Montana, the parody *Buffalo Bill and the Indians, or Sitting Bull's History Lesson* heightened its humorous ridicule by attaining new levels of cinematic realism. Instead of reveling in the fantastic, bloody encounters of victorious white pioneers, the film renders Buffalo Bill Cody's Wild West show as a pathetic, overstaged, circus-like rendition of the unfair conflicts between white horsemen and Native Americans. At the conclusion of the film, Paul Newman as the drunken, impotent Buffalo Bill miserably summarizes the gist of the national problem, a problem that is supposed to be transparent to the film's audience. After a conversation with the film's ex-slave character played by Robert D'Urville, who refuses his benevolence, Buffalo Bill ponders the nature of existence through obvious racialist terms the audience is led to debunk: "God meant for me to be white. God meant for me to be white. And it ain't easy. I got people with no lives. They're living through me. They're proud people, but they're people to worry about."[15]

Clint Eastwood's 1976 work and what followed would transform the dark humor of Newman's comment into a maudlin tale of rebirth. Eastwood produced a body of work to repudiate these contraconventional westerns, which he himself had been a part of, and reasserted the value of the militant white paternal figure known for harnessing communal belonging through violence. In dynamic distinction from the parodic elements connected to Altman and Newman's problem of the "proud people," the "people to worry about," Eastwood reinvigorated and reissued the main tropes of white power and the western genre itself after the mid-1970s.

Gone to Texas and the Origins of *The Outlaw Josey Wales*

In 1973 Clint Eastwood read a privately published novel mailed to him, unsolicited, by the author. The novel was titled *The Rebel Outlaw: Josey Wales*. Eastwood decided to purchase the rights and produce a film from the vantage of a rebel fighter from the slavery war on the border between Kansas and Missouri. The book's hero was a Confederate bushwhacker, lightly modeled on the historical criminal and terrorist figure Jesse James. An artist whose portraits of outlaw gunfighters with a mystical aura were on the radical edge of the genre, Eastwood might have been predisposed to respond to the unusual and singular vehicle, what he called "a very very appealing book" and a "story that needed to be told."

When Eastwood settled on *The Outlaw Josey Wales*, the western, the cinematic genre that had made him an international star able to direct and even to create his own production company, was then in sharp decline and thus considered economically unfeasible. Western films represented 30 percent of Hollywood's big-budget features in 1950, but 1958 was the final year that more than fifty of the films were produced in the US. By 1960 that number had fallen to twenty-eight. In the year after *The Outlaw Josey Wales* was produced, 1977, only seven westerns were made.[16]

Westerns that were connected overtly to the Civil War were also somewhat rare. Typologically, American westerns produced in the US tend to group in chronological time: cavalry films during the eradication of Native Americans of the plains (1855–85); the outlaw and gunfighter films, showcasing the lethal technological advancement of the metal cartridge, the repeating rifle, and after the completion of the transcontinental railroad (1873–90); and the problem of the frontier and Mexican revolutionary wars (1864–1920).[17] In the films of John Ford and John Wayne, the Civil War and slavery appeared sparingly and were used generally to initiate the plot, occasionally, as in *Jesse James* (1939), *Santa Fe Trail* (1940), or *Rio Lobo* (1970).

But the racial politics of 1970s westerns departed sharply from the racial liberalist ethos promoting nonwhite assimilation in the John Ford era of *The Searchers* (1956), *Sergeant Rutledge* (1960), and *The Man Who Shot Liberty Valance* (1962). Legendary actor John Wayne transformed his work, ending his career with somewhat singular reconsiderations of race, relative to his career arc. After providing James McEachin with small roles in *The Undefeated* (1969) and *True Grit* (1969), Wayne upended his onscreen interracial relationships with *The Cowboys* (1972), revising the superordinate-subordinate friendship of Wayne's Tom Doniphon to Woody Strode's Pompey from *The Man Who Shot Liberty Valance*. In *The Cowboys*, veteran actor Roscoe Lee Jones delivered a memorable, genre-defying performance as the dignified, erudite cook Nightlinger, who also possessed the ability to kill. The reformed racial attitudes depicted in *The Cowboys*, where Wayne's character dies three-quarters of the way through the film and Jones concludes the revenge action sequence, established a new threshold for interracial collaborations in westerns.

Eastwood's work in the 1970s contributed hugely to his own mythic arrival as cinematic icon. Part of his success was due to what was considered his extraordinarily canny depiction of race during the rise of a new version of Black cinema itself, one that proved financially significant and increased the circulation of Black artists.[18] As a transnational artist reworking the fictions of the western, progressive onscreen relations with and depictions of African Americans contributed to Eastwood's aura of defiant chic.[19] Shortly after *The Outlaw Josey Wales*, Eastwood would be called "The New John Wayne," "an icon of our culture," and, unlike Wayne, able to "capture both sexes."[20] During this era of his career, Eastwood worked closely with several Black actors: James McEachin, Albert Popwell, Felton Perry, and Vonetta McGee.[21] McEachin had a large role in Eastwood's first directorial credit, the 1971 suspense thriller *Play Misty for Me*, where McEachin played the streetwise friend, DJ Al Montone, a character involved in an interracial romantic relationship. The 1973 Dirty Harry vehicle *Magnum Force* coupled Harry Callahan with an African American partner (played by Perry). Eastwood went even further in the 1975-released *The Eiger Sanction*. That film starred Vonetta McGee, in her debut in a mainstream American film.

Previously, McGee had been in a western, costarring with Max Julien, *Thomasine and Bushrod* (1974), a film written by Julien as a Black western version of Arthur Penn's *Bonnie and Clyde* and with Black exodus politics similar to Sidney Poitier's 1972 *Buck and the Preacher*. McGee had launched her film career, like Eastwood, in an Italian western, Sergio Corbucci's highly esteemed *The Great Silence* (1968). With a screenplay by Franco Solinas and a score by Ennio Morricone, the film was set in Utah in the 1890s and featured bounty hunters and rapacious bankers as villains. McGee played Pauline, whose Black husband has been killed by bounty hunters, opposite murderous "lawman" Klaus Kinski and her protector, the voiceless Jean-Louis Trintignant. Her character is referred to over and over again as "the Negro." Eastwood almost certainly would have noted her appearance in the Solinas-written film when choosing her for the part of Jemima Brown in *The Eiger Sanction*.

Indeed, these forays into films featuring Blacks, and Leone's more direct turn to the realm of anticolonial politics with *Once upon a Time in the West* and *Duck, You Sucker*, seem to have boomeranged Eastwood in the direction of John Wayne's racial liberalism. He described *The Outlaw Josey Wales* as "a story that needed to be told." Moreover, pursuing the film seems decidedly connected to an observation on his part that a significant American point of view had disappeared from the national conversation about the cultural heritage of the nation-state as the actor entered middle age and began moving into other genres because the western seemed near the end of its utility. While his name recognition within the western had proved valuable commercially and been a springboard to other genres, it also tethered him as an actor to a limited past.

By the end of the 1970s, the western genre's commercial vulnerability was made sharply evident by the decision of United Artists to pull from theaters Michael Cimino's masterpiece of race, class, and corporate malfeasance, *Heaven's Gate*. Eastwood's own work had recognized the growing frustration with what had been the primordial American film genre. His most amoral film, the myth-laden 1973 *High Plains Drifter*, had presented a protagonist of fundamentally antisocial character. Lethal masculinity seemed unstable in the wake of the defeat in Vietnam and political upheaval of Watergate and Nixon's resignation. Important films like Dennis Hopper's *Easy Rider* (1969) and Cimino's *The Deer Hunter* (1975) called into question the validity of white chauvinism to resolve domestic and international conflicts with legibility and coherence. But by the decade's second half, *The Outlaw Josey Wales* formidably reversed those countercultural aims. It proposed a sacred moral motive and repaired the colonial divide between settler and Native. John Wayne's epistolary intervention with Eastwood over *High Plains Drifter* had, apparently, no small impact.

Eastwood began shooting *Outlaw* in fall 1975, becoming noted for his financial discipline as a director, the opposite of Cimino and the infamously bloated tour de force *Heaven's Gate*. Eastwood decided to have Philip Kaufman and Sonia Chernus adapt a screenplay from Forrest Carter's novel, later published as *Gone to Texas*, and, originally with Philip Kaufman directing, to create a tightly controlled realist film with minor humorous echoes of the noir tradition.

When *Gone to Texas* appeared, the book's author presented himself to the public as a self-raised Cherokee storyteller, actively engaged in the politics of racial Native uplift:

> Forrest Carter, whose Indian name is Little Tree, is known as Storyteller in [the] Council of Cherokee Nations. Orphaned at the age of five, he lived with his grandpa (half Cherokee) and his grandma (full Cherokee) in Tennessee until their deaths when he was ten. He's been on his own ever since. He has worked ranches in the South and Southwest and calls Dallas County, Texas, home. History is his main interest, especially of the South-Southwest and the Indian, and he uses the council storytelling method of the Indian passing on the history of his people. A number of his Indian friends will share the proceeds of this book.[22]

Eastwood's enthusiasm for the project came directly from the novel. He responded with prime affirmation to Carter's work, calling it "a moving, exciting story about real characters who come alive on every page," adding that the "plot has the ring of authenticity."[23]

Eastwood's association of authenticity with Carter turned out to be completely ironic. The entire book description, including the caveat of alms pooled with Natives, was false. By the time of the film's 1976 release, Forrest Carter had been revealed as the notorious public figure Asa Carter of Alabama. The author of *Gone to Texas*, a distinctly redemptionist Confederate fable, had, in fact, worked on the most famous white supremacist slogan of the 1960s, George Wallace's stump speech declaration for the presidency: "In the name of the greatest people that ever trod this earth, I draw the line in the dust and toss the gauntlet before the feet of tyranny. And I say: Segregation now! Segregation tomorrow! Segregation forever!"[24] The mainstream American press found the irony of an ex-arch-segregationist turned Cherokee humorous and untroubling. Until 2007, Carter's masquerade Native autobiography *The Education of Little Tree* was prominently featured on the Oprah Book Club reading list.

Though Asa Carter's Native disguise was effective through his death in

1979, in reality he was also a violent man and a belligerent racist. In the 1950s he organized a group called the "Original Ku Klux Klan," connected to the public assault on Black entertainer Nat "King" Cole in Birmingham in 1956, and responsible for castrating a Black man named Edward Aaron in 1957.[25] The writer of *Gone to Texas* changed his name from "Asa" to "Bedford Forrest" as an act of homage to the infamous slave dealer, Confederate general, and founder of the first Ku Klux Klan in 1866, Nathan Bedford Forrest.

Carter reinvented himself for the 1970s, coincident with the rise of the Native American movement, environmentalism, sexual freedom, and Black rights. In the words of Joseph Lowndes, this enabled him to move to a debate beyond the white supremacy of the US South, to a more global, antistatist project.

The move to indigenous identification thus allows Carter to begin to shift his investment in a purely biological white supremacist politics to a more consciously ideological antipathy to centralized authority—one that masks the racism of his earlier politics by demonstrating the more generally nefarious results of intrusive government.[26]

Carter's gravitation toward Native status seems odd, particularly considering his abandonment of George Wallace's white supremacy around 1970 as being too soft on the issue of racial segregation. Yet Carter's conducting a public masquerade as a Cherokee actually continues to participate in a project centrally concerned with the repudiation of Black Americans, consistent from the Revolutionary era.[27]

Since the work of Thomas Jefferson, one of the earliest Enlightenment-era figures concerned with the dynamic interaction among Native Americans, Africans, and Europeans, Natives have been assigned protoassimilationist qualities denied Africans. Jefferson noted that Natives were uncivilized but capable of "the most sublime oratory; such as prove their reason." Native American capacity for elevation seems strongly connected to an aesthetic capacity for white resemblance. Jefferson's evidence from "the traders who marry their women" encouraged him to write that perhaps "nature is the same with them as with the whites."[28] By 1808 and when he was president, Jefferson would declare to Natives themselves, "We shall all be Americans; you will mix with us by marriage, your blood will run in our veins, and will spread with us over this great island."[29]

In the identical sense of standards of beauty providing the basis for assertions of ethical value, since Natives were widely acknowledged as having a valid anterior land claim, the ethical ground of white settlers never relinquished the possibility of cohabitation and assimilation. Africans and Native Americans were existing in a state of nature, uncorrupted by civilization's excesses, but Jefferson proposed that the Blacks displayed an "eternal monotony, which reigns in the countenances," a deficiency in beauty bending toward a condemnation of intelligence—"more of sensation than reflection." Intelligence and beauty were qualities he ascribed to Native Americans as a part of their endowment of natural virtue.[30] In Forrest Carter, who proposed his own fantastic membership in the nation of slaveholding and literate Cherokee, Native belonging was a tactic complimenting African erasure.

Nor were the politics of a white supremacist–turned–Native American exclusively obverse to the ways that some Native people understood relations between themselves and Africans, a relationship with many low points. The antebellum Cherokees and Native nations inhabiting East Texas encountered Africans in the context of plantation slavery. The immediate postbellum western Native American nations faced Black soldiers as force multipliers during western territorial expansion. During the Civil War in the Trans-Mississippi theater, Black Union troops, especially the Kansas First and Second Regiments, battled frequently against Confederate forces made up of Cherokees, Creeks, and Choctaws. Rather than natural allies as victims of white-settler colonialism and imperial expansion, Native Americans and African Americans after the Civil War reached their epoch of sharpest antimony. The trajectory of the two groups' movement for rights and recognition in the twentieth century was also markedly different. Vine Deloria, a long-standing Sioux intellectual and writer, captured the difference with the analogy of the Black American as a "draft animal" from whom the right of assimilation was withheld, in contrast to the Native American constructed by white settlers as a "wild animal," whose assimilation was mandatory. "Policies for both black and Indian failed completely. Blacks eventually began the Civil Rights movement. In doing so they assured themselves some rights in white society. Indians continued to withdraw from the overtures of white society and tried to maintain their own communities and activities."[31] Wallace Coffey, the Comanche descendant of the historical figure Ten Bears rendered in *The Outlaw Josey Wales*, pinches exactly this tension as it unfolds into the present, writing sweepingly about the twentieth century: "Indian people didn't request affirmative action or equal opportunities; we requested the American Indian Religious Freedom Act. We wanted to be what we are."[32]

The articulated opposition is formidable: African Americans are understood as nearly sycophantic, seeking successful assimilation into American society, whereas Native Americans are protecting what remains of a cultural heritage. "Indians contrast with blacks for being noble and autonomous," thinks one critic of Carter and Eastwood, "and *stand in* for them as a form of cross-racial political commitment that was the legacy of the New Left" (italics mine).[33] If so, this is an extraordinary maneuver, one that enacts the explicit negrophobia of white supremacy but, by replacing Blacks with Natives, showcases the possibility of substitution and synecdoche for encounters with problems of ethics, civil rights, and remediative justice for a "postracial" age.[34]

But considering the Josey Wales stories primarily, Carter's authorial Native masquerade was not really designed to convince. His move marked a shift from immediate political intervention, including the practical mechanics of racial terror, to a larger project shaping a field of cultural discourse. In this manner, Carter engaged in what Antonio Gramsci referred to as a "war of position," using the novel and autobiographical memoir (*The Education of Little Tree*) to shape public tastes and attitudes toward a conflict that would reach a crisis point at a later date. Partly, Carter surpassed the crude belligerence of his earliest work and consummated an ideology of whiteness that harkened back to the myths of benevolent chauvinism obligatory in D. W. Griffith and Thomas Dixon Jr. Unlike the aristocratic myth of Southern rescue from *The Clansman*, Carter's *The Rebel Outlaw: Josey Wales* explored layered heroic exceptionalism around a figure from the rural yeomanry.

Filming the Civil War in Missouri

If films like *High Plains Drifter*, *A Fistful of Dollars*, and *For a Few Dollars More* were comfortably anachronistic, with a scenic backdrop implying an unchanging western landscape, a timeless zone tucked somewhere between postbellum and preautomobile eras, and always congruent with the ubiquitous technologies of the 1873 Winchester rifle and the Colt Single Action, short-barreled "Peacekeeper" pistol, *The Outlaw Josey Wales* offers multiple historical markers to locate and delimit the precise chronology of the film. Conversely, by isolating the Kansas Jayhawker "Red Legs" as the fanatic villains, an absolute ideal or pure principle that must be resolutely engaged and eradicated, the film suggests a war with time itself.

The movie is split into three territorial segments: the first in Missouri, with conversations between Josey and men who are doomed by the war; the second in Oklahoma and Texas, where the dialogue is mainly shared between Josey and Cherokee "chief" Lone Watie (Chief Dan George); and the final segment in Texas, on the border of Mexico, featuring the reborn community, signaled by the emotional and physical communion between Josey and Jayhawker Laura Lee (Sondra Locke). The total action of the film seems to take us roughly through the summer of 1865, paralleling the activities of two Confederate officers active in Missouri and who refused the armistice in April, preferring to invade Mexico, Major General Sterling Price and his subordinate "General" Joseph Shelby.

The film announces its seriousness with a "cold opening" sequence that transports the viewer to the peak of the Kansas-Missouri conflict, a historical epoch that began in late 1855 and is typically understood as the precursor to the all-out war launched at Fort Sumter in spring 1861. Josey Wales, a mild-mannered father and yeoman farmer from Cass County, Missouri, a western region of the state called "Little Dixie" located near the Missouri River, has just plowed an acre of ground for spring planting. Wales does not own slaves, and in this way his single-man sustenance farming represents the central myth conflating the prerogative of white supremacy and American westward frontier expansion.[35] Unexpectedly, one afternoon the Red Legs militia thunder into his homestead. Historically a band of about thirty men led by Captain George Hoyt, the film's Red Legs are shown carrying Wales's partially dressed, screaming wife in the direction of the barn after they have set fire to the main house, condemning "Little Josey," Wales's eight- or nine-year-old son, to the inferno. When Wales attempts to rescue the child, Captain Terrill (Bill McKinney), the film's fictional leader of the marauders and the name of one of the famous historic Kansas militia captains, slashes him in the face with a saber, knocking Wales unconscious and leaving him for dead.

In the prologue, similar in its import and style to the teaser sequence that plays while the credits run during Zinneman's *High Noon*, the film insinuates a connection to English historical romance, borrowing distantly from Thomas Malory's *Le Morte d'Arthur*. Following the destruction of the homestead by Terrill's men, the fifth minute shows a revived Wales reaching under the smoking foundations of his ruined home. He retrieves a holstered firearm and unsheathes the weapon, a Colt Army model 1860. (An anachronism, of course, pushing the historical time of the film roughly forward, placing the seemingly blameless Wales family beyond the plausible beginnings of the border war in 1855 and closer to its full conflagration.) He fondles and stares at the pistol, and decides to resume a former career that the domesticity of his life as farmer, father, and husband at the homestead have held in abeyance. Wales caresses the iron—which should be burning hot—but the flaming metal doesn't sear his flesh. His unholstering the weapon reproduces a new lineage for the hero, a Malorian moment of Arthur facing Excalibur and becoming royal, entitled, natural gentry.[36]

Wales has already buried his family, conflating anguished snatches of biblical verses from Genesis and the book of Job at the gravesite. Now, with his weapon, he uses both left and right hands, and fires more than seventy shots into a post at about twenty paces. After an afternoon at the firing post, he has regained his elemental strength, the lethal power he was born with, manifest through the technology of the gun. Between handling the hot iron and shooting into the fence post, he transforms into an ancient warrior, in the same way that the makeshift cross marking his family's grave is pounded into another shape, an X, or Saint Andrew's Cross, the core ensign of the Confederate battle flag. Bending the iron to his will and bending the shape of the cross, Wales is the mystic hero, the converter to a new religion of race war.

The film initially seems to encourage the view of a humble, innocent, yeoman farmer establishing competency, but that is a misreading about American masculinity. Wales is not acquiring lethal prowess for the first time; rather, he resumes a homicidal, technologically advanced expertise, which the natural law of vengeance now requires that he execute. While Eastwood suggested that the film identified the horrors of war "to people," the Civil War–era movie operated far better as an allegory to resolve two volatile US spaces of the late 1960s and early 1970s: the often private domestic sphere of male-female relations and the often public national sphere of racial relations.

After reacquiring his pistol expertise, an armed, ruminating Josey Wales is surprised a second time by another group of men on horseback. But these riders are sympathetic to his plight—his executed family and fired homestead. With a black flag (signaling they will give "no quarter" to their enemies in combat) as their herald, they ride up to a seated, nearly prone Wales. One of these men, wearing a Stetson hat, introduces himself and, in doing so, secures the film in the historical time of the Civil War: "The name's Anderson. 'Bloody Bill' is what they call me." "Bloody Bill" surveys the destruction and asks, "Red Legs?" Wales merely nods. Bloody Bill gives Wales an elementary lesson in politics and war. The Red Legs are from the West, Kansas (where the historical Anderson himself was from), and he and his men are going there "to set things a-right." Wales plaintively responds, "I'll be comin' with you."

The appearance of Bloody Bill Anderson in the film's sixth minute situates precisely the geography and history of the early sequence. Anderson was mostly a guerilla commander under Captain William Quantrill (another similarly ranked commander was "Cole" Younger of later Jesse and Frank James gang fame), and they operated in Lafayette, Johnson, Clay, Platte, Cass, and Jackson counties in northwestern Missouri, the last four of these counties on the border with Kansas. The acts of Anderson's band of guerilla raiders are debated today, but there is a fair amount of consensus that Anderson and his subordinate Archie Clement regularly committed atrocities, outright murder of unarmed people, scalpings and other mutilations, summary executions of disarmed soldiers, and robberies.[37] Combatants in the Trans-Mississippi theater labeled the guerillas simple outlaws, responsible for "indignities, murders, conflagrations, and robberies."[38]

While affiliating Josey Wales with Anderson secures the film's hero in temporal chronology and spatial geography, it also demands a relation with the similar name "Jesse James," a man whose older brother, Frank James, was a prominent member of the Cole Younger band operating under Anderson. In the last year of the war, sixteen-year-old Jesse James rode with Clement and Anderson, whose horses by then were adorned with scalps. When Audie Murphy had taken on the Jesse James role in Ray Enright's *Kansas Raiders* (1950), at the dawn of the cultural politics of racial liberalism, the narrator had imparted an antiromantic voice-over: "And so into the pages of crime history rode five young men . . . whose warped lives were to be a heritage to their teacher, William Clarke Quantrill."[39] In stark contrast, twenty-five years later, Eastwood would sanctify Forrest Carter's recuperation of the mythical outlaw in the post–Civil Rights Act era.

In a subsequent montage in blue filter, which shows Josey's increasing prominence as a skilled gunfighter always at the head of the charge and who fights beside a uniformed commander, we learn significant things about the conflict. The men ride on horseback under the black flag of "no quarter," always moving at a gallop. Arson is part of their mission, and when the director shows them firing a barn, the score emphasizes snare drums and fifes, transporting the Bicentennial era audience to a place of American patriotic valor by means of sonic cues. Close to the eighth minute of this prelude, though, the camera frames three pairs of dangling boots and Josey Wales beside Bloody Bill, who stares with satisfaction at the hanged men (the remainder of their bodies is cropped out of the shot). Anderson and Wales continue to charge the camera, and the score climbs to its emotional summit of patriotism with a fusillade of trumpets. The montage shifts when a federal howitzer fires and we see men on horseback with the American flag.

Wales's band's daring riding is then superimposed over shots of large numbers of federal troops and wagons and cannon. Bloody Bill Anderson (the historical figure was born in 1840) has now been replaced by a gray-bearded man who wears the uniform of a high-ranking Confederate cavalry officer, as do several of the soldiers in the troop. This same figure is soon shown lying mortally wounded, attended by Eastwood's hero, while the score shifts to a folksy harmonica dirge. Josey Wales, in his guerilla fighting outfit, oddly straddles the wounded officer and administers water. The man both grimaces and waves him off. Eastwood's character's gesture here, while the opening credits still run, and then at the conclusion of the first third of the film, when he consoles a dying Jamie, links the efforts directly to Blondie of *The Good, the Bad and the Ugly*, and the extension of solace to a dying Rebel soldier. In the two films, the moments of succor are deliberate invocations of blood or clan relation.

As the film proper begins, signaled by an ocular shift to full color, the audience is introduced to a debate about surrender. Should the guerilla fighters, bushwhackers, submit to federal authority? Their leader, Fletcher (John Vernon)—an apparent allusion to the historical Charles ("Fletch") Fletcher Taylor, one of Quantrill's raiders—suggests to the men that "full amnesty" awaits them if they ride into the Union camp, lay down their arms, and take an oath of allegiance. The guerillas under Fletcher ride into the camp to disarm, while malcontent holdout Josey Wales observes them through a telescope from a concealed hillside position. Once disarmed and in the camp, the men are told to recite an allegiance pledge to the United States, during which the Union soldiers shoot them down with rifles and Gatling guns.

Wales rides fearlessly into the camp, killing the exact number of Union soldiers necessary to equal the Confederate casualties. Eastwood and his screenwriters inserted the massacre of Rebel guerilas in the film to make a specific point, although the plot of Wales pursued by federal authority had already been established by his initial refusal to surrender. The Eastwood script goes out of its way to invoke and present a speaking part to another historical actor, Senator Jim Lane of Kansas, offered as the maestro of the massacre of surrendered, uniformed Southern troops. While Lane is not known to have murdered defenseless whites, he was a key political figure at the gateway to the American West in 1865. Senator Lane, more than other historical actors, enlisted African American soldiers during the war and then determined to remove them from garrison duty in the South. Lane sent twenty-five thousand Black soldiers, chiefly in the Twenty-Fourth and Twenty-Fifth Infantry Regiments, out of a total of fifty-four thousand federal troops, to the western US military command in the 1860s and 1870s.[40]

What, then, does the massacre, complete with a historical anchor, obscure?

Tropes of reflection by way of observation, surveillance, and capture enable the viewer to isolate central images in the film. These places of reflection are also attached to a dynamic of absence and erasure, a dynamic that is observed by Shawn Michelle Smith in *At the Edge of Sight*. The onscreen depictions operate doubly, "reinforc[ing] the invisibility of some things by overtly focusing on others. What is not represented is further obscured."[41] The efforts of films to convince audiences that they were not seeing what they were seeing bore a relation to the management of the cinema of the World War II period.

Writing at the end of the 1940s, as studios were preparing to turn out mammoth numbers of westerns, Ralph Ellison used the term *evasion* to describe the "manipulation of the audience's attention away from reality to focus on false issues."[42] Ellison pointed to the culture industry for the ritualistic circulation of "anti-Negro" stereotypes, and he implied politics as the driver of culture. The stereotypes enforced a series of illusions, centrally about the Civil War, helping to create "a tradition of avoiding moral struggle" about a violent conflict where Black Americans had played a key role.[43] Both the Civil War's Missouri terrain of arch-hostility and the Black mid-nineteenth-century presence were places of a remarkably coherent cinematic evasion. The displacement was matched allegorically. In the 1950s, the western worked vigorously to contain the complex oppositions of the Cold War, often erasing the domestic political transformations in favor of allegorical renderings of Latin American, Asian, and African geographies where Marxist-Leninist social philosophy spread and took on new contours, outstripping Western European referents prior to colonial independence. In the 1970s aftermath of many of the anticolonial independence movements, and counterimposition of despotic political regimes, the film industry evaded the representation of domestic civil rights and international Black liberation, while also understanding that classic racial liberalism had outlived its usefulness.

Of course, *Outlaw* features no credited Black performers. Thus, the first major evasion is putatively of African Americans and slavery, a topic erased from the totality of the terrain encompassed by the film. The absence of Blacks points to the film's interest in referring to cinematic conventions of the world after Griffith. The world of the historical archive is pursued only as a dimension of costume and artifact. In 1860, there were roughly 4,225,000 African Americans living south of the Mason-Dixon Line from a total American population of about 31.5 million.[44] In Missouri, where a little more than a million people lived in 1860, 114,000 were enslaved African Americans.[45] On the western border, where the film is set, lived about a third of that total,[46] most of them in the counties on either side of the Missouri River. In the Oklahoma "Indian Territory," where Josey Wales flees to begin the film's second act, 37,500 Native Americans, mainly Cherokee and Creek, but including others of the "Five Civilized Tribes," had been force-marched from Georgia and Alabama in 1835–36. In 1860, there were one hundred thousand Native Americans, assisted by nine thousand enslaved African Americans. In Texas, which officially became a state in 1847, there was a population of 421,000 in 1860. At that time, Texans had about 182,566 enslaved African Americans, about 43 percent of the total population. Between 1860 and 1865, however, at least ninety-seven thousand Black Americans were force-marched and sold in Texas, many of them hailing from Virginia.

Finally, at the conclusion of the Civil War, there were nearly two hundred thousand African American soldiers under arms in an almost entirely separate military branch called the United States Colored Troops. Rather than have them patrol the South and enforce the new federal laws of emancipation, the cavalry regiments, along with the Twenty-Fourth and Twenty-Fifth Infantry, were sent West, and from among these troops and other Blacks ridding themselves of the past of plantation slavery were formed something like 25 percent of the known "cowboys" working the large cattle herds, as well as the regiments of "Buffalo Soldiers" engaged in the Indian suppression wars of the 1870s.

While the fact of this number of Black people in "the West" of the 1860s requires a reconsideration of the films of the 1950s working to portray these territories as racially homogeneous, Eastwood's film is more radical in its deliberate historical evasions, erasures, and upendings. The most extraordinary revision to Carter's novel is the massacre. In *Gone to Texas*, Josey Wales and his sidekick, Jamie Burns, are bank robbers, congruent with the historical figure Jesse James, and Jamie is mortally wounded after the two successfully rob a federal bank. But the film proposes to glorify the men as heroic soldiers, freeing the characters from any possible taint as pillagers or brigands. The massacre becomes the film's most vivid and arresting early scene, determinedly revising an audience expectation of the Civil War as a conflict about slavery and human freedom or definitively affirming the presumption that it is not.[47]

The obvious analogue available to audiences proposes that the second Reconstruction, between 1954 and 1968, with historic legislation concerning education, voting, public accommodations, and housing, was also a kind of massacre of defenseless white Americans, suffering federal government intrusions. Relative to Eastwood's own understanding of the film and its allegorical conjunction with the war in Vietnam, the massacre might also offer an allusion to My Lai, the 1968 massacre revealed to the public in 1970, exposing American military commanders' field tactics as fundamentally genocidal and turning public opinion decisively against the war.[48] But the massacre in *The Outlaw Josey Wales* serves to insert an even more central distortion. During the US Civil War there were multiple massacres of civilians and surrendered soldiers. But the most famous, at Fort Pillow in Arkansas in 1864 and Lawrence, Kansas, in 1863, were conducted by Rebels against Black people and whites known to be sympathetic to slave emancipation.

The film's massacre cues a strong historical revision, utterly displacing the retributive violence of the race war that took place largely in Missouri but included Arkansas, Tennessee, the Oklahoma Territory, and Texas during the Civil War. Senator James Lane of Kansas (1861–66), played by Frank Schofield, orchestrates the massacre in the film, becoming the second named historical figure featured. Schofield's Lane even renders the senator's infamous words, to confiscate or condemn "everything disloyal from a Shanghai rooster to a Durham cow." A friend of Abraham Lincoln and a survivor of the 1863 Lawrence Massacre led by James Quantrill and Bloody Bill Anderson, James Lane recruited African Americans from Kansas, Missouri, and Arkansas into two regiments of Black troops, the Kansas First USCT and the Kansas Second USCT. The Kansas First was the inaugural Black unit to fight in the Civil War, at Island Mound in Bates County, Missouri, in October 1862, where they defeated mounted Confederate guerillas. "The rebels were mostly armed with shot-guns, revolvers and sabres, our men with the Austrian rifle and sabre bayonet. The latter is a fearful weapon, and did terrible execution in the hands of the muscular blacks," a serviceman told the *New York Times*.[49] By the time that Black soldiers were in the field in Missouri in 1862, an exceptionally vicious conflict with obvious racial overtones and genocidal practices was under way.

The killing of Black people in the Trans-Mississippi theater was not limited to the aftermath of large battles. In March of 1863, Cole Younger and others of Quantrill's men attacked a steamboat in Jackson County, the USS *Sam Gaty*, which had on board federal troops, white passengers, and scores of escaped African Americans, some now enlisted in the army. Within days, newspapers from Kansas to New York reported that Quantrill's men had summarily executed "contrabands"—perhaps ten, perhaps twenty.[50] The guerilla fighters also massacred federal troops after they took the railroad station in Centralia, stripping the men and then executing them. The largest massacre occurred during Quantrill's famous raid into Lawrence, Kansas. Stationed there in August 1863 were the recruiting centers for two regiments, the Kansas Fourteenth Cavalry and the Kansas Second USCT troops; twenty raw Black recruits were massacred, as well as Black civilians.[51] If it had not been clear before, after Lawrence, the Black Kansas troops were engaged in a blood fight. An abolitionist who had ridden with John Brown, Wisconsin cavalry officer James Pond, reported in his dispatch that during the engagement against bushwhackers at Baxter Springs, "the darkies fought like devils."[52]

Those Black soldiers almost certainly had little choice. Fighting with hellish intensity for Black troops was characteristic in the West. In 1864, at Poison Springs, the Kansas First received "no quarter" from troops under the command of General Thomas Shelby, who had been the largest slaveholder in Missouri. "No orders, threats, or commands could restrain the men from vengeance on the negroes."[53] After the battle, 117 men died—only days after the massacre committed by Nathan Bedford Forrest's men at Fort Pillow in Tennessee. That atrocity was the best-known battlefield massacre of surrendered troops that occurred during the Civil War, "out West," at Fort Pillow in Arkansas on the Mississippi River in April 1864. In the famous massacre, hundreds of African American soldiers of the Sixth Colored Heavy Artillery Regiment and the Second Colored Light Artillery Regiment, recently enlisted, attempted to surrender and were bayoneted and shot by Confederate troops under the overall command of Forrest. Black women and children, apparently impressed at the garrison as a labor force or in refuge from the nearby Edward Benton plantation, were also bayonetted and shot. Reports circulated that men were nailed to planks, thrown into cabins, and burned alive.[54] Two weeks later, on April 30, the Kansas Second avenged its sister unit at Jenkins Ferry, shooting Confederate wounded.[55]

When bushwhackers operated with impunity, such as in Marshall, Missouri, on August 5, 1864, they shot "five negroes in town and four a short distance from town."[56] On September 20, at Ft. Gibson, Cherokee Nation, the First Kansas USCT and the Second Kansas Cavalry were overrun, and the "whole force of the enemy then charged into my camp, capturing all of the white soldiers remaining there, and killing all the colored soldiers they could find. Only four out of thirty-seven of them succeeded in making their escape."[57] Inspired by and exceeding Asa Carter's mythology, the film, which organizes itself around a logic of historic fidelity, displaces and rejects the tribal feud under way on the "legitimate" battlefields of Missouri and Arkansas and the Oklahoma Territory, dramatically revising the Missouri conflict.

But the evasion is not simply the removal from Missouri of the Black soldiers and civilians, the victims of targeted assassination and systematic murder. Eastwood accomplishes what amounts to a double erasure, not merely removing Black people and the topic of African slavery from the film but accomplishing a keener silencing by substituting the massacre of Confederate guerrilas for Black soldiers as the original sin requiring the myth of the avenging Christ figure that is Josey Wales. The deceitful executions of the disarmed Confederates, in fact, revives the original blood feud of Wales. First his biological family is destroyed; then his warrior family constituted by oaths of blood vengeance is destroyed, making his motive for revenge doubly immaculate. Not even Forrest Carter's novelistic portrait of Wales had envisioned the sacrosanct and redoubled religion of blood vengeance that Eastwood and his team conceived and enacted for the film.

The Other

Both Carter, in his book, and Eastwood, in his film, are credited with sympathetic portraits of Native Americans. The most important representation of a Native American is the character Lone Watie, rendered in *Gone to Texas* (the later edition of *The Rebel Outlaw: Josey Wales*) as a late-middle-age warrior and cousin to Stand Watie, the famous Cherokee plantation slaveholder, Confederate general, and last Rebel commander to surrender his troops. Carter describes the character flatteringly:

> Like many of the Cherokees, he was tall, standing well over six feet in his boot moccasins that held, half tucked, the legs of buckskin breeches. At first glance he appeared emaciated, so spare was his frame ... the doeskin shirt jacket flapping loosely about his body, the face bony and lacking in flesh, so that the hollows of his cheeks added prominence to the bones and the hawk nose that separated intense black eyes capable of a cruel light. He squatted easily on his haunches ... occasionally tossing back one of the black plaits of hair that hung to his shoulders.[58]

Despite the fact that in the novel the two men meet as equals and easily join forces out of mutual respect and admiration, Carter's Wales harbors deep-seated prejudices. "Jest like a damn Indian," thinks Josey Wales about the experienced backwoodsman Lone Watie, "always buying somethin' red, meant fer foolishness."[59] When he translated the portrait into the film, Eastwood eliminated these lines of ridicule, but he altered the relationship in more fundamentally dramatic visual ways. The film reduced the novel's physically vigorous Cherokee character to a diminutive, nearly octogenarian sidekick played by Chief Dan George, who had been nominated for an Academy Award for his role in Arthur Penn's 1970 western satire *Little Big Man*. Affable and witty, George played Watie as a nearly senile ward to Eastwood's hero. The film's Native figure is more comic than physically dynamic, in some measure recapturing the paradigmatic relation from *The Birth of a Nation* between the heroic "Little Colonel" and blackface "Mammy," the dynamic duo whose heroic acts of violence enable that film. Though they are typically credited with softening the racism from the novel, in reality, Eastwood and his screenwriting team actually sharpened the visual dimensions of white dominance in adapting the novel to the film.[60]

The Outlaw Josey Wales was understood as a new achievement in historical accuracy since it featured "full-blood" Native American actors and actresses representing themselves, the Navajo language (rendered in monologue without subtitle), and the historical memory of Native American genocide. But the film also manufactures deliberately conflicting signals to misconstrue the capacity of particular characters, as well as the authority and know-how of Natives. The film's introduction of Lone Watie offers its most elaborate and poignant articulation of the conflict between Natives and settlers, staple elements of the plot for the most celebrated films in the genre like *The Searchers* and *Broken Arrow* (1950):

> LONE WATIE. I'm an Indian all right. But here in the Nation they call us the Civilized Tribe. They call us civilized, because we're easy to sneak up on. White man have been sneaking up on us for years.
>
> JOSEY WALES. Cherokee huh?
>
> LONE WATIE. Yeah. They sneaked up on us and they told us we wouldn't be happy here. They said we would be happier in the Nations. So they took away our land and sent us here. I have a fine woman. And two sons. But they all died on the Trail of Tears. And now the white man is sneaking up on me. Again.
>
> JOSEY WALES. Seems like we can't trust the white man.
>
> LONE WATIE. You bet we can't. I wore this frock coat to Washington before the war. We wore them because we belonged to the Five Civilized Tribes. We dressed ourself up like Abraham Lincoln. You know, we got to see the secretary of the interior. He told us, "Boy, you boys sure look civilized." He congratulated

us and he gave us medals for looking so civilized. We told him about how our land had been stolen and how our people were dying. When we finished, he shook our hands and said, "Endeavor to persevere." They stood us in a line. John Jumper, Chili McIntosh, Buffalo Hump and, eh, Jim Pockmark and me. I'm Lone Watie. They took our pictures and the newspapers said, "Indians Vow to Endeavor to Persevere." We thought about it for a long time. And when we had thought about it long enough, we declared war on the Union.

The film creates a usable past to entwine the rebellious projects of Wales and Watie and, in fact, to add another dimension of vigor to Wales's war against the federal army. Both men are shown as resisters against a corrupt federal government. Watie's oration, delivered in stovepipe hat and black frock coat, is equally comic and venerable. A stately, well-spoken man has earned, on account of white garb and acceptance on white American terms, the theft of his land and the death of the Indigenous population.

But after introducing the argument against assimilation and acquiescence to force, the film emphasizes the emptiness at the center of Watie's moving account. First, Lone Watie's name invokes the best-known Cherokee during the Civil War, Stand Watie. Watie fought battles in Arkansas, Missouri, and Indian Territory (modern-day Oklahoma) and participated in a massacre of African American soldiers at Flat Rock in September 1864.[61] The Cherokee were called "civilized" not because of a masquerade in Washington, where they donned coats like Lincoln, but because they had a written language and practiced plantation slavery. Watie himself is a complex sign of genocide as it pertains to Native Americans, killed and removed from the land but then also perpetrating another hidden genocide of Black victims of the Cherokee, who are removed from the film.

Watie's oration occurs with a mixture of sanctimony on the basis of the profile close-ups and the even, balanced narration of Chief Dan George. But Eastwood's Wales dismisses key portions of the artfully achieved framing narrative. When Watie first says, "White man have been sneaking up on us for years," he seems bitter but not defeated; he sounds hostile. But as the incendiary language intensifies, the camera shifts to Josey Wales, blurring the features of Watie in its foreground and blurring the vividness of his outrage. He repeats the line, perhaps his weightiest in the film, "And now the white man is sneaking up on me. Again." But the potency of Watie in this subsequent moment is utterly diffused. He had been occupying the shot alone, his face filling the screen to add gravitas to his tale of abuse and dismay. But we learn that when he smartly joins Wales, a white man, to the punitive government, "Again," Wales has left him and entered his house. Wales has dismissed the poignant narration of Native American struggle as superfluous.

When Watie follows the exhausted Wales into his own house, he continues the narrative of Indian removal and genocide. Wales, after presumably covering the distance from the Missouri River near Independence to the southwestern border of the Indian Territory, some two hundred miles away, makes himself comfortable while appearing to listen to the story. Watie tells a tale of betrayal and indifference from federal bureaucrats, but as he pays homage to his lineage, to other Native Americans like himself, Wales turns away and loses interest in the story and falls asleep, snoring loudly by the time Watie has concluded. The narrative event of telling the truth of the lives of Indigenous people is reduced to an afterthought or a piece of sleep-inducing pablum. Having soporifically seduced Wales with the tale of woe, the "Chief" smiles with satisfaction into the camera. The pleasure Watie derives from the snoring soldier is explicable by only two presumptions: either Watie is redoubling his effort to turn Wales in for a bounty to the Union troops, or Watie is a nurturing servant and ward, pleased with a natural obligation. The film shows it to be the latter.

While presented as a heroic Native American to the viewer, Lone Watie is actually a character of facades and masquerades. He invents stories to convince his white patron of his value, but the tales are relegated by Wales to simple instances of rhetoric. Watie assures Wales, "I used to have power," and that his credibility among Cherokees is connected to his having been ambassador to the White House of Abraham Lincoln. This claim of the negotiation between the Cherokees and the recent Lincoln administration is an absurd anachronism at the center of the character's mock assimilationist politics, as well as an interesting denigration of Lincoln as a racist historical figure (a sharp contrast to Griffith's reconciliationist celebration of Lincoln in *The Birth of a Nation*). It is 1865. Watie is an elderly man who has supposedly journeyed to Washington, if not in his youth, in his middle age; he claims to have adopted his dress from Lincoln, who doesn't become a national figure until the debates with Stephen Douglas in 1858; he describes a Native delegation having its picture taken, implying photographic technology and portrait themes in use by Zeno Shindler in 1851 but certainly more common in the later 1860s and 1870s. Later, the viewer learns that while Wales calls Lone Watie "Chief," the Cherokee man holds no real rank as an official in the Nation. Later in the film, Lone Watie dupes another Native American into misperceiving him as "some kind of a chief."

While Natives are mocked as royals, the heroic Wales is thoroughly beatified. The finale to the film's opening territorial segment, set in Wales's "native" Missouri, concludes with the boy Jamie facing the impossibility of surviving his wounds and yet reflecting on Wales as a Christ-figure: "Josey, I want to thank you . . . for saving my life." In the subsequent middle chapter of the film, as Josey Wales begins his interactions with Native Americans, Eastwood immediately doubles the presentation of Wales as a savior. At Zukie Limmer's trading post in the Oklahoma Territory, two Creek men offer muskrat hides for red cloth (a double allusion to Native and African "foolishness"). The Native men are lured toward a bad bargain by the offer of free whisky. As the Cheyenne woman, Little Moonlight, approaches the men considering Limmer's outrageous offer, she drops one of the bottles, perhaps as an act of rebellion, causing Limmer to beat her viciously. While Limmer strikes her with a stave, the Native men are shown in the camera frame, retreating from the scene, clutching the remaining bottle of rotgut. The Native men's indifference to her beating is sharply and swiftly contrasted by the arrival of the armed hero, Wales. As soon as Limmer notes Wales on horseback, he promptly ends the racist violence. In that way the film multiplies the power of the white avenger, who not only restores the myth of benevolent white supremacy but is also positioned as the masculine force capable of rescuing Natives from their own gendered indifference toward white malice.

The film offers multiple dramatizations of white sovereignty and Native subordination, typically reversing the stereotypes connected to ethnic knowledge and ethnically inscribed, non-Cartesian forms of calculation. At one point, for example, Lone puts his ear to the ground and warns Josey of an oncoming posse. "You gotta be an Indian to know those things," he says confidently. But the idea of ethnic knowledge is deliberately undercut and shown to be unreliable, as well as, in that situation, doubly incorrect. The Rebel outlaws are actually being pursued by another Native American, Little Moonlight, who has successfully tracked them. She then nearly kills Lone Watie in the ensuing failed ambush. The episode ends with Watie exposed as a character whose vanity makes him impossible to believe. "Glad you stopped me when you did," he says preposterously to Wales; "I mighta killed her." Native knowledge, by itself, without the guidance of white intervention, is either primitive or entropic.

Even while exceeding the containment of the Natives begun in Forrest

Carter's project and substituting the massacre of white Confederates for enslaved Blacks and freedmen, *The Outlaw Josey Wales* yet encountered the problem of the Civil War as a battle for the emancipation of the enslaved. The steadiness of the mocking, dry humor of Eastwood's characters over a fifty-year arc, from Blondie of *The Good, the Bad and the Ugly* to Walt Kowalski of *Gran Torino* (2008), suggests that Mel Brooks's gag-ridden but commercially successful 1974 film *Blazing Saddles* did not entertain Eastwood. The central chortle of Brooks's film was to place race at the center of a western and feature Cleavon Little as a Black sheriff rescuing a town from zealous land speculators. Exceptional Sheriff Bart, a Black cosmopolite who leaves life on the chain gang to suavely outsmart his rivals and save the day, was actually the version of the West that threatened the most. And it threatened because it was anchored more closely to historical reality.

Eastwood was highly versed in the western's tradition of occasional Black portraiture, from his on-set experience with Black actors on Leone's Spanish set for *The Good, the Bad and the Ugly* and in Don Siegel's *The Beguiled* (1971), with African American actress Mae Mercer, who played the character Hallie. But the social "frontlash" (appropriating Vesla M. Weaver's term)[62] of the middle 1970s, the inflation and restructuring of the American consumer economy connected to the oil embargo and the sharp resistance in the North and West to integrated schools, sharpened the public contradiction between democratically arrived-at national laws and the older social practices joined to the preservation of prestige in a deeply segmented social hierarchy ending an era of heavy industry. Italian westerns had ventured critiques of the colonial project at the heart of western expansion and territorial consolidation, but the wave of satirical westerns lampooning ideals of race and chivalry seemed to mark the genre's death knell. Eastwood's project defied the satires and apologetics. He not only revisited the field of the Civil War actions but would offer a heuristic device to engage the presence of Black westerners themselves.

CHAPTER FOUR

"Hold It Real Still"

Black Containment and Structures of Inequality in *The Outlaw Josey Wales*

Efforts will be made in such countries to disrupt national self confidence, to hamstring measures of national defense, to increase social and industrial unrest, to stimulate all forms of disunity. All persons with grievances, whether economic or racial, will be urged to seek redress not in mediation and compromise, but in defiant violent struggle for destruction of other elements of society. Here poor will be set against rich, black against white....

—George Kennan, "Long Telegram" (1946)

I thought TM [Thurgood Marshall] would be offended by any opinion which joined LFP's [Louis F. Powell's] equal protection discussion. TM had been extremely sensitive the entire Term regarding the Court's approach to the Bakke issue. He was livid over LFP's opinion which he regarded as racist.

—Justice William J. Brennan Jr., Papers of Justice William J. Brennan (1978)

Containment and Occlusion

After Quantrill's raid on Lawrence, Kansas, in August 1863, Union field commander Thomas Ewing Jr. issued Field Order No. 11, requiring Missourians to evacuate completely the counties in which Quantrill and Anderson were known to operate. The remaining houses, barns, and other structures were burned. A Union artist's protest against the removal of people from their lands, George Bingham's *Field Order No. 11*, starkly depicted Red Legs pillaging, killing, and presiding over the bodies of Missouri's men and women. Bingham's famous painting also shows a kerchiefed Black woman holding the prone body of a white woman beside a male corpse with blood pooled around his head, and it shows a Black man and boy, both horrified, fleeing the scene. While Bingham enforced the stereotype of Blacks as faithful and docile, he could not create a panorama of nineteenth-century life that excluded Black people from the tableau of rural Missouri on the border of Kansas. Perhaps somewhat surprisingly—particularly considering Eastwood's creation of onscreen intimacy in films like *The Beguiled* (1971), *Play Misty for Me* (1971),

George Caleb Bingham, *Field Order No. 11*, 1865–70, oil on canvas. Cincinnati Art Museum, Edwin and Virginia Irwin Memorial, Bridgeman Images, CIN403029.

and *The Eiger Sanction* (1975)—Black erasure seems to be the tactic of *The Outlaw Josey Wales*.

Eastwood's cinematic concerns emphasizing the pious and angelic dimensions of his Missouri guerilla characters in *The Outlaw Josey Wales* certainly shaped his decision to adhere to the overall dimensions of Black erasure from Carter's novel *Gone to Texas*. Joseph Lowndes, the ablest commentator on the political and cultural reorganization achieved by *Outlaw*, drives home the point about the nonexistence of Black people in the film:

> For a public caught between the militance of the New Left and antiwar movement and the emerging Right in the 1970s, the reconciliation between Josey, the antigovernment outlaw, and Fletcher, the government official, could be an easing of the political tensions of the era. But this is only possible insofar as blacks are made completely absent from the story. Such an absence is peculiar and seems forced in a historical depiction of a journey from Missouri to Texas

at the onset of Reconstruction. But the introduction of even one black character (or even an extra) would call into question the heroism of a protagonist who fought not just *against* an oppressive government that had indiscriminately wronged his family, but also *for* a society that was defined by its devotion to slavery.[1]

Lowndes believes that Eastwood resists even the faintest compromise of the hero Josey Wales's immaculate nature, a morality that would fall into question if Blacks appeared onscreen. But Eastwood's film is even more complicated than Lowndes perceives. Despite the film's fairly indistinguishable politics from Carter's novel and project, *Outlaw* wants precisely to demonstrate how Wales's heroism operates in the face of the weight of slavery and emancipation, Griffith's original problem in *The Birth of a Nation*, without becoming mired in the static racist binarism of the original polemic.

Bingham's *Field Order No. 11*, which imagined Blacks in a minor key of fidelity, was a noteworthy approach. Since sentimental realist parody was the main technique to represent angelic Natives, a similar mocking approach to Black portraits, already evidenced in films like *The Beguiled* and *Dirty Harry* (1971), made obvious sense to Eastwood. It was important to his vision and to the film, specifically as a western, to incorporate an obvious symbol revealing these central concerns.

The Outlaw Josey Wales does indeed include a deliberate, specific portrait of African Americans. There is a pivotal, anomalous representation of Black troops as Wales reaches the frontier of Texas, beyond an Oklahoma woodland that serves as the border to the terrain of the distinguishable "West."[2] The snippet of Black soldiers at the threshold of the recognizable landscape beyond the Civil War and into "the West" is a dynamic enactment of the white supremacist ideal of racial segregation and Black elision. The chosen relation is parodic and occlusive, hermetically sealed, fully encased—a kind of visual cinematic reenslavement within the larger dynamic of emancipation. Eastwood is able to quarantine and contain the instability represented by the Black soldiers in the film to the white Rebel hero, emphasizing and naturalizing Black concealment and absence within an obvious example of presence.

Contrary to Lowndes's reading, *The Outlaw Josey Wales* shows precisely how incorporating Blacks in a category of serene containment can even more thoroughly evade the imperative political crisis on which their representations insist. In this way, the film is able to work as an allegory with a false referent, a series of erasures and containments climbing to a master trope of false equivalence. Fredric Jameson's opposition of Georg Lukács to Brecht in the utility of modernist artistic techniques is instructive in conceiving of the manner in which presence can lodge a greater erasure: "Modernism would then not so much be a way of avoiding social content . . . as rather a way of managing and containing it, secluding it out of sight in the very form itself by means of specific techniques of framing and displacement."[3]

In addition to modernism's containments and displacements of reference, the crucial political valence of the term *containment* is paramount. Introduced by foreign policy expert and diplomat George Kennan, who advocated the "long-term, patient but firm and vigilant *containment* of Russian expansion tendencies," the containment strategy operates usefully in westerns retasked from the duties of the violent cold war 1940s and 1950s to the post–civil rights 1970s.[4] Containment, framing, and displacement actually become the precise technique of Eastwood's debut directing of a western film as he encounters the problem of Black emancipation. I have called attention to Leone's filmic reproduction of Black soldiers as a form of delimitation of space and time, and Eastwood duplicates the momentary insertion but to another purpose.

Before proceeding, however, we must ask this question: Why is it so easy to miss the appearance of Blacks in the film?

As the improbable trio of Rebel outlaw Josey Wales, Cherokee "Chief" Lone Watie, and Cheyenne woman Little Moonlight ride into the Texas town of Towash, on his way into a resupply at Dyer & Jenkins Dry Goods, Josey Wales divides and then realigns the most important constituencies of Americans whose fortunes have been radically altered by the war: Black men and white women. Towash, treeless and carved out of red dirt and sagebrush, with visible mountain ranges seemingly on all sides, is near the sandy desert. The town is an upstart work-in-progress, under rapid, expanding construction and containing the volatile mix of elements in the postbellum American West: cruel dandified hawkers of Native American scalps, uniformed Confederate amputees, jockeys conducting drunken horse races, fake elixir salesmen, and raccoon cap–wearing frontiersmen courting Native American women. Seven sequential shots frame the film's Black encounter: a wide-angle pan establishing Wales and the Native Americans and the Black soldiers; a tighter pan shot of Wales tying his horse, glancing toward the Black troops and establishing himself on the terrace of the dry goods store; and then a close-up of Wales only, his back to the store window looking out into the street; a tight, street-level shot capturing only the faded blue pants and red leggings

Chief Dan George, Geraldine Keams, and uncredited actors in *The Outlaw Josey Wales*, dir. Clint Eastwood (Warner Bros., 1976).

of Wales's nemeses; two return close-ups of Wales's face in profile from both angles; and the final shot, of Grandma Sarah and Laura Lee in the center of the frame, with the Black soldiers to Laura Lee's right.

In the wide-angle shot that pans slowly from right to left, Eastwood films himself as Wales and his Native American compadres approach the store. At the left edge of the frame, the viewer can pick out Black soldiers posing for a photograph. Six men stand and three kneel in front; one of the standing men is swigging from a bottle. A wagon crosses in front of the Black federal soldiers, and so do Little Moonlight and Lone Watie, as they exit the frame.

A second, tighter pan follows Wales as he dismounts and ties up his horse and makes the sidewalk in front of Dyer & Jenkins Dry Goods. Wales glances left toward the Black soldiers, who are no longer in the camera's frame; his visage betrays no notice—neither alarm nor scorn. He does not seem to recognize the emancipated black soldiers, the real object of the "damn war."[5] During the frames, the score offers an upbeat, racy banjo and violin duet of "The Rose of Alabama," the Black minstrel courtship song handed down to Jamie by his father when he performed maternal duties and sung by Jamie not long before his death.[6] Then the music dims to the bowed cello and bass as the camera shifts to the tight shot of four pairs of red leggings walking across the road, only the lower torsos of the men visible (joining them to the hanging cadavers from the opening credit footage). We return to another close-up of Wales, who spits in the street, his response to the Red Legs.

The camera then tightens to the immediate left, onto the first introduction

Paula Trueman (left) and Sondra Locke in *The Outlaw Josey Wales*, dir. Clint Eastwood (Warner Bros., 1976).

of the characters Grandma Sarah (Paula Trueman) and Laura Lee (Sondra Locke). Grandma admonishes Josey Wales for expectorating: "Nasty habit, young fella."[7] Her literal speech has an ironic dimension, marking her as the character who is the source of consistent false wisdom, culminating with the famous false equivalent for which the film is known. Josey is far from a "young fella," and murder, not spitting tobacco juice, is his "nasty habit." The words *nasty habit* bridge two vital collectives shown onscreen—the Red Legs bandits and the USCT soldiers sent west. These two groups are thus conflated, particularly because of the choice to characterize at least one of the Black soldiers as wanton, a public, daytime, street-corner drinker. (The drinking soldier glances in the direction of Laura Lee, a foreshadowing of the film's most malevolent glance made by a dark-skin man toward a white woman.) The "nasty habit" eases into an ironic description of freedom itself, presenting a justification for Jaimie's claim—which had only seemed bluster—before the guerillas were massacred: "I think it's them (the Union soldiers) that owe us an apology." The series of associations include the idea that emancipation itself is a submerged "nasty habit," now palpable, and that the allegorical referent belongs to what would have been considered "nasty" by George Wallace and Asa Carter—the public accommodations and voting guarantees of the Civil Rights Acts of 1964 and 1965.

Grandma is a proud Kansas Jayhawker, which is to say a radical abolitionist, though presumably a bigoted Negrophobe, based on her casual remarks to the store clerk about people who do not share her own background. (The store clerk also responds, "I'm a Hoosier, myself," his own false equivalent of prideful state association, though Grandma's refusal to handle goods from Missouri is of another category of antagonism than the "Hoosier," a nickname for residents of Indiana that some think is connected to the late eighteenth-century Black evangelist Harry Hosier, who was an intimate of renowned Episcopal Methodist bishop and traveling preacher Francis Asbury.) Her ward, her son's daughter Laura Lee, is presented as an innocent dreamer, who will examine the clouds and romantically connect them to fleeting aspirations in a way that Josey, who sees fearsome weather patterns commanding the destinies of humans and animals, cannot fathom. Though one is flinty and the other labile, both women are romantics and slightly clumsy evocations of the feminist movement.

Laura Lee, who becomes the most effective killer of Red Legs bandits after making love to Josey and being rendered inseparable from his commitments, seems director Eastwood's shrewd anticipation of hardline female figures in statecraft like Margaret Thatcher, Condoleezza Rice, Madeleine Albright, Theresa May, Hillary Clinton, and Angela Merkel. Eastwood's gender politics are deft, in the same way as both George H. W. Bush and George W. Bush were adroit racially, advancing Clarence Thomas, Condoleezza Rice, and Colin Powell into remarkably powerful executive and judicial branch positions. By doing so, the Bushes placed their regimes beyond the criticism of displaying obvious racial bigotry, offering instead what should be called "neo-racism," the promotion of Black figures who, as capable managers, allay the charge of broad discrimination while expertly carrying out the most mercilessly racially punitive imperatives of monopoly capital. This is fungibility on a bedrock of racist exchange.[8]

The nine-person Towash Black cavalry detachment is oddly outfitted, with infantrymen's rifles, 1861 Springfields (as are the Comanche warriors Wales meets later). These are United States Colored Troops, evoking the Twenty-Fourth and the Twenty-Fifth, sent west by Senator Lane immediately after the Civil War to fight Native Americans and immortalized as the Buffalo Soldiers. The inappropriate weaponry—the breechloading Sharp's carbine was the standard issue for mounted troops—seems partly a residue of Leone's critique as articulated by Blondie after the Branston Bridge assault: "I've never seen men wasted so badly."

The Black troops in this scene are nearly outfitted as fodder, as were their historic counterparts. In 1863, military historians were describing the fairly uniform low-rating and prospective duty of the Black troops. "As may be inferred from the language of the President's proclamation, it was at first expected that the colored soldiers would be employed almost exclusively in post and garrison duty."[9] Paid less than whites, if paid at all, Black soldiers were treated by the US Army typically as garrison troops and labor battalions and in multiple theaters were overworked on fatigue assignments and poorly provisioned, leading to their grave rates of mortality owing to disease. Equipped scandalously with "smooth-bore muskets, of very inferior and defective quality" or "old flintlock musket[s] altered to percussion," the troops endured desperate conditions unlike any other.[10] The Sixty-Fifth Regiment USCT, which never saw combat, was marched through Missouri in winter, many of the men without shoes, perhaps the reason why it had the second-highest casualty rate in the entire Union army, with more than six hundred men perishing from disease. But if this is indeed the manner in which the symbolism of the armed Black men is to be understood, notwithstanding the fact that 68,178, or more than one-third, of Black Civil War troops died (2,751 were killed in combat), the composition of the brief portrait also suggests that the ideal of extraordinary sacrifices for immediate emancipation were unworthy.[11]

Absence in Presence

The decision to reveal the Black men within the frames of the film in which they are prominent is as unusual as their obscurity. As historian David Blight asserts in his work *Race and Reunion*, during the first publication of the Richmond newspaper in December 1865, its first issue in seven months following the fire in the city that brought on Union victory, "Nowhere in the paper's reflection on the 'Past and the Present' was there a single mention of slavery or black freedom. That evasion would be critical in Southern Memory of the war."[12] Nor was the vanquished South the only source of censored memory. During the Grand Review in Washington, DC, on May 23 and 24, 1865, when some 140,000 federal troops paraded down Pennsylvania Avenue, not a single Black soldier, then making up more than 10 percent of the army, was included.[13]

The Black soldiers, nevertheless, present us with an opportunity to "repopulate space with all the obstacles and all the unknown images, which the illusion of transparency evacuated from it," in the words of critic Irit Rogoff.[14] Ostensibly, the Towash detachment of Black soldiers' decision to pose for a photograph is a celebratory moment, immortalizing pride and courage and self-emancipation by martial arts. But in the sequence involving the soldiers, only two shots bring them directly to the screen. The viewer is invited to consider the soldiers as players in a theater of war about them but in which they take no active part. Instead of fighting in the gun battle that will shortly unfold, the Black troops are posing for a photographer to create a set-piece, a diorama, a memento, a simulacrum distantly connected to the war. And it isn't possible to note their participation as a lack unless the viewer grasps that they are present. Their hazy role in the film, in fact, fully disintegrates, even for viewers who are looking for it. The men are completely silent, while the photographer, the puppet's marionette, commands them to "Hold it. Real still."

Similar to Stand Watie's anachronistic invocation of Cherokees photographed for a newspaper with the caption referring to their supposed vow to "endeavor to persevere," by accepting and succumbing to the dictates of photographic technology, the Black cavalrymen are both preserved by photograph and utterly erased from the film they are in. With their mismatched rifles and liquor jug, indicating the unlikeliness of their success in arms, to the abstemious religious avenger that is Josey Wales, they closely parallel Leone's rifleless Black prison camp laborers from *The Good, the Bad and the Ugly* (a composition brilliantly reconstituted by Francis Ford Coppola in brevity, but with startling impact, during the attack sequence against Vin Drin Dop in *Apocalypse Now*). But the activity in which they are involved also profoundly reverses these cinematic peers. Eastwood's Black cavalry serve as sealed mannequins who permanently occupy the silent margin of a film logic in which they are indeed central. Their most salient moment features them

"Hold it. Real still." Uncredited actors in *The Outlaw Josey Wales*, dir. Clint Eastwood (Warner Bros., 1976).

Uncredited actors in *Apocalypse Now*, dir. Francis Ford Coppola (American Zoetrope, 1979).

in an odd triptych, parceled into contained inanimate still-lifes by the porch posts of Dyer and Jenkins's store. They exist "real still," only for the ideal of being preserved, and in fact can only become the silenced representation of their service by silencing themselves in the present. But first the image must be dissolved.

As Wales purchases goods at Dyer & Jenkins, we have the single other reference to photographic technology in the film. One of Josey Wales's fellow bushwhackers, Simp Dixon, killed in Cotton Gin, has been photographed on the "cooling board." "Real photo" picture postcards of historic persons, including villainized Black people, reached popularity with the evolution of photographic print technology in the 1890s. After William "Bloody Bill" Anderson was killed in an 1864 gun battle with federal troops at Albany, Missouri, Union soldiers placed his cadaver in a chair and posed it with weapons and made multiple photographs, which were widely circulated. Especially important were the very late nineteenth-century and early twentieth-century photos of spectacle lynching, with two Black figures gunned down by vigilantes and marines later, Railroad Bill and Charlemagne Perault of Haiti.[15] The Black soldiers in Towash are celebrating emancipation, the belated Juneteenth, in fact. But with the help of "holdouts" like Wales, their fates will be transformed radically, and the photographs they are taking as national symbols of emancipation will be transmogrified into the picture postcards of lynching and national disaster.

The film's most stylistically chic gun battle concludes the Towash episode, a shootout in close quarters where Josey Wales impeccably guns down three Union soldiers (a fourth is slain by Watie). Embracing the position of Confederate avatar for this central portion of the film, Wales snarls, "Are you gonna pull those pistols or whistle Dixie?"—a taunt to initiate battle. After the shootout, a dying soldier crashes into the bottles sold by the Carpetbagger, who has revealed Josey Wales's identity, and Josey, in hurried flight, knocks the snake oil salesman into horse dung, which the man absentmindedly clutches to his chest. The Black military men are conspicuously absent.

One further scene implies the total symbolic containment and complete registry of nonbeing associated with the Black troops and the silence of photography. After Wales and Watie have escaped, the same photographer reproduces another group of Union soldiers opposite the Capitol Hotel: the four men slain by Josey Wales and Lone Watie. The men are laid out in the sun, one of them seminude, while the shopkeeper narrates a portion of the afternoon's events, emphasizing the smarmy commercial exploitation of his social class, as he prepares to exploit the forthcoming picture postcards of the new group of dead men. (Eastwood returns to this image in his 1992 film *Unforgiven*, bringing together the sphere of the immobilized Black and the cadaver in the form of the Black character Ned Logan, who is whipped to death and placed in a coffin displayed in public.) Like the trading post keeper Zukie Limmer, the aproned shopkeeper cheers, "I'd certainly like to share in any reward," before bragging and exaggerating about Josey Wales. "Knew him rather well, actually," the Hoosier explains, smiling to the camera. The chatty Dyer & Jenkins merchant places his hand over his heart, and the picture is snapped.

Like the three other commercial agents, whose convincing portraits highlight the film—Sim Carstairs at the ferry, the Carpetbagger selling elixir, and Limmer at the territory trading post—the entrepreneurial class of shopkeepers, salesmen, and traders in the film is shown as definitively corrupt. These are dishonest men without loyalty, absent masculine vigor, putrid, and venal. They are physically repugnant misogynists, sadists, and rapists like the Comanchero leader played by John Quade. Managed in the public spaces of a democracy by this class of men, the freed Black cavalrymen in the photograph are completely insecure. As soon as the opportunity to turn a profit on the picture postcards of their death prevails, after their work to help extirpate or corral on reserves the Native Americans, the about-face will happen without mercy. The Black troopers, who have completely disappeared after being photographed, are ultimately collapsible to the other photographed federal cadavers.

"Dyin' ain't much of a livin'"

The project of containing and erasing the Black presence in the film refers back to the drama of death and philosophical recognition from *Dirty Harry*, although *Outlaw* reverses the racial ingredients. In *Dirty Harry*, the opening pas de deux between Eastwood and Popwell is actually the weightiest and most vivid presentation of a cinematic trope dramatizing the justification of deadly force in the complete film. It rivals but finally exceeds the others for which Eastwood is well known. While the dramatic scene is doubled in *Dirty Harry*, the second occurrence, which results in the spectacle death of Scorpio (and seems to supply Harry's libidinal wish-fulfillment), is not between two rational characters: Scorpio is a deranged sociopath whose libidinal fulfillment is satisfied by extreme violations and penetrations of vulnerable innocents unable to confront him physically. *Outlaw* contains a fight to the finish between rational characters that shows the terms of life and death that legitimately rational men are availed.

After a series of battles, the hero, Josey Wales, is drinking in the Lost Lady, a saloon in the erstwhile boomtown Santa Rio. The town has become a desolate ghost town because "first the silver run out of Santa Rio, then the people run out, then the whisky run out, then the beer run out." The bonanza capital projects that began the hemispheric exploration by the Spanish in the fifteenth century and led to the Native genocide are imitated and reproduced in the nineteenth century by the English-speaking settlers but with a comic, absurdist, inebriated repetition. An especially competent-seeming bounty hunter enters the saloon, a man Wales has already surveilled as a possible threat as his band had entered the town. The two gunfighters have a brief, intense dialogue:

> BOUNTY HUNTER. I'm looking for Josey Wales.
> JOSEY WALES. That'll be me.
> BOUNTY HUNTER. You're wanted Wales.
> JOSEY WALES. Reckon I'm right popular. You a bounty hunter?
> BOUNTY HUNTER. Man's gotta do somethin' for a livin' these days.
> JOSEY WALES. Dyin' ain't much of a livin', boy. You know, this isn't necessary. You can just ride on.
> [Bounty Hunter exits; saloon regulars drink in relief; Bounty Hunter returns.]

BOUNTY HUNTER. I had to come back.
JOSEY WALES. I know.

At first, Eastwood's Wales offers a dialogue that seems a gentle critique of the history of western settler imperialism and its reliance on legions of landless, expendable, uneducated whites of the lowest class: "Dyin' ain't much of a livin', boy." But the confrontation also doubles back to the famous *Dirty Harry* scene and brings into the film the absent Black Americans. In *The Outlaw Josey Wales*, Eastwood whispers the conversation to another white man, a former soldier, and he diminishes him, refers to him as a "boy" and sends him outside. When the bounty hunter gathers his courage and returns, Wales skillfully, dispassionately shoots him down.

But there is a key distinction between the scene in *The Outlaw Josey Wales* and its silent, but obvious, intertextual allusion to *Dirty Harry*. In *Dirty Harry*, Popwell's Black character also wants to measure his ontological depth against a fellow gunfighter. Is he too capable of risking his life on the scale of Being? But to Inspector Callahan, the contest is unequal; it is, in fact, ludicrous or comic. Callahan disparages the Black man, exalts his technological apparatus, pulls the trigger, and smirks. The scene is funny.

In *Outlaw*, Wales sees in the bounty hunter an adversary who is a brother not unlike himself, worthy of fratricidal death, and thus not unworthy of fully complex existence. The bounty hunter stakes his life against fear and experience and loses, but he understands that he must risk death to find real meaning. The Black bank robber in *Dirty Harry* wants to know, too, but the framing undermines his opportunity to secure knowledge and meaning. His situation itself is already proscribed, and freedom is unavailable; the Black bank robber's only choices are meaningless death or the absolute confinement of prison. Like the hideous loss of life among Black garrison troops, the Black robber only has the choice of being wasted badly.

But the isolation of his drives within the body enforces the split observable more than a half century earlier when Griffith worked the minstrel types onto the screen: Mammy, Tragic Mulatto, and Bad Nigger. More repeatedly than virtually any other Hollywood director, Eastwood will be increasingly interested in working through dimensions of the stereotype as he engages Black characters as an actor and a director, through subsequent films like *Bronco Billy* (1980), *Heartbreak Ridge* (1986), *Bird* (1988), *White Hunter, Black Heart* (1990), and *Unforgiven* (1992). The tragic use of the comic recognition scene from *Dirty Harry* reverses what appears as a sympathetic continuation of a Leone-style colonial critique of the western exploration and seizure of Native American territory and mineral resources.

The Outlaw Josey Wales etches its Black people into a permanent geologic stratum of silence and displaces the event of enslavement onto a narrative of immigration. Ultimately, this work became congruent with the false racial equivalent narrative of "color blindness" that became so important to the creation of the American political New Right:

> The Old Right, North and South, had been on the wrong side of the revolution opposing the civil rights movement and reviling its leaders in the name of property rights, states' rights, anticommunism, and the God-given, biological inferiority of blacks. Largely moribund by the 1960s, the conservative movement reinvented itself in the 1970s, first by incorporating neoconservatives who eschewed old-fashioned racism and then by embracing an ideal of formal equality, focusing on blacks' ostensible failings, and positioning itself as the true inheritor of the civil rights legacy.... They insisted that color blindness—defined as the elimination of racial classifications and the establishment of formal equality before the law—was the movement's singular objective, the principle for which King and the *Brown* decision in particular, stood.[16]

So what is remarkable about *The Outlaw Josey Wales* is its operation as a western cinematic opera of the values of the New Right in 1976. The film is a significant visualization of the purported benefits connected to the maintenance of white supremacy in its recasting of the Civil War, a conflict seemingly unconcerned with the issue of enslavement. In terms of the myths that he mobilized, his conduct in the genre most associated with chauvinism, and the epoch in which he operated, Eastwood wound up supporting a transformation, described by Terry Eagleton, where "culture was no longer the antagonist of politics, as with the Olympian, anti-political aloofness of the Kulturkritik heritage, but the very syntax of it."[17] This shift in the cultural product as the conduit of politics had precedent in the Fordist era, but the silent presence of Black containment is also parcel of Eastwood's working to vault beyond the limits of the genre film, most importantly from the "B" genre to the prestige class.

The film exalts in dramatic tropes of *frontierism*, defined as "the attempt to resurrect an imagined, romanticized past inhabited by white archetypes triumphing over land and human others."[18] But even more so, the film is the expert cultural product in the shift away from the tactic of racial liberalism of the John Ford and John Wayne era, and to the equivalency of what Jodi

Melamed identifies as the era of antiracist "liberal multiculturalism," a part of the "unifying discourse for U.S. state, society, and global ascendancy and as material forces for postwar global capitalist expansion."[19] The importance of these officially sanctioned antiracisms is that they require full disconnection of racism and its effects from material conditions, and they bind antiracism indubitably from an expanding US-led, dollar ascendant, global capitalism. The racialization process, as it arcs from the liberalism of D. W. Griffith and John Ford to the multiculturalism of Eastwood and the neoliberal efforts of directors like Ang Lee and Quentin Tarantino, nevertheless has as its primary function "to make structural inequality appear to be fair."[20]

Slavery in *The Outlaw Josey Wales*

Although *The Outlaw Josey Wales* features no credited Black actors or speaking parts for African Americans, since the "Hold it. Real still" politics of emancipation are central to film, it is unsurprising that two key sequences address deliberately the problem of slavery, enabling Josey Wales to kill in favor of abolition.[21] A poor white man named Zukie Limmer operates a trading post in the Creek territory, near Wales's initial encounter with Lone Watie. Limmer is presented as a greedy bully, fleecing Native Americans in trade, using alcohol to control them, and beating Native American women. He is, however, a timid man when it comes to dealing with his own "kind," other white frontiersmen. In fact, though he attacks Little Moonlight, shouting, "Spilling Dog!" as soon as he realizes that a white man is watching him, he exhibits shame, controls his rage, and goes into the store for business. Inside, there are two bearskin-togged frontiersmen, rough trappers named Al and Yoke, who have a short discussion with Limmer:

> AL. What do you take for the squaw?
> ZUKIE. She ain't for sale. I mean, she ain't mine. She works here.
> YOKE. See that nose scar? Know what that means to a Cheyenne, hunh? One too many bucks. Little squaw likes the bucks, huh? Tell ya, Zukie, you put her on the bill too.
> AL. Huh, ah, ha.

Like Josey Wales, who seems to have continued the Civil War throughout the summer of 1865—Texas African Americans weren't notified of their freedom until June—and into the fall (as he makes his way into the Creek Nation, we see snow on the hilltops), the frontier trappers Yoke and Al are men who know the customs and heritage of the Native Americans but only as a means to literally rape them. (The Cheyenne are also the victims of one of US history's most infamous massacres, when federal troops executed and mutilated hundreds of women and children at Sand Creek, Colorado Territory, in November 1864.) The trappers are also, in fact, explicitly continuing the tradition of slavery, not yet outlawed by the Thirteenth Amendment, adopted in December 1865. Somehow during the conversation with Limmer, an exchange of cross-cultural legalistic rationales to justify the use of sexual violence against nonwhites, the audience recognizes the frontiersmen as meriting death. They drag Little Moonlight to a corner of the dugout and hold her down. Josey Wales enters the store. "You suppose these gentlemen will be able to discuss business before long?" Wales questions Limmer, sardonically.

Limmer and the fur trappers reproduce the dishonorable backwoodsmen Abe and Lige, killed earlier in the film by Josey and Jaime. These are desperate fortune hunters, ingratiating one moment, brutes the next, men who abandoned the Southern rebellion and are fundamentally untrustworthy. Little Moonlight holds an inverted Christlike pose, with only her face at the bottom of the screen. Her gaze is stoic and imploring as she readies herself for sexual assault, but her countenance beseeches Wales for rescue, repositioning Wales again as religious savior.

But the sin of violation of the Native woman is not the reason the trappers merit death. The white men become eligible ethical targets not because they are prepared to reenact the slavery of nonwhites but because they seek to carry out the logic of the bounty and reduce Josey Wales, another white man, to slavery, to reduce his white hide into a fungible commodity of exchange. And for this transgression, when they desist from rape to capture Josey Wales, they are shot down and spat on as punishment. This is an exceptional moment in the film, which had begun with the rape and murder of Josey Wales's wife. The rape sequence will, in fact, introduce a far more shocking and graphic sexual assault, making the film's politics clear. Only the violation of a white woman is a punishable crime.

Despite his intervention, the film never clarifies Wales's position on Little Moonlight's assault. Later, Wales is told by Chief Watie that Little Moonlight "kind of belongs to him" and that, in a sense, slavery was her natural condition. Wales retorts, "I don't want nobody belonging to me." Presumably, Little Moonlight, who does not speak English, has misread the situation of Josey Wales saving himself from slavery as saving her. The distinction is driven home with the most graphic sexual assault and prolonged threat of enslavement that unfolds shortly after Towash with the Comanchero. The most arresting onscreen moment of sexual violence occurs at the frontier beyond the frontier, the place where nation-state borders have lost their meaning and mixed-race bands of marauders vie with nomadic Native Americans and white explorers for plunder.

Eastwood, in his role of director, makes a series of fascinating choices to collapse the distance between the point of view of the viewer, the camera, and the vengeful hero Josey Wales, when Laura Lee, the film's only young white woman, is discovered hiding in the recesses of a prairie schooner after her wagon train has been attacked and all of the white men killed. The first man to discover her in her hiding place, and whose raw gaze of penetration performs the first blow in the assault, is the darkest-skinned actor that the camera centers on in the film. He gapes at her; another dark-skin Native man shows a pointed blade. The dark Comanchero pulls Laura Lee out of the wagon and dramatically rips open her shirt, exposing her breast. He then forces her to the ground and tears off her skirt, revealing her naked body. At this moment, Wales prepares to shoot at the man with his pistol, although the viewer understands it is only a pyrrhic gesture, proving only his morality and racial solidarity. The pistol would be ineffective at such a great distance, and firing would only give his position away, to men with rifles whose horses are nearby.

Wales's intercession would have been suicidal, assuring the ruin of the film's white characters. The rape cannot be stopped in any meaningful way except one: another white male character, the leader of the Comanchero band, intervenes and prevents the assault, invoking the transactional law of exchange value. In this neoliberal emancipation myth, unravaged whiteness will "boost [the] price" of commodities in an ancient network of slavery and piracy. After having curtailed nonwhite sexual violence against a white woman of childbearing age, like Colonel Mortimer's sibling in *A Few Dollars More*, Josey Wales is able to again shoot down the rivals. In his feminist politics of equivalency, Eastwood positions Little Moonlight as the retributive assassin against the would-be Comanchero rapist, shot in the groin. But ultimately it is emancipation itself that threatens white men with the possibility of enslavement and justifies their recourse to deadly force.

The False Equivalents: "No Offense"

This account privileges the film's necessary relationships with dimensions of the evolving American resolution of rendering voting rights and public access to American citizens irrespective of race and national origin. Unsurprisingly, during Eastwood's decision to pursue the project and subsequent filming, what has proved to be the most salient public racial antagonism harnessed to liberal discourse was beginning to take shape. In 1954, the Supreme Court had struck legislation barring Blacks from schools in the South, followed swiftly by a southern program of "massive resistance," ultimately requiring President Eisenhower to deploy military force to ensure that federal law was obeyed. A decade later and facing strong resistance, the apt politician and president Lyndon Johnson maneuvered through Congress the Civil Rights Act of 1964. Title VI, "Nondiscrimination in Federally Assisted Programs," sweepingly ensured that "no person in the United States shall, on the ground of race, color, or national origin, be excluded from participation in, be denied the benefits of, or be subjected to discrimination under any program or activity receiving Federal financial assistance."[22] The next year, enlisting domestic support for the Southeast Asia military buildup, Johnson initiated an expansion of "nondiscrimination," with an executive order requiring the government to use "affirmative action" in its hiring. The practical ideal was transferred to American higher education following the Watts riot of 1965, the Newark and Detroit riots of 1967, and the nationwide riots of 1968.

While many schools responded to the direct pressure from students, famously at Columbia and including armed takeovers at Cornell and Wesleyan, the securing of federal grants to research universities also assisted the dramatic shift in enrollments of Black students at elite private colleges in the US. Princeton went from a single Black undergraduate entering in 1960 to dozens by 1968; Yale went from 3 percent in 1966 to more than 8 percent in 1969.[23] Some schools used a language of "quotas" in their admissions practices to achieve the goals of dramatic racial realignment.

In 1976, the university system of California was sued by Alan Bakke, a rejected white male applicant for the medical school at UC Davis, alleging discrimination. At the time, conservative judges on the Supreme Court, like Louis F. Powell, author of the "Powell Manifesto" of 1971, which specifically identified culture as a battlefield where neoliberal market interests ought to confront radical left cultural icons like Herbert Marcuse, Angela Davis, and Eldridge Cleaver, believed that "achieving meaningful diversity" by taking race into account as an admissions criterion was permissible.[24] The ultimate decision, striking the idea of a "quota" as a legal unit to measure progress, began the systematic reversal of programs remediating racial inequality, that is, about ten years after they had begun. The point of conflation was to bend the "stigma and insult" of the original language in *Brown v. Topeka Board of*

Education (1954) back against itself and, as Justice Powell insisted, to argue that Bakke's rejection was connected to his association as a member of a stigmatized, insulted group. By rejecting the notion of racial "stigma" as fundamental to the Equal Protection Clause of the Fourteenth Amendment, Powell delivered the kernel of the rationale enabling the resurgence of white majority rights touted by Ronald Reagan in the 1980s. Powell decided that "the Equal Protection Clause is not framed in terms of 'stigma.' Certainly the word has no clearly defined constitutional meaning. It reflects a subjective judgment that is standardless. *All* state-imposed classifications that rearrange burdens and benefits on the basis of race are likely to be viewed with deep resentment by the individuals burdened."[25]

Using this argument, a person who came from the group representing the overwhelming majority of the population in a social order that regulated mortality (or longevity) along racial lines (a definition of racism)[26] successfully argued the false equivalent, that it was possible as a comparatively advantaged white to bear the same "stigma" as a person "burdened" with a legacy of state-sanctioned persecution and discrimination.

The turn to the Equal Protection Clause of the Fourteenth Amendment as a protection for white men against social remedies designed to reform structural racism was appropriately connected to Eastwood's method of revealing the Black soldiers in the film. The famous fourth footnote of Justice Harlan Fiske Stone's opinion in the 1938 *United States v. Carolene Products* was widely used to approve "exacting judicial scrutiny" of laws imposing on the Bill of Rights. *Carolene* introduced the ideal of strict judicial scrutiny because "prejudice against discrete and insular minorities may be a special condition, which tends seriously to curtail the operation of those political processes ordinarily to be relied upon to protect minorities."[27] Fascinatingly, in the film central to his western cinema oeuvre, Eastwood's technique of undeniably "special" Black representation could best be characterized by the words "discrete and insular," precisely the part of the 1938 decision that the film undermines.

Outlaw explicitly supports Powell's position on the Equal Protection Clause and, thus, the pending *Bakke* case, quite overtly. Once the Black soldiers have been successfully fragmented, encased, and displaced, the most obvious and precise resolution of the false equivalents of race and history occur within the multicultural Exodus community led by Wales. These dialogues are crucial to the film's overall presentation of neoliberal ethics and the anticipation of the Reagan regime of the 1980s and the successful repudiation of 1970s movements for public education and access to fair employment. As the Wales-Grandma-led "new age" family prepares to fend off a Comanche attack, where they will have to fight young, ideologically committed warriors who are in essence retaking territory and resources that the film implies are rightfully theirs and who would appear as sympathetic figures to the audience, Grandma Sarah, the proud Kansas Jayhawker, proclaims to the equally elderly Native figure Lone Watie:

> GRANDMA. You know, we sure are going to show them Redskins something tomorrow! No offense meant.
> LONE WATIE. None taken.

The episode is far from completely comic, emphasizing a point differentiating the prejudice of passion expressed in language but not held as an enduring belief. Grandma Sarah of Kansas at least partly represents the federal authority that has moved Watie from his Georgia, Tennessee, and Alabama lands. Building her confidence against overwhelming odds, Grandma expresses her courage with a vulgarity that slips into the linguistic logic that is about to rationalize genocide. But equally committed members of her community, who share her values—rights to private property through contract, title, beliefs, and, in fact, her household—know intuitively, and within the formal parameters of the discourse, that while she has invoked the logic of race war, explicitly the binary between being and nonbeing, she recognizes the contradiction and offers a sincere apology.

Lone Watie's response might not necessarily stem from a generous acceptance of the proffered apology. Instead, he takes on the world where colors, the signs of race and ethnicity, are only formal equivalents without any historical residues. Lone Watie must adhere to what Eduardo Bonilla-Silva and David Dietrich call "the collective expression of whites' racial dominance" or "color-blind racism."[28] To have a place in the expanding world of Kansans, passing property from one to the other, who have now united with their traditional and militarily skilled foes the Missourians in a new project of expansion, the Native American will have to accept the new order, which purports to a formal logic of color blindness.

The conversation is deliberately reproduced, like *Dirty Harry*'s ontological recognition doublings, a short time later. The "Redskins" have not endured as a redoubtable foe; in fact, now, they are distant confederates. The original Jim Lane Jayhawkers, of whom Grandma's son was actually a member, are now the villains. Thus, it is Grandma's turn to be on the receiving end of a ritualized exchange:

> LONE WATIE. Now, we're really going to show these palefaces something! No offense.
> GRANDMA. None taken. These freebooters are a slander to Kansas, attacking innocent women like this.

Despite the asymmetries in social hierarchies, colonial history, and linguistic valence, for Eastwood this is a pure analogy, an example of absolute transhistorical ethical value. The doubled exchanges suggest that prejudice resides exclusively in rhetorical figures and speech acts, and even when resentment or pique is stirred, rhetoric fully mitigates the offense. Precisely what is unavailable for consideration is the inequity of the comparison between a racial epithet connoting genocide from the majority and the minority's members simple reversal of the rhetorical terms for an analogy. But this is a decisive evacuation for the film, where the categories—Grandma's "Redskins" and Lone Watie's rejoinder, "palefaces"—can be reduced as perfect homologies: impolite epithets.

The application of transhistorical principle shorn of context was fundamental to the stated logic of Justice Louis Powell's majority decision for the Supreme Court on *Bakke*. One term (only recently retired by a professional sports team as an allusion to its capacity for fierce savagery) strongly conveys the idea of a barbarity that civilization must eradicate. As well as a history of genocidal execution, *Redskins* is a companion to *bucks*, as in the price paid for corporal proof of Native death. By contrast, the purported epithet *paleface* is actually an endorsement of the skin-color Western aesthetic hierarchy, representationally insignificant as a demeaning remark.

The film gives to its oldest characters the sharpest ideological points germane to the contemporary politics of *Bakke* and the harm of "reverse racism." By preserving, somewhat, the sympathetic aura of Eastwood's hero Wales, he remains unburdened by the flaws of political calculation. Wales is, however, connected to an important asymmetry in the film, hinted at early on. As the band of men—Wales, a wounded Jamie, and the Carpetbagger—had been hand-drawn across the river on Carstairs's ferry, the film contains a snatch of a Carstairs-sung alternate verse from the minstrel song "Dixie," considered the Confederate anthem. "Injun batter makes you fat or a little fatter, Look away, Look away, Look away, Dixie land." Carstairs, bedraggled, diminutive, and scheming, is attempting to ingratiate himself to Wales but instead displays only his insincerity. The point is driven home when the Carpetbagger proposes his patently insincere elixir to cure Jamie's not-yet-mortal wounds, an act of mendacity for which Wales punishes him by jetting brown tobacco spittle on the man's white jacket. When pursued by the federal authority in Missouri, the Carpetbagger, cleaning his jacket, furiously tells Josey Wales, "There is such a thing in this country called justice!" Wales replies to the man whom he has humiliated: "We got something in this territory called a Missoura boat ride." With that, Wales shoots the ferry cable, severing it and sending the ferry downriver in comic chaos, and the score reprises a spare banjo-and-tuba rendition of the "Dixie" melody, seemingly uniting Wales's nativist heroics to the anthem, but from the ironic point of view of the auteur.

Carter's book does not have as its center the feud between a vengeance-driven Josey Wales and Captain Terrill of the Kansas Red Legs. His novel climaxes with the rapprochement between Josey Wales and Ten Bears, when the Comanche chief decides not to pursue war against the settlers. The key line in the film conveying the resolution occurs when Wales presents his deal to Ten Bears, one that strikingly favors the new settlers, who offer only an annual tithe of cattle to the migratory Comanche in exchange for a permanent settlement, including the rights to convey title to property. Ten Bears, noted for the range of his intelligence, replies to Josey Wales's negotiation with contemptuous incredulity. "These things you say we will have, we already have," the Native American chief retorts to the bold interloper. But Josey Wales acts out the postsegregationist liberal logic of *Bakke*, replying swiftly, "I ain't promisin' you nothin' extra."

Here Eastwood utters the film's most revealing understatement, an oblique reference to Tuco and Blondie's original misunderstanding, one that implies the extraction of surplus value that is a core feature of colonial expropriation, plantation slavery, Native eradication, and the imputation of vertically scaled racial difference. Eastwood returns to the robust Nixon-era Republican ideological point of "root hog or die" to disrupt the notion that white settlers bear responsibility for the situation of colonialism. This idea that whites on the frontier could never owe taxation or reparation—"extra"—and must in some form be connected to or inscribed within a gratuity of surplus interior to bonanza capitalism, relies on the false equivalence of "redskins" and "palefaces" as much as the imaginary equivalence of the pictures of the live Black Union cavalry and the dead Union soldiers. The film works finally to center this logic, which is neoracism.

The Outlaw Josey Wales is a mythic revival of the western, which had fallen out of favor in the 1960s and 1970s, specifically as the extraordinary parallels with atrocities and meaninglessness of the Vietnam War increasingly demanded revisions of the standard generic myths of crusading white soldiers, lone gunfighters upholding transhistorical moral laws, and outlaws who were mythic Robin Hood populist heroes resisting a corrupt industrialism and progressive government. As Richard Slotkin convincingly demonstrates in *Gunfighter Nation*, the evolution of the "Cult of the Outlaw" western, a convention that *The Outlaw Josey Wales* deliberately extends, originated within a matrix of political and cultural events between wars in Korea and Vietnam and the exceeding of legal boundaries by the national chief executive. The Eastwood film comes three years after Watergate and the military "defeat" or absence of outright victory in Vietnam. In the film, an increasing arc of authority is claimed by the gunfighting hero, a chief executive in his own right, who makes treaties and goes to war against governments.

The film concludes with a wounded but in-control Wales riding away from Santa Rio. Carter had attempted a populist conclusion, uplifting the petit-blancs of Santa Rio into a new Athens, by having their deceit sufficient to foil the Pinkerton detectives, anathema figures to the historical Jesse James. But Eastwood makes the finale of his project the facing down of the white brothers, wrongly turned against each other in their first terrorist holy war by the baleful influence of a strong state. Thus, Eastwood must make a semiotic confluence with the powerful John Wayne symbolism that he had repudiated during the 1960s and early 1970s.

The obvious possibility that ends the film is that Josey Wales rides back to the Crooked River Ranch for a life of domesticity (the conclusion of Carter's Christian civilizationist narrative). Eastwood himself, when queried, suggested that he implied return. But the concluding shot of Josey Wales riding off is fully ambiguous, and, as he had said to Lone Watie before the beginning of the epic gun battle against the Jayhawkers, he might possibly return to the ranch in a year or two. Like Wayne's Ethan Edwards of *The Searchers*, who, having overcome the absolute genocidal imperative (even whites "contaminated" by Natives must be destroyed) in favor of the more liberal Jeffersonian bias (allowing for Native cohabitation as a subordinate), Wales heads off into the distance. Counter to Carter's novel, Eastwood misleads his audience at the conclusion of *The Outlaw Josey Wales*. The film implies that its hero will hang up his guns and become once again a productive father and rancher, a reasonable broker with the Natives. But the finale instead shows him alone, like *The Searchers* Ethan Edwards, unbeholden even to domesticity, able to resume the capacity for lethal action, the violent hero in the space of precondition, at the outset of another North American colonial encounter. Paraphrasing Aristotle's ideas of the formation of human society, seventeenth-century English philosopher Francis Bacon forecast this powerful twentieth-century western metonymy well before the advent of the cinema: "Whosoever is delighted in solitude, is either a wild beast or a god."[29]

CHAPTER FIVE

"Their Slaves, If Any They Have, Are Hereby Declared Free Men"
Ride with the Devil and the Contraband as Decorative Adjunct

> It will be difficult to compete with an Eldridge Cleaver or even a Charles Reich for reader attention....
> But one should not postpone more direct political action, while awaiting the gradual change in public opinion to be effected through education and information. Business must learn the lesson ... that political power is necessary; that such power must be assiduously cultivated; and that when it is necessary, it must be used aggressively and with determination.
> —Louis F. Powell, "Powell Manifesto" (1971)

> *Holt* — Why General, I am for the Constitution as it is, and the Union as it ware!
> *Lane* — Have you got any slaves?
> *Holt* — Yes, several at Kansas City.
> ...
> *Lane* — But suppose we restore the Union without Slavery, and cannot do it otherwise, what then, Holt?
> *Holt* — Wall, I'm for the Confederacy then. If that wins I knows I'll get my niggers sure.
> —"The War in Kansas and Missouri," *New York Times*, Sept. 4, 1863

Alexander H. Stephens, vice president of the Confederate States of America, famously proclaimed in his "Cornerstone Speech" that the "immediate cause of the late rupture and present revolution" was "our peculiar institution of African slavery" and "the proper status of the negro."[1] The "cornerstone" of the Confederacy, Stephens averred, rested "upon the great truth that the negro is not equal to the white man." But Stephens's foundation was never completely set. Free Blacks and the enslaved living on the war's frontlines grasped their leverage immediately. New Orleans freedmen, calling themselves "Native Guards," attempted to enter secessionist ranks in 1861 "to advance nearer to equality with the whites." During the Battle of Bull Run, Virginia native John Parker, attached as a laborer in Richmond, manned an artillery battery. Attempting to live long enough to free his family, Parker told a reporter from Reading, Pennsylvania, "We wish to our hearts that the Yankees would whip, and we would have run over to their side but our officers would have shot us."[2] The prevailing view against arming Blacks in the South was the view set out by Stephens. Confederate General Howell Cobb resisted his secretary of war on the question of enlisting enslaved Blacks, admitting, "If slaves make good soldiers, our whole theory of slavery is wrong."[3] In the war's final months, men like Stephens and Cobb saw their theory overturned, the cornerstone dislodged. The Confederate Congress passed an act to enlist "able-bodied Negro men" to "perform military service."[4] Probably no Black regiments of the enslaved ever took the field for the Confederacy, but Frederick Douglass feared that they had.[5]

Nonetheless, there are a handful of records, historical and fantastic, that depict militant Black support of the regime of chattel slavery and the Confederate States of America.[6] Among these are photographs and memoirs produced at the apotheosis of the Lost Cause era and official records from the conflict. In a photograph of a 1906 reunion of men who rode alongside William Clarke Quantrill in Missouri and Kansas during the Civil War, an African American man stands at the end of the third row on the right side of the photograph. The man was John Noland, and he worked as a scout for Quantrill.[7] Immediately prior to the guerillas' August 1863 raid on Lawrence, Kansas, a Black scout belonging to Quantrill's cavalry rode into Lawrence and reported back to his fellow Confederates.[8] Other Black men are known to have been connected to the band.

During the Baxter Springs Massacre in Kansas in October 1863, Rube, a "yellow negro," working as a Union army teamster found himself pressed into guerilla service. In the immediate aftermath of the battle, the guerillas prepared him for execution, until it was learned that Rube had secretly informed, harbored, and then helped escape from Kansas City Captain Todd of Quantrill's marauders. The mercy he found was tantamount to reenslavement. "After Captain Todd had related to us these facts [Rube's acts of fealty], none of the boys desired to harm Rube and we took him on South with us."[9] In March of 1864, the Eleventh Missouri Cavalry conducted engagements against bushwhackers who had fled ten miles south of Missouri into Izard County, Arkansas, and killed a "negro desperado," a man named Wildwood Jack.[10] Black martial figures who were effective at killing white soldiers, and particularly Black men capable of skillfully operating on either side of lethal partisan divides, remain troubling to incorporate in culture machines of teleological narrative myth.

Quantrill's Raiders Reunion, 1906. B. James George Sr. Photograph Collection (P0010). 000435. State Historical Society of Missouri, Photograph Collection.

Film director D. W. Griffith encountered this dilemma as a prime challenge, choosing the appropriate site for Black fidelity and valor. On the one hand, he needed to vilify the Blacks he created to symbolize the maneuvering between the two worlds of civilization and barbarism: the wanton, lascivious (and putatively self-generated) mulattoes. But by the dawn of the cinematic age, the Lost Cause writers and filmmakers were disconcerted by the tradition represented by John Noland or William Mack Lee (Robert E. Lee's Black attendant) or Silas Chandler, another noted armed Black Confederate. The violence those men were capable of might too easily be associated with the heavyweight boxer Jack Johnson, the gargantuan Black screen star of the 1900s. The most vivid display of martial Black loyalty in *The Birth of a Nation*, the film that anchors cinematic renditions of the cavalry rescuing besieged homesteaders, would fall to the Lost Cause icon Mammy, a white woman in blackface, who fearlessly uses brawn to defend Southern whites against Union troops.

Griffith's Black Union soldiers, mainly played by whites in blackface, represented savages and cowards. This tradition of male portraiture emphasizing fecklessness, indolence, and ineptitude remains even seventy years later, in neoliberal standards like *Glory* (1989, dir. Edward Zwick). Even as a method to emphasize contrast in the development of its Black protagonists, the film overdwells on ignorant marauders and witless brats among the ranks of loyal, self-sacrificial Black men. In the same film, we see the white commander, Colonel Robert Gould Shaw (Matthew Broderick), in the role of white savior, occluding the Black soldiers, including those played by established stars Denzel Washington and Morgan Freeman.

The middle era of westerns, with civil rights actors and racial uplift activities of the NAACP, would only occasionally represent enslaved Africans docilely accepting their fate. Woody Strode evoked the representational difficulty of these issues, the irrevocable presence of possibly loyal, possibly subversive Blacks alongside the threat of savage rebellion, most famously with his portrait as the titular Sergeant Rutledge in John Ford's 1960 film, a character-type he reprised for television audiences on *Rawhide* (the western series that featured a young Clint Eastwood) in January of 1961.[11] Strode's ultrapatriotic, utterly loyal-to-his-comrades fighter, articulated a middle distance in prestige genre films between servants like Ernest Whitman's Pinkie in *Jesse James* (1939) or Everett Brown as Big Sam in *Gone with the Wind* (1939) and the more emphatic heroic conventions performed two generations later by Sidney Poitier as Buck in *Buck and the Preacher* (1972) or Jim Brown as Lyedecker in *100 Rifles* (1969). Arguably, the palpable unrest of Black Americans in the wake of 125 rebellions[12] following the assassination of Martin Luther King Jr. accounted for some of the reluctance toward robust treatments of racial encounters and reflections on enslavement. Yet, as we have seen, Eastwood demonstrated awareness of the issue in the split-second, contained encounter with Black troops in *The Outlaw Josey Wales* and the unmentionable fact of race that yet explains the portrait of Morgan Freeman's Ned in *Unforgiven*, the Black character within the orbit of racial tropes including hypersexuality, general dishonor, and gratuitous suffering. But it took forty years after *Sergeant Rutledge* before a major studio film attempted to capture the central dilemma of slavery, the Civil War, and the West.

Taiwanese American director Ang Lee directed and cowrote, with James

Schamus, *Ride with the Devil* (1999), adapted from Daniel Woodrell's novel *Woe to Live On* (1987), radically encountering the crisis of enslaved Black gunfighters in the West brokering physical freedom.[13] Even more remarkable than a redeployment of the civil rights era concerns of *Sergeant Rutledge*, Lee's film was, in effect, a remake of Eastwood's *Outlaw Josey Wales* with the photographed black soldiers in the middle of the frame.

Lee inserted the dynamic between enslaved and free, absent from *The Outlaw Josey Wales*, while reviving the classic racial liberal ethics of the 1950s. The turn to race within the context of a film about Confederate guerillas makes sense considering the reordering of the terms of national political life embodied by the presidency of Bill Clinton (1992–2000), a former governor of Arkansas and the first Democratic Party president elected to two-terms since Franklin Roosevelt. Clinton, defended by the novelist Toni Morrison during the investigation leading to his impeachment as "our first black President" and "Blacker than any actual black person who could ever be elected in our children's lifetime,"[14] suavely implemented a new convergence hatched by the Democratic Leadership Council, which he had chaired. Distinction between Republican and Democrat, the American Right and Left bipartisan political polarity, became increasingly indiscernible. The "neoliberal" dismantling of the New Deal and Great Society social welfare programs, financial market and government deregulation, enhanced criminal penalties for the poor, and the willingness to apply lethal technologies in overseas conflicts accelerated from the helm of a putative ally of the worker.[15] Clinton represented "a new and significant political conjuncture between private capital and party politics on the left," a fascinating coordination between populist feeling and corporate privatization.[16]

Nonetheless, the new model of conciliation opened the door for heightened revanchism. In the most contested American election since 1876, the Supreme Court overruled the extended vote count in the state of Florida, thus enabling the victory of George Bush, the first president seated since Benjamin Harrison who did not win the American majority vote (followed by Donald Trump in 2016).

The Bush administration implemented a massive reorientation and recategorization of rights and values and deployment of power. Following the widely and repeatedly televised terrorist acts on September 11, 2001, distinctive elements of the national culture pivoted toward pre-Watergate American attitudes about empire and a global military footprint. Among the more startling signs was military planners' decision to revive the Vietnam era counterinsurgency "Phoenix Program."[17] That program had reputedly been responsible for the deaths of more than twenty thousand Vietnamese secretly accused of National Liberation Front sympathies.[18] In spite of the specter of the military program having been little more than a mandate for the assassination of civilian dissenters to American foreign policy aims, twenty-first-century American legislators and government officials returned to the controversial program after the passage of the USA Patriot Act [Uniting and Strengthening America by Providing Appropriate Tools to Intercept and Obstruct Terrorism]. The legislation formally rescinded the prohibitions against domestic surveillance practices conducted by the CIA and the military, bans that had been imposed after the sensational Church Commission hearings of 1975.[19] The Patriot Act, a "most sweeping expansion of government surveillance authorities," accessed the technology of the digital information age to revive a Cold War–era agenda of coercive state acts that had included targeted assassination.[20]

Ride with the Devil both incorporates and anticipates the worlds of these concerns. The circulating iconography of global Blackness had shifted from Eastwood's era, with ever sharper distinctions circulating between Blacks in positions of wealth and power and precarity: the merchandising phenomenon connected to Michael Jackson, the "King of Pop"; the Los Angeles riots following the exoneration of policemen for the videotaped beating of motorist Rodney King in 1992; and the recognition of Michael Jordan as an icon for athletic excellence and as a commercial sports-apparel engine, as much as circulated representations of Clarence Thomas on the Supreme Court and Condoleezza Rice as national security adviser.

Lee's western is confined to the Civil War era, 1861–65, and he concludes his film with a powerful territorial symbolism for liberty by way of westward travel. While functioning within the same orbit of violence as *The Outlaw Josey Wales*, the film features key moments of deadly conflict between Confederate guerillas, unarmed civilians, and Union soldiers. The film is a diptych, and in its first half, it appears to celebrate and sympathize with the two scions of slaveholding families, Jack Bull Chiles (Skeet Ulrich) and George Clyde (Simon Baker). Their chivalry and dash are emphasized by their dress and their amorous affairs. The deaths of these principals constitutes the film's surface liberal agenda: the two slaveholding characters appear punished for ancestral misdeeds, and their own fathers have already paid with their lives for their "sin" of keeping others in bondage. The main implicit ethical principle of the film thus parallels the ideological work of *The Birth of a Nation*, which, by superimposing the child-savage dichotomy onto its Black representations, sought not simply to justify slavery and postbellum reenslavement but to venerate the contemporaneous establishment of racial apartheid in the 1910s. By requiring all of the plantation patriarchs in Lee's film to have been killed for the crime of slavery, the film, like *The Outlaw Josey Wales*, is consistent with Louis Powell's determined suturing of corporate mercantilist triumph and white privilege in the *Bakke* decision, which I read as an extension of Powell's 1971 procorporate "Manifesto." While the Ronald Reagan era is commonly regarded (along with Margaret Thatcher's United Kingdom) as the moment of delivery of neoliberal economic policy and sharply more punitive racial regulation, the domestic transformation reached its peak under President Clinton.[21] By then, Powell's argument—that the injury of "reverse racism" actually existed because of remediation efforts toward the descendants of the enslaved—had become implicit. New stereotypes of dysfunction in need of state regulation (like "super predator" and "crack baby") appeared, unleashing the vertically arrayed forces of historical inequity that would impact the distribution of resources into the future.[22]

Lee's film reproduces a full complement of the myths of American social and racial class relations that were being reordered in the 1990s. At the film's foundation, he emphasizes the manner in which recent immigrants and enslaved Blacks prop up the aristocratic regime symbolized by Chiles and Clyde. The bubbling mass below is arrayed between struggling white freeholders, forced out from rich riverside land by slaveholders, jobbers, and "Pukes," the illegitimates, the last of the frontier's whites, whose labor is already outmoded by machine-age agricultural technology. These white men in the guerilla camps who might have aspired to slaveholding and could only have reached that plateau through intermediate careers as overseers, are portrayed by actors James Caviezel as "Black John" and Jonathan Rhys Meyers as Pitt Mackeson.

The character "Black John" is the direct historical analogue to "Bloody" Bill Anderson, who in the pre-*Roots* era of *The Outlaw Josey Wales* could briefly appear onscreen without fully stigmatizing the project as a white supremacy polemic. But even American audiences would need to be shielded from a historical actor like Bloody Bill Anderson twenty years later and the rise of academic discourses in fields like African American Studies.[23] In any event, these characters are presented onscreen as intense psychopaths—skilled fighters and courageous—but unredeemable men.

Remarkably enough, though, the bounds of good taste created by discourses of racial liberalism have an impact here. Meyers's characterization of the deranged murderer Mackeson, an analogue to the historical figure Archie Clement, the most notorious guerilla murderer in the conflict in Missouri, seems to draw inspiration from the Scorpio character played by Andrew Robinson in the Eastwood *Dirty Harry* film of 1971. Lee will handle the audience's expectations with a reversal that characterizes modernism; neither of the murderous characters will use the word *nigger* or be seen onscreen committing race war murders. Only three characters use the word *nigger* onscreen—the main character, Jake "Dutchy" Roedel (Tobey Maguire), George Clyde, and Cave Wyatt (Jonathan Brandis)—the three bushwhackers most sentimentally inclined to treat the film's Black character fairly.

Lee drew from the popular biography of William Quantrill *The Devil Knows How to Ride*, by Edward Leslie, from which the film also derived its title. But Lee was specifically invested in pursuing the dilemma that Eastwood had already invested himself in: enabling strong white empathetic connection with not merely the Confederate States of America but a more obvious totem of white militant terrorism and analogue to the "Viet Cong" National Liberation Front. For Lee, a Taiwanese immigrant whose films include several westerns and display an abiding interest in observations of white American life, the Civil War was emphatically an epic tragedy because of its fratricidal dimension, not on account of its abolitionist result. The result of the Civil War, naturalizing citizenship by way of the Fourteenth Amendment for people born in the United States, is the definitive act creating the terms for modern ethnic American life.

The erasure in favor of the Civil War as a misguided fratricidal contest taking the lives of approximately 750,000 human beings is not a controversial position and is precisely the same point of departure for the iconic Hollywood director Steven Spielberg in *Lincoln* (2012) as it was for Griffith. But Lee's outsider status as an immigrant director, his edginess and radical daring, is not so much in his capacity to recognize or infuse Black people into the western, as it is to recuperate the Missouri guerillas, the Civil War's most violent actors, and by extension the founding myths of the Ku Klux Klan and white terrorist organizations, the exact network of concern for *The Birth of a Nation*. If Eastwood's *Outlaw* had absorbed the moral dilemma of enslavement by incorporating and sealing off Black portraits, Ang Lee returned to the most obvious topic of racial liberalism and would disavow the idea of evil.

Lee's production designer Mark Friedberg claimed on seeing the film that he could finally sympathetically ally himself with the South on account of the expertly drawn historical detail.[24] Similar to Eastwood's lauded verisimilitude in *The Outlaw Josey Wales*, which improved the realism of costume, scenery, and speech, Lee's film sharply elevates the pretension for historical accuracy in measures like dialogue, set design, onscreen violence, Missouri landscape, and costume. But these measures are always fully politically ideological. American historical cinematic epics are premised on a fallacy: the peopling of an uninhabited North American continent by European immigrants. In other words, American films that are obsessed with history typically reject the objective of historical accuracy, negating especially Native genocide and African enslavement. In the words of Susannah Radstone, echoing Fredric Jameson, the film "substitutes the pleasures of nostalgia memory for historical consciousness."[25]

The capacity for historical accuracy in scenery and production to enable access to liberal empathy exposes a site of slippage peculiar to invocations of racial liberal tolerance. Ancestor film *The Birth of a Nation* formidably grounds itself in the era's best historical sources, like Woodrow Wilson's 1902 *A History of the American People*. The fifth volume of the series opened with a catalog of Radical Republican and Black-led government abuse that caused the "veritable overthrow of the Civilization of the South."[26] Griffith, whose work was designed to show the vigilante method of overcoming the Black-led Reconstruction, nonetheless opened the second half of his film with a caveat: "This is an historical presentation of the Civil War and Reconstruction Period, and is not meant to reflect on any race or people of today."[27]

Operating in the less-contentious environment of the 1930s, when racism had been successfully codified for more than a generation, *Gone with the Wind* could devote itself to a fully sympathetic South and fully benign, in fact, benevolent slavery, sharecropping peonage, and convict-lease labor. Southerners made heroic by a reconfiguration out west included the multiple cinematic productions of Owen Wister's *The Virginian*, starring Gary Cooper in 1929 and Joel McCrea in 1946. John Wayne's Ethan Edwards of *The Searchers* (1956) would announce boldly, "I figure a man's only good for one oath at a time. I took mine to the Confederate States of America." While perhaps the most deliberate and formidable recuperation of the Southern combatant following *The Birth of a Nation* is Eastwood's Josey Wales, it is difficult to ignore the strong theme of divisional reconciliation in western films, Griffith's ambition.

Ride with the Devil is understood as well beyond the aims of a reconciliation of North and South that sacrifices Black people to do so. Because it does

Tobey Maguire approaches a group of uncredited actors in *Ride with the Devil*, dir. Ang Lee (Universal, 1999).

indeed feature a Black lead actor, like *Glory*, the film is thought opposed to the myth of benevolent slavery and the sentimental portrayal of the Southern soldier. While the credits run, we watch the film's protagonist, Jake Roedel, ride a horse through the grassland of Lafayette County, Missouri, on his way to a farm near Lexington for a wedding. Roedel dismounts, greets armed guards, and walks swiftly past tables laden with chicken, sliced ham, potatoes, and cakes. At this banquet he greets by name a Black man in dress coat, golden vest, and white gloves, while several Black women in aprons and Black children in leather shoes smile and greet him. It is during this brief second or two of film time when the credit line of the African American actor Jeffrey Wright appears. Lee presents his viewer with twelve African Americans working as servants during the wedding of Asa Chiles's daughter. All these people, who we understand are enslaved, are extremely well dressed. In fact, the four grown serving men are uniformed: black dress suits, golden vests, starched white shirts, and white gloves.

The Chileses have a two-story brick colonial home, which seems about twenty-five feet deep and forty feet wide, eight rooms around a central hallway and stairs. The identically dressed, white-gloved Black serving men, and their children shod in ankle length leather shoes (definitely not brogans), suggest not merely the upper-class status of the slave-owning Chiles family but the genuine wealth of the small-plantation class and the attendant artisan manufactures of a nearby town. If Chiles has eight or nine healthy adults working inside, or even as trained mechanics, he might be presumed to have ten or twenty times that number in the field, making him one of the wealthiest slaveholders in all Missouri. While this scene is one of peaceful contentment for the viewer, emphasizing the genteel, polite side of slavery, with its competent white-gloved smiling servants tending the ample wedding feast of well-dressed, portly families, it also recognizes that the luxury rests on bondage. Unlike parts of Missouri where slavery was an incidental fact of life, Lafayette County, on the southern side of the Missouri River and one county away from the Kansas border, enslaved exactly one-third of its population in 1860.[28]

During the feast that follows the wedding ceremony, Horton, the neighbor who has provided the armed guard, precipitates an argument with a German family, the Bowdens, by saying, "There are Union men among us. Schmidt and his cohorts have a militia at Independence. And his Lawrence cohorts have eyes and ears amongst us, even here." This scene, leading to a verbal altercation that reveals the tension between pro-Union slaveholding or anti-abolitionist Missourians and secessionist Missourians, is cinematically ironic. Throughout the shots of Horton's worried apprehension, in the misty background of the scene, Lee shows the disloyal "eyes and ears" of enslaved Blacks, the most reliable sources of information for Union soldiers once the Missouri conflict came fully under way, and who appear in the shot as mainly torsos and gloved hands. The exclusive optic of the camera reduces the enslaved workforce at the Chiles farm to white gloves, a reduction to corporality but successfully dissected and accumulated into parts, but at the same

Unknown actress (left foreground), Skeet Ulrich, Tobey Maguire, and Kathleen Warfel in *Ride with the Devil*, dir. Ang Lee (Universal, 1999).

time suggesting a synecdoche capable of taking the information and supplying it to the attackers who will return that evening. At first, the film narrative resists the implication of this contradiction about the sources of multiple "eyes and ears" that detract from Southern unity. The conflict can only initially be understood between white men and on white men's terms.

Missouri's Southern sympathizers held a convention for secession in June 1861, though Lee's film seems to take as its start the year before. The film's protagonist, Jake Roedel, is born in what he calls "Germany," and his father Otto is shown as a millworker who prefers sharpening cutlery to attending the Chiles gala wedding. Teenage Roedel is not overbound by tradition or submissive to his father but rather speaks up and proclaims his new American identity. Thrifty, self-improving Jake studies and writes avidly, has affluence enough for spare candles to read by at night, and has a young swift horse at his disposal. In these significant ways, Jake, the son of a skilled mechanic, adapts new knowledges and represents the striving "middle class," categorically quite different from his wealthy slaveholding friend Jack Bull Chiles, who is cared for by the servants. More salient, Roedel is not even remotely connected to the "Pukes" of the bottom of the Missouri social order, the drunken "poor southern white trash" and "dirt-wallowing, elemental brutes, suspended in a comatose state between bouts of primitive violence," the model Missourian Mark Twain used for Huckleberry Finn's father, Pap.[29]

No opinionated antislavery crusader, the elder Roedel wishes to send his son to St. Louis with relatives to sit out the imminent hostilities coming to their county. At this stage, Lee introduces a few more elements of social class magic that seem strongly in keeping with the ideological arc of the film. Jake's father makes no principled resistance to what the wealthy Chiles family represents, the oligarchy of Southern slaveholders. Otto Roedel (John Judd) tells his son that ethnicity is a permanent barrier to successful assimilation; Jake will "always be a Deutschman, a German to them, no matter with who you are friends." Similar to a 1950s vital centrist liberal, the immigrant father resists the extremes of both abolition and the expansion of enslavement into new territories. He emphasizes that "for us," the mechanic and the immigrant, "this is no war." Impartial to the hostilities, he hopes to send his son to St. Louis, where the federal government holds power. Indeed, this is precisely the film's conclusion, that Jake Roedel, a modular figure for enlightenment-based reason and human-rights liberalism, had no position in the fight.

Seemingly on the same night as the wedding, Jake rides off after hearing the hoofbeats of riders and deducing that the Kansas "Red Legs" are striking in the county, apparently at the home of the most prosperous slaveholder, Asa Chiles. When Jake arrives at the Chiles home, the viewer sees an outbuilding beside the two-story brick house in flames and hears shouts of "Where is he?" and the sound of breaking glass. Duplicating the conflagration that begins *The Outlaw Josey Wales*, Lee shows Red Legs brigands firing the house and dragging the gentle patriarch Asa Chiles out front and mercilessly shooting him down.

The villains, Jake is told by Jack Bull, who conceals himself with Roedel's help, are "Jayhawkers, Jake, Lawrence men." The execution of the elder Chiles is juxtaposed with a shot of three Black adults and six Black children. They appear to be an African American family of nine, all attired in night shirts, the females not in kerchiefs but in bonnets with pleated ruffled brims, looking on at the carnage and conflagration. Since we never observe the backstory of the principal Black character, Daniel Holt (Jeffrey Wright), the audience conflates these images of contented work and Victorian nightdress as the backstory for Black enslavement. Obviously, Lee has fundamentally encountered Eastwood's mythmaking but with what is actually only a mild difference in presence. The Jayhawkers are crucifying male slaveholders while the enslaved look on in silent witness. The viewer is asked to weigh the crime of stolen labor and heritable bondage and to consider whether it rises to the cost of punishment by death.

Lee inserts Blacks in precisely the place that Eastwood and Asa Carter were at pains to erase and contain them, and he eliminates the rape-vengeance complex from the film. Rather than kidnapping and rape-vengeance, the film operates on an Abrahamic imperative of observing the father's law. What is necessarily submerged, however, is the primal American "sin"—not the enslavement of African Americans but *partus sequitur ventrem* (the offspring follows the belly), the legal principle by which all children of enslaved mothers are considered born into slavery to ensure slave increase.[30] The adoption of *partus sequitur ventrem* is a violation of patriarchal law, an abrogation of genealogy and declension, the central code of English property rights.

Lee's portrait of the Chileses destruction corresponds to the representation of the conflict in Caleb Bingham's *Field Order No. 11* (see chap. 4). Lee seems here to be closer to a reenactment of the painting, with Red Legs soldiers shown pillaging and presiding over the bodies of Missouri's slaveholding but perhaps loyal men and women, while enslaved Blacks react with horror. In Lee's swift shooting, it is unclear whether the assortment of Black

Uncredited actors in *Ride with the Devil*, dir. Ang Lee (Universal, 1999).

people are as terrified as their owners or if they see the event as providing a chance for liberty.

The matched bitterness of the conflict is evident in a subsequent scene at Hugh's trading post on the Missouri River. Jake Roedel and Jack Bull Chiles, who the audience believes are the film's principal heroes, are shown as young soldiers of asymmetrical war as it is now known, and we don't recognize Chiles at first because of his shoulder-length hair, mustache and stubble, and blue uniform. The two men are dressed in the clothes of men they have murdered, and they masquerade to lull the federal soldiers, who outnumber them, into a false sense of security. The encounter is with five Union teamsters who are apparently distant from their larger body of troops. But though there would be a difference between teamsters and front-line troops, especially cavalry, Lee exploits this scene as an opportunity for a pointedly violent gun battle, where a quick draw and unerring precision are the assertive marks of the bushwhackers' masculinity and technological competency.

For the sequences of violent pistol action, Lee especially works through "Black John" and Pitt Mackeson. While the frightening battle is inaugurated by Roedel himself—"So you were in on Lafayette?" he shouts to one of the men, announcing his own deadly violence as an act of retribution in reprisal to the hanging of four bushwhackers—after the soldiers have all been shot dead, the store owner, a balding, clean-shaven middle-aged man, is shot in the back, while begging for his life. The man who shoots him, Pitt, seems the youngest of the bunch and a guerilla fighter who has been turned into a sociopathic killer from the trauma of the war. He is inured to violence, unable to experience an identification with his victims, and he finds pleasure and satisfaction in impulsive cruelty. Pitt sets the store on fire over a protesting Roedel, who attempts and fails to restore an ethical framework to their deadly crusade. Lee, who does not provide any Union soldiers in the film with important speaking roles, sets up the central conflict between righteous vengeance and homicidal mania, a conflict not merely between white men who are in deep conflict over slavery but one that occurs between white men on the same side of the battle line.

With this unstable ethical balance, Lee introduces the real hero of the film in the next scene, Daniel Holt, though Lee renders this principal, at first, without speech. Jeffrey Wright has to perfect the talents of a mime in the first half of the film, until he can break through at the halfway point. It would be worthwhile to say that the editing of his performance and the relative screen time he receives in comparison with Maguire and Skeet Ulrich are excellent examples of historic racial bias in American film—were the other cinematic choices available to him not so pathetic. It would also be like saying that a film director and film studio could envision serious historical drama for a Black American audience.[31]

At the fourteenth minute, we have a shot of Roedel, Jack Bull, and their knowledgeable older friend Cave Wyatt, a historical figure who rode with the notorious Bill Anderson in Missouri.

> ROEDEL. Whose guns are those?
> CAVE. You mean Holt over there. You'll get used to him. That's Holt. That's George Clyde's pet nigger. Don't call him that in front of George though; George don't like that.
> ROEDEL. He carries those?
> CAVE. He's a damn fine scout. A good Yankee killer too. You know him and Clyde growed up together. When Jim Lane's boys come for Clyde, Holt sent three of them to heaven. So he rides with us now. 'Cause them Yankees wanna kill him real bad.
> ROEDEL. Yeah, well, a nigger with guns is still a nervous thing to me.

During this discussion the camera goes three times over to George Clyde and Holt, whom Woodrell's novel identifies as "the oddest comrade thinkable,"[32] quickly and efficiently cleaning and reassembling a shotgun and several 1860 Colt pistols (notoriously gummed by black powder after a single firing and prone to rust) and apparently also casting lead balls. The men squat beside

Jeffrey Wright (left) and Simon Baker in *Ride with the Devil*, dir. Ang Lee (Universal, 1999).

their equipment and a small fire with a blanket rigged between the trees. The idea that Holt, a "nigger with guns," might, in a sense, enjoy killing white men on account of the injustice of his own enslavement is an outlying fact, diluted by his rapid and efficient movements in the sequence, which seem to connect him with the other serving Blacks we have glimpsed in the camp earlier.

Watson and the Shark

Holt is obviously an expert with firearms and munitions manufacture, but he is ineligible as a carrier of these killing tools on his person before the fight begins because, as Roedel has asserted for himself and the others, "a nigger with guns is still a nervous thing to me." But Lee seems to have conquered Eastwood's dilemma: the Black man—but not woman—exists in the theater of operations. Instead of fundamentally disallowing Black images with the post–Cold War containment logic of "Hold it. Real still," Lee crops, shades, blurs, and partitions his Black subjects, evoking tactics in keeping with the color-blind logic familiar to neoliberalism.

Roedel is reluctant to rely on armed Blacks, not for the reason articulated by Southern gentry, that they would not or could not fight, but rather as a young person who knows the reflections of immigrants and Northern sympathizers, that Blacks with guns are liable to free themselves and seek out their own self-interests. The discussion also reveals the public discourse of Black inferiority—"That's George Clyde's pet nigger. Don't call him that in front of George though"—that is overturned by the bushwhackers' odd war without allegiances. It also reflects the onus and imperative for the fight, to defeat abolitionism, another set of moral obligations that can't be stated.

The marauding band dines at a rough Southern homestead, a two-story house reproduced by the production company approximating the farm of Zerelda James and Reuben Samuel, the home of brothers Frank and Jesse James, who joined the Missouri bushwhackers in 1863–64. In an important moment, Roedel's allegiance to the Confederacy as a German is challenged, as his father had earlier predicted. The camera frames the sociopath Pitt Mackeson to emphasize the peril that his hero may face when his identity is scrutinized. "Jake may have been born a Dutchman," his planter friend Jack Bull Chiles reminds the crowd, attempting to secure Jake to an impeccable proslavery ideology via his own rich-man's genealogy, "but my Ma and Pa practically raised him. He's as Southern as they come."

While the camera focuses on the escalating menace awaiting the film's protagonist, in the back left corner of the frame is Holt, a framing that recalls John Singleton Copley's 1778 painting *Watson and the Shark*. An undoubtedly abolitionist painting, it features an African male figure at the apex of the compositional triangle, men in a lifeboat appearing to lend a lifeline to a youth under attack by a shark. But the image, thinks scholar Albert Boime, is less weighty than that; the Black male figure is neutralized, fully contained: "It is understandable that in Copley's painting the black man—despite his prominent position—remains an invisible man whose capacity to act in the real world is blocked. In the end he functions as a decorative adjunct to the composition, as empty of potential action as the rhetorical shallowness of the colonists and the inflated bombast of their Tory critics."[33] Holt's portrait is connected to this problem of the Black image in American painting and iconography. Lee struggles with the same "decorative adjunct" condition, of meaningless yet prominent representation. But the instability of Blackness in the composition defies an exclusively "decorative adjunct" reading.

What Boime's reading obscures from *Watson and the Shark* is the possibility that the angelic-seeming Black seaman may have an interest in having the victim die or suffer a grievous wound. The shark pools in the Atlantic were artificially sustained and enhanced on account of Africans thrown overboard from slave ships, many still living. Any nexus connecting an African man, a white sailor or scion of shipping fortunes in grave jeopardy, and a destructive natural force like a wild animal must take this into account. Black indifference, contempt, and derision for Western projects is a register that becomes particularly available in the ambiguity-laden visual field. Lee's film brings in

John Singleton Copley, *Watson and the Shark*, 1778, oil on canvas, Ferdinand Lammot Belin Fund, 1963.6.1. Courtesy National Gallery of Art, Washington, DC.

the veil of self-interest at the conclusion, fostering a rereading of the essential scenes of the film, but it is also possible to begin the film from this standpoint of Black subjective (or sovereign) self-interest.

Lee's film also actively wants to evade such a reading of autonomy for its Black central character. Holt is cast as a strong humanistic force that directly balances his humanism with malevolence. He mediates the peril for the misguided, naive, and reckless white boy, Jake Roedel, who figuratively swims with the sharks of white supremacy. Without the balancing force of Black service, the American striver lacks safeguards from the social order excess, the overavenging figure, in the form of Mackeson, the sign of distorted, ugly, unreasonable violence.

Holt's difference from the other men and his capacity as the moral center of the film is slowly drawn out as the gun battle breaks out in the farmhouse. With all of the bushwhackers crouching in the difficult-to-defend wooden

Jeffrey Wright and Jonathan Rhys Meyers (foreground) in *Ride with the Devil*, dir. Ang Lee (Universal, 1999).

house, Holt prepares alone for battle after being thrown his weapons by George Clyde, humming what seems a snatch of a slave song, a spiritual, to himself. Soon the situation will be announced as totally desperate, and in a breakout move, Holt will be assigned the crucial position of leading a daring escape, literally knocking down the farmhouse walls, running through federal fire and gaining the horses in a nearby glen. The operation requires bravery and raw strength, and Lee seems to draw from a wealth of historical myths of Black fighting men—from Bunker Hill's sharpshooter Peter Salem and William Henry Lee, who rode alongside George Washington, to York, who performed unusual feats of physical prowess with Lewis and Clark, to the Civil War heroes.

Roedel attempts to redeem his ethical point of view by going to lengths to spare the life of a captured neighbor fighting for the Union and throw legitimacy behind his own odd-seeming anti-Union and anti–civilized warfare behavior. "We're only asking to be treated like the soldiers we are," he mouths to the bruised Alf Bowden, who stares at him with what we later learn is contempt and simmering rage that his German-born neighbor has joined the marauders. At this crucial moment, when Roedel's youthful idealism reaches its second test, Lee gives us Holt, for a split second, in the center of the frame, a place that he won't occupy again until the climax of the film. Again, Wright is left with a mime's role; he has no dramatic lines. He is again in *Watson and the Shark*, a centrifugal point to which Jake angrily asks, "What are you looking at?" The camera then turns to Wright, who looks briefly in

Jeffrey Wright in *Ride with the Devil*, dir. Ang Lee (Universal, 1999).

the direction of the eyes of Roedel, and then looks away in self-absorbed contemplation, while picking his teeth. There is a marvelous economy of movement and gesture in the brief glimpse. This depiction evokes Leone's framing of Blondie during the gun battle finale and Eastwood's Wales glancing grimace of distrust at Fletcher when he is requested to disarm.

The sequence of shots, concluding with Wright in the center frame for the first time, seems a non sequitur, until eight minutes later when the audience learns that the man that Roedel freed has returned to their hometown, Lexington, and murdered Roedel's Union-loyal father. Holt's silent judgment, it seems, had been a moment of foreseeing the likely doom of Jake's naive act. Holt's Black perception is connected to his inhabitation of what Fred Moten calls "the cut," "the ongoing improvisation of a kind of lyricism of the surplus—invagination, rupture, collision, augmentation."[34] It is this rhapsody of the Black gaze in "the cut" that Jake misinterprets and that Holt's successful performance of life in bondage enables him to proffer. Woodrell had used this language to define Holt's precarity: "As with most niggers his life was puppeted by slender threads of tolerance at all times."[35] But the onscreen performance redeems another dimension of subjective assertion, a cut.

Lee drives home the increasing alienation of Roedel as a character who is neither comfortably a "Puke," a homesteading farmer, nor a slaveholder. As one of the few literate bushwhackers, he is asked to read captured letters from Unionists, and initially he refuses to violate the sanctity of these intimate, private communications. But when he does so, after some threats from the murderous Mackeson and with the general agreement from the rest of the men, we learn of the cultural and educational indigence of these illiterate warriors and the imaginative world that is opened up to them as the prose is read aloud. Lee frames Holt during the narration of Northern farm life in a shadowed moment of isolation, braced against a stone fireplace, all that is left of a pillaged, ruined house. Holt seems to need something to protect his back as he casts his eyes to the firelight to grasp the story. While he is entertained and entranced by the reading, his thoughts about the ruined home and desecrated hearth differ from those of the rest of the guerillas.

The shift of the film from incorporating the German immigrant into the slaveholding South, distinct from its sociopathic dimensions, and into a sphere encountering the problem of the fullest dimensions of American freedom in its encounter with the western film begins definitively at the forty-second minute, when the young bushwhackers are preparing winter camp. Here Lee gives a complete frame to Holt; his body occupies two-thirds of the frame, the area from his chin to the top of his hat is the bottom to top of the screen; the audience is required to recognize his fullness and his pensiveness regarding his new allegiances and quarters. This is a fully redemptive gesture, in terms of shot selection reproducing Black people in Southern territorial spaces, the Civil War itself, and western cinema. It also connects to Sergio Leone's similar top-to-bottom full-frame closeup of Woody Strode in *Once upon a Time in the West*. The question returns to *Watson and the Shark* and its creator, Copley, as abolitionist and inventor of tokenism. In the same situation, does Wright's Black man serve as a seminal figure in the triadic relation or, as Boime has argued, "despite his prominent position—[he] remains an invisible man whose capacity to act in the real world is blocked," a figure who "functions as a decorative adjunct to the composition," "empty of political action"?[36]

In fact, Ang Lee aggressively pursues the question of the value of Holt as a majestic but powerless figure in the winter camp scene by beginning a series of upendings that will reach a powerful early climax. The three white bushwhackers—Roedel, Jack Bull Chiles, and George Clyde—are seen at work shoveling out a hillside cave, while Holt keeps guard on an embankment above. He spits inelegantly, leaving saliva on his face, recalling Eastwood's Josey Wales. In one view, this makes sense: he is considered the hands-down best scout and gunfighter among the men, though in the course of the film we never see him shooting a weapon and then having the camera show us a federal soldier collapse (again, a convention that also swings backward to consider Holt as unwilling to cause the death of Union soldiers). But, by the racial logic of slavery, the heavy labor should be his, and it is strange to see white men shoveling while a Black man watches, the reversal of the audience's expectation. Also, we soon find the aristocratic men resenting or sloughing off the indelicacy of heavy labor. While Roedel admits there is "something soothing" to their digging, George Clyde soon stops shoveling and pontificates about easier, more sensual ways to spend the time. The rough domestic scene concludes with Holt conducting labor from above, this time using a rope to hoist a heavy log into position as a sill, seemingly with little aid.

The dugout home of the four bushwhackers serves as the set for the first sharpening of the drama of racial position, social class, and the western. The young widow Sue Lee Shelley (Jewel) visits the men, bringing supplies. All are taken with her beauty and voluptuousness, but the young aristocrats Clyde and Chiles, sons of slaveholders, forthrightly assert their proprietary right to begin courtship. They introduce only each other and consider only the two of them appropriate rivals for the young woman. Holt, who has shown himself through his valiant mime abilities on earlier occasions to have a powerful sense of *sentir c'est apercevoir*, speaks his first lines of the film to Roedel, who has stood awkwardly aside after George Clyde has handed him the dinner basket, treating him like a servant.

Lee shoots the scenario with Holt standing above the dugout, slightly off to the side, again evoking the Copley portrait and a series of triangulations in the frame. Holt slyly smiles to himself, but, again, and this is Wright's gift and determination to use craft to overcome some of the more obnoxious limitations of Black portraiture in cinema, his Holt understates the dramatic affect. But the gesture is noticed by Roedel, who is always vacillating between being the inquisitive, rational ethicist raised as an outsider to traditional Southern society and the cold-blooded killer who upholds the racial order. He repeats the line that he used in his earlier discussion with Holt:

ROEDEL. What are you smiling at?
HOLT. I see to that mule.
ROEDEL. Wait a second. What did you say?
HOLT. I say I look to him. You better go on in there. Let that woman see your face.

The courtship advice is clearly privileged intimate terrain, and Holt, now an avuncular figure, is asserting himself over Roedel. Roedel blusters in response, "Damnation Holt," and rebuffs the Black man for interfering in his personal life. Then he observes the directions, restating them in the language of a social superior. "Now you see to the lady's mule while I check on what she brung to eat." Lee reminds us of the place of power in this discourse by giving the final shot in the exchange to Holt, who is well-satisfied with the young boy's obedience. Roedel is the only member of the four-man band unable to grow facial hair. The audience also has to consider the fact that we have definite evidence of Holt having managed a bout of sexual desire for Sue Lee (*mule*, of course, bringing into the conversation "mulatto" and interracial sex), which dramatically complicates his final observation of Sue Lee in the film.

Inside the dugout, the men are following courtship rituals completely at odds with their guerilla war under the rules of the black flag, a war of pillage, murder, summary execution, and rape. As the men enact a performance of genteel manners, doffing their hats and exchanging grandiloquent pleasantries with Sue Lee, she tells them, "My, aren't you bushwhackers the gentlemen." As she leaves, she remarks about her deceased spouse, a man from a family similar to the Chileses but who served in the regular army according to the regulations of civilized combat: "We all suffer, but he suffers no more. He was a good husband to me. For three weeks he was a good husband, but he didn't last." As she conducts the discussion, she stands in the simple backwoods doorframe of the dugout, addressing the Southern aristocrats who will be ruined if the war is lost and the slaves are freed (or their accumulated capital is lost). Beside her stands the immigrant from Germany, who has already mastered advanced technological skills but who has to adopt the mien of servant for social acceptance among the Pukes, farmers, enslaved, and gentry.

Holt carries firewood into the dugout at the precise moment that Sue Lee reveals that her husband "didn't last." Wright's gravitas takes the sequence of sharp symbols beyond the antebellum joke of "a nigger in a woodpile." The racist proverb that indicates Black theft conceals another meaning: Blacks have accumulated the woodpile. Fundamental to Holt's character (and Wright's performance) is the unacknowledged act of provisioning the white men and the woman in the hut, his well-done job. The visualization of the accumulation made possible by slavery alongside the articulation of white male slaveholding impotence begins a series of sharp triangulations of the three positions of slaveholder, slave, and middle-class striver. There is also a subtle suggestion in the situation of a mutual desire by Sue Lee and Holt for one another, for whiteness and blackness each desiring its opposite.

Holt marches directly into the dugout with the wood, brushing Sue Lee, who is shocked to find herself sharing a Southern interior domestic space of any kind with a Black male. She responds with affront and near-fright:

SUE LEE. What's he doing here, inside?

CLYDE. Ma'am this nigger's with me. His name is Holt.

SUE LEE. Well, wouldn't he be more useful off in a field plowing?

CLYDE. Oh no, I reckon not. No ma'am, that's one nigger I wouldn't try to hitch behind a plow. I wouldn't try that.

SUE LEE. Well now.

Lee leaves implicit Sue Lee's objection to an armed Holt inhabiting the domestic interior of the South. The scale of the violation and the loss represented by shared domestic space is summarized in Woodrell's novel with the line, "It looks like we're going to win the fight and lose the war."[37] But Lee's film centers on George Clyde's response, the young patriarch's mounting anger and irritation. He smiles superficially, but his pleasure with the young woman is now curiously gone, perhaps inexplicably so. He seems perturbed to have his masculinity and social class authority challenged in spite of having asserted "this nigger's with me." But the discussion and his response also reveals the unstable social class values of the bushwhacker camp anyway, where presumably the best rider and most accurate shot have the roles of leadership. Quantrill always maintained that the South, if it had adapted his strategy of unkind, murderous war, could have easily defeated the North. But Sue Lee's remark that in the pursuit of liberation from the "Yankee invader" they are overturning the conventions that structured the meaning of their

Jeffrey Wright and Jewel in *Ride with the Devil*, dir. Ang Lee (Universal, 1999).

lives (a point in the film that will be made shortly by her father-in-law), pertains also to the literal fight. As a skilled gunman, Holt might "save the South" if he were granted more responsibility, a gesture toward the larger problem of Black enlistment in the Confederate army. Clyde's answer also has an undercurrent of Holt's imminent revolt; he wouldn't try to hitch Holt behind a plow because Holt has more useful martial work to do, but he also might not allow himself to be hitched.

A moment later, the gaffe is extended and made more serious, requiring complete exculpation. Sue Lee extends a courteous invitation to the band for a meal at the home of her former father-in-law. She glances in Holt's direction and confesses:

> SUE LEE. Umm, I'm not sure about him. Mr. Evans...
> CLYDE. You ain't got nothing to worry about on that score. You needn't worry about Holt. I'll be taking Holt with me to the Willards tomorrow. We won't be coming to your dinner.
> SUE LEE. Mr. Clyde, honestly, I didn't mean to speak ill of your nigger.
> CLYDE. He's not my nigger. He's just a nigger who I trust with my life every day and night, that's all.
> SUE LEE. That's very high praise.
> CLYDE. Yes Ma'am, it is.

The defense of the man introduced to the audience as "George Clyde's pet nigger" (we find out a few minutes later that Holt, who now takes over the film, is free) is spirited and completely within the bounds of slave/master paternalism. If there is any truth at all to Southern apologists' observations of amicable relations between enslaved and master written before 1865, the reports hang on this peg, that the endowment granted the enslaved brought pleasure and esteem to the master. But the powerful words, "He's not my nigger," have been spoken, even if in the next breath, Clyde has to push Holt back, away from the comforts of paternalism and into the broad category of enslaved nonwhite.

Jack Bull Chiles makes a deliberate attempt to restore the conventions of chattel slavery and the paternal authority of masters when he chastises Holt for failing to touch his cap along with the others when Sue Lee says upon leaving, "Good night, all." In this dramatic moment, Clyde is prepared to fight a white man: "He don't need no telling, Chiles!" But Holt defuses the situation. "It's all right, George. Night, Missy," he responds and to which Sue Lee surprisingly replies by completely recognizing him as a named individual: "Good night, Holt." To his friend he proclaims, "Wan't nary a hardship, George." The determination to contain the pressure of the exchange and diffuse the tension is a fascinating glimpse into the strong human center of the character.

Lee reminds us of the purpose of this by doubling the scene for us, as the film now pivots directly to the immigrant and the Black American as the heroic centers of consciousness. After seeing Sue Lee to her horse and establishing exclusive place of prominence in the courtship ritual, Jack Bull returns to the dugout, where dinner has been equitably divided. He offers Holt his main protein, his bacon, as olive branch, and Holt accepts the lagniappe easily, replying, "I could eat more." George Clyde mocks the scene by also offering Roedel his bacon, collapsing the social status of the young German immigrant to that of the enslaved African, while turning the scene comic. When Roedel humbly requests the meat, Clyde ridicules him. "Well, I'll just shit it out by the oak tree in the morning and you can just go and help yourself." This play tenders a crucial distinction between the two slaveholders, Chiles and Clyde, one of whom clings tenaciously to the convention of genteel racism and the other, who associates the bourbon chivalry with excrement.

Race and Literacy

Chiles's arrogant tenaciousness to Southern aristocratic conventions becomes more pronounced in an ideological conversation that occurs between him and Evans, the owner of the farm. Roedel listens as his friend explains the enduring vengeance against Kansas and defends, without recourse to religion, the agrarian Southern seigneurial system over the nineteenth-century ideological innovation, the schoolhouse:

EVANS. You ever been to Lawrence, Kansas, young man?

CHILES. No, I reckon not Mr. Evans. I don't believe I'd be too welcome in Lawrence.

EVANS. I didn't think so. Before this war began my business took me there quite often. As I watched those Northerners build that town I witnessed the seeds of our destruction being sown.

CHILES. The founding of that town was truly the beginning of the Yankee invasion.

EVANS. I'm not speaking of numbers nor even abolitionist trouble making. It was that schoolhouse. Before they built their church even, they built that schoolhouse and they lettered every tailor's son and every farmer's daughter in their country.

CHILES. Spelling won't help you hold a plow any firmer. Or a gun either.

EVANS. ... No it won't Mr. Chiles, but my point merely is that they rounded every pup up into that school house because they fancied that everyone should think or talk the same free-thinking way that they do. No regard to station, custom, propriety, and that is why they will win because they think that everyone should think like them, and we shall lose because we don't care one way or another how they live. We just worry about ourselves.

When Mr. Evans says, "they lettered every tailor's son and every farmer's daughter in their country," the camera swings to Jake Roedel, the machinist's son born in Germany, who reads and writes better than anyone in his company of Missourians We are reminded that much of Roedel's value as a member of the guerilla unit is from his cultivated intelligence as much as his capacity for violence. (The film does point out, however, that everything he does as a guerilla fighter only backfires to destroy him.)

The question of white working-class and immigrant access to literacy is immediately paired with Black access to the same technology. It turns out that Holt harbors a silent desire to become literate, though he begins the journey asking to be read to and marveling in the power of the disembodied narratives. In their dugout, Jake is reading a dense book with a two-word title of roughly eighteen letters. Both men are in the hidden space of the dugout, absent the upper-class sons of slaveholders, who are courting the local belles, angling to reproduce their broken class. At this time, Holt reveals that he has been clandestinely keeping a packet of letters. In 1847, Missouri passed a dramatic law outlawing literacy not by condition but by race: "No person shall keep or teach any school for the instruction of negroes or mulattoes, in reading or writing, in this State."[38]

HOLT. Roedel, nobody never learned me letters. When you was reading the mails out loud it was something the likes of which I'd never heard. Got me thinking you might sometime try it again.

ROEDEL. So you packed those and been keeping 'em all this whole time? Might not be too amusing. Might be the boring words of one stranger to another.

HOLT. No, the one you read from the mother was fine. You recall it? She say things I enjoy to hear.

ROEDEL. All right. Here it goes. [Reads letter of man joining federal army] . . .

HOLT. It could come to where maybe you could like that man.

ROEDEL. Yeah. In other times it would not be so bad.

HOLT. I think though I like the one from the Mama the best.

ROEDEL. Holt, where's your mother?

HOLT. Kansas or the kingdom. I don't know. I know she's sold into Texas. I reckon she in Texas.

ROEDEL. How was that? Was that George that sold her?

HOLT. Naw, sir. George and me growed up neighbors. It was George what bought me out when Massa Henry passed. He ain't have no means for my Mama or my sister.

ROEDEL. So Clyde owns you?

HOLT. No sir, not in greenbacks and coppers no how. No, he don't own me that way. No. He made it out a gift.

During the reading of the letter, prior to Jake's first personal inquiry into Holt's past, an inquiry that begs the question of social death and the Black subject, the camera captures the two young men. Jake is lodged in the foreground reading, Holt beside him in the shot but blurry and a foot or two behind him. But something startling becomes apparent. At that moment, it becomes clear that the men are the same color epidermally; the ideal of morphology as a signal mark of absolute difference has been dissolved. Holt's response to the letter of his enemy, "It could come to where maybe you could like that man," indicates the power of knowledge to shape choice in perception, affiliation, and belonging, as well as the depth of his alienation as a subject whom the law withholds from the episteme.

In the men's subsequent, even deeper, conversation and reckoning with the full meaning of slavery and its shaping of the American identity, they

Jeffrey Wright, with Tobey Maguire, in *Ride with the Devil*, dir. Ang Lee (Universal, 1999).

begin to face squarely the real crisis of slavery and what the Civil War's consequences would be, an issue that Missourians encountered directly within the earliest months of the conflict. On August 30, 1861, Union general Charles Frémont issued a blanket emancipation in Missouri, the first in the United States: "Real and personal property of those who shall take up arms against the United States, or who shall be directly proven to have taken an active part with enemies in the field, is declared confiscated to public use, and their slaves, if any they have, are hereby declared free men."[39] The revolution in wartime Missouri had not been rebellion and dissolved union but emancipation.

The full meaning of Fremont's order powerfully disturbed Abraham Lincoln. The American president responded quickly to the proclamation, fearing its repercussions all along the border but especially in Kentucky: "I believe there is a great danger at the closing paragraph, in relation to the confiscation of property and the liberating of slaves of traitorous owners, will alarm our Southern Union friends and turn them against us."[40]

Frémont and Lincoln's conflict—which Lincoln ultimately ended by removing Frémont from Missouri after Frémont insisted that Lincoln himself rescind the order, which led further to his loss of command in another theater of the war—emphasizes the pragmatic conflict in the area of politics, and the area of military affairs in the field, that was sometimes echoed as a division within the Republican Party among the radicals and the moderates. But these divisions never quite reflected the position of the liberals, whose best symbol by the 1860s was Frederick Douglass. Douglass believed in the full capacity of Blacks as citizens, but the overwhelming majority of American whites—North and South, Democrat and Republican, Abolitionist and Copperhead, Radicals (who wished to see Southerners punished for their rebellion) and Republican conservatives (who attempted to restore union and end war as speedily as possible)—cared little about Black freedom or Black rights and hoped not to have to deal overmuch with Black people.

In the Missouri of Roedel and Holt, an enslaved man named Dred Scott had initiated a ten-year-long legal battle to gain his freedom, beginning in 1846 amid much of the drama playing out in St. Louis. In 1857 the Roger B. Taney–led US Supreme Court decided that Scott, and anyone else of African descent, was ineligible for citizenship. Roedel the scholar has to come to terms with these precedents, as he increasingly takes the law into his own hands to defend slavery and the South, while he begins to realize the ever larger problem of injustice. He reads to Holt from a letter written by a Unionist who lives in St. Louis:

ROEDEL. "They [secessionists captured in Gratiot prison] are traitors, but also human. If you looked in on them, you would not believe that they were, for they so resemble scarecrows now. Father believes the war will go on and on but is ever more committed to the struggle. He manages to send ever greater numbers of slaves up north to freedom and away from the grasping hands of their masters, who even in the midst of all attempt to lay claim to them. The Confederates claim that we strike at their liberty and rights, but what kind of liberty is it that takes away the liberty of others? The war will end . . ." Has it been an hour yet?

HOLT. No. Ain't an hour passed yet. Roedel, you know my name?

ROEDEL. It's Holt.

HOLT. No, my whole name. My whole name is Daniel Holt. Daniel. Like that lion den man. You know his story?

ROEDEL. Of course I do.

HOLT. They throwed Daniel to the lions, but he weren't never ate. Daniel. That's what my momma named me.

During this summative moment, Lee uses three different shots: a tight close-up of Roedel, with Holt blurred and in the foreground left quarter of the screen; a tight close-up on Holt, with Roedel blurred and in the right upper fifth of the screen; and a wide shot of both men filling the right half of the screen, the left half taking in the winter pasture and wooded hillsides. Holt and Roedel are presented at odds and not mutually understanding one another, and the balance they finally achieve exists in nature, but one in which they still tilt to a side.

During the drama of tilted unification, Roedel reads a letter to Holt from a Union man in St. Louis, someone who would have views very much like his own deceased father. He is reading for Holt's pleasure and as a diversion while his comrade Jack Bull makes love to Sue Lee. But the contents of the letter increasingly reverberate with the most fundamental crisis in their lives, slavery, and then the context, his reading the letter to a formerly enslaved man, becomes a moment of embarrassing and unforeseen radicalism. In fact, Roedel seems to abridge the letter itself, which seems to end, "Someday this war will end . . . slavery." All Roedel can bring himself to say is that "Someday this war will end," followed by an abrupt cessation of speech and a puckered face staring at the page in something like disbelief. To put into words the emancipation is obviously too destabilizing, too potentially an act of authorizing Holt's liberty. But it is also a warning to the audience that the liberalism of the agents of enlightened reason can always silence itself, remove, censor, or contain language, and reshape the contours and message of freedom to suit their own needs.

But in the next sequence of the minidrama, we learn that Holt has an inner narrative, or metanarrative, a self-generated creation myth that does not rely on the law of white Western rationalism freeing him from bondage. Rather, his Black mother has powerfully and psychologically freed him as a precondition of existence, by giving him the name of "that lion den man" and transferring the meaning of the ancient myth to his own life. It is worth noting, too, that Holt's biblical metanarrative is a source of protection against the interpellative power of the law, which, relative to the *Dred Scott* decision, completely denies him citizenship.[41]

After the death of Jack Bull Chiles, Holt and Roedel return to the woods to fight the war in the spring and summer of 1863. The guerilla war has now become an openly terrorist conflict and a race war; Roedel's capacity to conduct youthful chivalry has utterly ended. (It is also at this moment that the historical record divulges one of the rarely recorded examples of a Black woman being gang-raped by guerillas.)[42] Riley Crawford, a character based on the historical youngest member of Quantrill's riders, welcomes the mixed pair back regaling the new savage war, "scalping every nigger we can find. Except, of course, our own." A glance from George Clyde elicits the bracketing from Crawford, the state of exception for Holt, the sense of his conditionally commuted death sentence.

And now the racial tensions that had been put to the side in 1861 and 1862 are brought to the fore. At camp, the men play cards and trade in scalps, evidence of savage war that is repulsive in principle to Jake, whose repugnance to the scalps of Blacks and Dutchmen like himself is observed as a sign of disloyalty. The blending of scalps of Germans and African Americans by the bushwhackers over cards at camp fully collapses the status of Roedel and Holt, a point made explicitly by Pitt, who chides Roedel threateningly: "You two sure got to be pals." Holt is also demoted since he no longer serves George Clyde exclusively. Now, with low-standing Roedel as his main white friend, he is required to serve in the camp kitchen alongside other Black men in aprons, who, like Leone and Eastwood's totems, only appear for a split second in the film.

Uncredited actor, Jeffrey Wright, and Tobey Maguire in *Ride with the Devil*, dir. Ang Lee (Universal, 1999).

The Lawrence Massacre and Black Erasure

The film's violent culmination occurs with the infamous August 1863 raid on Lawrence, Kansas, during which perhaps two hundred unarmed and defenseless men were slain, after most of them had been robbed and promised safety. Led by Quantrill, nearly three hundred armed bushwhackers rode more than fifty miles from Missouri into Kansas to sack Lawrence. The bushwhackers were believed to have been motivated by the deaths of several secessionist women in a weakly constructed Kansas City jail that had collapsed. The historical figure Bill Anderson lost one sister and had two others badly injured; in the film, "Black John" loses three sisters.[43] The Lawrence raid was purportedly engineered as a reprisal, and although Quantrill and the bushwhackers hoped to kill all the men, they were to take pains not to injure women and obey the codes of chivalric behavior that they hoped to show the federal soldiers had violated. The film goes to great lengths to propose the "valor" underlying the infamous act of mass murder. Black John shouts at a healthy but gray-haired Kansan in the street: "Old Man! Old Man! Where is your army? Who are we to fight?" He then spits on the man and throws him down but deigns his victim unfit for slaughter.

Neither Roedel nor Holt participates in the killings, as both are portrayed as reluctant members of the band in the ride west. Roedel realizes that the group of farmers and "puffs" cannot effectively combat trained federal cavalry, and Holt, who recognizes his and Roedel's soldierly difference from the majority of the riders, goes into the deeper ideological contradiction of their participation in the reprisal ride, a Dutchman and a formerly enslaved Black man: "No more fools than you and me, Roedel." Holt's consciousness of his own precarity and utter marginalization is one of a few cues Lee provides his audience to perceive the historic tragedy. The blend of realist filmmaking and myth departs radically from Woodrell's novel, which had notably striven for verisimilitude.

In the historic Lawrence massacre, the first victims were unarmed federal recruits on Massachusetts Street. There, two companies of soldiers, "one white, one colored," bore the brunt of the assault. The men set upon and summarily killed were enlisted in the Second Kansas United States Colored Troops and the Fourteenth Kansas, whose casualties were supposedly twenty-two men killed or wounded. Woodrell reproduces the scene from Roedel's perspective:

> I saw a whirl of men split off and ride into a camp of recruits near the center of town. They were yet in slumber inside their white tents, and we fired into their bedrolls and brought them crawling out. It was all niggers. Uniformed niggers raised extra frenzy with the boys, and the hectic potshotting and dodging went up a notch. I think two or three niggers made it to the brush bottoms of the river and escaped. I don't know. I thought they were an army, and I guess I got one.[44]

Lee decides, however, to fully isolate Holt in his narrative of exceptional Blackness by erasing the Second Kansas United States Colored Troop from his treatment. The book Lee relied on for historical accuracy, written to glorify Quantrill in the wake of the author's personal relationship with a contemporary mass murderer, concluded that "the unarmed blacks had been alerted by the gunfire and fled."[45] The popular writer Edward Leslie bases his view on an eyewitness report from Reverend Richard Cordley, who published an account thirty years later and noted that, oddly enough, the people explicitly marked for death—Jayhawkers, abolitionists, and able-bodied Black men— "fared the best":

> For this reason the men who were specially marked for slaughter fared the best, for they knew what to expect and took themselves out of the way. There was a large number of military men in town, but scarcely one of them was killed, except the unarmed recruits who were shot in their camp, almost in their beds, at first onset. Soldiers knew they could expect no quarter, and

so took care of themselves. The same was true of the colored people. They knew what kind of men slavery had made, and they ran to the brush at first alarm, and comparatively few of them were killed. But the raiders made no discrimination.[46]

Other reports were less confident than Cordley about the escape of the Black troops. Two newspaper accounts from August 1863 reported that "twenty-five negro recruits were shot dead,"[47] and "two small camps of recruits on Massachusetts street (one white, and the other colored) were surrounded, and the poor defenseless fellows, without a gun in camp, and begging most piteously for their lives, were pierced through and through with bullets, and all but four of the two unfilled companies left mangled corpses on the ground."[48] Deciding not to ennoble an atrocity, Lee finds common cause with what David Blight defined as the reconciliationist take on the Civil War: he simply eliminates the Black troops from the Lawrence massacre entirely.

While we see several white men executed, the Black Americans, mostly escapees from Missouri, are depicted as ready-made corpses. The camera pans Black cadavers being stacked like cordwood. It is through Holt's eyes that we briefly see the well-dressed, piled men. This adds to the image of their summary, perfunctory executions, but it also is in keeping with the long-standing convention of keeping Black action offscreen. Oddly, during the historic massacre itself, few young Black men were killed, as the film suggests. "The colored people were pursued with special malignity," eyewitness Cordley recalled. "Most who were killed were the old and decrepid [sic]."[49] In other words, the guerillas were known to have killed the elderly Black men. The film emphasizes the elderly spared.

Among the Kansas Black dead were ninety-year-old "Old Uncle Frank," lame by rheumatism; "Uncle Henry," burned alive in a building; and Benjamin Stonestreet, the Baptist preacher, shot in front of his daughter. Black babies and children were reported thrown into fires. At the Eldridge House the guerillas are reported to have been told Black children were in the fire and to have responded, "We will burn the G-d d—-d little brat up."[50]

But in the curious economy of the Hollywood feature film that purports to convey historic accuracy, gray-haired Black men, like Joel Chandler Harris's amanuensis Uncle Remus, are inappropriate fodder. Their deaths run counter to the stereotype of the plantation in and of itself as a salubrious haven for aged Black people, while being also cinematically awkward and not

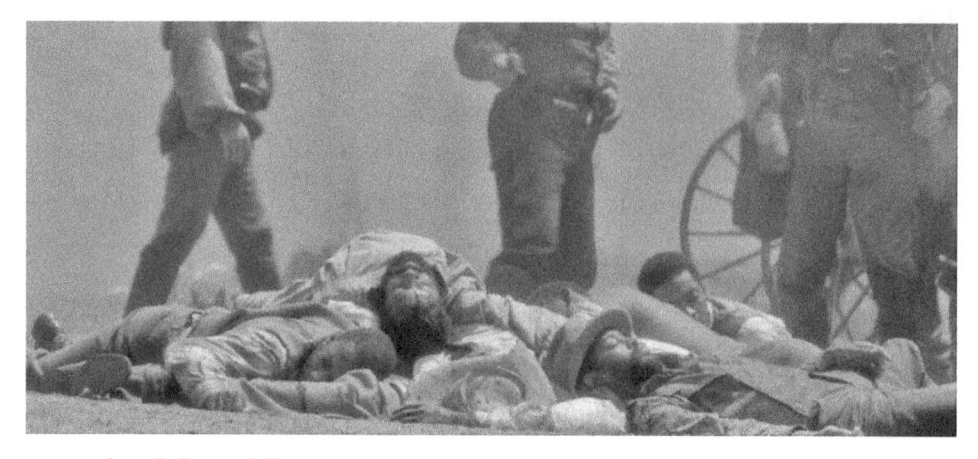

Ride with the Devil, dir. Ang Lee (Universal, 1999).

especially meaningful for white audiences to merit being filmed. Lee counters the Black erasure in the massacre with the image of five or six Black military-aged men who apparently will arouse the audience's empathy, the possibility of Black necropolitics vitiating the possibility of Black entertainment value. In the twenty-plus years since the film's release, the digital world has exploded with the circulation of "onscreen" Black male death, typically poor and nearly exclusively of youth.

Lee's removal of the executed Black elderly men also corresponds to the impossibility of violating one of the twin Black bulwarks of Lost Cause mythology: Uncle Remus, the sexless male companion figure to Mammy, created in the last quarter of the nineteenth century somewhere between the Daughters of the Confederacy, the magazine the *Confederate Veteran*, and Joel Chandler Harris's Brer Rabbit tales appearing in an Atlanta newspaper. The stereotype generated by Harris in the era of Southern redemption recast Stowe's Christian evangelist martyr Uncle Tom as a richer Indigenous Uncle Tom figure for the South, a lodestone of folklore who could take to the screen in *The Birth of a Nation* (safely as Mammy Jane's husband) and by the era of the talking film with Shirley Temple in the form of Bill "Bojangles" Robinson.

The elimination of the dead Black elderly men is also magnified by the fact that for Roedel and Holt the most significant conflict during the massacre occurs when Pitt Mackeson attempts to execute an older man and boy in a hotel where Roedel, Holt, and two Missouri farmers are eating, away from the fray. When Roedel objects to sending the Kansans outside with Pitt to their deaths, an objection seconded by Holt and the farmers, he is promised that retribution will follow, which it does. In other words, the plot shifts as Roedel and Holt save an old white man during the Lawrence massacre, an irony about the historical difficulty of Black men being saved and then subsequently being erased when the atrocity is recalled in a modern film.

There is also the difficulty of dramatic balance in sifting through American atrocities. Lee could have asked for nothing more wrenching and ethically fixing in the film than to have shown one of his principals murdering a disabled Black senior citizen. He is keenly motivated by whatever historical accounts he can find. He has his second-tier principals Pitt Mackeson, Turner Rawls, and Cave Wyatt all involved in famously recounted episodes of the massacre. He used versions of the death of Judge Louis Carpenter, who was killed while in the arms of his wife, and reproduced the action around the death of Edward P. Fitch, whose wife attempted to preserve his picture from their burning house.[51] In another homage to the record of verified events, Cave Wyatt goes into the home of Charles Reynolds and fails to recognize as male a Mr. Winchell, shaved and dressed in women's clothes and masquerading as an invalid.[52]

Lee's version of the Lawrence massacre is chiefly complicated for us by the addition of Holt's perspective. By focusing briefly on the deaths of young military-age Black men rather than relatively helpless older men and children, Lee effectively rescues the Lost Cause sensibility in the midst of calling some of the aims of the Confederacy into question. At one point a bushwhacker attempts to drag Holt out into the street and, the audience presumes, execute him like the other Blacks. Roedel fights the man off, shouting, "This man's with us, you fool! That's George Clyde's nigger, you fool!" The inadequacy of the reprieve is evident on many levels, because while it effectively chastises the drunken bushwhacker, it reinforces Holt's difference from the other men on the scale of being. Only the recourse to his existence outside of humanity, "George Clyde's nigger," seems capable of saving him from a violent death. Holt is not passive in the encounter. He does not merely seek to defend himself against the ruffian, but he also shows a violent passion against Roedel and his magic words of reprieve, "George Clyde's nigger."

In the immediate aftermath and flight from Lawrence, Lee invents a heroic epic battle between Union cavalry and the bushwhackers under Quantrill's leadership. Roedel is under accusation by Black John and by extension Pitt Mackeson for having "spared" the lives of the old Kansas hotelier and a young boy. In the exchanges in town, where Roedel uses elaborate codes of courtesy to address women, he distinguishes himself from the drunken rabble marauding through the town and engaging in war crimes. All of the sentimental relations between Roedel and Holt in Lawrence are Lee and co-writer Schamus's concoctions. Novelist Woodrell left Holt's role to a single line of unique Black solidarity: "I saw Holt at The Eldridge House, standing with Quantrill's nigger, an older man called Nolan."[53]

After the raiders are attacked by Union troops, Pitt Mackeson, the sociopath and a leading figure in the bushwhacker hierarchy, turns on Roedel and begins shooting. At this crucial moment, Roedel is partially rescued by Holt, the only man to witness the nefarious action and who begins to take action himself, sighting Pitt with his pistol, who disappears into the trees. Of course, Holt is an unreliable witness and savior, whose testimony can hardly counter the word of white Mackeson and whose actions, if gleaned by any of the others, will merit him the same unsavory death that has been accorded the victims of the Lawrence massacre and which Holt has actually faced. At this point, before the cascading effects of this realization settle, Holt is shot by the Union gunfire and is seriously wounded.

What follows is an extraordinary turn of events. First, George Clyde dismounts and rushes to tend to the fallen Black man, crying, "Holt, come on, I gotcha!" Clyde is immediately shot in the neck. Thus, Holt exposes himself to danger to save and redeem Roedel, and is shot, and then Clyde rushes to comfort and nurture Holt and is killed. The economy here favors masculine heroics over feminine nursing, which is punished by wounding or death. Lee also is invested in finishing off the gentry in the film. (Clyde's one act in the Lawrence massacre is to pitilessly execute a Polish man who has befriended

Simon Baker and Jeffrey Wright in *Ride with the Devil*, dir. Ang Lee (Universal, 1999).

"Their Slaves Are Hereby Declared Free Men" 167

him, out of naked self-interest to be sure, but an obvious construction of the exclusivity of concerns between the declining gentry at the end of the agricultural age and the ascending immigrant bourgeoisie and industrial class.)

Clyde's exaggerated gesture of sacrifice can be read as a reconciliation of civil rights in the western twentieth-century fantasies of fictive kinship between white and Black men, where white men take up their paternalist burdens. Lee, however, dilutes even that reformist move by depicting Holt moaning over the dying Clyde, thus imbricating Wright's portrait of Holt with Sidney Poitier's Noah from *The Defiant Ones*, an extraordinary and template-like depiction of a Black man in American letters, traceable to Twain's Huck and Jim and ultimately Stowe's Uncle Tom cradling little Eva. (Eastwood offers a cognate rendering in *Unforgiven*, where faithful Ned Logan stitches up William Munny.) It is valuable to be reminded of the precise contours of Uncle Tom's caretaking at the death of the child:

> The child suffered much from nervous restlessness, and it was a relief to her to be carried; and it was Tom's greatest delight to carry her little frail form in his arms, resting on a pillow, now up and down her room, now out into the verandah; and when the fresh sea-breezes blew from the lake,—and the child felt freshest in the morning,—he would sometimes walk under the orange-trees in the garden, or, sitting down in some of their old seats, sing to her their favorite old hymns.[54]

Although Holt seems doomed after his wounding, when Clyde has been shot, he experiences a lightning bolt of renewal, recovers from the misery of his

Jonathan Brandis, Jeffrey Wright, and Tobey Maguire in *Ride with the Devil*, dir. Ang Lee (Universal, 1999).

injury, reverses his position, and cries out to nurse his mortally wounded friend.

In Lee's understanding of American race relations, this maudlin heroic act must be matched and overcome by the remaining white men in the film in a kind of Johnsonian affirmative action Great Society gesture. It is not enough for Holt to wish to sacrifice himself again to save his white benefactor (the complex shading of Clyde as slave master, friend, and patron is carried through to the end); rather, his striving to do this must be surpassed by the general standards of homosocial love and friendship available among the Missouri guerillas, though, of course, with the exception of the alienated psychopath Pitt Mackeson. This is the strident color-blind neoliberal maneuver of the film. If or when Blacks show themselves to be loyal and self-sacrificing, then enfranchised, financially secure whites will join and, in fact, surpass their efforts. In the sequence of shots that show Holt kneeling over the rapidly expiring George Clyde, it is unclear why Cave Wyatt must have another man hold his horse and rush over to pull Holt away, a move that will be seconded and supported by Jake Roedel, who leaves the firing line and runs over to help Cave drag Holt away from the action. Holt has to be forcibly removed from the body of his slave master, a necrophilia added to the hyper-emotionalism and a suggestion of a Baraka-like critique being made of a Black attraction to a white erotic object ending in death.[55] But the conclusion is obvious. Holt's overemotional fixation in the dead object threatens his life, requiring white men to endanger themselves to rescue the ex-slave. Saving the savage from himself is, as Stuart Hall and Edward Said showed a generation ago, at the foundation of the orientalist philosophy undergirding Western imperialism.

The sentimentalized portrait of relations between white and Black men in the specter of danger was active and available to writers in the 1860s, though they tended to see them as comic. The eyewitness Cordley observed the Lawrence massacre, including this scene:

> The cashier of the Lawrence bank crawled under a sidewalk. Nearby was an old colored man who had sought the same refuge. Being a pious old man, he called mightily upon God to save him. His cries could be heard half a block away. The cashier suggested that "the Lord will hear him just as well if he did not pray quite so loud, and the raiders couldn't." He hushed for a minute, but soon began to "cry aloud" again. The cashier thought it prudent to find a quieter, if less pious hiding place.[56]

Clyde's death symbolizes the end of the antebellum era of the film; the slaveholding gentry is no more. Roedel and Holt's relationship as equals appears capable of unfolding on terms of mutuality. The film thus eliminates any vestige of slavery at this point, although the men are moving farther South to escape the Union army, in the direction of Arkansas and Oklahoma, areas controlled by or nearer to the armies of General Price, cavalry General Shelby, and Cherokee General Stand Watie. (This triumvirate of Confederate officers is nearly a Holy Trinity in the sacred origin mythologies of the western genre, from *The Virginian* onward, and is a reference point for the John Wayne character in *True Grit*, whose cat is named General Price.) Southern Missouri counties had fewer slaves because the soil was richest along the Missouri River, where large hemp farms were located. But the Deep South Brown Farm, refuge for Roedel, Holt, and Sue Lee Shelley, is a resplendent showpiece of agricultural abundance—a place of wonderful interiors, ample food, and fat cattle in the midst of war—a place from which even a covered wagon will become available for the trek west. It is completely clean of the taint of slavery.

As the two principals recuperate from their wounds, and as Roedel vies with Holt for top billing in the narrative by the introduction of the marriage plot, Holt finally establishes his central subjective distinction, apart from the legacy of enslavement and subordinate service to the rebellion. Cave Wyatt implores the men to join the Regular Army of Price after their wounds have healed, and Roedel and Holt exchange a guarded, confidential conversation about their allegiances:

ROEDEL. I'm going to kill Pitt Mackeson.

HOLT. You going to join up with them regulars?

ROEDEL. Fight for the cause. What about you?

HOLT. You really asking me? What cause you think I got, Roedel?

A chorus of violins begins to play, cueing strong viewer sympathy, and Roedel invokes the legacy of their fallen comrades. Holt replies:

HOLT. And they's both good and dead Roedel. Just as dead as they can be. Where's that leave you and me. Where's that leave me?

ROEDEL. Right here.

HOLT. Yeah I knowed we was right here. Ain't nowhere for me. Reckon I just don't understand it. That day George Clyde died. It changed me. I felt something I ain't never felt.

ROEDEL. You felt that loss, that hollow feeling.
HOLT. Naw. What I felt was. Free.
ROEDEL. I thought that's what Clyde give you.
HOLT. Now that wan't really his to give now was it? George Clyde. I believe I loved him. But being that man's friend wan't no different than being his nigger. And Roedel, I ain't never again going to be nobody's nigger.

Roedel's misinterpretation of Holt's feeling is the single strongest moment of the film, insisting that despite shared experience and social affinity, there are mountains of difference that defy understanding.

The misapprehension is consistent with the film's bending away from Woodrell's interpretation of Holt to Ang Lee's. In the novel *Woe to Live On*, Holt's gradual awareness is not of the friendship denied between himself and George Clyde but rather his kinship to the slain Black soldiers in Lawrence:

> I wondered if all the war I had slopped through had gone for naught, so I said to Holt, "Holt, was all that fighting for naught?"
>
> I lit a candle while I waited on his answer.
>
> "How would I know?" he said. The little flame flickered and did shadowy things on our faces. "What it is I do know is all them dead niggers in Lawrence. I can't toss them dead niggers out of my mind."
>
> "It was a lot of dead types in Lawrence," I said.
>
> "They didn't spare a single nigger."
>
> "They didn't *want* to spare anybody, Holt."
>
> "Jake, what I think of the boys is this: niggers and Dutchies is their special targets. Why was we with them?"[57]

While Lee shifts the portrait away from racial solidarity toward the trope of devoted Black fealty, he retains the key question of slavery and existence. In *Ride with the Devil*, Holt's possible feeling of freedom (not the attainment of the protection of the law for the exercise of rights on the body in space, but for the ontological capacity to engage the question of existence and existentiality outside of the white patriarchal logic of chattel slavery) is predicated on the death of the white gentry. It is also connected to the place where white ownership, power, friendship, and evaluation collapse.

Conclusion

Although *Ride with the Devil* seems to successfully show that the shared space of the western is available to Black and white protagonists, as it was in historical reality, the notion that mutual understanding is available is importantly withheld. This is the failed terrain of reconciliation that can't be bridged between Roedel and Holt in the camera's frame balanced by the landscape.

At the conclusion of the film a series of mythic schemes collide, and Lee returns to the problem of *Watson and the Shark*. For the first time, we find out unequivocally that Holt is both taller and broader-shouldered than the increasingly boyish and juvenile Roedel. In a shot emphasizing his longing, his isolation, and his sexual desire, Holt stares at sleeping Sue Lee and her infant in the wagon. The viewer recognizes that Holt has ushered Roedel, forced to hide while they make their way through Union lines in Kansas, into a future free of the war that had included the complexities of racial conflict on account of interracial allegiances in the West.

Roedel is on the brink of new opportunity. But Holt is headed south, to Texas, in an allusion to Forrest Carter's novel. This is a prescient comment on the mission on which he is engaged, as he travels to Texas to free his mother, in what seems to be the spring of 1864, with a full eighteen months or so of slavery yet to be endured by Africans there. Instead of riding west to freedom, Holt is riding south and into the nation's past, a place of mythic, ritualized, and barbaric African erasure, a series of imbricated procedures endemic to the genre of the western itself.

At this moment in the revisionist historical epic, the Black costar abandons the pragmatic realism of the collaborationist for the full-bore romanticism of the quixotic, the suicidal gunfighter's errand to rescue his mother and sister from enslavement. While the sentimental quest appeals to the unrequited justice for the other missing enslaved Africans in the film, it rudely inserts the counterlogic of *partus sequitur ventrem*, the antipodal legal designation of African American maternal lineage and descent to the western's logic of *partus sequitur ferramenta*, or descent linked to iron tools, or perhaps *partus sequitur telum*, descent through the weapon. This is the core of the debate of Black being and Black property in market-organized Western society, where the rational market in every instance must be undergirded by armed force.[58]

At this sweeping climax, Holt is denied the film's full endorsement. Lee always protects the screen and the viewer by keeping young Roedel in sight, who, in another kind of Copleyesque triangle, remains the camera's balanced center, its fulcrum, the plateau of its tripod. Finally, Holt is on horseback, and, after he spies Sue Lee and the child, he shares two frames with the teth-

Jeffrey Wright and Tobey Maguire in *Ride with the Devil*, dir. Ang Lee (Universal, 1999).

ered horses grazing; Roedel shares his frame with the saddle. As Holt spurs his horse on, the back of Roedel's head, like a gunsight, centers the image of the frame, before the film concludes with its final visible human image, Roedel, a head and shoulders, spanning from the top of the screen to the bottom, center shot. The final frame shows the galloping Holt, becoming smaller and smaller, eclipsed by the sublime majesty of the natural landscape. Without Roedel in the frame, the country itself, the natural environment, envelops and finally entombs its Black character. It is ultimately an effective containment of the problem of Griffith's intertitle of 1915, "The bringing of the African to America planted the first seed of disunion."

And it is precisely this point that the film has been working toward, a rupture and opening. The conversation occurs figuratively as Holt and Roedel protect the body of the white woman, the slaveholder who never relinquishes her patrimony and who was actually impregnated by Jack Bull Chiles, who is also enabled to stride forward posthumously into postbellum relations. Jack Bull Chiles's capacity to reproduce himself after death, and for the blood myth of the unreconstructed Southern paternalist to be conveyed down through his daughter, is evidence of the lingering and strong residue of enslavement and permanently antagonistic relations that haunt the film at its conclusion and constricts the attempt at a symbolic liberty in its closing frames.

This is the same residue that I am arguing ultimately eclipses the avowed liberal frame of the movie and, after a fashion, connects me to the Afro-pessimist who would preclude the possibility of Black subjectivity in any sort

Ride with the Devil, dir. Ang Lee (Universal 1999).

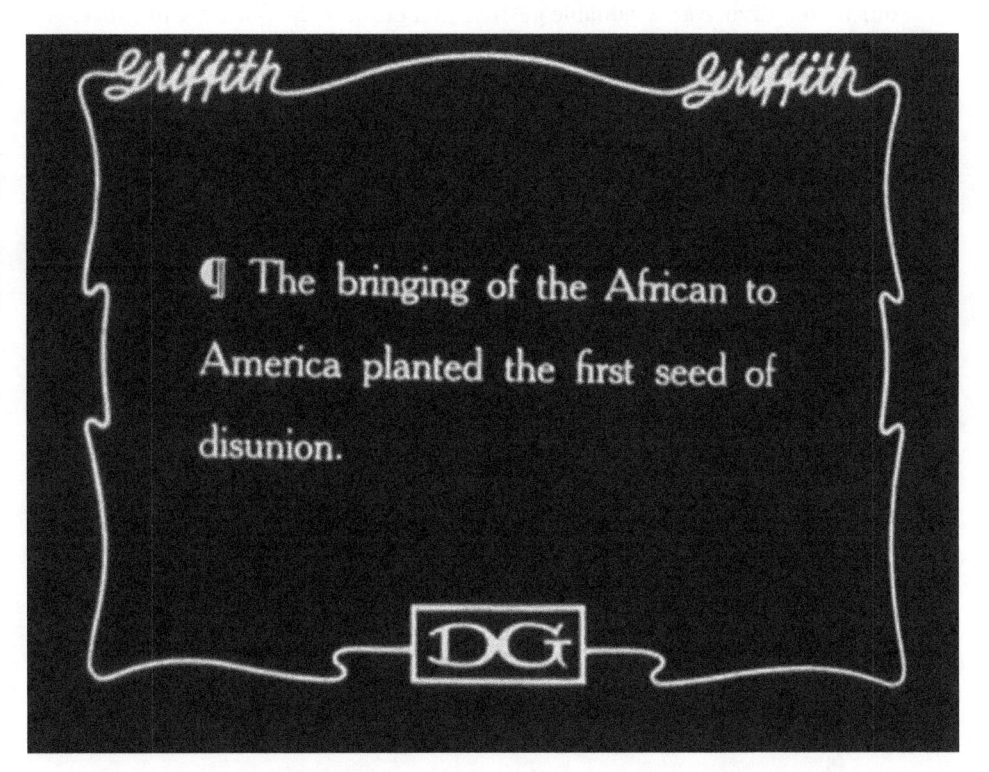

Intertitle from *The Birth of a Nation*, dir. D. W. Griffith (David W. Griffith Corporation, 1915).

of western narrative. Lee's immigrant modernism, his insistence on a western metanarrative of possible bonanzas if the Enlightenment vision can be rescued or remastered—and which operates with familiar synchrony to Sergeant Rutledge's strophic rejection of possibility: "I wasn't nothing worse than a swamp-running nigger"—is not fully disjoined from Holt's antistrophic decision that he is "never again going to be nobody's nigger." In both films the fearless veteran Black scout triumphs through his relation with the young white acolyte, who must struggle against the traditional rules of his military bureaucracy (bushwhackers and Union court-martial respectively). And in both films, the conclusion elaborately demands that any relation between the Black Native and the white male heir must be mediated by the body of a white territorial woman.

Lee's courageous film seeks a reinsertion of Black presence in America during the Civil War, a valuable gesture that ensures the film's significance. But Lee overvalues the transgressive capacity of Copley's inclusion of the Black sailor among dramatic principals. He embraces the flaw of the equivalence that aligns him with the John Ford of *Sergeant Rutledge* and the Clint Eastwood of *The Outlaw Josey Wales*. But finally the film is irrevocably marked by its uneasiness in being caught portraying onscreen the fullest evidence of a sentient Black subject.[59]

CHAPTER SIX

"I Am That One in Ten Thousand"

Django Unchained and the Black Exceptional State

... the American homeland is the planet.
—*9/11 Commission Report* (2004)

Certainly, with the demise and collapse of American imperialism in South-East Asia, you can see that almost inevitably U.S. imperialism wants to concentrate on the Indian Ocean and on Africa.
—Walter Rodney, *Walter Rodney Speaks* (1975)

President Cowboy

The disastrous box-office performance of Ang Lee's *Ride with the Devil* tempered the possibility of a strong revival of the western following the amazing success of the other 1990s films in its class, Eastwood's *Unforgiven* (1992) and Kevin Costner's *Dances with Wolves* (1990). Although audiences of the later 1990s showed no deep thirst for the western genre's strong drink of the frontier and the ethics of deadly force, the tropes of the cowboy continued to successfully resonate across American political life. American presidents have made ample use of the western genre to demonstrate purposefulness and ancient resolve in their communication with the public. The political allegories available from western films have obtained to both state actors and regular citizens during the unfolding of the new millennium's terms of American imperial expansion and practice, especially to political upstarts. More than even Ronald Reagan and Lyndon Johnson, in the vein of the buffalo hunter and Rough Rider Theodore Roosevelt, President George W. Bush styled himself as a Texas rancher, cattleman, and cowboy. Bush laboriously buttoned the legible tropes of the western genre to himself and his public performance of the presidency. Frequently wearing cowboy boots during his regular West Wing presidential duties, and attired in jeans, Stetson, and plaid shirt on his ranch in Texas, Bush presented himself as a homespun, pious, self-made, rugged, forthright, formidable individual. His cowboy self-presentation helped him to disavow the image of pampered, Ivy League, capricious, third-generation aristocrat, whose grandfather had been a bank director and senator, and whose own father had already served as president of the United States.

The facade of the forty-third presidency and its claims of virtuous leadership was, in some ways, congruent with the manner in which it was achieved. Bush owed victory, during the infamous "hanging chad" 2000 electoral recount in Florida, to "a few dozen Republicans," hired guns who had "swarmed outside" the Miami-Dade election office to disrupt officials, shouting, "Voter fraud!" and "The fix is in!" The insurgency presumably caused the election board in the county to end the hand recount of 10,600 ballots from "largely black-populated precincts" that "machines had been unable to read."[1] A prototypical American Enterprise Institute model and telling result of the Powell Manifesto of 1971, the protestors' ranks were filled with Republican congressional staffers. Their victory was not, to be sure, an organic counterpoint to the grassroots activism of the Left but, rather, a parachute brigade of drilled operatives deployed to strip the franchise away from Black citizens and remove them from the electoral process.[2]

The result of the election was immediate. Within months of taking office, the new president launched successive, indiscriminate military actions. This inauguration of a new era of American militarism relied on sweeping legislation like the 2001 congressional Authorization of the Use of Military Force, which secreted lethal military action into the hands of perhaps eighteen people, most of them the president's handpicked cabinet officers. But the racial optics of this regime were new and unabashedly "liberal," in terms of the representation of African Americans. The Bush White House included Black Americans Condoleezza Rice and Colin Powell as National Security Advisor and Secretary of State, respectively. Powell had previously served as National Security Advisor under Ronald Reagan, and Rice would serve in both positions in the Bush administration, the highest public posts held by Blacks before Barack Obama's election as president.

When in October of 2001 the Taliban-led Afghan government offered to turn over to a neutral country the individual named as the architect of the terrorist attacks in the United States in September 2001, the Bush White House refused, saying, "There's no negotiations."[3] The president, born in 1946, rationalized his stark "good-versus-evil" and "us-versus-them" approach to statecraft in interviews by using the rhetoric from the popular western television shows and films of his youth, images of Hollywood-derived masculinity he had assiduously cultivated as part of his political image. Certain journalists sneered at the correlation between the images of boot-wearing cowboy and the inheritor of successive generations of wealth. ABC News anchor Peter Jennings, on-air for many consecutive hours on September 11, 2001, repeatedly questioned Bush's absence from "command" in Washington and suggested that he "show up in a more vigorous way."[4] Jennings more than implied that rather than a fearless John Wayne, the American president was cowardly in the face of danger. Nonetheless, Bush had no qualms about emphasizing the pose of veteran cowboy pugilist once safety was assured. He chose the language of the heroic gunfighter and lawman over evidence to attest his determination to eradicate belligerents he called "evildoers." Instead of diplomacy and "negotiations," he would use military force against the enemy and "smoke 'em out" of mountainous redoubts that had earlier foiled the Soviet military. Expressing his ethical sensibility through the medium of televised reproductions of the postbellum West, Bush proclaimed that he wanted his adversaries, "Dead or Alive," an obvious indication of his preference for deadly force.[5]

The entry of the ominous "Dead or Alive" language of the mythical West into the often analytical and precise lexicon of international diplomacy exhumed other related edicts, such as "Indian country," an unambiguous metaphor for perilous enemy territory appropriately encountered with unsparing force. The military's declarations about Natives that went on to operate powerfully in the public imaginary is infamously captured by General Philip Sheridan's purported statement, "The only good Indian is a dead Indian," as the US Army began more methodical territorial occupation of the West after the Civil War.[6] The genocidal practices of warfare, massacre, and removal to reservations were central techniques of internal territorial consolidation. In the western theater the logic of massacre crossed racial and ethnic boundaries, occurring even in the first quarter of the twentieth century against Black Americans—East St. Louis, Missouri, in 1917; Elaine, Arkansas, in 1919; and Tulsa, Oklahoma, in 1921—and the latter two mass killings involved US troops. The preeminence of the Hollywood western of the 1950s would seem primarily responsible for the emergence of the term "Indian country" or "Injun country" during the Vietnam War by military personnel. Used widely to justify extermination-style warfare practices, officers like Colin Powell explained the massacre at My Lai with reference to it. A decade later Native American national names for large-scale military operations and later weapon systems and platforms came into prominence. By the time of the US invasions of Afghanistan and Iraq in the twenty-first century, "Indian country" had entered widespread use by military commanders and news journalists, as well as official government documents.[7]

Several spectacle moments marked the military contest as a deadly global theater, quite different from its stated goals of punishing Al Qaeda and bringing that group's leadership to justice for criminal acts. When the morality play's villain, Osama bin Laden, appeared to be cornered in a mountainous region of Afghanistan called Tora Bora, Secretary of Defense Donald Rumsfeld redirected the commanding general of American military operations, Tommy Franks, to prepare a plan to invade Iraq.[8] Bin Laden escaped. Months later, George Tenet, director of the Central Intelligence Agency, provided Secretary of State Powell a set of either forged documents or a deliberate and extensively misleading interpretation of secret evidence. At that time the highest ranking Black American official of all time, Powell did not carry the burden of obvious white supremacy, a key tenet of imperialism, in his pronouncement to the UN, an important quality contributing to his claims to impartiality. Powell went before the United Nations Security Council, demanding a resolution to invade Iraq because he could "prove" the existence of facilities manufacturing weapons of mass destruction. After the invasion drawn from Franks's 2001 plans, inspectors and intelligence officers searched in vain for the facilities and technology, which were never located and apparently simply never existed.

The war became an opportunity for private companies with overt ties to the presidential administration like Haliburton, Brown and Root, and Blackwater to engage in both sovereign state destruction and sovereign state rebuilding. During an early video of the Iraq invasion, as American military and privately contracted snipers target militants, a contractor turns to the camera after a successful "kill" and says, "Fucking niggers."[9] The appearance of the epithet during a US military engagement raised questions about the ideological nature of the state-perpetrated conflict, as well as the situation of constitutional protections of free speech unbound by military law, as well as the obvious suture of slavery and segregation in the United States and genocide and imperial practice abroad. Considering these tensions and predicaments, and in spite of weak box-office performance in the later 1990s, western films would resurface as interpretive and didactic vehicles in national life.

The election of Barack Obama, the first American president of obviously African descent, was an occasion for the dramatic revision of traditional measures of value and volitional constructions of identity and systems of racial representation. The ascension of the Ivy League–educated, confident, and skillful president made it impossible not to concede the immutable presence of Blacks, and, although Obama himself was not descended of Africans who had been enslaved, his achievement made manifest the rightful belonging of Black people in the highest councils of the nation and the iniquity at their previous exclusion by law and custom.

Seemingly resisting the arc of American presidential history since John F. Kennedy's "New Frontier" acceptance speech at the Democratic National Convention, Obama purported to be a declarative end to the militant adventurism that characterized the "cowboy" presidencies of Texans Lyndon Johnson and George W. Bush, full-scale invaders of Vietnam, Afghanistan, and Iraq, respectively, and the clandestine "gunfighting" work of Ronald Reagan (a former film star who also wrapped himself in cowboy regalia) in the Caribbean and Central America. Anxious to reassure Americans of his status quo bona fides (many Americans doubted Obama's ability to survive assassination), Obama reappointed as secretary of defense a man who had served in the Bush administration, and, in his first year, kept in place the same economic advisers and financial managers who had either been in government or were heading Wall Street investment banks, men many believed should have been criminally charged for their role in precipitating the financial system's collapse in 2007.

A political centrist without any firsthand military experience, Obama called for "a new era of responsibility," emanating from "honesty and hard work, courage and fair play, tolerance and curiosity, loyalty and patriotism— . . . the quiet force of progress throughout our history."[10] Crafting a foreign policy strategy tailored away from blatant military entanglements, Obama seemed to regard Middle East interventionism with a wary eye. Not a full twelve months in office, he was awarded the Nobel Peace Prize, partly in recognition of his efforts to end an Israeli attack on Palestinian territories. But during his Nobel acceptance speech, which he dedicated to the American military, Obama asserted a remarkable distinction from the tradition of other winners of that prize. Although he acknowledged that he was "someone who stands here as a direct consequence of Dr. King's life work," meaning he was the beneficiary of the world of revised legal protections and enfranchisement struggled for by nonviolent tactics, Obama clarified the eschatological difference between his new position as head of state and his old stance as a Black American whose most perfect recourse to injustice had been nonviolent action in King's tradition: "I face the world as it is, and cannot stand idle in the face of threats to the American people. For make no mistake; Evil does exist in the world. A non-violent movement could not have halted Hitler's armies. Negotiations cannot convince al-Qaeda's leaders to lay down their arms. To say force may sometimes be necessary is not a call to cynicism—it is a recognition of history; the imperfections of man and the limits of reason."[11] Captivated, perhaps, by his deputy Samantha Power's argument in favor of force to end genocide,[12] Obama thus delivered a classic defense of "just war" doctrine during the awarding of a peace prize, suffusing the situation with irony.

A biracial man whose white mother's family hailed from Kansas, Obama was an ambitious, dutiful, neoliberal manager who served American nation-state and Western global interests. Fond of insisting that "in no other country on earth is my story even possible,"[13] Obama affirmed regularly that he believed American military action grew out of the exceptional nature of the nation-state. He saw the United States of America's global military interventions motivated not by economic need but by ideologically based "enlightened self-interest." Second, he declared that the US "has helped underwrite global security for more than six decades with the blood of our citizens and the strength of our arms." Excluding the fact that the election took place during the "Great Recession," the worst economic disaster since the Great Depression, and that the opposing party ran a female candidate for vice president, a strategy attempted for only the second time in major party history, Obama's election seemed to signal an alignment between the possibility of the public expression of racial fairness and the private execution in the voting booth of such a preference.[14]

Eastwood's snapshot of contained Black soldiers in *The Outlaw Josey Wales* alludes to an obvious parallel in national politics since that time: the fixed, absent-present Black Democrat voter. Having served only a few months in the Senate and regularly simply voting "present," Obama became a viable national candidate because he had carefully refused to assert principled allegiances, all the while carrying with him a loyal Black electoral base of support.[15] But news stories emphasized the nature of Obama's presidency as evidence of the existence and health of multiracial democracy in the United States and proposed that the final taboo of the racist regime, the impossibility of electing a Black president, had finally been laid to rest.[16] The media coverage rarely considered what Obama represented for white people.

Obama, again, a person whose white, Dunham-family origins were west of the Mississippi, represented something quite extraordinary to white Americans: his achievement characterized truly limitless possibility. If a person fixed in the "antagonistic" category as a Black subject could achieve the presidency, then the dream for whites of unlimited bonanza remained intact.[17] In other words, the election of a person stigmatized by his racial background might signal the end of Frederick Jackson Turner's "the end of frontier." To whites, only 6 percent of whom identify nationally as "very often" feeling both sympathy and admiration for Blacks, and 34 percent of whom do so "not very often or never,"[18] and who tend to think of being socially defined as a Black person as akin to being diagnosed with a deadly disease, the successful run for the presidency by one from the maligned group indicated the capacity for extreme levels of prosperity. As a Black person living in the White House, Obama actually was a living avatar of the concept of a new bonanza frontier.

Obama's representational magic was the result of a variety of complex factors. A graduate of private schools, he had nearly completed his education prior to the affirmative action reversals building on the *Bakke* decision and turned into national mantras under Reagan, Bush, and Clinton. At the same time, Obama was young enough to have never himself known segregation. He did not have biological ties to anyone systematically discriminated against in the United States and no lived experience or traditional family heritage linking him directly to the Confederacy. When asked about his historical privilege relative to other persons identifying as Black Americans, he referred to his Luo grandfather, who had been tortured in Kenya under the British government's concentration camp pacification system there following World War II, as well as his career as a domestic servant, though Obama knew neither his grandfather nor even his biological father, having met his male parent on a single occasion.[19] It was impossible to consider Obama an avenging descendant of Black slaves. Empowering Black ultraelites like Susan Rice, the daughter of a Federal Reserve Bank chairman, Obama exemplified the success of a young Black privileged elect groomed early to take the helm of the nation-state. On the cover of a magazine or a campaign poster, Obama signaled indelible Black achievement, but he remained a person whose experience as *Harvard Law Review* editor and US senator was practically impossible for other Blacks to duplicate. He was utterly exceptional.

Obama, "shy about race for much of his presidency," was characterized in some quarters as obsequiously conciliatory toward Confederate sympathizers and racists.[20] His foreign policy, which waffled and had mutable "lines in the sand," was similarly ridiculed. "It's so at odds with the John Wayne expectation for what America is in the world," thought one ranking official, who, however, conceded, "It's necessary for shepherding us through this phase."[21] The era of the cowboy, the violent unilateralist with a moral code of vengeance and an economic logic of bonanza as archetype for American behavior, was thought, by some, at an end. At the same time, the first Black president seemed uninterested in any overt gesture signaling a decisive repudiation with the rhetoric and symbology of the proven racist American past.

The Western Genre's Exceptional Triumph

Before Obama concluded his first term in office, a tenure that was noteworthy for staving off double-digit unemployment and curtailing the most aggressive forms of inflation, a western genre film won considerable acclaim with a gambit that was unprecedented. Quentin Tarantino's 2012 film *Django Unchained*, the most financially successful western to date, deliberately sought to confront the overlapping issue of the western, slavery, white supremacy, and the myth of Black inferiority. The film opens on a beige mise-en-scène of desert, sand, and boulders, taken over by the backs of shackled, whip-scarred, Afroed, Black men.

No other film set in rocky, arid, sagebrush landscapes featuring its main characters regularly on horseback and wearing gun belts, using repeating rifles, and fighting pistol duels against adversaries matches the $425 million commercial success of *Django Unchained*.[22] The film, which won awards for its actors and its writing, is difficult to surpass for reducing the ethical problem of hereditary chattel slavery into a Manichean ethical justification of homicide to overcome wrongful bondage. The crude ethical polarization that the film promotes is obscured by the dizzying series of colliding surfaces that are its postmodern storytelling method. The gleeful pursuit of the righteous grotesque kill distinguishes Tarantino from the modernist racial liberal ethics of Ang Lee. The agonized but understated fighter Holt, portrayed by Jef-

Jamie Foxx in *Django Unchained*, dir. Quentin Tarantino (Weinstein Company / Lantern Entertainment, 2012).

frey Wright in *Ride with the Devil*, is the tortured ambivalent of high modernism, superseded by Jamie Foxx's postmodern Django, a hero of glinting exteriors without reference. The choice to burnish facets paid dividends. The controversial director found immediate approval from the intellectual crowd of the Ivy League, like several Black faculty at Harvard, including economist Lawrence Bobo and media-savvy literature professor Henry Louis Gates Jr.[23]

The film portrays the unlikely friendship between a traveling German dentist named King Schultz (Christoph Waltz) and a liminally enslaved man named Django (Jamie Foxx). Always signaled by his professional credential, Dr. King Schultz has abandoned the life (but not the affect) of the urbane bourgeois for the bonanza fortunes of nomadic bounty hunter, a profession whose sole reward is lucre and that he performs exclusively as juridically sanctioned murder. Set in the immediate antebellum era, the film features the white and Black pair of bounty hunters in the identifiable landscapes of the American South, Southwest, and West, as far as Colorado.

The film opens on Django as a wretched, anonymous member of a chain gang coffle, being force-marched through Texas. With one exception, Django spends the film avenging himself against the overseer class of plantation functionaries and liberating his wife from a cruel slave owner named Calvin Candie (Leonardo DiCaprio), a professional trainer of slave gladiators and amateur phrenologist.[24] In the course of the film, Django himself becomes a skillful pistoleer, using legal documents and his capacity for mimicry to evade peril and rescue his spouse.

The film resembles a fascinating postmodern collage of alternating media spectacles: its hero is endearing, witty, and perspicacious, like the sitcom star Gary Coleman of *Diff'rent Strokes*, but now physically endowed; the action sequences offer the violent gore of an over-eighteen video game or adult cartoon, illicit juvenile entertainments (western-themed video game *Red Dead Redemption 2* was announced in full-page advertisements in the *New York Times* in 2018 and netted $725 million in sales within days of its release);[25] and the ethical conclusions are as easy to arrive at for the audience as sympathy for victims and condemnation of perpetrators of the mass shootings. The video game, with its motif of endless slaughter, in conjunction with the devastating reality of the American spectacle mass-shooting (including especially its undocumented Black urban form) carnage, functions as a vector for the audience to regard the hyperviolence of film as guiltless entertainment and suppressed terror.

Tarantino's film surpasses the false equivalences posed by the racial liberalism of *Ride with the Devil* in one central aspect. Tarantino appears to suggest that a film audience might putatively accept a Black hero as the attentive center for the western. But his overture of top-billing to an African American actor is a ploy, in the manner in which undervaluing (or failing to quantify) the excitement of African Americans wanting to vote for a Black candidate (obvious after the unusual success of Jesse Jackson in 1984 and 1988) for US president was a ploy. Technically, it is impossible to call Jamie Foxx the star of the film, in the manner of an Eastwood or Wayne hero. In the first seventy-five minutes of a 165-minute film, Foxx occupies center frame alone for perhaps seventy-five seconds, and he has no sequential lines longer than a sentence. Django is usually disadvantaged or disabled or appearing onscreen accompanied by a chaperone, typically fellow lead actors Christoph Waltz, Samuel L. Jackson, or Leonardo DiCaprio. Their speaking parts dominate the film. It makes more sense to think of these directorial choices as serving the construction of a new sort of titular marquis performance for the Black heroic lead, a simulacrum. This Baudrillard-like precession of the simulacrum,[26] whereby the representation of a Black western hero from a mainstream film company actually precedes its existence in reality, is obnoxious in its mendacity and relation principally to other mass-culture artifacts, negating the possibility of real life being symbolically captured in the heroic gunfighter model at all.

The situation of an African American as US president and one as starring in a western film is equally singular, equally odd. During an early campfire scene, designed to show the affection building between Dr. King Schultz and Django, the camera looms over Foxx crouching on the bottom left of the frame, and when it focuses on Christoph Waltz, it positions him in the center and photographs him from his feet up. Because of blocking and the seemingly neutral power of the camera to enlarge or diminish different actors, the scene resonates with the famous image of President Obama in the situation room awaiting reports of the demise of Osama bin Laden in Pakistan during the raid of 2011. In the White House–approved photograph,[27] Obama seems distinguished not at all as commander in chief. Rather, the lone Black man appears with shoulders hunched at the margin of the photograph, a minor, ancillary figure to the deadly decision, putatively directed by a crowded table headed by white principals: the Assistant Commanding General of the Joint Special Operations Command, the Deputy National Security Advisor, and the Secretary of State.

The Tarantino film proves quite useful in paralleling the journey of ultimate triumph of an exceptional Black hero, able to overcome slavery through

Jamie Foxx and Christoph Waltz in *Django Unchained*, dir. Quentin Tarantino (Weinstein Company / Lantern Entertainment, 2012).

martial arts and targeted killings, and the president, who in spite of his Black appearance, which is to say, his unconventional or antitraditional mien, proved adept at expanding executive branch powers to control information and extrajudicially kill abroad in order to survive in office. The film *Django*

Pete Souza, *Situation Room*, 2011. White House / Official White House Photo.

Unchained takes for granted a circuit of power sweeping upward from slave to master enforced by violence, but Tarantino enacts the relation with the irruptive gap that always contrasts expectations. The film's earliest scene signals Django's unusual affinity for King Schultz, a mirror to the unusual facility Obama was noted for in his complex and asymmetrical political partnerships, which included recasting Bush-era cabinet members in key roles.

But the collaboration between Django and Schultz occurs across a breach of credulity. When approached by a white male stranger, Django speaks out truthfully and reveals crucial information about white men cruelly enforcing the rules of the slave regime. At this exceptional moment, the film resists the bank of traditional African American culture, like the venerable folktale conditioning Blacks to taciturnity, "You talk too much anyhow." Even the paternalist tradition of Joel Chandler Harris's "Uncle Remus" tales is rife with the problem of truth-telling or any sort of loquacity by the powerless to the powerful. Frederick Douglass, in his 1845 narrative, a work that has achieved the standing of the Old Testament relative to the telling of American slavery, described the outcome of a Maryland encounter of truth-telling between master and enslaved: sale in handcuffs to Georgia. "It is partly in consequence of such facts, that slaves, when inquired of as to their condition and the character of their masters, almost universally say they are contented, and their masters are kind."[28]

In contradistinction, Tarantino imagines an encounter in which a Black man sold into backbreaking enslavement away from family, force-marched for weeks and shivering in the cold, unfamiliar with words that come into English from the Norman conquest (like *positive*), is addressed by the foreign-sounding white man, whose words are disorienting enough that the white male natives will ask him to "speak English" and yet trust him implicitly:

SCHULTZ. Amongst your inventory I've been led to believe is a specimen I am keen to acquire. Hello you poor devils. Is there one amongst you who was formerly a resident of the Carrucan plantation?
DJANGO. I'm from the Carrucan plantation.
SCHULTZ. Who said that? . . . What's your name?
DJANGO. Django.
SCHULTZ. Then you're exactly the one I'm looking for. Do you know who the Brittle brothers are? Who are they?
DJANGO. Big John, Ellis, Raj. Sometimes they call him Lil Raj. They was overseers at the Carrucan Plantation.

In the exchange, it is impossible for Django to know that King Schultz will rely on him to make an identification; however, it might be quite reasonable to assume that after the information has been shared, the relationship will end. In this early case of the bounty or targeted killing motif, it is curious that the "bill" provides no details of the suspects' physical identities, an omission that calls into question the precision possible in targeted killing. Nonetheless, Django responds truthfully, speedily, offering up all of his valuable human intelligence and putting himself in the position to be punished by his owners. The scene contradicts much of what is known about the slave experience and disposition of the enslaved. Rather than a portrait of slavery, the film elaborates two symbiotic positions: the blank enslaved designed by European romanticism

Django Unchained is deliberate in its connecting the western genre to the slave narrative. DiCaprio's Candie identifies Django at their initial meeting as a "cowboy," extending the western into the Mississippi plantation segment of the film. DiCaprio's character then makes the Obama allegory impossible to avoid when he identifies Django by way of multiple exceptionalist references: "Bright Boy," "an exceptional nigger," and "one in ten thousand." Once interpellated into this role of exceptional Black, an act that could only have symbolic heft if undertaken by the slaveholding plantocracy,[29] Django begins to assert and distinguish himself vis-à-vis the enslaved Blacks and poor whites. After attacking a white rider, Django berates another restive enslaved man, Rodney (Nigerian Sammi Rotibi), a member of the coffle of enslaved men on their way to the unfolding doom of life on the Candyland Plantation: "You flash that bad look at me again, I'll give you a reason not to like me. Now move, nigger! You niggers are gonna understand something about me. I'm worse than any of these white men here. You get the molasses out your ass, and you keep your goddamn eyeballs off me."

The trope of the "Black slaver" or "One-eyed Charlie" (a reference to Don Chaffey's 1973 film *Charlie One-Eye*, starring Richard Roundtree)—the oppressed person who ruthlessly oppresses others who share a fate that person might expect but has conditionally escaped—is the "role" played by Django throughout the rest of the film.

The situation of being distinguished from fellow Blacks parallels a signature, career-defining move made by candidate Barack Obama. In 2008, attempting to win the Democratic Party nomination, Obama famously debrided himself from Black people who foreswore the language of transracial neoliberalism. After politically benefiting from his relationship with Chicago minister Jeremiah Wright to ground his own organic authenticity (Wright's church is at the end of the subway line to the Southside and is, with Westside Chicago in 2020, unequivocally, the epitome of the world's Black badlands, "Indian country," or, the essence of geographies capable of conveying Black belonging), Obama denounced Wright after the right-wing media began circulating clips of the minister's sermons critical of American foreign and domestic policy, edited for sensational effect. In Obama's famous "race speech" at Philadelphia's Constitution Hall in April 2008, he began to lay out a precise terrain of his own inscriptions of what are typically referred to as "centrist" politics and imply that racism had not produced actual injustice requiring government redress but mainly "perceived injustice." He proposed that Blacks like Wright had made ocular errors and expressed "distorted views" that besmirched "the greatness and goodness of our nation":

> On one end of the spectrum, we've heard the implication that my candidacy is somehow an exercise in affirmative action; that it's based solely on the desire of wide-eyed liberals to purchase racial reconciliation on the cheap. On the other end, we've heard my former pastor, Reverend Jeremiah Wright, use incendiary language to express views that have the potential not only to widen the racial divide, but views that denigrate both the greatness and the goodness of our nation; that rightly offend white and black alike.
>
> But the remarks that have caused this recent firestorm weren't simply controversial. They weren't simply a religious leader's effort to speak out against perceived injustice. Instead, they expressed a profoundly distorted view of this country—a view that sees white racism as endemic, and that elevates what is wrong with America above all that we know is right with America; a view that sees the conflicts in the Middle East as rooted primarily in the actions of stalwart allies like Israel, instead of emanating from the perverse and hateful ideologies of radical Islam.

While Obama's use of ocular metaphors is a crucial bridge back to the imaginative world created by the camera's eye, he hedged during this first speech, "I can no more disown him than I can disown the black community." The disowning occurred a few short days later, and, again, precisely in response to a news cycle. Tellingly, the broad cross-racial success of the film *Django Unchained* seems not unrelated to its hero's similar public enactment of ethnic repudiation.

The Gap and the Allegory

The basic grammar of deadly violence superficially rewards the audience of *Django Unchained* with scenes of gory, comedic, violent spectacle, but a series of jarring anachronisms reveals the ambition for political analogue at the heart of the project. The film foregrounds these anachronisms to advance a revisionist counterpolitics. It opens with a D. W. Griffith–style textual insertion on its frame announcing two competing chronologies, both "1858" and "Two years before the Civil War." The American Civil War began in 1861, or, three years after 1858. Tarantino makes no mistake here; rather, early on he sets the terms for a revisionist past, addressing himself to a moment beyond a Steven Spielberg or Tom Hanks (or Ava DuVernay) version of modernist realism in a romance package of wish fulfillment. Rather than a mapping of the future and history as a fact maintained by academic institutions and newspapers, the film hints that publicly recorded memory is itself merely an opportunity of overt historical revision. Tarantino uses his postmodernism to guide him into the position of regarding the sequential chronologies of history as an overdetermined metanarrative, a dispensable relic. At the same time, by invoking the war as a necessary parameter in the historical arc of his film, he satisfies (and stimulates) the contemporary political appetite for a reductionist Abrahamic world of resolve against the Islamic caliphate and everything else that involves militant resistance to Western consumer society.

But where *Django Unchained* is imperative and revelatory is not in the mode of its deliberate juxtapositions of antebellum time with contemporary events or the revision of history to ensure that deadly force in Black hands eradicates the condition of bondage. (Among many places, the trope of Manichean Black violence as the ultimate spoiler of slavery was in the popular militia movement of 1995.)[30] The crucial operative mode of the film is its allegorical dimension. I would prefer the older sense of the Greek term, *alle + goria*, which means "other speaking in public," a rough designation for symbolic speech acts. I am less interested in the dichotomy struck by the romantics limiting allegory to a mechanical "translation" or substitution.[31] If allegory operates as a missing referent, or better, the technique of making "absent things seem present,"[32] there is a remarkable shared theater of operation, a reinsertion of presence, between the film's putative protagonist, Django, and the president of the nation during the moment of its release, Barack Obama.

Postmodern stylistic techniques and philosophical concerns alone do not account for *Django Unchained*'s deliberate violations of scrupulous historicism. In the most deliberate overture (among several) to diegetic postmodernist techniques, Tarantino removes the distance between past and present and, thus, the film and reality. The noticeable presence of this gap, the interludes in credulity, are places where the film insists on the viewers' reflection on the allegorical relationships. These places of rupture have notable political effect.

The philosopher Giorgio Agamben has developed a useful idea that helps us understand the obvious allegories between the film's dramatizations and the function of the modern western state and its principle of constitutional governance. Rather than states providing laws to satisfy empowered citizens, Agamben notes parallels between contemporary democratic state functioning and "the camp," the warren of temporary placement for stateless refugees and political prisoners. "In our age, the state of exception comes more and more to the foreground as the fundamental political structure and ultimately begins to become the rule. When our age tried to grant the unlocalizable a permanent and visible localization, the result was the concentration camp."[33]

With the refugee settlement or concentration camp as their likely home, inhabitants of the new state are governed by the temporary suspension of lawful rule that becomes permanent, the "state of exception." One critical commentator of Agamben's work, who faults Agamben's account for failing to incorporate the literature on constitutional law, refines the idea of the exception to indicate a problem of a cleft: "a situation where all legal order is suspended. The move from a specific, procedurally circumscribed authorization to an informal suspension corresponds to the conceptual shift—from the exception understood as an alternative rule to the exception as a gap or void in the law."[34]

The "gap," where the law, history, or even simple credulity are suspended, operates in Tarantino's work as a postmodern storytelling technique, a narrative device emphasizing a noticeable cleavage and insisting on allegory. In these moments of suspension, the audience has the opportunity to recognize the space between the law of credulity in the film's neorealist romance plot, now disabled, and the substituted allegorical logic and space, the exceptional condition.

The filmmaker's most obvious or self-conscious example of this gap insisting on political allegory occurs at the end of a gory fight to the death between two slave gladiators, and during a scene that brings together in the same room the three principal actors Waltz, Foxx, and DiCaprio. At the eruptive mo-

Spilling Skittles in *Django Unchained*, dir. Quentin Tarantino (Weinstein Company / Lantern Entertainment, 2012).

ment of spectacle destruction indicative of imminent death, after a fighter has his arm loudly broken and is blinded, a bowl of Skittles, a colorful, gummy children's candy that hit the US market in the 1980s, spills conspicuously onto the floor in front of the camera. In that postmodern interlude, which demands that the film audience awaken from the fantastic cocoon of the theater and its ensemble of soporific effects emphasizing continuity with the illusion unfolding onscreen, the director insists we break into the present.[35] Tarantino invokes the demise of Trayvon Martin, the boy who in early 2012 was returning home from a convenience store, where he had purchased an Arizona iced tea and Skittles, when he was murdered by an armed white vigilante who had accused him of trespassing. Tarantino, whose film was released on Christmas Day in 2012, clumsily or ostentatiously, or even cheaply perhaps, thus pairs white domination of Black people over two temporal spheres, the slave regime and the contemporary moment of Black public persecution by armed vigilantes and police.[36]

The film maximizes these irruptions between diegetic antebellum time and the theater present. A few minutes into the drama, Waltz, the surprise star of the film (who received an Academy Award for his role as Best Supporting Actor, in spite of the fact that he has more lines, by far, than any other performer), explains to the doomed slave trader Dicky Speck, "I only shot your brother once he threatened to shoot me, and I do believe I have one, two, three, four, five witnesses who can attest to that fact." He is referring to the Black men in the coffle.

Here the film calls attention to the contradiction between King Schultz's failed application of Rousseau's natural law on account of the formal pragmatic adjustment to it made by the US Constitution's "three-fifths compromise." The enslaved, each accounted as three-fifths of a person for congressional representation in the House of Representatives, have been fully nullified as citizens by the Supreme Court's March 1857 *Dred Scott* decision outlawing the court testimony of "beings of an inferior order . . . altogether unfit to associate with the white race, either in social or political relations."[37]

King Schultz, whose dainty European affect fully belies the fact that he regularly both misperceives his New World environment and then also easily dominates its witless inhabitants, is wrong. Black testimony has been removed from legal tribunals. In consequence, Schultz has no witnesses according to law. The architect of the legal decision, Maryland's Supreme Court Chief Justice Roger B. Taney, thought that since the Constitution freed no slave, its privileges could not have applied to Black people generally, who possessed "no rights which the white man was bound to respect."[38] Black Americans were living not under law but in a state of exception. In other words, King Schultz's authority on the level of the operation of the story line in the film is unstable, unsubstantiated, and illegitimate from the opening. Schultz's subsequent position, which he goes on to clarify as "a legal representative of the justice system of the United States of America," an arbiter of law, legal proceedings, detention, and punishment, is completely untenable. Technically, Schultz is introduced to the audience as the figurative trope aporia, a deliberate example of a contradiction calling attention to the fact.

Schultz's violent mastery of Americans and partisan representation of the law is connected to what he more fully stands for, which is the operation of a similar economic principle to that of Clint Eastwood's Blondie in *The Good, the Bad and the Ugly*. When purchasing Django from an injured and unwilling Dicky Speck, he shouts "Sold American!" The comment collapses American business practice with compulsory transaction and draws attention to slave-trading itself, a mirror to the pending forced sale of the men on the chain gang.

In the seconds before the commerce with the Specks becomes violent, Schultz scoffs at Ace Speck's unwillingness to dither, reprimanding the trader, unwilling to sell Django: "Of course he is for sale!" Schultz stands at first for the laissez-faire market, whose absence of contractual regulation he enforces with his lethal firearm technology. He advocates its principle as the most neutral arbiter of human relations that needs to unfold without hindrance.

This market operates regardless of the volition of the seller, an ominous allusion to the arrival of the European colonial system in the Americas and its asymmetric real estate transactions with Indigenous people.

In the market that King Schultz enforces, everything is a commodity and has a price, in the same manner in which he regularly introduces himself, Django, and the horses they ride, flattening the circuit of relation among people and commodity goods. The point is emphatic, because the opening scene mimics *The Outlaw Josey Wales* and its Zukey Limmer trading post. Allowed the use of a horse, coat, and boots, Django, like Creek Little Moonlight, who willingly gives herself to Wales, follows a deadly stranger into slavery. King Schultz believes that vending commodity goods on the market is an inviolable principle, one sanctioning his own commercial participation in the slave trade.

The presence of five other chained men on the coffle is an opportunity for Tarantino to allow his paternalism to clash openly with the postmodern departure from a historical teleology. The film premises that any death caused by a white man can be fully legitimated to the juridical order without any possible recourse, which is to say the supportive network of laws exists on the basis of invocation and that homicide can be committed without condemnation from an ethical tradition like Christianity. King Schultz, as his own witness, is capable of justifying multiple murders without any of the fairly dense legal entanglements, especially witness testimony to wrongdoing, that habitually precluded other western heroes from deadly violence, but principally in the Ford dramas *The Searchers* and *The Man Who Shot Liberty Valance* and even in Eastwood's best publicly received western at this writing, *Unforgiven*. By contrast, in Tarantino's film the law—and the state behind it—is theoretically positioned as omnipotent *summum bonum*, its inviolability enhanced by the total absence of any semblance of its structure: the courtroom, the jail, the military, the slave patrol.

Empty Black Relations

In the same way that Taney's *Dred Scott* decision removes Black existence before the law, Black people in Tarantino's vision lack a shared nativity, heritage, legacy, and conceivable national connection outside their morphology as it exists as an aspect of difference and distinction for whites. The opening and closing of elements of shared confluence of interest is the key neoliberal tenet operating in the film. Do Blacks have any common ground that offers them an opportunity for relation beyond the market of transaction other than morphology, which is to say, a relation of sameness, a mimetic relation? And unlike Richard Fleischer's reproduction of enslavement in *Mandingo* (1975), Tarantino wishes to invigorate the politics of authenticity in the visualization of enslavement by reproducing African Americans as preponderantly dark-skinned. Tarantino, like Henry Louis Gates Jr. and John Ridley in the film *12 Years a Slave* (2013), creates a slavescape that undeniably looks like the people of Africa but demands that Black difference in speech, in particular African speech, be fully eradicated. Black appearance is strenuously pursued, to the point of casting Nigerian, Senegalese, and Kenyan actors as third- and fourth-generation Black Americans, but African sounds are silenced. By contrast, throughout *Django Unchained* and reaching its crescendo with the woodsman and kennel warden Mr. Stonesipher, Tarantino deploys whites whose speech is less legible, less open to meaning and interpretation, further into idiomatic idiosyncrasy than any Blacks, who all speak an easily understood version of English.

For Tarantino, there is considerable difference and linguistic range among whites, but Blacks are reduced, linguistically and epidermally. For the most part, the men are whole-bodied muscular brown cruiserweights, and for the most part, the women are lithe brown courtesans, all speaking in similar varieties of English, mutually intelligible to themselves and to whites. (Tarantino uses the captivity and romance narrative plot of Django resuming his marriage mainly to erase the preoccupation of Fleischer's *Mandingo*, which was the spectacle and sexual violence of the slave regime and the consequence of both.) In fact, the rap music of Rick Ross and Tupac, which jarringly trumpets during transitory moments of the film (recalling similar anachronistic musical interludes in western films such as B. J. Thomas's "Raindrops Keep Fallin' on My Head" in Altman's *Butch Cassidy and the Sundance Kid*), is more idiomatically obscure than the speech of enslaved African Americans. But the message is clear: shared language tradition will not operate as collectively common African ground.

In fact, the film repeatedly insists that there is not, nor can there be, any mutually shared tradition among Blacks other than morphology, and certainly not the shared experience of slavery. These men and women have no recourse to a folk project that will contest the vicious industrial labor commodity conditions that they face. There is no mutual past, even of experiential anguish, available to draw from to sustain them against the centurylong labor transformation observable in the film, the transition from agricultural labor directly to spectacle entertainment. The fundamental language and as-

Jamie Foxx in *Django Unchained*, dir. Quentin Tarantino (Weinstein Company / Lantern Entertainment, 2012).

piration to contract-based private property relations are drawn from the whites. But the film goes even further and separates natural-rights discourse from American neoclassical thinkers like Thomas Jefferson, rerouting it to the European Enlightenment by way of nineteenth-century French and German romanticism, heralded by its references to Goethe, Wagner, and Alexander Dumas made by Schultz. More troubling, the film concludes with Django parroting the scientific racism of Calvin Candie, whose belief in phrenology and interest in breeding and culling fighting men places him in the eugenicist camp. Before killing his final victim, Django brags to the enslaved man Stephen, "I am that one in ten thousand," and wears Candie's clothes and smokes tobacco from Candie's ivory cigarette holder in the film's resolving frame.

Here the rational market principle is braided to enlightenment individualism in the same way that Django's Black exceptionalism is made to fall under the broader arc of American exceptionalism evident in the imperial response to the 9/11 terrorist encounter. That goal is completely legible by the allegorical middle of the film and the conflation of Franco Nero's 1966 Django with Foxx's Django, at which point the exceptionalist nature of the film is excruciatingly clear. Only one black person trapped in the misery of a slave narrative can become the apotheosis of the machine-gun-from-a-coffin wielding gunfighter from the 1966 western *Django*. The whip-scarred, shackled, Black men, who have communally survived an overland journey from Natchez-over-the-Hill, the famous trading station of enslaved Africans, to arrive in what appears to be west Texas, are understood as a collective of random agents awaiting an individual main chance through the ends of a particular beneficence, or white paternalism, which they respond to passively. Tarantino reproduces a similar scene of caged Black men who must free themselves but are reluctant to do so at the conclusion of the film.

Understanding Black people as without the ability to have relationships with each other outside of contracts provided by Western epistemic or juridical frameworks is the logic that allows King Schultz to give a gun to an enslaved man.[39] After ascertaining Django's identity and unlocking his leg shackle, King Schultz hands a loaded shotgun (he later misidentifies it as a "rifle," another gap in his credibility as a weaponry expert) to an enslaved man still chained, whom he has not freed. He says, "Could you hold this for a moment?" At this point in the film, King Schultz has demonstrated immaculate gunfighting talent, but on what logic does he imagine a shared confluence of interest with the enslaved man?

Schultz's ongoing improbable paternalist discussion with the chained men builds on the absurdist moment of handing over the weapon escalating to a climactic address. After setting his own price for Django, who readily complies with his directions, and coercing the wounded and unwilling Speck to sign a bill of sale, King Schultz addresses the now armed group of black men:

> Now as to you poor devils. So as I see it, when it comes to the subject of what to do next you gentlemen have two choices. One: Once I'm gone, you could lift the beast off the remaining Speck, then carry him to the nearest town. Which would be at least thirty-seven miles back the way you came. Or two: You could unshackle yourselves, take that rifle, put a bullet in his head, bury the two of them deep and make your way to a more enlightened area of this country. Oh and on the off chance that there are any astronomy aficionados amongst you, the North Star is that one.

Schultz's pedantic, aggressively didactic speech operates as a moment of managerial control designed to obscure the third choice. Why don't all of the Black men kill Schultz and Speck, and take all the horses to create the best possible opportunity for freedom?

Schultz points out only the most obvious solution that coincides with his own goals. More viable than the overland trek of thousands of miles to Canada are the nearby Indian Territory of Oklahoma, the foreign country Mexico, which outlawed slavery in 1834, and even the Black Caribbean republic, Haiti.[40] The legal changes of the 1857 *Dred Scott* decision have turned Amer-

"I Am That One in Ten Thousand"   197

ica into a slaver and bounty hunter's paradise; immediate escape from the contiguous US territory is the best path for Black freedom, especially after having committed deadly violence. But the neoliberal narrative seeks to silo the choice of the suddenly freed men to the one of exceptional post–World War II northern and European laws and markets, which exposes the main contradiction of the market rationale that sustains the plausible logic of the film's plot. Blacks are not entitled to define their own terms and territories of citizenship under the law; they are cast into a permanent state of exception. The myth of exceptionalism, by contrast, the capacity to outstrip the constraints imposed by episteme, operates here as a discourse chiefly to emphasize the hard limit of categorically available patterns of existence.

This scene of racial liberalism between King Schultz and the enslaved men effectively extends the occlusions of Eastwood and Lee, which had emphasized different methods of filmmaking and plot construction to isolate and seal off the Black figure from representation in western films. The unspoken logic of Tarantino's plot device of the expert ranging bounty hunter is ethically less coherent than the predecessor films. As the certified agent of the Texas court, what logic prevails to prevent him from shooting down the newly defiant chained men and selling their corpses? Once the chain-gang men have become runaways, Schultz's legal and fiduciary interest shifts, and he has motive to hunt them down and return them to slavery for the bounty. The most sought-after villains in a racialized slave society featuring a Black-and-white, slave-and-master dichotomy are Blacks suspected of violence against whites.[41]

Rather than an enforcer of the law, Dr. King Schultz is presented to the audience as a dandy assassin, a technologist who only pursues white people who have been condemned; he never expresses any interest whatsoever in returning a fugitive alive to produce his bounty. Tarantino's script positions a cosmopolitan European bourgeois, secure in his lofty education on natural rights and free markets, as the readily identifiable, Manichean "good" white man. (The film even includes a shot of Django touching Schultz's corpse with affection.) The "bad" white men that Schultz kills are "homegrown" white Americans, unlettered chauvinists, slave traders, overseers, rustlers, thieves, highwaymen, and backwoods idlers, whose unregulated and backward capital acquisitions threaten the stability of the market. Schultz systematically removes them. (Django shoots two of these white men in the groin, symbolically positioning himself as the eliminator of their generative capacity as a class and fulfillment of King Schultz's vision.) The logic of the film suggests that the English declension-variety of the capitalist slave system too long retains the cold logic of "nigger" as permanent chattel to drive the bonanza capital project of North America and "catch up" with the rest of the "western" world. Tarantino's unending exploration of his audience's desire for Black violence against the white minion, the most accessible agents of the plantation regime, fully resonates with an ethical formula so uncritical as to retain the main features of structural inequity.

As in Lee's *Ride with the Devil*, the large German immigrant group to the mid-nineteenth-century United States exemplifies the machine-tool mechanic conducting the shift from agricultural life to industrialization. The gap in the portrait is the distance between King Schultz's reason and his passion, the difference between the immaculate Kantian categorical distinctions and the romanticist considerations signaled by his lengthy retellings of Goethe and the implication of Herder's folk philosophy and Wagner's music. King Schultz, an 1848 refugee, who appears to willingly sacrifice his life and the lives of the people he cares about because his romantic passions prevent him from logically forgoing a "kill," actually offers the audience an abbreviated window onto the twentieth century. There, the rationally expert German war machine, fighting on all fronts, internally and externally, and endlessly killing out of romantic passion, loses its wars for imperial ascendancy. But the catastrophic finale of the German romanticist national ideal is the destruction of the territorial imperial goals of the British and French, leaving the Americans, with their conspicuously Native, European, and African mixed-race nation, as the hegemon.[42]

The Manicheanism and the Mass-Culture Artifact

Tarantino borrows directly from the superficially ethical pulp genre, including the 1966 Sergio Corbucci *Django* (a film about a lone gunman, played by Franco Nero, who uses the surprise technology of the belt-fed machine gun to rescue a Mexican town from predators) and the Martin Goldman–directed 1972 Fred Williamson vehicle *Legend of Nigger Charley* (about a trio of escaped slaves defending their freedom in the West). But Tarantino's updating relies for its ethical concerns on the ideal of slaveholding and the maintenance of the slave regime as a fundamental evil, from which recuperation or conciliation is unavailable. This is a profoundly Manichean postmodern effort, which grounds its ethics in its contemporary unwillingness to brook compromise or tender shared humanity with slaveholders. This unwillingness to negotiate with antagonists on the other side of the Manichean divide is directly analogous to the contemporary problem of the War on Terror and the existence of more radical Islamists than can be killed.

Tarantino tour de force films like *Pulp Fiction* (1994), *Jackie Brown* (1997), and *Django Unchained* are postmodern arcades of collected lines and collages of scenes from 1970s B movies. His audience would not be able to recognize the new product as part historical reassembly without the digital archive and its deep access to the analog material past, the world of film, audio, and video of the twentieth century. Tarantino thus expands the superficial entertainment value of the B film genre by exhuming it as a historical artifact and layering intertextual significations into a contemporary collage reassembled to address new political problems.[43] Early in his career Tarantino exhausted explicit representations of violence and racialized sexuality in the films *Reservoir Dogs* (1992) and *Pulp Fiction*. After achieving wealth and cultural influence, he began a series of explicit historical revisionist films with *Inglourious Basterds* (2009). *Django Unchained* is the second film in this series. In these revised accounts of war and slavery, no onscreen foe escapes the wrath of the God of Abraham. The films are Manichean fantasies whose prime climactic moments involve violent retribution to the "evildoers" of modern Western political history. All of these films are a struggle over the past, where the contemporary conglomerate of market states attempts to define absolute categories of exception, goodness, and purity, even when the films acknowledge the villainous complicity of the market state.

But despite his stylistic choices and even his personal antagonism, in the western, Tarantino cannot avoid the cinematic terrain of forerunners like John Ford's *The Searchers*. Even with the film's commitment to postmodern aesthetics, *Django Unchained* harnesses itself to the ethical concerns of racial liberalism, the melodramatic predicament of the "protest novel," the genre belittled by James Baldwin in 1949 and Ralph Ellison in 1963.[44] While the admonitions of the heralded Black modernists were directed against liberal sentimentality, as well as Marxist overdeterminism, the dilemma for the protest art form or Manichean ethical drama is its mechanical reduction of any ethical problem to a "good" or "evil" choice.[45]

Tarantino adeptly balances the needs of an American mass audience—the audience of the films of Steven Spielberg and Oprah Winfrey, baby boomer cultural icons whose media efforts have created the central tropes of American national identity and visualizations of the conflicts of the American past. The unity between talk-show host Winfrey (a journalist known for bringing the news into the talk-show format and for regarding "viewers as consumers ... who need to be kept entertained")[46] and Spielberg is evident by way of the closure that Tarantino understands between dimensions of historical experience. With the films *Inglourious Basterds* and *Django Unchained* he is reproducing in postmodern historical revision the Spielberg modernist realist duo describing the legitimate and rare instances of the overcoming of the concentration camp in *Schindler's List* (1993) and the titular slave ship of *Amistad* (1997). In an interview, Tarantino races to join the propagandist of American racial segregation to the Nazi Party icon Adolf Hitler, hyperbolically claiming that Dixon's *The Clansman* "really can only stand next to *Mein Kampf* when it comes to its ugly imagery."[47] The analogue of slave regime white supremacists and Nazis was famously introduced by Stanley Elkins in the *Sambo* psychological history of American slavery in 1959. The resultant reduction of historical horror to the Polish crematorium and the plantation are the Spielbergian nodes of American historical experience made legible to the popular audience. The sharp mis-equivalence of the two systems and the dangerous erasure made by Tarantino's enclosure are brought out in a nugget by Wilderson: "Jews went into Auschwitz and came out as Jews. Africans went into the ships and came out as Blacks."[48]

But this is the problem of the Manicheanism—the elimination of context and relativism, the pursuit of "morally exclusivist and politically separatist" absolutes—that emphasizes a rigid typology over a humanistic, individual precision.[49] The commanding Manichean vision is the vision of Abraham. They are also authoritarian visions, as complementary with Far Right revisionist spectacles that bring contemporary technology to bear on the problem of sustaining white supremacy during different historical epochs, while "left"-wing elites and monopoly capitalists readily harness the technologies of biology and chemistry to control and redirect population growth of the nonwhite world.

Django Unchained evinced a basic plot grammar of spectacle killing but made the determined Manichean ideological point that Black death could only be occasioned by whites or through whites. There was an underside of consequence to this purported solidarity of the director and writer on behalf of enslaved Black people. The existence of a Black folk or popular unity is inconceivable. The character Rodney simmers with rage at Django, the ordinary reaction of an enslaved man witnessing the exclusive privilege of the exceptional Black. As Django surmounts the last hurdle before the film's

Sammi Rotibi, Evan Parke, and Omar Dorsey in *Django Unchained*, dir. Quentin Tarantino (Weinstein Company / Lantern Entertainment, 2012).

denouement, Rodney finds himself chained to Django in a mobile dungeon. Django miraculously breaks his bonds and destroys the white horsemen leading the coffle to the LaQuint Dickey mining company, in a sequence indicating that a "just kill" is actually anyone embedded within the framework of slavery at all—any white person who is not actively abolitionist.

Before he returns to achieve his vengeance and rescue his bride, Django looks at Chester, Chicken Charly, and Rodney, and there is no moment of shared freedom or twined future, no recognition even of mutually endured hardship and injustice. Rather, Django is portrayed as a man or a possible man, and the others are chattel, who, despite the death of the whites directly enforcing their bondage, are too timid to move instinctively from beyond the cage of their confines. Rodney looks at Django, who rides boldly away, with cautious envy and admiration. But it is unclear if the metaphysical leap beyond slavery can take place for him. Nonetheless, the significance of the moment is always the possibility of the individual's distinction in the face of the sluggishness and backwardness of the ethnic community. While Blacks in the movie have only whites to blame for their condition, without exceptionalism, their access to an alternative future remains bleak and improbable.

The most important scene in the film eradicating the notion of Black common ground or shared imagined community occurs in the wake of Django's triumphant gun battle at Candyland. After defeating all of his armed foes, Django says to the cook and the courtesan, "All you Black folks, I suggest you get away from all these white folks." Then Django tells Cora the cook and

Sammi Rotibi in *Django Unchained*, dir. Quentin Tarantino (Weinstein Company / Lantern Entertainment, 2012).

Candie's mistress Sheba, two thoroughly invested "house" slaves, to bid their mistress adieu. As Cora completes the words, "Goodbye, Ms. Lara," Django shoots from upstairs at the surviving emblem of the plantation aristocracy, standing in a doorway below him. Unlike the other victims of Django's pistol, her body is not dismembered in a torrent of blood. Nor is she the victim of rape, which would seemingly correspond to the film's fascination with intertextual reference to the cinema of the 1970s, particularly Fleischer's *Mandingo*, and reverse the terms of white male sexual dominion over black women depicted in the film.[50] Rather, the white woman's body is yoked through a doorway in the manner of a vaudeville foil being pulled off the stage.

Tarantino has a noteworthy and complex sense of gender in the western, one informed by precedent like Ruby Dee's role in *Buck and the Preacher* (1972) and Vonetta McGee's performance in *Thomasine and Bushrod* (1974). His film features incongruities or anachronisms designed to improve the gender balance in the film, like a multiracial public dinner including Django, Sheba, and the hostess from the Cleopatra Club. But it is hard to maintain Django as the ethical western hero who shoots down unarmed women, so Lara Lee Candie's death must be rendered comedically. At the same time, her violent elimination nonetheless signals the arch trope of racial Manicheanism deployed by the film. It is, of course, Django's single moment of racial confraternity with other Blacks and his only unsupervised attack on an aristocrat. Held as equally culpable for the crime of enslavement as the more direct profiteers and brutalizers, Lara Lee is a "just kill" for being part of the plantation machinery. Nonetheless, the onscreen feat is extraordinary: a defenseless, unarmed woman is murdered, and the audience laughs.

Tarantino accents the claim in two ways, as both a "natural" association and as ridiculous. Deprived of a mutilated corpse, the film audience regards her death absent any cognitive work on the complexity of the injustice of the slave regime, or how that injustice, signaled at the epistemic level by Calvin Candie's interest in the science of phrenology, might be undone. There is no opportunity to reckon with the gender collusion of plantation mistress with master, in spite of her diminished standing. Tarantino's Broomhilda (Kerry Washington), who well knows Lara Lee's active work in the slave regime, does not avenge herself against her mistress; rather, she awaits Django on horseback outside. The film's contradictions insist on absent heroic presence here, where genre convention is defied and the racial Manichean ethics are given trump standing. Part of the work of the elimination is to prevent the audience from encountering its own culpability for the contemporary "just kills" conducted by the drones, mercenaries, or specialty military forces, campaigns that inevitably kill noncombatant women and children. The deus ex machina attempt to erase the villain, and the audience's mistaken insertion of comic release instead of measured consideration, opens up another gap, a void, where we become aware of an absent referent, an absent analogue.

The insincere and misguided essentialism of Django's lasso—"all you black folks"—has its apotheosis earlier, in the space where discourses of natural rights, European romanticism, colonialism, industrialization, and scientific racism collide. King Schultz informs plantation owner Calvin Candie of the racial origins of Alexandre Dumas to assert that because of his racial ancestry, Dumas was necessarily a philosophical abolitionist. Schultz calls the biracial, white-skinned and blue-eyed Dumas "Black," alluding directly to Obama, whose Euro-American and Kenyan ancestry is also regularly reduced. (Obama wrote in 1995 that "if I had come to understand myself as a black American, and was understood as such, that understanding remained unanchored to a place.")[51] But for Tarantino's heroic project to occur, the other Blacks in the film, but particularly Django, can afford no such philosophical commitments to a cause like abolitionism or a collective identity rooted in a locale, which would inform their choices toward violence.

"Black" Django has just witnessed and, in fact, partly orchestrated the eating by dogs of D'Artagnan, a man renamed after a Dumas character from *The Three Musketeers*. The intervention Django makes, as King Schultz offers to pay for the doomed man's life, is the culminating act of distancing himself from the coffle of men sold into the slave-fighter market. The assorted rivalries among the Black characters in the film are presented as fully capable of surpassing the conflict between white and Black.[52]

This is the precise parallel to Obama's repeated assertions of distance from Reverend Jeremiah Wright, an act of recusal since he had powerfully collapsed his voice and political work with Wright's ministry in *Dreams from My Father*. At Morehouse College in 2013, after the national Black electorate had delivered all it might, Obama reminded the college graduates of his work on the Affordable Care Act but emphasized to them his inability to enforce the laws and remedy the world made by racism: "Nobody cares how tough your upbringing was. Nobody cares if you suffered some discrimination. And moreover, you have to remember that whatever you've gone through, it pales in comparison to the hardships previous generations endured—and they overcame them."[53]

Taking for granted a familiarity that he never used, ever, in addressing predominately white audiences, and relying fully on a contested historical teleology of unceasing improvement after emancipation, Obama endorsed for Blacks a classic "respectability" politics in dress, speech and appearance, hard work, sacrifice, and unremunerative ethnic obligation.[54] When in 2015 one of the nation's poorest communities in Baltimore rioted after a young man's death in police custody, he dismissed the protesting crowds as "thugs."[55] He adopted a steady message of improved Black fitness to merit inclusion, a common message of racial essentialism.

Tarantino accepts such racial essentialism as fully natural, and it is an assumption that undergirds his racial liberalism. At the moment of purchasing Django's wife, Broomhilda von Shaft, King Schultz, the liberal arts professor to the fraudulent dilettante Calvin Candie, looks at the books in the library and begins a Socratic dialogue. What would Alexandre Dumas think of Candie having named enslaved men after characters from *The Three Musketeers*? Nearly reproducing Obama's language on Jeremiah Wright, Schultz declares Dumas's approval of the naming practices a "dubious proposition." Then he explodes, "Dumas was Black!"

While the news clearly surprises the ignorant slave master Calvin Candie, the assertion is a dramatic Manichean reduction. It proposes, in spite of the obvious examples of house slaves like Stephen (Samuel L. Jackson), who has just helped his master outwit the bounty hunters, that all blacks are abolitionists. Schultz rejects the irony in the naming practices widespread throughout slavery, insisting that heroic romantic naming and heroic romantic acts bear a one-to-one relation. Naturally, the sleight of hand is completely invented by Tarantino. Dumas, whose mother was from Normandy and whose father was a famed biracial colonel, conspicuously declared that he was white.[56]

Furthermore, Dumas went to lengths to complicate the point on slavery and slave trading in France during the Napoleonic era. In the 1843 novel *Georges*, the eponymous biracial hero trains himself to fight racial injustice, culminating with his decision to lead a slave rebellion. But Georges's abilities and intentions are not fundamentally at odds with the character portrait of his older brother Jacques Munier, a free biracial captain and fighter who views the slave trade as "a perfectly legal industry." Munier, in a chapter titled "The Philosophy of the Slave Trader," decides "as soon as this free creature had become a slave by a circumstance beyond his control, Jacques saw no difficulty in dealing with her as her owner."[57] The same view is parroted by King Schultz at the beginning of the film when, after coercing the "specimen" Django's sale and leaving the wounded Willard Speck at the mercy of armed, enslaved men, Schultz asserts that he is capable of "making this slavery business pay." Dumas gives a sympathetic, honorable character the view that slave-catching and depriving natural rights is wrongdoing, but once the commodity relation has been introduced, an actor reasonably seeks personal immediate interest and has "no difficulty in dealing" with the enslaved as "owner." Django's careful act, immediately before killing the members of Calvin Candie's funeral party, is to recover the bill of sale for his wife, Broomhilda (and presumably himself), from the body of Dr. King Schultz (whose romanticism has made him a fiery abolitionist and results in his death). If enslavement is barbarity, and the heroic figure Django is capable of protecting his freedom by force of arms, why does he return to the contractual logic of the *Dred Scott*-era law to buttress his claim?

The film purports to show Django's escape from enslavement, but it concludes with a vengeance killing that, in fact, emphasizes the sharp limits on the deadly capacity attained by Django. He kills Stephen, the other "bad nigger," or exceptional Black person, shooting him in the kneecaps and then leaving the "house nigger servant" to be burned alive in the explosive apocalypse of the dynamited plantation house. Tarantino takes this achievement quite seriously, a depiction of the Old Negro overcome by the New Negro, the seigneurial liege clad in his "house nigger servant uniform" of feudalism replaced by the dandy who looks forward to the Enlightenment's rule of law and contracts to secure his conjugal, domestic, manorial happiness.

But the credo of eliminating the exception as a condition of peace has the effect of making the practice of eliminating the exception the rule. Why must the one decision that Django makes about a killing completely on his own and without the condition of legal prophylaxis be against precisely his own kind? Because, as Giorgio Agamben writes in his genealogy of the shift in democratic theory and practice, there is "a continuing tendency in all of the Western democracies, the declaration of the state of exception has gradually been replaced by an unprecedented generalization of the paradigm of security as the normal technique of government."[58] The generalization of security paradigms among Western nation-states unleashes fantastic violence, supplemented by a discursive network of ethical claims from the exceptional state, a layer of ideological force that amounts to the "instrumentalization of international morality."[59]

Tarantino contorts Dumas's racial identity into this same sort of instrumentalized, Manichean morality and to interpellate, to call into social existence, his Black hero, Django. The entire procedure of interpellation is to disguise the violence of the state, and Tarantino's method of redeeming or fully heroicizing Django relies on the polar morality of the Manichean dynamic, racial essentialism, an overture to the "Mandingo" fight between Black contestants. Like Obama, who repudiated his lineage to the Black territory of minister Jeremiah Wright, the film Django requires not the Black subject's dismantling of the slave regime but destroying its successful enslaved operators, thus preserving his own exceptional status.

CHAPTER SEVEN

"Why Don't They Kill Us?"

Django Unchained and the Politics of Deadly Force

> Given the farflung responsibilities of the executive branch for law enforcement, and the large complements of personnel required to discharge these responsibilities, it would scarcely be surprising if there were not isolated examples of abuse of this investigative function. ... I do not believe it raises a constitutional question.
> —William H. Rehnquist, "Federal Data Banks, Computers, and the Bill of Rights" (1971)

> The list goes on ...
> —Barack Obama, "Remarks at US Air Force Academy Commencement" (2016)

Before being elected, presidential nominee Barack Obama made his fondness for the world of computer technology evident in a unique way: he rejected the federal campaign matching funds for his candidacy.[1] He was then setting records for small donations collected by way of the internet and understood that despite having to betray the principle of removing unfettered donations to political campaigns, he would be able to protect himself and act with speed and authority to advertise his brand where he was vulnerable. The tools of remotely gathered information and networks were natural to him, and he gathered them as president as his predictable adversaries set up. During the Obama presidency, the American Enterprise Institute went on to produce political activist groups like the Tea Party, a contingent of the Far Right that throttled Obama at every legislative turn. Typically depicting Obama as a Pollyannaish liberal, the Tea Party expressed its agenda using western tropes of militancy and fierce, even suicidal, independence. When the Tea Party Republican congressmen Eric Cantor of Richmond, Virginia, Kevin McCarthy of California, and Paul Ryan of Wisconsin wrote a book laying out their principles, they titled it *Young Guns*, aligning their own uncompromising political hostility to the upstart heroes of the 1988 western film starring Emilio Estevez, Kiefer Sutherland, and Charlie Sheen. The film reproduced the legend of fabled western gunfighter Billy the Kid and his gang.[2] Young Gun Ryan went on to become the running mate of presidential hopeful Mitt Romney in the failed 2012 bid for the presidency.

The Right, led in Congress by the Young Guns, labeled Obama a concession maker who mishandled national and international affairs, leading to the decline of prosperity and American dominance. Partly in response to critics of presidential vigor, Obama increasingly showed himself to be interested in the big data tools of state power and digital protectionism. Reversing himself on other campaign promises, like the closure of the detention base at Guantanamo Bay, Obama increasingly told Americans, "You can't have one hundred percent security and also have one hundred percent privacy and zero inconvenience." Warning Americans that civil liberties would be foreshortened, he said, "We're going to have to make some choices as a society."[3] Obama never donned the gear nor subscribed to the anecdotes of the Hollywood cowboy in the ways of his predecessors Reagan and Bush. But at least one of his cowboy acts—since 1938 an intransitive colloquial verb meaning "to drive a vehicle in a reckless manner," and, by 1972, a noun used in the financial arena that was synonymous with unscrupulousness—merits investigation.[4] One journalist claimed that "Obama's great achievement—or great sin—was to make the national security state permanent."[5]

The Homeland Security Department, which oversees 22 government agencies, the 17 intelligence-collection agencies, and the US military, all with access to private communication company databases, constitute the state security apparatus, which officially cost almost $1.3 trillion in 2020.[6] Between 2008 and 2016, Obama made the HS bureau and the surveillance method a permanent part of government. He was attracted to and had benefited from big data collection, and silencing journalists with lawsuits for data breaches domestically and destroying enemy combatants abroad using unmanned aerial vehicles were his preferred means of exercising state power, means that enhanced presidential impunity. Obama's instincts about the misuses of authority, partisan loyalty, the legacy of mass movements and democracy, and the right to privacy had actually been on display during the Jeremiah Wright campaign crisis (see chapter 7). The sound bits reproduced by the right-wing media networks had little substance and were archival, Obama knew that Wright had little power to hurt him, and Wright had some incentive to serve as a martyr on Obama's behalf. But as Obama escalated his disavowal of Wright to a denunciation, he revealed future components of his strategic political thinking that might guide state militancy: "But when he [Jeremiah Wright] states and then amplifies such ridiculous propositions as the U.S. government somehow being involved in AIDS, when he suggests that Minister Farrakhan somehow represents one of the greatest voices of the twentieth and twenty-first century, when he equates the United States' wartime efforts with terrorism, then there are no excuses. They offend me. They rightly offend all Americans. And they should be denounced, and that's what I'm doing very clearly and unequivocally here today."[7]

Although Obama avowed as his main foe "perverse and hateful" and "radical" Islam, his condemnation of "ridiculous propositions" and his willingness to speak metonymically for "all" the American people were better signals of the direction of future policies. It was obvious to Obama that he needed to make an example of easy targets that would whet the appetites of his detractors, that he needed scapegoats, in fact, who might absorb the residual racism threatening his own position. He was exhibiting an ability to adopt a political philosophy coherent with the sweeping Bush Doctrine, a promulgated creed of preemptive lethal action on the part of the state: "[The United States would] not hesitate to act alone, if necessary, to exercise our right of self-defense by acting preemptively. . . . We must be prepared to stop rogue states and their terrorist clients before they are able to threaten or use weapons of mass destruction against the United States and our allies and friends. . . . The greater the threat, the greater the risk of inaction—and the more compelling the case for taking anticipatory action to defend ourselves."[8]

The necessity of violent intervention is based on the preservation of the US state, but Bush nonetheless rationalized the violence as a harbinger of democracy. Bush, in the eyes of analyst Philip Bobbitt, articulated only a tactic, not a doctrine, and in the process "vitiated the legal and strategic strengths of both democracy promotion and counterproliferation, and invited a charge of empire seeking."[9]

Obama was rarely accused of empire seeking, but his instinct to sacrifice Blacks who publicly questioned the narrative of American nation-state "goodness," whether Jeremiah Wright, Louis Farrakhan, or Cornel West, was an outspoken comment on his mild sense of ethnic obligation to the Black imaginary community and strong sense of geopolitical danger from overclose association. While he needed a good turnout of Black voters to win the election, Obama, handily in the months before the vote, partitioned himself off from the Black radical communities that construct themselves supranationally. Although Obama's stepfather had been Muslim, it was reflexive for him to deride Chicago religious leader Louis Farrakhan, head of the Nation of Islam, the Muslim sect founded by Elijah Muhammad and made famous by Malcolm X.

Obama, like many other nationally regarded Black people, understood easily that Black Americans who vigorously pursued diaspora and Islamist conjunctions were persona non grata in American establishment circles. He perceived that to become a viable national political force, it was necessary to disavow publicly prominent Black Americans who understood *Blackness* as a supranational term, distinct from "obtaining market access, equal citizenship, or integrating black people into a common national subjectivity."[10]

The Target List and the Bounty Kill

While the program of drone killing begun during the Bush presidency was initially aimed at Al Qaeda leadership, during the Obama presidency it became the program of choice to address troublesome adversaries, many of them members of organizations that had not existed in September 2001. Three state killings were especially important as the War on Terror began to shift its territory from the Gulf States and Mediterranean states and coincide with a new frontier in East Africa and the Arabian Peninsula: Osama bin Laden, the purported architect of the terrorist attacks on September 11, 2001; Anwar al-Awlaki, an American citizen, and his children; and Muammar Gaddafi, the president of Libya and 2002 founder and head of the African Union (the original organization was founded by Kwame Nkrumah and Julius Nyerere in 1963).

The use of deadly force is the central question raised by the western, and, following Slotkin's critique of the genre in *Gunfighter Nation*, because they are nearly direct interventions, we are required to habitually note the interaction between the films and their contemporary political analogues. *The Good, the Bad and the Ugly* is often credited with introducing a series of ethical concerns that were amoral and suggesting, as I have argued, that subjects are concerned more fundamentally with the aesthetics that define their politics and thus undergird the creation and enforcement of the law. But the genre privileges the demonstration of the unfairness of violence against the weak and more regularly justifies the use of deadly force in the defense of the powerless and innocent.

If "regeneration through violence" is a governing feature of the genre, *Django Unchained* adds a rider, an ethical axiom that is profound. In an ultra-violent testimony, more akin to a video game or a cartoon than to even Peckinpah's surreal level of onscreen violence, a central rule is to be observed. The possibility of volitional "Black-on-Black" violence is omitted, with two consequential exceptions (Django and Stephen; Django and D'Artagnan). In other words, the film has at its center a primary sentimentality, a purity, insisting that the parameters of deadly force in the antebellum world oscillated exclusively along the fault line of unethical white violence against Blacks and the fantastic dream world of retributive Black violence against whites.

The meager operation of Black violence is made considerably more plain in the film's second half when Calvin Candie articulates the central question at the cleavage between western and nonwestern understanding. At the film's penultimate dramatic moment, as Candie theatrically unravels the deceptive ruse, Candie explains to his guests that from his position as slave master, he has only a single question about Black submission to the regime of slavery. "Why don't they kill us?" he asks, as he details the kamikaze opportunities of individual Blacks to execute whites and overcome the private condition of enslavement by retributive violence and martyrdom.

The question of counterviolence by Blacks against whites has been raised twice before in this film. The opening chain-gang scene and the Tennessee plantation bounty hunter slayings are two occasions in which Tarantino deliberately shows armed Black people. Black fidelity to slaveholding families or to individual agents of the slave regime is a complicated point, but Booker T. Washington observed that, if they had been treated with decency, "the slaves would have laid down their lives" during the Civil War "to defend and protect the [white] women and children who were left on the plantations."[11] But the Blacks in the film are shown as less interested in killing or rather eradicating whites for indecency or brutality than in imitating whites and inhabiting their predesigns.

The film's exceptional Blacks—Django, Broomhilda, and Stephen—are not necessarily prone to resent or kill whites; rather, they are all marked by their extraordinary capacity to imitate the whites in the position of ownership power, a mimetic reproduction of themselves as internally indistinguishable from whites and completely consistent with their values and desires.[12] The uncomplicated endorsement of the imitations may explain the reason why Django, the natural killing machine, dispatches almost exclusively the lowest class of whites, generated as fodder in the plantation and western landscape, characters who are typically drawn without any backstory or onscreen lines to express themselves.

The audience is left to ponder the distinction among extrajudicial death, moral killing that is illegal, and completely immoral lethal force. Django, armed by King Schultz with his preferred weapon—the concealed, two-shot Derringer—murders Big John Brittle. (The film features three men killed in this fashion by the concealed weapon of the assassin.) He kills "Lil Raj" Brittle with a discarded pistol, after bull-whipping him into submission. Tarantino gives us blue-filter flashbacks of Django and Broomhilda running across an open field and being chased down, caught, whipped, and branded by the three Brittle brothers. With this history in place and with the two brothers in the act of roping to a tree and whipping another black woman, the audience is encouraged to understand their summary killing as justifiable. In the logic of the film, of course, the violence is almost entirely orchestrated by King Schultz, whose court "warrant" is the publicly exculpatory means that prevents them from being shot down. (Why the shrewd "Big Daddy" would allow the duo to remove the cadavers of the Brittle brothers from private land without negotiating a fee is yet another assertion of the economic wasteland of the South.)

But as liars and pretenders and violators of custom, the bounty hunters are marked for death by the plantation head, Big Daddy. In this second sequence, which King Schultz and Django have anticipated, Schultz allows Django the privilege of shooting the owner of the plantation. Tarantino has a slight problem here, and he reuses the flashback technique to fill in a nefarious backstory to help ease the path toward a satisfying act of onscreen murder aligning with the Manicheanism of the film. Countering the blued, blurred mysticism of Django's enslaved flashback, Tarantino's Big Daddy has a conversation recalled in a brightly lit, realist segment, where the audience learns that the owner of a plantation who looks fondly on the sale of "nigger gals" is actually the founder of a Ku Klux Klan–style hooded terrorist organization. He plans to whip Schultz to death and castrate Django in a states' rights, bourbon aristocratic show of force against the judicial overreach of the national federal government and its court system. The problem for Django and Schultz is one of surveillance and perception. Since all the men are hooded, how can they identify the ringleader? In addition, why must they determinedly kill the plantation head? Nor are they preemptively killing to ward off the genre's fate worse than death; only the audience is privy to the flashback.

In the violent sequence showing the heroes attacking the core symbol benefiting from the plantation, Schultz detonates an explosive, an analogy to the Predator drone's Hellfire missile descending on unsuspecting evildoers. As a hooded Big Daddy flees on a white horse from the spectacle, he is the lone person tracked by Schultz, holding a Sharp's carbine. In an onscreen example of a "just kill," Schultz then offers Django, unproven at long-range weaponry, a chance to try a shot. As Django sights the horseman, his hood comes off, verifying that he is indeed Big Daddy, and Django fires, instantly

Don Johnson in *Django Unchained*, dir. Quentin Tarantino (Weinstein Company / Lantern Entertainment, 2012).

splattering blood over the neck and mane of the galloping horse. Tarantino uses the anachronism about the Ku Klux Klan, formed immediately after the Civil War to suppress Black rights, as another gap calling out to the allegory. Nathan Bedford Forrest founded the Ku Klux Klan immediately after the Civil War, and Tarantino relies on a kind of "Blue State" sentimental abhorrence toward the terrorist group to offset the plot problem.

Django and Schultz have no way of positively identifying the masked men to justify their shooting. The viewer finds that Django shoots Big Daddy effortlessly, and Schultz tells him approvingly that he is a "natural." (I am completely bracketing the Tarantino paternalist association of Black men as "super-predators" prone to violence.) But the "natural" part of the killing is that both men are capable of effortlessly identifying a fully masked man they have met on a single occasion. In this way, the anachronistic gap of the Klan sequence compels the allegorical tie to the work of the Obama administration, which had "approved the killing of twice as many suspected terrorists as have ever been imprisoned at Guantanamo Bay."[13] The duo of master and slave have exchanged places with the surveillance satellites and the military "Predator" drones, capable of tracking without being seen, determining guilt, and administering deadly justice.

The appearance in the narrative of nature as the provider of the exception, in this case the exceptional skill with lethal technology, works, of course, as the neoliberal comfort with a fixed social hierarchy and a compressed middle class and large working poor.[14] On the side of the social environment as the predictive factor of behavior, Django seems a man to have endured more than three decades of enslavement before stumbling onto his "natural" gifts, clandestine surveillance and lethal firearms expertise. A European militarist, really a kind of Prussian Junker (and in the genre of the western requiring us to make a connection to Peckinpah's foil, German general Mohr from *The Wild Bunch*) is presented as the lever enabling Django's self-realization. The conflating points bring to the fore the possibility of militarism and authoritarianism, King Schultz's overmeticulous overtures to judicial practices notwithstanding. In Peckinpah's meditation on the dilemma of violence as the means to overthrow tyranny, because violent acts reproduce violence-traumatized people who speak only the language of violence, exactly reproduced in the wars of Afghanistan and Iraq, it is not the killing of the federale General Mapache that brings on the war of extermination but the unplanned and more casual shooting of the German officer. In *Django Unchained*, King Schultz's death by Candie's bodyguard, Butch, precipitates the first onscreen orgy of violent bloodshed.

The film reproduces unproblematically the execution of men condemned by the legal apparatus and, finally, in Tarantino's recourse to a sharply polarized ethical system dividing good and evil, anyone connected to profit or comfort from the slave regime itself. Django and Schulz's work as bounty hunters is in a sense simplified by the western tropes that seem to imply their transit through the uncolonized territories of Colorado or Montana; here, the bounties that Schultz and his ward, who sits at his feet during the film, collect are always exclusively of white men. In 1858, however, in the United States the most regular and advertised bounties were of typically unarmed Black men and women. Obviously, this is another irruptive space that the film silences but a tension that rides along the purportedly "legal" and remunerative killings. In 1859 there are hundreds or thousands of sometime bounty hunters, but they are not in the western mythscape; they are the enforcers of the plantation slave regime, and they order the southern town.

Django Unchained thus operates both to erase the reality of its plot as it substitutes unusual actors, as Obama signaled liberal antiracist ideals while effecting antiliberal policies. Only a single scene in the film deliberately considers King Schultz's tactic to kill instead of turning over to the court the targeted men. He convinces Django, from a concealed position hundreds of yards distant, to shoot an unarmed sodbuster innocently plowing a field, accompanied by his young son. The audience views a humble yeoman farmer sentenced to die. Django hesitates, conflicted not by the tactic of remote, un-

Jamie Foxx and Christoph Waltz in *Django Unchained*, dir. Quentin Tarantino (Weinstein Company / Lantern Entertainment, 2012).

suspecting execution, a condemnation of the wanted gang leader Smitty Bacall, for whom Django has no personal evidence of wrongdoing, but because the shooting will take place in front of the child, a witness who must view the act as simple, lawless murder. Echoing *The Outlaw Josey Wales*, Tarantino includes the child's desperate, "Paw? Paw?" after Bacall falls into the sod, slain from a distance great enough to seem heavenly. The child's cry is contextually comic because the Manicheanism introduced channels sympathy toward a single shooting victim in the film, King Schultz. The lack of meaning connected to the cry also begs the question of the level of resistance or threat that might require Django to shoot the boy. Nonetheless, the combination of Schultz's deadly authority through the accusatory handbill and his having stirred Django's resentment of whites ("Kill white folks and get paid for it, What's not to like?") absolutely justifies the death from on high.

While Schultz works from a death list vetted by a Texas judge, and produces court-ordered writs of capture or execution on some occasions, during the Bacall shooting he works only from a wanted poster. To mark his initiation into the band of remote executioners, Django, who can now read well enough to sound out the simple evidence for death from the poster, receives a ceremonial parchment. After the shooting, King Schultz offers as a present to Django the completely banal poster, indeed as banal as Schultz's rationalizations have been for the killings without trial. But this is precisely the "political unconscious" of the film that the audience accepts as indubitable: *Django Unchained* inscribes the validity of reliable mercenary killing of remote, appropriately stigmatized targets. In effect, Django, by killing strangers whose felonies injure a state that does not recognize him as a citizen, operates as a mercenary, satisfied by money and racial feud. The state that he supports with lethal force has outsourced its capital punishment contracts to private companies who conduct legally plausible state business tangential to but not synonymous with ethical justice, and always for private accumulative gain. At first Django is made uncomfortable by the relation, but, as he goes on to comport himself as a "Black slaver" in keeping with the ruse to "rescue" his spouse by vaulting her into the world of the sanctity of the legal contract, he becomes inseparable from his category, habitually condemning other Black people to death in order to secure his desires.

Django's first bounty "kill," accomplished at a distance on the basis of a mass-produced circular, exactly like the bills used to pursue runaways like himself from the slave regime, and the gap occasioned by the debate that is necessary to compel his application of lethal technology, allegorically signal our return to the Obama presidency. It has been noted that the sniping of the unsuspecting victim, whose crime has been alleged but not proven, also simulates the specter of activity around drone killings.[15] The pivotal shooting of Bacall symbolically joins Django's project to King Schultz's. But the film's conclusion deliberately collapses Django with the other white lead, his putative nemesis, plantation owner Calvin Candie. Significantly, Django does not kill Candie; he does, however, appropriate Candie's clothes, his style, his affect, his claim as sovereign, and his righteous use of violence.

Killing Geronimo, Killing Hope

Of the countries that have authorized American Unmanned Aerial Vehicles, several are notorious for severe autocratic rule, collaboration with Islamic militants and terrorists, and corruption: Afghanistan, Djibouti, Ethiopia, Kuwait, Niger, the Philippines, Qatar, Seychelles, United Arab Emirates, Yemen, and Saudi Arabia. US drones operating in the Arabian Peninsula are based in Saudi Arabia, an infamous authoritarian monarchy that in 2018 murdered and dismembered at its Turkish embassy an American-based journalist, Saudi Arabian Jamal Khashoggi. The drones operating in zones of hostility are under the control of the Department of Defense, and their actions are reported in Pentagon briefings. US drones on patrol where war has not been declared, in Yemen and Somalia, for example, are run by the Central Intelligence Agency, and their activities remain secret. But the Rubicon for drone use was whether a United States citizen was an appropriate mark for targeted killing or if constitutional protections required due process. As early as 1971, the contentious issue of the rise of technology, data collection, and surveillance had been presented to Department of Justice assistant attorney general and Nixon appointee William H. Rehnquist. Senators of a Judiciary subcommittee asked Rehnquist "whether the constitutional rights of individuals were violated by Government surveillance in cases where there was not probable cause to believe that a particular individual had committed a crime."[16] Rehnquist testified that there probably was "collection of information" in excess of "statutory or constitutional" provision, as well as "unauthorized dissemination" of citizens' data. But, in the years immediately prior to Watergate and the broad censure of the intelligence community by the Frank Church committee, Rehnquist dismissed any wide "violation of any particular individual's constitutional rights." He was confirmed to the US Supreme Court a year later, where he cast the deciding vote in the *Laird v. Tatum* case, which found nothing wrong with domestic US Army surveillance of American citizens. Rehnquist became Chief Justice of the Supreme Court in 1986.

In June 2010 an attorney named David J. Barron at the Department of Justice created a memorandum called "Applicability of Federal Criminal Laws and the Constitution to Contemplated Lethal Operations against Shaykh Anwar al-Aulaqi." Barron's "kill-list memo," as it came to be called, included citations from a civil rights decision, *Shuttlesworth v. City of Birmingham* (1963), and compared the work of CIA officers to the Alabama minister Fred Shuttlesworth, who had defended students attempting to integrate lunch counters in 1962.[17] Like William Rehnquist's testimony to the Senate Committee in 1971 denying constitutional violation by military intelligence agencies, the DOJ memo denied Awlaki's Fourth Amendment right of safety of his person and Fifth Amendment right of due process "in time of war or public danger," which would have permitted him his day in court and revealed, perhaps, the state's evidence against him. A federal court noted some concerns about "the risk of erroneous deprivation of a citizen's liberty," but both the *Hamid* court and the Department of Justice used a similar noun to articulate their ultimate support. For the court, the Justice Department "need not blink at those realities" of due process, and for the operational authorities, the "'realities of combat'" "would not require the government to provide further process to the U.S. person."[18] In a sense, the recourse to realism and the obvious validity of evidence was the government's assurance to its citizens of their most basic right.

While the "reality" of Yemen, a designated hostile zone, authorized government planners to freely kill a citizen, the DOJ memo cited the American *Garner* law enforcement case to rationalize deadly force without a warrant because the case had successfully asserted that "the officer has probable cause to believe that the suspect poses a threat" and "the importance of the governmental interests . . . justify the intrusion."[19] This rationale makes it difficult to conceive of territories where missile-firing drones might not be applicable for use, like the US-Mexico border or other areas perceived as "troublesome." As if in anticipation, in Baltimore, Maryland, an airplane, donated by security philanthropists to the police department after the protests and street unrest in 2015, flew overhead, photographing the city with multiple cameras, until a lawsuit ended the flight in 2021.

The 2010 memo (released to the public in 2014) had strong proscriptive capacities. If the state could confidently execute citizens without a public adjudication process, the most fundamental curtailment of a democratic right, then the state brooked no opposition to its efforts to monopolize data, both by harvesting the private information of the citizen and controlling the information made available. The secretly vetted data was the information that might prove innocence or guilt. The three dimensions of the Bill of Rights—freedom of speech in the First Amendment, exemption from warrantless search and seizure in the Fourth Amendment, and the due process of the Fifth Amendment—were subsequently inveighed. Once the logic of the memo was in place, the most dramatic "just kill" of the post-9/11 period occurred in 2011. President Obama delivered "Geronimo," the code name used by White House and Department of Defense planners for the operation against and the person of Osama bin Laden.[20]

The Black president Obama, with the identifiably "Muslim" middle name of Hussein, oddly resembled as similar a group of conflated symbols as Tarantino's Black character Django. Initially, Obama secured himself to the same American exceptionalist narratives that had operated under the presidential administration of his predecessor, George W. Bush.[21] With his stunning Iraq fiasco, Bush had returned to the unilateralist foreign policy of the early Vietnam era. If Obama did not make the claim for state exceptionalism as plainly as Bush, he was more comfortable in the exceptionalism of his own position as a mixed-race American chief executive. His Pacific Ocean childhood and white household roots granted him an almost Orientalist sense of fundamental allegiances with Western allies in opposition to Asia and Africa, as indicated by his expanding the targeted kill list. Obama would not preen the cowboy like Bush, but the statecraft choices he made have revealed him in some fashion excelling the violent authority of his predecessors. In the film *Django Unchained*, Django's decision to kill Bacall in the presence of his family (who, presumably, must be confronted offscreen and pacified so that the corpse can be removed and exchanged for the bounty) reminds the viewer of precise analogues from 2010 and 2011. In those years, very high-profile US drone killings were authorized against people living where the continental precision between Asia and Africa is obscure: the militant cleric Awlaki, the editor Samir Khan, and later Awlaki's son.

The projected limits of contemporary civic life found their measure in the triangle of surveillance, intelligence gathering, and the publication of the news of state sanctioned acts, so many of the interlocking features germane to Tarantino's black character Django. Late one Sunday evening, the president went before the American public, claiming that "after a firefight," American soldiers "killed Osama bin Laden and took custody of his body."[22] A "senior Pentagon official" added that following "prepared religious remarks, which were translated into Arabic by a native speaker," Bin Laden's body was buried at sea.[23] The next day the English-language international press reported that Bin Laden "was killed along with a son and two other men who fought during the raid, ending any hope of arrest and prosecution. A woman used as a human shield during the raid was also killed."[24] Although the co-leader of the terrorist group Al Qaeda, Ayman al-Zawahiri, remained at large, the chief executive declared an important milestone in the efficacy of intelligence gathering and the necessary application of deadly force.

The early reports, it turns out, were patent falsehoods, held together by American media tropes traditionally used to convey violent acts perpetrated by the state: (1) Bin Laden refused to be taken alive and insisted upon his own death; and (2) he was a coward, incapable of maintaining the ethical conduct of civilized Western man and his codes of patriarchal responsibility. The immediate, salacious use of these tropes tether the presidency of Bush, the evangelical Christian avenger, to the putatively ultraliberal presidency of Obama and onward to the openly reactionary and lethal presidency of Donald Trump. Almost without peer in the annals of television-era US statecraft, the forty-fifth US president would revel publicly in describing the deadly state-sanctioned violence that was used against a "whimpering and crying and screaming" Abu Bakr al-Baghdadi. "He died in a vicious and violent way, as a coward, running and crying. . . . He died like a dog."[25]

Obama showed his exceptional traits by securing the middle of this cowboy executive brigade. His measures had been more subdued than the gleeful overpromising of Bush or the later evident bloodthirst of Trump. But the miracle of the righteous targeted killing of the malevolent began to look less sacrosanct within hours of his press conference. A day after his initial announcement, modifications occurred to the story of the manly battle with "Geronimo." "The SEAL team stormed into the compound—the raid awakened the group inside, one American intelligence official said—and a firefight broke out. One man held an unidentified woman living there as a shield while firing at the Americans. Both were killed. Two more men died as well, and two women were wounded. American authorities later determined that one of the slain men was Bin Laden's son, Hamza, and the other two were the courier and his brother."[26] The news claimed now that identity of Bin Laden's corpse was certified after "one of Bin Laden's wives identified his body" and a picture taken by a commando "processed through facial recognition software suggested a 95 percent certainty." But National Security Advisor John Brennan—considered by Obama insider David Axelrod to be "like a John Wayne character"[27]—and who had insisted that the soldiers were prepared to take Bin Laden alive, now specified that Bin Laden was shot above his left eye at the end of a forty-minute gunfight. Brennan also admitted the possibility of nonviolence on Bin Laden's part: "Whether or not he got off any rounds, I frankly don't know."[28]

The *New York Times* corrected the gunfight narratives on May 4, 2011, in its front-page story "New US Account in Bin Laden Raid: He Was Unarmed." Reporters accorded the "discrepancies" in the Obama administration's "dramatic story about a successful operation" to "their haste to provide details . . . to an intensely interested public."[29] By May 5, the entire account was revised yet again: "After the SEAL members shot and killed Mr. Kuwaiti and a woman in the guesthouse, the Americans were never fired upon again. . . . When the commandos reached the top floor, they entered a room and saw Osama bin Laden with an AK-47 and a Makarov pistol in arm's reach. They shot and killed him, as well as wounding a woman with him."[30] The operation to seize the globe's most wanted man was beginning to seem more like targeted killing and outright murder of the defenseless, guilty by association.

Finally, the same press reporter who had revealed the military coverup of the My Lai massacre in Vietnam, news coverage that helped garner public opinion against the war, and who also exposed the systematic torture at America's Abu Ghraib prison camp in Iraq, proposed what became a plausibly compelling contrarian narrative. American publishers refused to print his account. According to Seymour Hersh, Bin Laden surrendered but was simply executed.[31] Identified by DNA weeks earlier, gunless Bin Laden was thought to have been shot by American snipers in front of his wife, his corpse ripped by bullets so many times as to have prevented his recognition or even the physical integrity of a cadaver. What's more, the number-one enemy of the Western world appeared not to have been hiding at all but to have been living "on the reservation" (like the Apache rebel who fought against western expansion that was the origin of the code name) in the custody of the Pakistani government.

The question became, then, why was he killed? If seventy-nine American soldiers represented an overwhelming military presence, why was it necessary to use deadly force? Rather than a trial revealing publicly a preponderance of state evidence and the arguments from the defense explaining Bin Laden's American training, rationale for the attacks, and the global collaborators involved, the press reported mainly that pornography had been located on dozens of computer storage drives. In 2013, *Esquire* reported that duffle bags of opium had been found. Pornography and drugs had turned up at the site of earlier state foes, as in the 1980s at Manuel Noriega's, the deposed Panamanian state chief.[32] No other bodies or evidence from a "firefight" were ever produced, a lacuna similar to the missing evidence of weapons of mass destruction that had been claimed to justify the 2003 invasion of Iraq.

Zero Dark Thirty (2012), a film depicting the assassination, was soon made with cooperation from the CIA and DOD.[33] The film controversially suggested that Bin Laden's whereabouts were unveiled by torturing detainees. However, an assassination team of nearly eighty heavily armed men shooting a surrendering elderly man whose trial was thought to have been crucial to the unraveling of an international conspiracy, and apparently also shooting unarmed housewives, and then justifying itself as honorable and ethical, does not have a cinematic analogue. Where was the "dramatic story" that the White House could deliver for the "intensely interested public"? The standard tropes of forced captivity, exploitation of the weak, and futile kamikaze resistance were incredibly more resonant orientation points than the reality of overwhelming violence, assassination, dismemberment, and the renunciation of evidence, trial, and judgment before punishment. A series of false statements from Obama undergirded a broader revelation about the conflict after his presidency had ended. By 2019, the *Washington Post* reported that "senior U.S. officials failed to tell the truth about the war in Afghanistan throughout the eighteen-year campaign, making rosy pronouncements they knew to be false and hiding unmistakable evidence the war had become unwinnable."[34]

Black exceptionalism directing the western epic had enabled the mimetic reproduction of the state failures of the past.

Despite the existence of considerable reasonable speculation that multiple states had known the whereabouts of Bin Laden, coincident with the evidence that the US military showed a curious failure of coordination and resolve during the 2001 attack of Tora Bora, where Bin Laden was believed to have found refuge, the decision to use deadly force in the charade (King Schultz's word to describe the visit to Candieland) of his apprehension was uncontroversial and brought Obama uniform praise. Bin Laden appeared to have released tapes and videos in which he relished the 2001 destruction and mass murders in the United States. With the willingness to use deadly forces against US citizens who had not been convicted of crimes and a keen sense of the narrative theater necessary to mollify a public curious about the figure most associated with the consumption of government resources and the direction of national priorities for more than a decade, Obama felt emboldened to look further down range for additional bounties. The assassination of Bin Laden took place during what was widely recognized as the "Arab Spring," a term used to describe antiautocracy protests in western Asia and northern Africa in 2010 and 2011, that resulted in the abdication of Egypt's president Hosni Mubarak and jeopardized the reign of long-standing seigneurial regimes, excluding Saudi Arabia. The decision to kill Bin Laden instead of bringing him to trial signaled the heavy support for retributory killings across a spectrum of geographic entities and tested the edge of state-sponsored assassination, as both retribution and prophylaxis.

With the resumption of the ideology in place that could sanction and justify preemptive violence, the ideal of prodemocracy, Western-friendly states open to private property, geologic resource exploration, economic relations, and Western humanistic regulatory governance became plausible mandates for "regime change." The conditions for preemptive violence, now in the 2010s, differed from what had been proposed for Saddam Hussein's Iraq (weapons of mass destruction), Manuel Noriega's Panama (narcotics trafficking and firing on US troops), or Coard's post-Bishop Granada (threatening US medical students). Having now fully outstripped the "loss of Vietnam" mentality surrounding the war that could not be celebrated, the US-led or weapons-sourced collectives of "Western" military states became capable of "gun-for-hire" operations. The extraordinary example here is the overthrow and killing of Libyan president Muammar Gaddafi, a professed Afro-Arab and the unusual head of a so-called "Arab" nation who emphasized his country's ties to the African continent. The participation of Obama as the rationalizing Django, the natural maestro of the law and the explanatory podium who had taken his country with little pushback into new terrain of monitoring and lethal resolve, was crucial now. A Black head of state in the Euro-American posse made the violence color-blind; it would be impossible to gain media traction describing the attack as racist. On the surface, such identity politics seem too puerile for efficacy. And yet, Tarantino's screenplay gems, like the reference to Dumas's race, were the raw ingredients of his Academy Award for Best Screenplay.

The African Gaddafi was killed in October 2011, after nine months of civil war. Rebel militias in eastern Libya were aided militarily by the NATO countries Italy, France, the United Kingdom, Canada, and the United States. In a televised address in which he drew comparison to American military action in Fallujah, Iraq, and Waco, Texas, Gaddafi vowed to end the rebellion in Benghazi, which he also declared to be conducted by Al Qaeda. The television address and its inflammatory rhetoric were used as evidence of imminent war crimes, and western governments decided that he must be punished in advance. In February 2011 a United Nations Security Council resolution passed, "condemning the violence and use of force against civilians" and "rejecting unequivocally the incitement to hostility and violence against the civilian population."[35] As the Libyan army fought protestors and armed rebels, three weeks later the UN Security Council authorized a "No-Fly Zone" (apparently spanning the totality of the coastal cities and shipping lanes), a diplomatic term for aerial military operations that typically degrade a standing military, beginning by attacks on its air force, air defenses, and communications.

The UN had approved force—"all necessary measures"—in order to "protect civilians and civilian populated areas under threat of attack." President Obama decided to interpret the mandate as authorizing military activities— "we would need to bomb his forces attacking people," he told Britain and France—and preemptively extending the attacks to Libyan military forces themselves. In April, reminiscent of George W. Bush's proclamation to Saddam Hussein in 2003, Obama signed a letter with Nicolas Sarkozy, president of France, and David Cameron, prime minister of the United Kingdom, writing that "it is impossible to imagine a future for Libya with Gaddafi in power." The NATO alliance then bombed the entire country, especially the strongholds of government loyalists, enfilading Gaddafi's compounds with missiles in Tripoli and leveling his birthplace, Sirte, killing members of his family and entourage. Once the Libyan military was limited to the ground, the rebellion, aided materially by Italy, France, and the UK, picked up speed. The rebel militias considered themselves ethnically Arab and were accused of genocidal murder against immigrants from West Africa and people who looked like them in Tawergha, Libya.[36]

In October, Gaddafi was in Sirte when his convoy was struck by missiles. Captured alive, he appears in a video that was later released of his final minutes. While Gaddafi is typically described as being killed by angry Libyan resistance fighters, there are also accounts of his murder by French agents who had been directing a US drone strike, coordinated by intercepting Gaddafi's telephone number.[37] At the time of the Libyan leader's death, the country had roughly 105 tons of gold reserves valued at $6 billion, the most in Africa, and had proven oil reserves of forty billion barrels, the most in the world. A year after Gaddafi's death, the US ambassador to Libya, Christopher Stevens, and members of his security team were killed in a Benghazi villa, typically described as a "consulate" in the American press. According to Horace Campbell, Stevens died "caught in the midst of the COIN [counterinsurgency] strategy of switching sides to engage the jihadists of the east," a series of negotiations and reorientations involving the American CIA and oil company interests far away from the embassy in Tripoli.[38]

After French president Sarkozy lost the election in 2012, he was indicted and accused of taking more than €40 million from Gaddafi for his election campaign in 2007. In 2016 the British Parliament revisited the decision to join forces with France and the US in the attacks, determining that "UK strategy was founded on erroneous assumptions and an incomplete understanding of the evidence," including taking Gaddafi's bellicose rhetoric "at face value."[39] If the French president actually wished to eliminate a rival whom he had fleeced, and if the British government eventually did wash its hands of the affair, what exactly did the Americans gain? Obama's willingness to reconnoiter, target, and condemn an African head of state made him legible as a gun for hire on the international stage. He was a reelectable cowboy in the drama of imperial resource extraction in the multinational neoliberal age. The willingness to kill gruesomely and even unseat a sovereign theatricalized across the globe his willingness to cut a notch on his pistol. Nevertheless, the trophies would win him no merit with Hollywood cowboy Clint Eastwood, who would lecture the Republican convention a year later. Among the things Eastwood ridiculed Obama for before the GOP audience was his support of the war in Afghanistan.[40]

Obama's turn from the maestro of domestic hope and change to the collector of international bounties of Arabs and Africans in the year leading to his reelection campaign resembles the arc of Django from barefoot on slave coffle to the gunfighter in the Calvin Candie suit. The Tarantino film's conclusion of the rivalry between two exceptional enslaved men is instructive. As a proponent of Afro-Arab identity and unity, Gaddafi was an exceptional head of state. Unlike several of his Mediterranean neighbors, Gaddafi cultivated ties with Africa south of the Sahara, and he served in 2010 as head of the African Union. The American press accused him of importing "mercenaries from African countries" to uphold his regime.[41] Gaddafi was also the globe's loudest proponent of the geopolitical configuration the United States of Africa, or federal continent system, featuring a unifying continental African passport, currency, and military. Gaddafi also professed a pan-African view[42] and remained wary of temporal closures like "postracial" and "postcolonial," insisting up to his end that African people "must watch out for colonial forces, which spy on us and aim to steal our riches."[43] Mainstream media found the NATO invasion tenable partly as a result of Gaddafi's ethnic infidelity. "His relations with his Arab neighbors are unstable," reported the American press; "his rambling rants at Arab League meetings have long ruffled counterparts, Saudi Arabia among them."[44] Long-range kills legitimized by fiat manifestoes from secret courts and satellite telephone data leading to recorded disembowelment are the currency for the donor class bidding on political cowboys they can trust.

Following Gaddafi's death, Libya would endure the devastation of a nearly ten-year civil war, won or brokered eventually by an army backed by Russian mercenaries working for the Wagner company and Egypt. Al Qaeda in the part of northwest Africa called the Maghreb (the name is Arabic for "western") has taken control of the trading routes and many of the cities in countries immediately south of Libya, like Mali, Niger, and Burkina Faso.

Despite its willingness to embrace strong-arm tactics to unseat recalcitrant politicians who saw themselves as Blacks in Africa, the Obama presidency was repudiated with a strong and violent counterreaction by the Right, leading to the election in 2016 of Donald Trump. A proud white nationalist, Trump was a fervid opponent to nonwhite immigration, a labeler of Africa generally as a land of "shithole countries," and economic protectionist. Fascinatingly, the emergence of more palpable white bigotry set in motion an unforeseeable rejection of racist symbolic iconography. In August 2017, a band of white supremacist marchers rallying in Charlottesville, Virginia, in favor of Confederate statues clashed with demonstrators, and the violence resulted in the death of a peaceful female protestor. Trump blamed "many sides" and refused to condemn neo-Nazis and white militias.[45] The national response to the mounting racial conflict produced the immediate removal of Confederate monuments on city ground in Baltimore; indeed, the climate of national animus had been strenuous earlier in the year and had contributed to monument removal in New Orleans.[46] In June 2020, after the videotaped public killings of several Black men in police custody, dozens of monuments were removed nationwide and, under pressure from Black athletes and officers from amateur and professional athletic organizations, the state of Mississippi removed the Confederate battle flag from its state flag (as South Carolina had done after the murder of nine Black churchgoers, including a state-elected official, by a white supremacist in 2015).[47]

In a manner that had not occurred since the most tumultuous moments of the 1950s and 1960s, Americans (and citizens of other countries across the globe) reflected on the public meaning of slavery, the politics behind the commemoration of the Civil War and imperial heroes, and the legacy of racial discrimination.[48] Typically, however, these requiems often masked political agendas to smear Trump as a racist in order to garner support for a Democratic presidential candidate whose congressional record of appeasement to white supremacy had already garnered him the moniker of "champion of yesterday's sordid compromises."[49]

The pan-Islamist circulation of anti-Western ideology had outstripped the racist confines of the Arab North and the Black center. The work of Black exceptionalism in power flavored by the cowboy cadence of the westerns had achieved a sad but probably predictable goal. Pierre Lapoque, district head of the United Nations Office of Drug Control, metaphorically described the situation around Gao, an ancient city and corridor from the West African South to Libya, where it is now estimated that thirty-five tons of cocaine transit through: "Northern Mali is the Wild West."[50] American foreign policy—as well as American entertainment—had introduced those western film tropes in the Middle East and Islamic Africa. As my shell-shocked friend at the edge of the what had recently been the rebel zone in Côte d'Ivoire had said, "*Clint Eastwood, c'est mon père.*"

Conclusion

The Return of the Native

Taya. Did you always want to be a soldier?
Chris. I wanted to be a cowboy and I did that and thought I was meant for something more.
. . .
Soldier. Welcome to Fallujah, the new Wild West of the old Middle East.
—*American Sniper*

The first two decades of the new millennium have seen a revival of the western film genre in popular culture on a scale that would have been difficult for Ang Lee or Clint Eastwood to envision during the 1990s. As of this writing, according to the Internet Movie Database, the internet's most definitive film catalog, there are 610 western film projects in some phase of studio production; approximately 550 films were released between 2011 and 2020; fewer than half that number (239) were produced in the decade prior, 2000–2010; and between 1990 and 2001, when the genre-reviving films *Dances with Wolves* (1990) and *Unforgiven* (1992) were made, an even smaller number (24) were produced. Under the cinematic genre "western," IMDb catalogs 8,562 total films.

It is impossible to avoid the conclusion that the steady prominence of the genre is owed to the multiple unprecedented events that have reshaped the contours of day-to-day life in the United States in the twenty-first century. The paramount reason for the resurgence is the substitution of the 1946–89 Cold War with the 2001–present War on Terror. The western film genre is the traditional American mass-culture heuristic available to explain ideological conflict, and the exhausting public climate demands new modes to rehearse and debate desirable ethical conduct.

The key difference between the Cold War and the War on Terror is that while the latter operates and transforms the national economy into a structure absorbing an unending series of low-grade conflicts and military interventions, it is publicly legible to Americans as episodic civilian killings, sometimes deaths of thousands of people, sometimes televised live. The Cold War afforded the possibility of deadly violence in remote Asian theaters of war, like Korea and Vietnam, but the lethality extended to the public was typically confined to the virtual threat of mass death from atomic and nuclear weapons technology. Distinguishable as a murderous ideological campaign, the War on Terror—specifically connected in the minds of its Islamicist ideologues to the adventurism of Western nation-states that began more or less in concert with the demise of the Soviet Union[1]—produces killing spectacles designed precisely for maximum distribution and reviewing on networks, cable, and internet feeds. The September 11, 2001, mass killing is an epitome of the project. (The impact of the militant Islamic groups opposing Western hegemony has been telling. White supremacist militants have moved to the tactic of live-feed public massacre via real-time circulation of the carnage on the internet.) Connected to the militarization of day-to-day life, from airport security to police officers in schools, are the series of economic market panics and outright financial system collapses in 2000, 2001, 2008, and 2020 that have powerfully rearranged the postwar Keynesian framework of regulatory government intervention into consumer society.[2]

The economic depressions, perpetually resolved by government-deficit spending and lending to the largest corporations and private banks, sharpen the basic contradictions of American exceptionalism and globalization, offering rewards for a smaller and smaller group. The economic system of the nation-state seems only to honor merit and competitiveness at its lowest levels, and the values of high achievement and excellence among the middle classes prove unable to rebalance the vast accumulation and expropriation model exercised by the top tier. The most successful nation-state models are now scaling downward and resemble the city-states that dominated the earliest periods of global capitalism.

Where is the next frontier bonanza? How should American citizens understand their difference and historic specificity? Does the ideal of exceptionalism, a providential writ for a chosen people in a chosen land, remove Americans from obligations to history, from conundrums like the genocide of the Indigenous populations; the depopulation, land acquisition, and repopulation of a continent; the history of slavery; the problem of the climatological degradation of the planet? Is the frontier now definitively closed, the "perennial rebirth" for bonanza capitalism fully at an end?[3] The promise of the stunning affluence of new markets and cheap labor from globalization seems confined to the elites. Where is value now in ordinary American life?

The western film shows every capacity to continue to mold popular attitudes in response to the unique conditions of the American nation, including the shifts to the market state, the contradictions of multiracial democracy, and conflicts over global hegemony. The genre has also become so essential and malleable that it overlaps and insinuates quite easily with its cousin, the war film, which for the United States in the era of ascendant militant nationalism takes on heavy responsibilities of both public history and ideological repair. Eastwood's 1986 film *Heartbreak Ridge*, a folksy tale of a romantically inept Marine gunnery sergeant, Thomas Highway, preparing his ethnically diverse troops for the fight that none could ever have imagined would ever take place—the invasion of the Caribbean island Grenada—presents the same commanding project of racial reconciliation observable in the Sylvester Stallone *Rocky* and *Rambo* franchises. The films suggest that the embrace of the interracial and interethnic composition of US society justifies militant intervention abroad by proving the moral fitness of the US.

Eastwood's work in the 1990s and the new millennium has become even more popular with audiences and influential in tracking the changes in national ideals. Nonetheless, these are not new achievements of the genre. During the classic era of the western, with the 1948 John Ford film *Fort Apache*, we see a range of liberalist concerns: sectional reconciliation after the Civil War, assimilation of immigrants and the ethnic outsider, the problem of reparation and equity in the treatment of oppressed minorities like Native Americans. Ford's most perceptive films, such as *Fort Apache* and *The Man Who Shot Liberty Valance* (1962), which centrally figure Native Americans, Latinos, and Blacks, are structurally concerned with mythmaking and contrast sharply with recognizably sourced history. Ford insisted in both films on an extradiegetic encounter with newspaper reporters and politicians to emphasize the genre's powerful role in "print[ing] the myth." Leone and the Italians, especially the screenwriter Solinas, inserted a more complicated racial and ethnic politics into the genre. Eastwood, without recourse to the external storytelling devices, has centered more and more on mythmaking in his films following the success of *The Outlaw Josey Wales*. If Eastwood isolated and confined Blacks and made a mythic equivalency with Natives, Ang Lee and Quentin Tarantino have more comfortably returned to the ethics of racial liberalism in ideology and in using the idiom of high modernism and postmodernism, respectively.

In more recent films like *Gran Torino* (2007) (whose protagonist, Walt Kowalski, reprises the Thomas Highway character from *Heartbreak Ridge*) and *American Sniper* (2014), Eastwood returns deliberately to the project of equivalence and exchange that marked his career at the turning point of *The Outlaw Josey Wales*. While *Gran Torino* superficially addresses the problems of deindustrialization, racism, and immigration, Eastwood's award-winning and commercially successful action-drama *American Sniper* opens with the ethical problem of the Bush Doctrine, the "anticipatory action to defend ourselves."

American Sniper

American Sniper's protagonist, Chris Kyle (Bradley Cooper), is a US sniper on a rooftop in a bombed-out town in Iraq, at some point in the 2000s, a chronologically amorphous moment that marks the beginning of digitally archived time, a place where "the present [exists] as an object of future memory."[4] Scanning rooftops, Kyle spots a man talking furtively into a cellphone while looking down at a US convoy of infantry and Abrams tanks. The next shot shows a woman leaving the house and handing an explosive to a child as both of them speed toward the soldiers. Kyle relays the objective information about the locals to his remote management team, including the observation that the explosive is "Russian-made," and his teammate contributes the hard cynicism of realpolitik. If Kyle misjudges the threat and shoots unarmed civilians, the military tribunals will convict him of unlawful killing and sentence him to prison.

In his effort to construct Chris Kyle as the apotheosis of the D. W. Griffith archangel of judgment, Eastwood here powerfully reverses Pontecorvo's *The Battle of Algiers*, where bombings against Arab or French civilians are imbricated so complexly as to disable a reflexive allegiance with either victim or perpetrator. In *American Sniper*, Eastwood works diligently to secure a residual malevolence within the pan-Arab Iraqi population, habitués of a badland where combatants, collaborators, spies, thieves, and extortionists always already occupy a desolate war zone. They are people who have failed to accede to the logic of the invaders, whose lethality is marked by fire raining from the sky. They have failed to evacuate to the refugee camps, and now they fail to collaborate eagerly with the occupying force.

As the child approaches the convoy with the bomb, a shot rings out, and we are transferred back to Kyle's Edenic childhood; he is on a hunt with his father and has killed his first buck. These scenes, too, occur in archived time, presumably the 1970s or very early 1980s, but resonate fully with both the earlier decade of the 1960s and the later decade of the 1990s. It is impossible to lodge the father and son interactions within any precise historical context that might govern their ideology: is it the 1968 riots era, Watergate era, Iran Hostage era, Iran-Contra/Panama era, or Monica Lewinsky era? After the successful, ritualized "first kill," Wayne Kyle adjudges his son "a natural" (and doubly emphasizing the paternalism of the same scene in Tarantino's *Django Unchained*). The celebratory moment ends abruptly as the father instructs the son to regard his rifle and not the slain animal as his sacred object. Like the ritualistic Arthurian moment firing at the fence post in *The Outlaw Josey Wales*, *American Sniper* is about *partus sequitur telum*, the descent through the weapon, and the mythic realm of American initiation of boyhood to manhood.

Josey Wales kills men in "peacetime," calling into question the distinction between peace and war. Chris Kyle's fictionalized actions recreate the agon of a real-life Arthurian hero, naturally synced with a technology of death, a Philoctetes whose bow is the component of victory and whose wound is his theology of patriotism. *American Sniper* contains a more outright allusion to *The Outlaw Josey Wales* when Kyle, stateside between tours of duty, runs into a man at a garage who tells him, as dying Jamie told Josey-as-savior, "You saved my life."

Attaching Christianity to the valence of the totemic weapon, the deer-slayer scene quickly shifts to a church service and sermon about Paul in the book of Acts and the process of judgment. Young Chris Kyle pockets a miniature Bible, which he lays on his chest of drawers alongside a football, a group of 1/32nd-scale American Vietnam-era soldiers, and a cigar box, inserting the rigorous prophet of Christianity into a tableau of sacred objects: the dream of war in miniature, the sport that simulates war, and the theology of the war of salvation. Downstairs, the family dines, recalling the week's event, when scrawny younger brother Jeff Kyle has been beaten on the schoolyard. A muscular, large, domineering father, Wayne Kyle preaches to his sons a mantra of biosocial determinism that renders the world into three categories: feckless sheep, predatorial wolves, and altruistic sheepdogs "blessed with the gift of aggression" who are "the rare breed that live to confront the wolf." Spliced in between the father's homily are scenes of children ringed around Jeff's schoolyard fight. A lone, small Black boy yells, "Punch him, punch him!" as a heavy boy pummels Jeff. By focusing on the Black child's vitriol, Eastwood reverses James Baldwin's famous point of Black people as "improbable aristocrats."[5] Rather, if the world is not one of "color-blind" racially exchangeable equivalency, the children who are isolated as minority sheep are simply prone to look to the abject force of the wolf as a guardian. Minority groups offer no particular ethical guidance.

The next shot shows young Chris Kyle battering the face of the boy who has beaten his brother. The violence of the fight is shocking, and the crowd of children shriek for a victim's blood without any ethical concern, a strong echo of Peckinpah's *Wild Bunch* and its rejection of childhood innocence. Wayne Kyle ends the meal and his role in the film by threatening his sons with a beating if they submit to the passivity of the sheep or the predation of the wolf. He concludes by asking his oldest son, Kyle, "Did you finish it?" The boy dutifully and obediently nods in assent, cementing the two logics of authority in place: biologically determined categories of existence and submission to patriarchy, God's law.

Eastwood carefully symbolizes the conjunction of the biologically determined laws into a cinematic archetype. He leaves the boy behind and reveals the fully formed adult Chris Kyle as a cowboy. From the rear the camera shoots an adult Chris Kyle, attired in jean suit, boots, and Stetson, having emerged through the open doors of a barn. The camera turns to his face, and the cattleman's straw hat halos actor Bradley Cooper in a pose of angelic righteousness. We learn that he is now a champion bronco circuit rider. His brother, Jeff, goes on to say, "We're cowboys, living the dream." After a bad breakup with a girlfriend who cuckolds him and then degrades him as "just a lousy ranch hand," Kyle watches shots of the aftermath of the 1998 bombings of US embassies in Africa and instantly decides to join the military. He chooses the elite Navy Sea Air Land "SEAL" unit, because despite its challenges, he "never quits."

Suturing the hardy, wise, ur-American cowboy figure to the post-Vietnam American soldier is the act that John Wayne was unable to achieve in the aftermath of the Vietnam loss. Eastwood accomplishes the feat. Using heroic guardian-hunter myths visible in even countermyth films like Michael Cimino's *The Deer Hunter*, Eastwood creates a biopic of the legendary American shootist in Iraq, the sniper who provides "overwatch," protecting the innocent American soldiers from violent extremists, the political realist archangel above the fray who protects the "regime change" work of the moral idealists.

If John Ford had superseded the Progressive-era racism of Griffith with the "racial liberalism" of the Cold War, Eastwood's patient triumph in American cinematic arts capitalizes on the available discourses of the culture at hand to recuperate militant nationalism in the aftermath of Vietnam and the public unwillingness to endorse the imperial nation-state. The five decades spanning the distance between the downfall of Richard Nixon and the popularity enjoyed by Barack Obama demonstrate the successful arc of his project, neoliberalism's investment in domestic color-blind politics and regime change as an international economic tool.

Eastwood safeguards his film from a fatuous celebration of these aims of expanding imperial control on two structural levels. First, in one sense, the film is a tragedy because the hero, Chris Kyle, dies at the hands of another veteran. Although Kyle is celebrated as a family man and father, he will never enjoy the serenity of the patriarchal world beyond the battlefield and its opportunities for increase. Second, the film emphasizes the tragic component connected to the hero in the mold of Philoctetes, the unstaunched wound. Kyle is haunted by the traumatic shootings that he has carried out, despite the fact that they are justified by the legal and ethical framework of the American military. The trauma outstrips the moral framework he had in place to rationalize his deadly violence and is ultimately resolved only in a nexus of his willingness to accept "overwatch" from his wife and her choice of supervisory guardianship, an army psychiatrist.

Nonetheless, the film works to amplify the mystique of American innocence, the "greatness and goodness of our nation," as Obama put it, by way of two main narrative terrains. One segment appears to occur on an urban desert battlefield, which is, of course, really a series of police actions, searches, occupations, and disarmaments conducted by the American military against Islamist radicals and criminal gangs. The other territory is the idyllic exurb of the domesticated, debt-free or financially secure cowboy married to the character Taya, a female spouse developed exclusively in terms of her romantic and emotional attachment to Chris Kyle and her having given birth to a son and a daughter. They occupy exclusively a quotidian Texas suburban domestic world of extended vistas of sunny skies, clipped grass, new cars, freshly painted interiors, and scrubbed family barbecues not substantially differentiated from the place of Kyle's childhood or the San Diego where the couple met and courted.

Despite the stability of the tropes, the narrative of protector, savior, patriarch, and law enforcer, the film eliminates the circumstance of onscreen violent death without the value of heroism. In fact, the viewer is positioned to desire that Kyle become even more effective in his killing and eliminate more Iraqi militants. The "recurring concerns about excessive killing and civilian deaths" that marked the historic "overwatch" role in the conflict, and the immoral deeds of known battlefield actors in Iraq, like Navy SEAL Eddie Gallagher or the Black Water contracting firm, are displaced.[6]

Because the audience knows that, "9/11" notwithstanding, the most egregious possibility for swift global death occurs by way of an encounter with the American war machine, Eastwood sustains the ethical dimension of the film by way of a counternarrative of "evil," in another exceptional manner to sustain the plot of heroic cowboy gunfighter. He pits Navy SEAL sniper Chris Kyle against a Syrian nemesis, a former Olympian, now a determined jihadist for Zarqawi's Al Qaeda band in Iraq, then, later, apparently a soldier for a successor, al-Masri. The foil character possesses lethal prowess so ineluctable that once he lays "eyes on our guys," which is to say if they are ever surveilled by this godlike force, the American soldiers, including the expert trained SEALs, can be presumed dead. The enemy sniper provides not only a worthy, ruthless opponent, but, critically for the plot, which erases the issue of the original motive for invading Iraq (as Eastwood had done with Granada), he is one who has also sworn allegiance to Osama bin Laden (whose murder, dismemberment, and disappearance have enabled him to emerge spectrally as the archvillain of twenty-first-century American historical theater).

Stylistically, the enemy sniper, Mustafa (Sammy Sheik), is set apart by his gear of Nike track shoes, sweatpants, and a tied scarf that strongly resembles a Black American "[hair]doo" rag. In spite of Syrian origins, Mustafa, called on the phone by a random Iraqi on the streets charting American movements, occupies the space of the native, and during the final engagement in Mosul is shown living with a wife and child. But the film reveals no motive on his part, emplacing a comfortable binary conflict that splits the world into US combatants and "savages," the word that the soldiers use to describe their enemy, unethical kamikazes inhabiting "Indian country."

Kyle regularly calls his wife "in the world [of civilization]" on satellite telephone, inadvertently revealing the extreme levels of violent conflict and threat that he endures. The audience grieves with Taya Kyle, who begs her husband to abandon his sheepdog warrior mission and return home to raise his family. After killing Mustafa and risking the lives of a dozen "sheep" he is sworn to protect, Kyle tearfully calls his wife to confess that he is ready to submit to the domestic chore. (The irony that the putatively equitable gender portraits in this film and others like *Zero Dark Thirty* coincide with the fuller incorporation of American women into the project of militant imperial expansion is unrelievingly obvious.)

But Kyle chooses his return home as a second choice, after he has made a decision that seems certain to result in heavy US casualties and even his own death. Eastwood finally conflates the overwatch and protection of family with that of the soldiers in Iraq and shows Kyle choosing the warrior life; the result is the Elysium. Although Chris Kyle successfully defeats his Al Qaeda adversary, by risking his "family" of other American troops to do so, he calls into question the vanity of heroism, as well as the possibility of personal sacrifice and protective "overwatch" in a full-scale war. If it were limited to its battlefield scenario, the film could be read as suggesting that even the best American heroes are engaged in a suicidal project in Iraq, like the enemy of zealots they fight.

To advance the project of color-blind equivalence, Eastwood selects an African American SEAL to survive the rigors of war alongside Kyle, though the character is not developed in screen-time equal to Kyle's other fallen comrades. "D[andridge]" (Cory Hardrict), the only person from Kyle's BUDS group (Basic Underwater Demolition School team members from the grueling SEAL "Hell Week" training) to have remained unscathed, supports Kyle's decision to reduce the war to the single combat between snipers and to risk the lives of the other soldiers by attempting a shot from more than a mile away. Unlike the cynical Marine spotter from the film's opening frames, who unites both the antagonisms of overactive legal administration that will imprison Kyle for a "mistaken" kill, akin to the problem of Inspector Callahan in *Dirty Harry*, as well as the sociopathic bully who relishes the death of others while they themselves prefer rearguard action, subordinate "D" affirms Kyle's fundamental ethical sense. "It's your call, Chris," he tells him. "If you got it [the twenty-one-hundred-meter improbable shot], take it man."

After Mustafa is shot through the eye and the other white troops bemoan over the radio that their position has been compromised, D celebrates the revenge killing by repeating the painfully ironic words uttered by American president George Bush within weeks of the 2003 invasion of Iraq, "Mission accomplished." Eastwood ends the heroic action of the film with the Black soldier, the only member of the original SEAL team alive after four tours of duty, remembering to hold up the evacuation trucks to secure "The Legend" Kyle, the last man leaving the battlefield. The gesture bears relation to more famous portraits of Black protectiveness from *The Defiant Ones* and the original statement in *The Birth of a Nation*.

The extraordinary dimensions of the fantasy of the duel between the culturally blackened jihadist savage and the civilized American protector, along with the denouement of the revenge Iraq-action portion of the film being ethically sourced through the lone Black actor are necessary for a precise end. Eastwood substitutes the crisis of knowledge in politics and the film—the controversy over the invasion, the clash of civilizations, the Project for a New

American Century's "Rebuilding America's Defenses"—to reintroduce a miniature crisis of equivalency. The problem of what has already happened to get the viewer to a place of judgment about which character has the right to exist becomes overtaken by the problem of different characters' more basic rights to occupy space. The sniper must unhesitatingly kill Iraqis to save the American soldiers sifting their way through the cities of rubble.[7] The remorse that the film encourages is the remorse that more Americans were not saved by Kyle having killed more Iraqis. It is the ultimate ethical crisis of equivalency, the ultimate ethical crisis of moral relativism, and finally the crisis of form triumphing over content. Context, history, and meaning do not matter; they are displaced, erased, and contained, like the problem of the Black soldiers in *The Outlaw Josey Wales*. Since the nature of the conflict does not ultimately have significance—conflict is only a stage for the display of fearlessness, technological mastery, and martial expertise—certainly the choosing of a side during the Civil War is irrelevant.

The film concludes with Taya Kyle closing the door on a disturbed man who resembles her husband's brother, Jeff, the weakling sheep who first flunks paratrooper school and later becomes a disaffected marine who rejects the battlefield after his deployment. An intertitle informs the viewer that the man will murder Chris Kyle that day (though it does not reveal that Chad Littlefield was murdered, as well), thus turning into horror the scene of joyful family conviviality and marital reconciliation witnessed a moment before. As the credits roll, Eastwood runs homemade footage shot from an overpass onto the Texas highway showing people honoring the funeral cortege of the historical Chris Kyle. A portion of the slain soldier's public ceremony occurs at an indoor Texas stadium, the same arena used by the Dallas Cowboys. The stadium arena seems the fitting place of honor for the larger-than-life man-of-war, "The Legend" who successfully surveils the battlefield and scores 160 "kills" (Kyle apparently believed he had shot more than three hundred Iraqis, double the official tally) and whose lesson in the film was to move from "helping" by killing so many "insurgents" that the official numbers cannot reflect his true lethality, to nurturing the conflict's badly disabled veterans. The therapy for the men Kyle treats is target shooting, and we learn that the remedy is effective when in response to hitting the mark, a legless, one-armed soldier asserts, "I finally got my balls back."

American Sniper reveals the remarkable stability of the network of concerns in Eastwood's films since the mid-1970s. Even when directors have attempted to rework Eastwood's project, in the case of Ang Lee's *Ride with the Devil* or Quentin Tarantino's *Django Unchained*, provocative attempts to recast Black actors as principals in the western and to rewrite the legacy of chattel slavery and the Civil War in Missouri, they founder by failing to wrestle with the more conspicuous problem of racial liberalism. The western films, especially in the figure of John Wayne and the Golden Age of John Ford westerns, begin dramatically incorporating the thematic project of immigrant and ethnic acculturation, sectional reconciliation, and racial hygiene central to D. W. Griffith's mythic historicism (leaving aside the multiple contradictions of race and power representations in *Birth of a Nation*). Eastwood effectively revised the colonial critique of the Italian filmmakers, which had made more transparent the compromises of racial liberalism, and then he helped to restore the genre to its Golden Age ideals and the concert project of militarization and neoliberal accumulation.

No Country for Old Men

Multiple recent noteworthy films and cable television series have used the western genre to portray the contest of civilizational clash, democratic value, and what Max Weber condensed into the title of his famous work as "the protestant work ethic and the spirit of capitalism."[8] (The Kevin Costner series *Yellowstone* is exemplary and operates fundamentally as a vehicle to repatriate a Chris Kyle–like hero to the western land and reconcile him with his father.) While the challenge to this network of concerns within the western is certainly limited by the genre materials at hand, two humorists, eclectic satirists, have made an important intervention, especially in terms of systematic repudiation of the ideological arc of colonial violence. The most sharply critical contemporary film to engage the mythic western and the problem of colonialism and regeneration through violence was the 2007 Joel and Ethan Coen film *No Country for Old Men*, adapted from the 1988 Cormac McCarthy novel by the same name.

The film structure of *No Country for Old Men* partly parallels the triumvirate ethics-of-beauty motif of *The Good, the Bad and the Ugly*. *No Country* presents three central characters and overlapping story lines: lawman Ed-Tom Bell (Tommy Lee Jones), the hunter and industrial worker Llewellyn Moss (Josh Brolin), and Anton Chigurh (Javier Bardem), a professional assassin. Both Moss and Bell are born-and-bred Texans, military veterans, hunters, and men who adhere to an unstinting moral code of self-reliance based on the purported values of the Old West. They are also linked as a father and son, like Angel Eyes and Blondie. Resembling Sheriff Ed-Tom Bell, Moss is a figure of superficial, stylistic ethical morality and, further down, one of deep historical erasure. Bell and Moss are irretrievably tied to each other by the film's conclusion, when the childless sheriff stares longingly and mournfully at Moss's dead body on a gurney at the morgue. Ed-Tom sees Moss as a lost son, like Van Cleef and Eastwood in *For a Few Dollars More*. "Sorry we couldn't help your boy," the El Paso sheriff consoles Ed-Tom. But unlike Leone's two films, *No Country for Old Men* leaves the younger man eclipsed and the older man emotionally ruined.

The audience is lured into believing that Llewellyn Moss is the bona fide American hero, cleaned up slightly from the McCarthy novel.[9] Moss is the likable good old boy, the snuff-dipping, mustachioed, cowboy-boot-wearing man of legendary simplicity and ironclad value. While hunting antelope in the Texas brush one morning, Moss finds a half-dozen dead Mexican drug runners and $2 million. Chigurh is the man sent to find the money.

Moss is tough. He shoots a dog with one hand after having been shot and having swum a river and breaking down, drying, and reloading the pistol. But he is also a welder, and it is 1980. The steel industry decline has completely arrived, blunting or even eradicating the fortunes of the skilled laborer Moss, who states as the significance of his folly is made plain to him, "If it can be welded, I can weld it." No longer able to afford to live on the land with which he seems in harmony, Moss lives in a trailer park with his nineteen-year-old wife. The drug money he finds is his chance at the bonanza as the steel unions are decapitated and heavy industry is transferred abroad.

Like Eastwood's Chris Kyle, Moss is a soldier-cowboy who seems to embody the myth of the hardy, taciturn western pioneer ("Quit your hollerin,'" he says to a silent Carla Jean early on). His teenage wife, who works at Walmart, reveres him. When told by Sheriff Ed-Tom that Moss is in mortal danger—"These people will kill him. They won't quit"—Carla Jean stoutly replies, "He won't either; he never has. He can take all comers." Moss is a Vietnam veteran, who served in the air cavalry for "two tours" between 1966 and 1968, in other words during the massive escalation of American force and the change of strategy from counterinsurgency war to war of attrition. Moss represents the force that shifted from a more or less selective war against armed combatants to a far less discriminating one of attrition that destroyed organic material—human beings, animals, forests, water supplies, and so much more—using calculus, grids, and cartographic designations. Moss serves in Vietnam during the Tet Offensive, the escalating strategies of destruction, and the My Lai massacre. He has at least one time gone voluntarily.

Moss's embeddedness in these narratives of horror and violence is brought out in his most sentimental moments, not during his portraits of callous resolve. He says to his wife, the last time he sees her, "I shall return," playfully and knowingly quoting General Douglas MacArthur's famous lines about the Philippines. While MacArthur's language is typically characterized as sinewy American resolve in the face of triumphant Japanese totalitarianism during World War II, it also carries the residue of American imperialism into Asia, the original capture of those islands from Spain, and then war against Emilio Aguinaldo and the Filipino independence movement. Moss's playful inclination seems innocent but, like MacArthur, with his close tie to the corporate media titan and Sinophile Henry Luce, has the possibility to invoke the most vitriolic antidemocratic and expansionist tendencies.

Chigurh, who, in the narcissistic vacuity of American society, is thought of as "raceless"—in that to be without race is to be white, and only whites can consider a world without race, and the maneuver itself is an illusion designed to erase the sources and enrichment strategies of European power—is the native transformed into an implacable killing force, a near total death relation. He is Leone's "Tuco," but with his intensity never relieved by humor, completely unsentimentalized, a force that does not operate from the motive of material accumulation or the origin myths sustained by an unimpeachable history, neither the organic social world nor the future of unlimited desire. Chigurh is described to Moss by Carson Wells (Woody Harrelson), the one person who knows him, in these terms: "I'd say he doesn't have a sense of humor.... You don't understand. You can't make a deal with him. Even if you gave him the money back, he'd still kill you for inconveniencing him. He's a peculiar man. Might even say he has principles. Principles that transcend money or drugs, anything like that."

With a minor exception (and in the strongest departure from McCarthy's novel), the Chigurh character is absolutely effective in murdering adult white men, beginning and most graphically with a sheriff's deputy inside a police station, using only a pair of handcuffs as weapon. Afterward, Chigurh washes the blood from his own wrists, blending the representation between Christlike savior and Pilate-like bureaucrat of empire. Both the teleology of salvation and the rise and fall of empire are inadequate to comprehend the figure. The next murder is conducted with a cattle stun gun, a tool that demands two conclusions. First, it completely shows the industrial-regulatory function of the death relation, the transformation of organic matter to inorganic matter. Second, it shows the willingness on Chigurh's part to understand his opponents as cattle, to depart from the stand of humanism. Chigurh kills string-tie-wearing gangsters who underestimate him; leather-voiced night clerks; balding vintage F150 drivers; affable chicken farmers; three rival Mexican drug dealers; and, in his finale, the widow Carla Jean Moss, just returned from her mother's funeral. His single act of clemency comes against the owner-operator of a gas station, who wins a coin flip and is spared, and who only slowly and horrifyingly realizes how close he has come to death. But arguably, Chigurh's most notable "kill," one accomplished absent any onscreen ratiocination, is of the business executive who has hired him. The executive is marked by his strong accounting sensibility.

Javier Bardem, the actor who plays Chigurh, is made-up and physically duplicates a minor character from Peckinpah's *The Wild Bunch*, the major American western to call into question the cultural politics of the genre. Chigurh resembles the Indian from the split shot in *The Wild Bunch* who menaces Freddie Sykes after he's been wounded, abandoned by Pike Bishop and the gang and forced to hide in the mountains. The Indian, who wields a machete, is a horrifying figure, and it is difficult to assess precisely what is terrifying about his pasty whiteness and physical size. But the terror joined to the image stems precisely from the leathered blankness in the face that is similar to whiteness yet retains the possibility of a strong difference. In this place of bloodless Frankensteinian reanimation, the character emphasizes a central fear that recalls for the viewer the horrifying face of the white girl in *The Searchers* who has been forcibly Indianized. The great horror is not merely whiteness that has been violated or tainted; it is whiteness deraced, stripped of its core power.

Uncredited actor in *The Wild Bunch*, dir. Sam Peckinpah (Warner Bros., 1969).

Javier Bardem in *No Country for Old Men*, dir. Joel and Ethan Coen (Paramount, 2006).

The portrait by Javier Bardem of Anton Chigurh was in concert with novelist Cormac McCarthy's intention. The spectral villain of *No Country for Old Men* is racially ambiguous and confounding to the stereotypical westerners. "'What did he look like? Was he Mexican?'" Sheriff Bell asks a teenager in the novel. "'I don't think so. He was kindly dark complected is all,'" replies the boy. The narrator has already described Chigurh as having eyes "blue as lapis." But the brief detail that might be associated with northern Europeans is deliberately qualified, emerging in the same scene that Chigurh threatens a gas station proprietor with what can certainly be considered an antiwhite racial epithet, "I guess that passes for manners in your cracker view of things."[10] Bardem invokes the alchemical Frankenstein force that prevails under multiple conditions.

While I have tried to show that the morality of heroes of virtue like Josey Wales relies on a similar bedrock of assumptions as the heroes from *The Birth of a Nation*, the Coens' creation of Chigurh counters the avenging Christ narrative with the Native's pagan form of vengeance and bloodlust, the animation of the death relation and its incommensurability with the narrative of bonanza capital. In the conclusion of the film, Chigurh walks away from a car wreck, blood streaming from his face, his arm broken; he is a terrifying, horrific figure, outside of the logic of reason, incapable of being substituted for or made equivalent.

A similar point about the pending doom embodied by the figure of Chigurh is made deliberately at the film's middle, when he languorously assassinates the western assassin, the established, technically capable military hero. Chigurh detains, interrogates, and leisurely kills Carson Wells, a former Green Beret officer turned corporate mercenary. Wells is a self-defined "day trader," and he attempts to barter for his life, first with $14,000 from an ATM (the triumph of not just fungible specie but instantaneous electronic delivery) and then with the true bonanza, $2 million. Ostensibly, the viewer might be fooled into believing on the surface that the two characters are mirror opposites, like Blondie and Angel Eyes in *GBU*, but this is a misreading. Wells represents the best in his class; he is the model of what can be achieved for the film's white men vis-à-vis accumulation. (It also sheds light on Chigurh's choking comment to the spared gas station attendant, whose accumulative path has a matriarchal tinge, inconsistent with the trope of Western patriarchy—"You ... you married into it?").

Wells has already confronted Moss, who exists in a social class below him, in a demeaning conversation where he categorizes Moss's life of labor, a conversation in which Wells makes clear his capacity to manage and define Moss. Moss resists Wells initially but later reconsiders, calling him at the hotel room in an attempt to barter, thus placing himself in the position of Angel Eyes in *GBU*: Moss will be found dead three-quarters of the way through the film, and the denouement actually lies elsewhere, with Sheriff Ed-Tom and Chigurh.

Chigurh shoots Carson Wells in his hotel room, suddenly, while the telephone rings, because he is in fact the death relation, the philosophical antipode evolved from the binary relation of good and evil and black and white that governed Western concepts from the medieval era through the Enlightenment and that was then given over to the fungible relation of the taxonomy of the following centuries. This is the essence of the film and the philosophical misunderstanding made by all the principals throughout. They claim that they can't understand the terms of the relation to Chigurh ("sugar" to Moss, and thus an allusion to the Triangle Trade and colonialism), precisely because Sheriff Bell, Carson Wells, and Moss are evacuating the history of the European colonization of Texas and Mexico.

Paying homage to *The Good, the Bad and the Ugly* and *The Outlaw Josey Wales*, the Coen brothers' film departs from the McCarthy novel and deliberately inserts the encased Black centripetal force in its strategic middle, as it moves from a film with survival and bonanza as its telos to a meditation on reckoning, suffering, and death. As the putative hero, Llewelyn Moss, leaves the hotel room where he has been discovered both by the Mexican cartel and the deadly agent of finance capital, he is transported by the only Black character in the film. The viewer then learns that Moss is not the hero of the film and that the juxtapositions between Moss and the deadly character Chigurh demand a side-by-side categorization of details. The Black driver in far-out Laredo offers an unsolicited piece of advice: "You shouldn't be doing that. Even a young man like you." Moss says with irritation and suspicion, "Doing what?" To which the man replies, "Hitchhiking." A Tiresias-like figure of deliberation (and the one to whom Moss is not shown to offer payment), the Black deliverer counsels Moss away from his linear assumptions and fungible logic, to accept (or pursue) the curved force that would pull him to the center of the project, toward his destiny with death, which would in turn offer Moss the chance for redemption rather than erasure.

The sentimentality the film exposes is revealed in extraordinarily moving narrations made by Tommie Lee Jones, a superior actor in a career-defining role. He opens by expressing his bewilderment at the modern criminal, homicidal maniac, and sociopath who kills for pleasure, sport, and to satiate embedded psychopathological drives. The sheriff contrasts the contemporary world and its imponderable murderers with the mythological tales he knows of the lawmen from another era, the "old-time sheriffs who never wore a gun," who seemed able to serve and heal the public that they served without violence. Sheriff Bell "never missed a chance" to hear these narratives of maintaining legal order without deadly coercion. But before the film's conclusion, the viewer becomes aware that the "old-time sheriffs who never wore a gun" in places like Comanche County settled parts of America named to commemorate with irony their utter pacification—the standard western term for genocidal killing and historical erasure—of the people who had lived in these territories. They were the immediate heirs to an utter obliteration of space and humanity. Bloody settlement, mass killing, and population displacement haunt the land, and the project itself has only recently ended. The Mexican border (and the "lawless" violence of the cartels) is barely at bay, awaiting any opportunity to reemerge, like a force of nature, a vortex of violent hostility.

The inadequacy of the mythic view that would accord settlement of the ancient conflict of colonialism is brought home to Sheriff Bell by his cousin, an old Texas Ranger who has been crippled in a meaningless gun battle with an outlaw. Ellis (Barry Corbin), who has recently sent to the museum an ancient single-action pistol, their uncle's "thumb buster," like the weapon of Josey Wales, reminds his younger cousin of the killing of Bell's grandfather's brother in 1908: "Seven or eight of 'em come up there. Oh, wanting this, wanting that. Uncle Mac went back to get the shotgun. Well, they was ahead of him. Shot him in his doorway.... They just sat there on their horses, watching him die. After a while, one of 'em said something in Injun and they turned and left out."

Ellis's spartan narration is designed to teach his younger, heralded, and able-bodied cousin the lesson from a man familiar with living with loss: "What you've got ain't nothing new. This country's hard on people."

And this reveals the other lesson in the story, rendered with understatement. As recently as the era of his own father, Sheriff Bell's people were battling it out, to the death and with no quarter, not against Mexican drug lords but Native Americans. In fact, the narrative of the drugs and the Mexicans is a kind of subterfuge or gloss-over of a larger and more formidable historic plate collision. It isn't necessary for motive or reason to interfere, "wanting this, wanting that"; the geography and the ethnic actors themselves predicate the deadly conflict. Bell shows no capacity, no illumination on this simple point of the "settlement" of the country. He remains wedded to his romantic but painfully shortsighted history of his own relation to his father. This is the lesson that the sheriff receives, and it affirms his decision to retire, an admission of his strong desire to continue to live in the world of illusion.

The sheriff closes the film by narrating to his skeptical spouse a twin dream. In one adumbrated reverie, he has gone to town and lost money given to him by his father, the patriarch's bonanza. The more completely recalled vision is a deeper, primordial paternal creation myth in which his father, on horseback, rides ahead with fire in a horn, a black-powder-era technique, transmitting light and heat to penetrate darkness and cold. But this ideal of a white man like himself pushing ahead with a technology wrenched from the gods to make the world habitable is a dream from which he wakes up.

ACKNOWLEDGMENTS

I would like to thank a few of the many people who have contributed to this project during its gestation over the past two decades, though the mistakes here have been made on my own. First, my sons Nathaniel and Mitchell, who grudgingly and then less grudgingly responded to John Wayne and Clint Eastwood movies as suitable entertainment during our time in Bouaké in Côte d'Ivoire. I continue to grapple with the transference between my affective response to some of the films in this study and the nostalgia produced from family memories of watching western reruns on the black-and-white Philco portable on the back porch during the 1970s. In retrospect, Richard Slotkin, whose *Gunfighter Nation* has laid the foundation for my understanding of the role of western films in American life, was the best professor whose courses I missed entirely in undergraduate school. He surprised me with a note of encouragement as I undertook this work. I first started thinking of the Italian westerns of Sergio Leone in the context of Gillo Pontecorvo's *The Battle of Algiers* in my English seminars at Alassane Outtara University. My colleagues Eugene Nguessen, Daouda Coulibaly, Vamara Koné, Pierre Kramoko and Aloa Alexandra Akpo offered unique friendships and intellectual rigor. In Atlanta, my students at Emory University, particularly Peter Witzig, contributed to the earliest pairings and dissections of western genre films and their black and nonwhite representations. At Johns Hopkins University, the students who endured the multiple courses roughly called "Clint Eastwood, Race, and the American Western" deserve special mention. Among them, several students were exemplary: Vanessa Richards, Steph Saxton, Ian O'Connor-Giles and Arron Long-Lewis, who signed up for the class twice. It was in ENG 389, spring 2017, that I actually noticed that there were uncredited African Americans performing in *The Outlaw Josey Wales*; I had been astounded by the Africans in Leone's *The Good, the Bad, and the Ugly* some years before.

In English departments of the United States today, it is challenging to write a book of this kind, which is guided by close reading of plot and the contextual political and historical circumstances encasing a series of films. Written between other projects, this book is unique in my work as an example of almost exactly what I would write if I were free of academic professional duties or the obligation to connect with any audience. On account of generous colleagues who have helped to sustain my view that there are politically responsible benefits associated with textual criticism and juxtapositional historicism of the work of art, I am particularly grateful. I would like to thank my colleagues in the Department of English at Johns Hopkins, especially Christopher Nealon, Andrew Miller, Drew Daniels, Mark Thompson, and Jeanne-Marie Jackson, for reading this manuscript and for making many helpful suggestions. My colleagues in history, François Furstenberg, Peter Jelavich, Nathan Connolly, Angus Bergin, and Matthew Crenson, were also generous and helpful with my related work in 2020. Mitch Cram of the English department provided many invaluable and expert services in the production of the final manuscript. From the Hopkins Political Science Department I would like to thank Sam Chambers, Vesla Weaver and in particular Robbie Shilliam for close readings and useful suggestions. Professor Daniel Desormeaux of the French and Comparative Literature Department also offered a rare insight. Martha Jones and Jean Hébrard provided a room with a view.

I benefited from the sabbatical support of the John Simon Guggenheim Foundation and the Dean's office in the Krieger School of Arts and Sciences at Johns Hopkins University during stages of the drafting of this manuscript. I would like to thank the current dean, Christopher Celenza; the former dean, Beverly Wendland; Assistant Vice Provost Denis Wirtz, Provost Sunil Kumar, and the university's president, Ronald J. Daniels. Regina Brooks of Serendipity Literary Agency deserves credit for her work on my other project from this year, *Shelter*. I would also like to thank copyeditor Joe Abbott, and, at Johns Hopkins University Press, my editor Laura Davulis and other Press staff.

I have appreciated the feedback and conversation from my external colleagues Roy Scranton and Michael Szalay. Christopher Phillips was most helpful with sources. I owe a scholarly debt to Theodore Van Alst, who read the manuscript for the press and encouraged me to rethink the roles of Native Americans in western films. Nathan McCall reminded me of the significance of the western genre for black Americans, and Horace Porter, Jerry Watts, and James A. Miller are always alongside me. My lifelong friend Christian

Allen exposed me to Ang Lee's *Ride with the Devil* and generously discussed the films. I have benefited from his professional expertise in cinema; his encyclopedic memory of dialogue, character, and scene; and his professional appreciation for the action genre.

NOTES

Introduction

1. Frantz Fanon, *The Wretched of the Earth*, trans. Richard Philcox (1961; New York: Grove, 2004), 31.

2. The resonance and circulation of Italian and Hollywood "westerns" in West and Central Africa during the twentieth century has been notable, if not profound. Mauritanian-Malian filmmaker Abderrahmane Sissako said, "Spaghetti Westerns have marked my entire film culture. They were very important for me" (155). Scholar Tsitsi Jaji has coined the term *Cassava Westerns* to capture the layers of embedded borrowings and commentaries on the genre as it is practiced in West Africa. See Tsitsi Jaji, "Cassava Westerns: Ways of Watching Abderrahmane Sissako," *Black Camera* 6, no. 1 (Fall 2014): 154–77. Historian Didier Gondola describes postwar Kinshasa as indelibly shaped by migrant labor and Hollywood westerns. "Young people, especially, parlayed their vision of the Far West from the screen into the street, creating in the process a unique hybrid blend that conflated the Hollywood version of the drifting cowboy with local elements of manhood and fashioned township gangs after frontier posses." Didier Gondola, *Tropical Cowboys: Westerns, Violence, and Masculinity in Kinshasa* (Bloomington: Indiana University Press, 2016), 66. And in British-controlled southern central Africa, including modern-day Zimbabwe, Zambia, and Malawi, "by the end of the Second World War, for many African moviegoers the 'cowboy' and the cinema had become synonymous." James Burns, "John Wayne on the Zambezi: Cinema, Empire, and the American Western in British Central Africa," *International Journal of African Historical Studies* 35, no. 1 (2002): 103.

3. One of the more exceptional features of the elimination of African Americans is found in the 2013 film *12 Years a Slave*, which features as its Black principals Nigerian and Ugandan performers. The symbolism and the decisions the Black British filmmaker made about the spoken language in the film were quite fascinating: Black Americans are not "Black" enough to serve as facsimiles in their own story; also, specifically, there seems to be the idea that their language is not "English" enough. By contrast, apparently, any white actor has the linguistic capacity to carry out the role of a mid-nineteenth-century character.

4. Joseph E. Lowndes, "Unstable Antistatism: The Left, the Right, and *The Outlaw Josey Wales*," *International Journal of Politics, Culture and Society* 16, no. 2 (Winter

2002): 237–53; and Joseph E. Lowndes, *From the New Deal to the New Right: Race and the Southern Origins of Modern Conservativism* (New Haven, CT: Yale University Press, 2008).

    5. James T. Sparrow, *Warfare State: World War II Americans and the Age of Big Government* (New York: Oxford University Press, 2011), 251–52. While Sparrow notes that the main benefit of full employment was "for whites," postwar America presented "astonishing" economic activity, and "military spending kept the economy running at high capacity well into the 1970s."

    6. Regents of the University of California v. Bakke, 438 US 265 (1978).

    7. Dan Steinberg, "Jeffrey Wright Defends 'Redskins' Name," *D.C. Sports Bog* (blog), *Washington Post*, Sept. 24, 2013, www.washingtonpost.com/news/dc-sports-bog/wp/2013/09/24/jeffrey-wright-defends-redskins-name. Wright, a DC native and lifelong football fan who claims Powhatan ancestry, says that "if you go back and you look at the origins of the word, it was actually the Native Americans themselves who first referred to their own kind as red, to differentiate themselves from white." *The Oxford English Dictionary* records the word circulating in English translations of French *peaux rouges* in 1769, and Natives themselves use the term in the early nineteenth century: French Crow "I am a red-skin . . ." But by the time the term appears in James Fenimore Cooper's 1823 *Pioneers*, *redskins* is increasingly associated with race war and genocide—"There will soon be no redskin in this country." A century later this connotation had become widespread and transnational, as indicated by James Joyce's use in *Ulysses*: "there would soon be as few Irish in Ireland as redskins in America." Wright proposes that the sports team name "Cowboys," as a symbolic antipode and signal of the genocidal agent, was "more offensive" and insists on the appropriateness of the term as part of his intention to defy "white racists determin[ing] meaning and value." Nonetheless, "Redskins" as a twentieth-century name for a sports team in the geographic area of the Algonquin, Iroquois, and Tuscarora is significantly more objectionable by category than names like "Seminoles," "Indians," and even "Braves."

Chapter 1 • Black Representations in the Western

    1. Jane Meyer, *Dark Money* (New York: Doubleday, 2015), 331, 321.

    2. Michael Barbaro and Michael D. Shear, "Before Talk with Chair, Clearance from the Top," *New York Times*, Sept. 1, 2012, A1.

    3. Gerald Boyd, "Reagan Says Panel 'Retreats' on Budget," *New York Times*, March 14, 1985, A1.

    4. Norman Mailer, "The White Man Unburdened," *New York Review of Books*, July 17, 2003.

    5. Evelyn A. Schlatter, *Aryan Cowboys: White Supremacists and the Search for a New Frontier, 1970–2000* (Austin: University of Texas Press, 2006), 2–6; Ann Burlein, *Lift High the Cross: Where White Supremacy and the Christian Right Converge* (Durham, NC: Duke University Press, 2002); Michael Rogin, *Ronald Reagan, the Movie, and Other Episodes in Political Demonology* (Berkeley: University of California Press, 1987). On the creation of ethnomythic history as a shared precondition for society, see, for example, the use that John Rawls makes of the idea of the background of political culture in his theory of justice. John Rawls and Erin Kelly, *Justice as Fairness: A Restatement* (Cambridge, MA: Harvard University Press, 2001). For more on the idea of social imaginaries,

see Charles Taylor, *Modern Social Imaginaries* (Durham, NC: Duke University Press, 2004); and Benedict Anderson, *Imagined Communities: Reflections on the Origin and Spread of Nationalism* (London: Verso, 2006).

6. See Arnold R. Isaacs, *Without Honor: Defeat in Vietnam and Cambodia* (Baltimore: Johns Hopkins University Press, 1983); Arnold R. Isaacs, *Vietnam Shadows: The War, Its Ghosts, and Its Legacy* (Baltimore: Johns Hopkins University Press, 1997).

7. Ian Haney-Lopez, *Dog Whistle Politics: How Coded Racial Appeals Have Wrecked the Middle Class* (New York: Oxford University Press, 2014), 23–24.

8. Haney-Lopez, 24.

9. Mark Shiel, "Banal and Magnificent Space in 'Electra Glide in Blue' (1973), or an Allegory of the Nixon Era," *Cinema Journal* 46, no. 2 (Winter 2007): 98; Austin Fisher, *Radical Frontiers in the Spaghetti Western: Politics, Violence and Popular Italian Cinema* (London: I. B. Tauris, 2011), 188.

10. In the 1970s, "more cop shows were aired than at any other time." In 1973, *Time* magazine recorded twenty-nine crime shows on the network schedules. Roger Sabin, *Cop Shows: A Critical History of Police Dramas on Television*, with Ronald Wilson, Linda Speidel, Brian Faucette, and Ben Bethell (Jefferson, NC: McFarland, 2015), 3. "Cops and Comedy," *Time*, April 16, 1973, 72. Crime shows, including the westerns *Gunsmoke* and *The Cowboys*, included ABC's *Chopper One*, *Griff*, *TOMA*, *The Rookies*, *The Six Million Dollar Man*, and *The Streets of San Francisco*; CBS's *Kojak*, *The New Perry Mason*, *Mannix*, *Hawaii Five-O*, *Barnaby Jones*; and NBC's *Adam-12*, *Banacek*, *Columbo*, *Ironside*, *McCloud*, *McMillan & Wife*, *Chase*, *Faraday and Company*, *The Magician*, *Police Story*, and *Tenafly*.

11. Katherine Becket, *Making Crime Pay: Law and Order in Contemporary American Politics* (New York: Oxford University Press, 1997), 106.

12. This scene is so crucial to the formation of the law-and-order detective that it is sometimes erroneously collapsed with the more specific deployment of lethal violence against the Black "menace" in the 1983 film *Sudden Impact*, where the same detective utters the more famous slogan, repeated by Ronald Reagan in March of 1985 vetoing tax increases, "Go ahead, make my day." Shiel, "Banal and Magnificent Space," 105.

13. See Sigmund Freud, *Beyond the Pleasure Principle*, trans. James Strachey (New York: Norton, 1961).

14. Loic Wacquant, "From Slavery to Mass Incarceration: Rethinking the 'Race Question' in the US," *New Left Review* 13 (Jan.-Feb. 2002): 55.

15. Richard Slotkin, *Gunfighter Nation: The Myth of the Frontier in Twentieth Century America* (New York: Harper, 1993), 350.

16. Rebecca Wanzo, "The Cosby Lament: Rape, Marital Alibis, and Black Iconicity," *differences: A Journal of Feminist Cultural Studies* 29, no. 2 (2018): 96–125, 100–101; see also Melanie Klein, "Mourning and Its Relationship to Manic-Depressive States," in *The Selected Melanie Klein*, ed. Juliet Mitchell (New York: Free Press, 1987), 149.

17. Slotkin, *Gunfighter Nation*, 350.

18. Achille Mbembe, "Necropolitics," *Public Culture* 15, no. 1 (Winter 2003): 11.

19. There is a broad range of material available to consider these questions. I have found the following particularly useful: Ira Katznelson and Martin Shefter, *Shaped by War and Trade: International Influences on American Political Development* (Princeton, NJ: Princeton University Press, 2002); Richard I. Immerman, *Empire for Liberty: A His-*

tory of American Imperialism from Benjamin Franklin to Paul Wolfowitz (Princeton, NJ: Princeton University Press, 2010); W. Michael Weiss, *Cold Warriors and Coup D'Etats: Brazilian-American Relations, 1945–1964* (Albuquerque: University of New Mexico Press, 1993); Charles S. Maier, *Among Empires: American Ascendancy and Its Predecessors* (Cambridge, MA: Harvard University Press, 2006); William Appleman Williams, "Empire as a Way of Life," in *Americans in a Changing World: A Short History of the United States in the Twentieth Century* (New York: Harper and Row, 1976), 353–83; Richard H. Immerman, "Halcyon Days and Growing Pains: 1950–1961," in *The Hidden Hand: A Brief History of the CIA* (Sussex, UK: Wiley, 2014), 35–69; James H. Meriwether, "A Torrent Overrunning Everything: Africa and the Eisenhower Administration," in *The Eisenhower Administration, the Third World, and the Globalization of the Cold War*, ed. Kathryn C. Statler and Andrew L. Johnson (Lanham, MD: Rowman and Littlefield, 2006), 175–96.

20. See, e.g., Tania Modleski, "Clint Eastwood and Male Weepies," *American Literary History* 22 no. 1 (Nov. 2009): 136–58. Modleski observes in Eastwood a masquerade of purposeful civic chauvinism masking sentimental despair and absolutely akin to the "female sentimentality" heavily critiqued in the work of Lauren Berlant for its inconsequence. "If the danger with female sentimentality is that it elevates suffering over the will to political action, the danger of Eastwood's sentimentality—'his sacrifice, suffering, and mourning'—as exhibited in *Gran Torino*, is that it in fact *passes itself off as a 'socially transformative' act*" (154).

21. See Mark Gottdiener, "Hegemony and Mass Culture: A Semiotic Approach," *American Journal of Sociology* 90, no. 5 (1985): 979–1001; Sylvia Wynter, "On How We Mistook the Map for the Territory, and Reimprisoned Ourselves in Our Unbearable Wrongness of Being, of *Desêtre*: Black Studies toward the Human Project," in *A Companion to African American Studies*, ed. Lewis R. Gordon and Jane Anna Gordon (Malden, MA: Blackwell, 2006), 107–17; T. J. Jackson Lears, "The Concept of Cultural Hegemony: Problems and Possibilities," *American Historical Review* 90, no. 3 (June 1985): 567–93.

In a semiotic critique of the explanatory power of Antonio Gramsci's Marxian term *hegemony*, the sociologist Mark Gottdiener helpfully develops the philosopher Louis Althusser's refining of the term *ideology*, explaining that "people cannot understand the real forces in the social formation that produce social events, because these function in ways not readily apparent. Their interpretation of the events perceived by consciousness, therefore, is an imaginary one, and it is the representation of this realm that Althusser terms 'ideological.'" Gottdiener relies on the work of English Marxist Paul Hirst to refine the realm of ideology more completely. Hirst writes that ideology is broadly considered the field of imaginary social relations: "Ideology is not 'Consciousness,' it is a representation of the 'imaginary.' This 'imaginary' relation is not the experience of consciousness of an already constituted subject—it is in the imaginary that the subject is formed as subject" (983).

Gottdeiner's observation suggests that the ideological, instead of articulating a hierarchy of oppositional relations, is the realm, in fact, that makes possible imaginary relations at all. It provides a place where multiple symbols and discourses collide and, in turn, lead to the formation of a worldview—one that is not required to conform to the facts of "real" life but that allows human beings to understand themselves as subjects, as agents, as actors, as citizens. The ideological, in this sense, is both more vast and less ominous than the system of communicative forces by which power might be projected or tasked from one class or group onto another.

At the same time my thinking here is strongly shaped by the field of Black Studies, which resists the sweeping generalization of "people cannot understand the real forces in the social formation that produce social events." Black Studies views that certain knowledges and observations will also be deliberately repressed, disavowed, or erased, and that the point of view that keeps Africans at the center of the discussion helps to retrieve this buried knowledge. From time to time in the discourse of Black Studies, the "real forces" are not opaque by any means at all. Sylvia Wynter describes the arc of Black Studies growing out of Stokely Carmichael's call for "Black Power" in 1966, through the discipline's "reterritorialization" by the "postructuralist and 'multicultural' literary theory and criticism" of Henry Louis Gates Jr. (109). I am using the term "Black Studies" specifically to pay heed to Wynter's caution about hegemonic reterritorialization. But "real forces," such as the condign power wielded by the state indiscriminately against Black people, gains its legitimacy precisely by obscuring its origins with the imaginary relations such as patriotism and law and order or, for that matter, "broken windows" policing.

Related to the workings of ideology, or imaginary relations that are the precondition for imagining subjects, is another technical term that contributes to the modern understanding of the role of mass culture in shaping the attitudes and beliefs in advanced industrial societies: *hegemony*. Originated by Antonio Gramsci, and an advance in the theoretical workings of the classic Marxist dynamic interplay between the materially productive "base" of society and its "superstructure" effects that manage the resources, hegemony was an early twentieth-century intervention to explain "the 'spontaneous' consent given by the great masses of the population to the general direction imposed on social life by the dominant fundamental group." Gramsci quoted in Lears, "Concept of Cultural Hegemony," 568.

22. Stanley Corkin, "Cowboys and Free Markets: Post–World War II Westerns and U.S. Hegemony," *Cinema Journal* 39, no. 3 (Spring 2000): 74. It should also be said that Wayne's socially conservative perspective on race relations was completely in line with the Truman era social politics during the era in which he secured his position in American cultural life. Truman, who was the single force responsible for desegregating the American military, which had a more immediate impact than the Supreme Court's decision to end segregation in American schools, addressed the National Colored Democratic Convention: "Let me make it clear, I am not calling for the social equality of the negro. . . . The highest type of negro say frankly that they prefer the company of their own people." Andrew Alexander, *America and the Imperialism of Ignorance: US Foreign Policy since 1945* (London: Biteback, 2011), 261.

23. Lani Guinier, "From Racial Liberalism to Racial Literacy: *Brown v. Board of Education* and the Interest-Divergence Dilemma," *Journal of American History* 91, no. 1 (June 2004): 95.

24. Jodi Melamed, *Represent and Destroy: Rationalizing Violence in the New Racial Capitalism* (Minneapolis: University of Minnesota Press, 2011), 10.

25. See Ralph Ellison, "The Shadow and the Act" [originally published in *The Reporter*, 1949], in *Shadow and Act* (New York: Random House, 1964), 273–81; Frantz

Fanon, *Black Skin, White Mask*, trans. Charles Markmann (1952; New York: Grove, 1967), 139–40. *Home of the Brave* (1949) was a mixed offering, the film itself scorned by such Black intellectuals as Ralph Ellison and Frantz Fanon but offering probably the most complex individual performance of a Black character available in the era, by James Edwards. The Hollywood mass-distributed movies of the later 1940s are far from the exclusive examples of black cinematic representation. Film scholar Allyson Field argues cogently and with good evidence for the multiple examples of films made by Black filmmakers, as early as the 1900s and 1910s, that presented the ideology of Black uplift. See Allyson Nadia Field, *Uplift Cinema: The Emergence of African American Film and the Possibility of Black Modernity* (Durham, NC: Duke University Press, 2015).

26. "When it comes to sit-ins and marches, you can pass me by," was a vintage Strode quote. Walter Burrell, "No Marches and Picket Signs for Woody Strode," *New Journal and Guide* 3 (June 1967): 14.

27. For examples of black radical responses outside of categories of civil rights protest, see Nikhil Pal Singh, *Black Is a Country* (Cambridge, MA: Harvard University Press, 2004); and Timothy Tyson, *Radio Free Dixie* (Chapel Hill: University of North Carolina Press, 2000).

28. Cedric Robinson, *Forgeries of Memory and Meaning: Blacks and the Regimes of Race in American Theater and Film before World War II* (Chapel Hill: University of North Carolina Press, 2007), 83–92.

29. Toni Morrison, *Playing in the Dark: Whiteness and the Literary Imagination* (New York: Vintage, 1993), 25, 3.

30. Ellison, *Shadow and Act*, 276–77.

31. John Wayne, *Playboy*, interview, May 1971, 80.

32. Wayne, 80, 80, 82. See also Lawrence Jackson, *My Father's Name* (Chicago: University of Chicago Press, 2012). Just as a case in point, my grandfather, who was seventy-six years old when Wayne took part in the *Playboy* interview, was the son of a man named Edward Jackson, who was enslaved between 1855 and 1865. So, while the event of US chattel slavery was three generations removed from me, a three-year-old child in 1971, it was only a single generation for my grandfather.

33. Quoted in Slotkin, *Gunfighter Nation*, 513.

34. Philip Durham and Everett L. Jones, *The Adventures of the Negro Cowboys* (New York: Bantam, 1966), 13–15.

35. Mary Lea Bandy and Kevin Stoehr, "Eastwood and the American Western," *Ride, Boldly Ride: The Evolution of the American Western* (Berkeley: University of California Press, 2012), 244.

36. David Sterritt, *The Cinema of Clint Eastwood: Chronicles of America* (New York: Wallflower Press, 2014), 132–33. See also Peter Biskind, "Any Which Way He Can," in *Clint Eastwood: Interviews*, revised and updated, ed. Robert E. Kapsis and Kathie Coblentz (Jackson: University Press of Mississippi, 2012), 150; Patrick McGilligan, *Clint: The Life and Legend* (New York: St. Martin's, 2002).

37. Richard Schickel, *Clint Eastwood: A Biography* (New York: Knopf, 1996), 291.

38. Kurt Hackemer, "Union Veteran Migration Patterns to the Frontier: The Case of Dakota Territory," in "Reconsidering Civil War Veterans," special issue, *Journal of the Civil War Era* 9, no. 1 (March 2019): 84–108, 86–88. Hackemer reviews the contem-

porary scholarship with special focus on the economic history work of Chulhee Lee, "Health, Information, and Migration: Geographic Mobility of Union Army Veterans, 1860–1880," *Journal of Economic History* 68 (Sept. 2008): 862–99.

39. Owen Wister, "To the Reader," in *The Virginian: A Horseman of the Plains* (New York: Macmillan, 1902), vii.

40. See, e.g., Alex Ross, *Wagnerism: Art and Politics in the Shadow of Music* (New York: Farrar, Strauss and Giroux, 2020), 148.

41. Robinson, *Forgeries of Memory and Meaning*, 92; see also Scott Simmon, *The Invention of the Western Film: A Cultural History of the Genre's First Half-Century* (Cambridge, UK: Cambridge University Press, 2003).

42. Gregory S. Jay, "'White Man's Book No Good': D. W. Griffith and the American Indian," *Cinema Journal* 39, no. 4 (Summer 2000): 19–20.

43. As James Merrell points out in "Second Thoughts on Colonial Historians and American Indians," *William and Mary Quarterly* 69, no. 3 (July 2012): 451–512, the contemporary use of terminology by historians—words such as *contact, discovery, settlement, wilderness, backwoods,* and *forest*—is conscripted to "an archaic but still living discourse that keeps American history tethered to the very 'European structures of thought' faced by America's indigenous peoples centuries ago" (459). See also William L. Hixon, *American Settler Colonialism: A History* (New York: Palgrave Macmillan, 2013), esp. chap. 6, "They Promised to Take Our Land and They Took It: Settler Colonialism in the American West," 113–44; the classic Dee Brown, *Bury My Heart at Wounded Knee: An Indian History of the American West* (New York: Bantam, 1970); Francis Jennings, *The Invasion of America: Indians, Colonialism, and the Cant of Conquest* (Chapel Hill: University of North Carolina Press, 1975); Russell Thornton, *American Indian Holocaust and Survival: A Population History since 1492* (Norman: University of Oklahoma Press, 1987); Daniel Richter, *Facing East from Indian Country: A Native History of Early America* (Cambridge, MA: Harvard University Press, 2001); and the more recent Ned Blackhawk, *Violence over the Land: Indians and Empires in the Early American West* (Cambridge, MA: Harvard University Press, 2006); and Julianna Barr, *Peace Came in the Form of a Woman: Indians and Spaniards in the Texas Borderlands* (Chapel Hill: University of North Carolina Press, 2007). Even mainstream and apologist US historians today admit that British colonialism and American state consolidation "killed or displaced tens of thousands" and "continually violated treaties," invoking the specter of genocide and land theft. Gordon S. Wood, *Empire of Liberty: A History of the Early Republic, 1789–1815* (New York: Oxford University Press, 2009), 2, 121. Relative to the possibilities of D. W. Griffith conflating animus toward Natives and Blacks and seeking to erase the histories of both groups, it is worth remembering that one of the earlier works of imaginary art depicting triangular race relation is James Fenimore Cooper's leather stocking tale *The Last of the Mohicans*, which sutures the doomed Mohican Uncas with the doomed mulatto character Cora Munro.

44. Richard Schickel, *D. W. Griffith: An American Life* (New York: Simon and Schuster, 1984), 212; quoted in Jay, "'White Man's Book No Good,'" 26.

45. David Blight, *Race and Reunion: The Civil War and American Memory* (Cambridge, MA: Belknap, 2001), 2.

46. Blight, 38.

47. John J. Collins, "The Zeal of Phinehas: The Bible and the Legitimation of Violence," *Journal of Biblical Literature* 122, no. 1 (Spring 2003): 3–21:

> In the N[ew] T[estament], identity is no longer tied to ethnicity or to possession of a particular land. What this literature shares with Deuteronomy, however, is the sharp antithesis with the Other, whether the Other is defined in moral terms, as sinners, or in political terms as the Roman Empire. Both Deuteronomy and the apocalypses fashion identity by constructing absolute, incompatible contrasts. In the older literature, the contrast is ethnic and religious, but regional. In the apocalypses, it takes the form of cosmic dualism. In both cases, the absoluteness of the categories is guaranteed by divine revelation and is therefore not subject to negotiation or compromise. Herein lies the root of religious violence in the Jewish and Christian traditions. (18)

48. John H. Mollenkopf, *The Contested City* (Princeton, NJ: Princeton University Press, 1983), 16–18, 40–41, 125–35.

49. Martin Luther King Jr., "Why I Am against the War in Vietnam," April 4, 1967, New York, Riverside Church.

50. "Third World Project" is Vijay Prashad's term; see his "Dream History of the Global South," *Interface: A Journal for and about Social Movements* 4, no. 1 (2012): 43–45. Prashad understands the TWP as successor to the Bandung Non-aligned Movement and brought down by the mid-1970s Atlantic Project. See Yousef K. Baker, "Killing 'Hajis' in 'Indian Country': Neoliberal Crisis, the Iraq War and the Affective Wages of Anti-Muslim Racism," *Arab Studies Quarterly* 42, no. 1–2 (Winter/Spring 2020): 46–65, 48–51; and David Harvey, *The Condition of Postmodernity: An Enquiry into the Origins of Cultural Change* (Cambridge, MA: Blackwell, 1990), 152–53.

51. Joan Baez (but not The Band) took "The Night They Drove Old Dixie Down" to no. 3 on Billboard's Hot 100 in October of 1971; Neil Young did not have chart success with "Southern Man"; and Lynyrd Skynyrd's "Sweet Home Alabama" reached no. 8 on the Billboard Hot 100 in October 1974.

52. My description of the antebellum South as a place of "rank injustice" is being challenged all the time. For a more sanguine view of Black and white interactions in antebellum Virginia, see Melvin Patrick Ely, *Israel on the Appomattox: A Southern Experiment in Black Freedom from the 1790s through the Civil War* (New York: Vintage, 2004).

53. Virginia—Race and Hispanic Origin: 1790–1990, Table 61, https://web.archive.org/web/20141008120207/http://www.census.gov/population/www/documentation/twps0056/tab61.pdf.

54. Sterling A. Brown, "The Negro Character as Seen by White Authors," in *A Son's Return: Selected Essays of Sterling A. Brown*, ed. Mark A. Sanders (Boston: Northeastern University Press, 1993), 149–83. In the early 1930s Brown broke ground by identifying six recurring stereotypical portraits of Black people in American literature, as well as in uncollected articles for the popular press (especially the *Nation* and *Opportunity*), showing their appearance in popular film: Contented Slave, Comic Negro, Brute Negro, Tragic Mulatto, Local Color Negro, and Exotic Primitive. Ralph Ellison, "Twentieth Century Fiction and the Black Mask of Humanity," in *Shadow and Act* (New York: Random House, 1964), 24–44; Morrison, *Playing in the Dark*.

55. Reebee Garofalo, "Crossing Over," in *Split Image: African Americans in the Mass Media*, ed. Jannette L. Dates and William Barlow (Washington, DC: Howard University Press, 1990), 90, 101; William Barlow, "Commercial and Noncommercial Radio," in *Split Image: African Americans in the Mass Media*, ed. Jannette L. Dates and William Barlow (Washington, DC: Howard University Press, 1990), 189–266.

56. Corkin, "Cowboys and Free Markets," 71.

57. Patricia Fernandez-Kelley, *Hero's Fight: African Americans in West Baltimore and the Shadow of the State* (Princeton, NJ: Princeton University Press, 2015). Fernandez-Kelley identifies the process of "capital regression," or massive disinvestment, that is euphemistically called "white flight," which enabled a process of predatory commerce and what she defines as a "distorted engagement" practice between Black citizens and liminal institutions (schools, welfare and medical bureaus, and subsidized housing) that instituted a program of palliation, acute regulation, and symbolic violence (190–211).

58. Robin Wood, "Papering the Cracks: Fantasy and Ideology in the Reagan Era," in *Movies and Mass Culture*, ed. John Belton (New Brunswick, NJ: Rutgers University Press, 1996), 203–6.

59. George B. Tindall, "Southern Strategy: A Historical Perspective," *North Carolina Historical Review* 48, no. 2 (1975): 127. See also Kevin R. Phillips, *The Emerging Republican Majority* (New Rochelle, NY: Arlington House, 1969).

60. Immerman, *Empire for Liberty*.

61. Bruce Schulman, "Comment: The Empire Strikes Back—Conservative Responses to Progressive Social Movements in the 1970s," *Journal of Contemporary History* 43, no. 4 (2008): 698–99.

Chapter 2 • The Good, the Bad and the Ugly *and Critique of the Colonial Aftermath*

1. Renata Adler, "The Screen: Zane Grey Meets the Marquis de Sade," *New York Times* Jan. 25, 1968, 25.

2. Marcia Landy, "'Which Way Is America?': Americanism and the Italian Western," *boundary 2* 23, no. 1 (Spring 1996): 43.

3. Bosley Crowther, "A New Western Anti-hero," *New York Times*, Feb. 6, 1967, D1.

4. Landy, "'Which Way Is America?,'" 41–42.

5. Martin Conway, *Western Europe's Democratic Age* (Princeton, NJ: Princeton University Press, 2020), 58.

6. D. W. Ellwood, "Italy, Europe and the Cold War: The Politics and Economics of Limited Sovereignty," in *Italy in the Cold War: Politics, Culture and Society*, ed. Christopher Duggan and Christopher Wagstaff (Oxford: Berg, 1995), 26.

7. Mario del Pero, "American Pressures and Their Containment in Italy during the Ambassadorship of Clare Booth Luce, 1953–1956," *Diplomatic History* 28, no. 3 (June 2004): 427. The approved National Security Council paper on Italy of April 1954 read, "Even 'an extreme rightist government,' though 'almost certainly authoritarian, probably ultra-nationalist and opposed to European unity,' would be 'far less dangerous than a Communist regime.'"

8. The satire was difficult for audiences to read. The deliberately antiracist and anticolonial Italian films, irrespective of the racist and colonial residues of their production, were misunderstood and showed the vulnerability of the documentary and

pseudo-documentary in its portrait of cinematic realism. The problem was the historical gap or the incapacity of the audience. Audiences found themselves unable to recognize the authentic language of eighteenth- and nineteenth-century racist tracts ennobling white supremacy, mistaking these obvious critiques of British and French eighteenth-century philosophers for Nazi-era pronouncements, which they then ridiculed as the filmmakers' misdirected hyperbole. The filmmakers had actually exposed nearly two centuries worth of bowdlerized texts, sanitized consecutively by editors to keep Enlightenment thinkers and their direct descendants safe from obtruding, cruel political bias.

9. Quoted in Christian Uva, *Sergio Leone: Cinema as Political Fable* (New York: Oxford University Press, 2020), 35.

10. See Sohail Daulatzai, *Fifty Years of "The Battle of Algiers": Past as Prologue* (Minneapolis: University of Minnesota Press, 2016).

11. Stuart Klawans, "Lessons of the Pentagon's Favorite Training Film," *New York Times*, Jan. 4, 2004, AR26.

12. Ryan Davis, "Homemade DVDs about Informing Give Police Clues; Information from Film Has Led to One Arrest; Anthony Has 'No Culpability,'" *Baltimore Sun*, Dec. 4, 2004, 1A; Peter Herman, "'Stop Snitching' Figure Sentenced to 20 Years: 'Skinny Suge' a Co-producer of the Intimidation Videos," *Baltimore Sun*, June 26, 2010, A7.

13. Thomas Weisser, *Spaghetti Westerns: The Good, the Bad, and the Violent: A Comprehensive Filmography of 558 Eurowesterns and Their Personnel, 1961–1977* (Jefferson, NC: McFarland, 1992), n.p.

14. See Donald Clarke, "The Genius of Ennio Morricone: 'I Didn't Know I Was Doing Anything New or Revolutionary,'" *Irish Times*, July 7, 2020, 7.

15. Uva, *Sergio Leone*, 75.

16. These latter 1960s films are typically regarded as the most direct declarations praising revolutionary violence on behalf of oppressed masses of peasants to overthrow fascistic and racialist oppressive regimes. Damiano Damiani: *A Bullet for the General* (1966); Sergio Corbucci: *Django* (1966) and *The Great Silence* (1968); Sergio Sollima: *The Big Gundown* (1966), *Face to Face* (1967), and *Run, Man, Run* (1968).

17. Richard Slotkin, *Gunfighter Nation: The Myth of the Frontier in Twentieth Century America* (New York: Harper, 1993), 15. See also Pauline Turner Strong, *American Indians and the American Imaginary: Cultural Representations across the Centuries* (Boulder, CO: Paradigm, 2012). Strong writes that "the capture of a defenseless settler by Indians . . . [had become by the twentieth century] a conceptual model for representing American relations with currently more threatening Others" (72). See also Kathryn Zabelle Derounian-Stodola and James Levernier, *The Indian Captivity Narrative, 1550–1900* (New York: Twayne, 1993).

18. Frantz Fanon, *The Wretched of the Earth*, trans. Richard Philcox (1963; New York: Grove, 2004), 6.

19. Slotkin, *Gunfighter Nation*, 14–15.

20. See Edward L. Ayers, *Vengeance and Justice: Crime and Punishment in the 19th Century American South* (New York: Oxford University Press, 1984); Christopher Waldrep *Roots of Disorder: Race and Criminal Justice in the American South, 1817–80* (Urbana: University of Illinois Press, 1998); Douglas Blackmon, *Slavery by Another Name: The Re-enslavement of Black Americans from the Civil War to World War II* (New

York: Anchor, 2008). For an account of how the constable system designed to control urban freedpeople before the Civil War transformed into a police system that began aggressively incarcerating Black people after emancipation, see Adam Malka, *The Men of Mobtown* (Baltimore: Johns Hopkins University Press, 2018). The slave patrol as the bounty hunter is a key element of imaginative fascination for some of the best historical fiction written by African Americans; see, e.g., David Bradley's *The Chaneysville Incident* (New York: Harper and Row, 1981); and Edward P. Jones's *The Known World* (New York: Amistad, 2004).

21. The use of the term *mestizaje* to locate Tuco, presumably born into a landed peasantry and with a sibling who successfully joined a Catholic brotherhood and rose through its ranks, is only a preliminary way of signaling the motile non-Anglo, non-peninsular or creole Spanish ethnic positions available in the Southwest during the 1860s, a generation after the successful defense of Mexican independence. There are no determinative signals in the film to Tuco's belonging to equestrian Native American nations, like Comanche or Apache ("Indios"), as he is also unlikely to belong to the Afro-mestizo caste (a quarter million living in New Spain by the mid-eighteenth century). As someone speaking Spanish and English and familiar with Catholic ritual, he seems (ironically for the film) grouped into the "gente de razon"—the people of reason—the 1821 Spanish census category that included "peninsulares, criollos, afromestizos, mestizos, and all Indians who recognized *solely* the sovereignty of Spain." The plasticity of settlements on the northern frontier, and the regular entry of new, competing, and assimilating settlers, complicates the understanding of the ethnic and racial blending that emerged as a Mexican nationality. Maria Josefina Saldana-Portillo, *Indian Given: Racial Geographies across Mexico and the United States* (Durham, NC: Duke University Press, 2016), 119. See also Gary B. Nash, "The Hidden History of Mestizo America," *Journal of American History* 82, no. 3 (Dec.1995): 941–64, esp. 945–54.

22. "The Treaty of Guadalupe Hidalgo," Article IX (1848), National Archives, www.archives.gov/education/lessons/guadalupe-hidalgo.

23. Mahmood Mamdani, "Beyond Settler and Native as Political Identities: Overcoming the Political Legacy of Colonialism," *Comparative Studies in Society and History* 43, no. 4 (Oct. 2001): 654–56.

24. Jacques Rancière, *The Politics of Aesthetics: The Distribution of the Sensible* (2004; London: Bloomsbury, 2013), 8. See also Paul Gruyer, "Thomson's Problem with Kant: A Comment on 'Kant's Problem with Ugliness,'" *Journal of Aesthetics and Art Criticism* 50, no. 4 (Autumn 1992): 317–19.

25. Christopher Frayling, *Spaghetti Westerns: Cowboys and Europeans from Karl May to Sergio Leone* (London: Routledge and Kegan Paul, 1981), 61.

26. Quoted in David Macey, *Frantz Fanon* (New York: Picador, 2001), 139.

27. Dorothy J. Hale, "Aesthetics and the New Ethics: Theorizing the Novel in the Twenty-First Century," *PMLA* 124, no. 3 (May 2009): 899.

28. The racist occlusion of Natives in cinema has an incredible history, beginning, in a sense, with Ernest Alfred Dench's 1915 essay, "The Dangers of Employing Redskins as Movie Actors." Dench considered it dangerous to work with Native people at all: "it is necessary to have armed guards watch over their movements for the least sign of treachery." Gretchen M. Bataille and Charles L. P. Silet, *The Pretend Indians: Images of Native Americans in the Movies* (Ames: Iowa State Press, 1980), 61–62; Theodore C. Van

Alst Jr., "Ridiculous Flix: Buckskin, Boycotts, and Busted Hollywood Narratives," *Great Plains Quarterly* 35, no. 4 (Fall 2015): 322. Jay Silverheels, a Mohawk man who played the character Tonto on the television series *The Lone Ranger*, criticized activist groups in the 1960s who protested stereotypical representations of Native Americans as limiting the capacity of Indigenous actors to earn a living. See Jay Silverheels, "Lo! The Indian Image!!!," *Indians Illustrated* 1 (July-August 1968): 9. Vine Deloria described the Tonto character as "the supreme archetype of the white Indian" in Vine Deloria Jr., *Custer Died for Your Sins: An Indian Manifesto* (1969; Norman: University of Oklahoma Press, 1988), 200–201.

29. It is not precisely clear if Tuco is born in what became Texas or in New Mexico. His heritage as a Mexican, part Amerindian Native, and part Spanish conquistador invokes doubly the legacy of colonial conquest by multiple imperial powers. I read the position his character occupies as having more rather than less in common with Leone's character played by Gian Maria Volontè in *For a Few Dollars More*, "El Indio," an internally colonized subject, with access to a borderland that would also impose another style of hegemony. "Internal colonial theory may not apply so neatly to ethnic Mexicans as to Navajos, but the basic elements of conquest, occupation, and domestic domination of a people and their land are present in both cases," suggests John R. Chavez. See his "Aliens in Their Native Lands: The Persistence of Internal Colonial Theory," *Journal of World History* 22, no. 4 (Dec. 2011): 797.

30. Frayling, *Spaghetti Westerns*, 64.

31. While I want to avoid a network of overdetermined effects that can accompany the critique at the heart of the Black subject in the West's reduction to fungibility, it resolves an incredible phenomenon of contemporary perception of Black people and the crisis of racism, which is fundamentally a crisis of manipulated premature mortality, a "state-sanctioned or extralegal production and exploitation of group-differentiated vulnerability to premature death" (Ruth Wilson Gilmore, *Golden Gulag: Prisons, Surplus, Crisis and Opposition in Globalizing California* [Berkeley: University of California Press, 2007], 28). Police forces consistently rationalize the use of deadly force against Black suspects that they encounter by invoking their likely adult maturity when, in fact, the suspects, like Cleveland's Tamir Rice, are often very young children. Alternatively, managerial bureaucracy (often supported by healthcare and police force professionals, as well) insists that Black adults of advanced age are actually "youthful" and undeserving of compensation in the form of salary, healthcare prophylactic or benefit, or housing subsidy, or even the more fundamental validity of their historically informed lived experience (independent of whether or not they acknowledge racism as a condition destroying vitality). Fungibility helps to explain how Black young people are perpetually mature and Black adults are perpetually neophytes. The concept helps us to account for the ways that not only the ancestry connected to race but the time of the racialized subject is organized, traded, derivatively amortized, and bartered.

32. Frank Wilderson III, *Red, White & Black: Cinema and the Structure of U.S. Antagonisms* (Durham, NC: Duke University Press, 2010), 89–90. Framing it in this manner enables me to sidestep, for the time being, Wilderson's strongly stated opposition to Natives, or the "Red," occupying a "Black" position. I am also informed here by Iyko Day's reading of this issue in her "Being or Nothingness: Indigeneity, Antiblackness,

and Settler Colonial Critique," *Critical Ethnic Studies* 1, no. 2 (Fall 2015): 102–21. Day teases out strains of the important critique on Black ontological opportunities in the western episteme and Native goals for individuation from settler regimes. Glen Sean Coulthard rejects the idea of mutual or shared sovereignty between Natives and European settlers; see Glen Sean Coulthard, *Red Skin, White Masks: Rejecting the Colonial Politics of Recognition* (Minneapolis: University of Minnesota Press, 2014). According to Day, "the main argument in *Red Skin, White Masks* is to categorically reject "the liberal recognition-based approach to Indigenous self-determination. This is not a politics of legitimizing Indigenous nations through state recognition but rather one of refusal, a refusal to be recognized and thus interpellated by the settler colonial nation-state" (111). This rejection of recognition and interpellation places Native subjectivity in a parallel but incommensurate position with people of African descent, who are rendered in the American context for their labor but, in the process of slavery, enslavement, and slave-making, are significant as signs of fungibility and gratuitous violence. See also Jared Sexton, "The *Vel* of Slavery: Tracking the Figure of the Unsovereign," in *Otherwise Worlds*, ed. Andrea Smith, Jenell Navarro, and Tiffany Lethabo King (Durham, NC: Duke University Press, 2020), 95–117. Sexton forcefully maintains a dichotomy of persecution and exclusivity so vast as to split the world into Black and non-Black, the hereditarily enslaved Africans on Western Hemisphere plantations, and everyone else. Sexton explains his perspective on the global ramifications of African enslavement since the fifteenth century: "slavery is already and of necessity the study of capitalism, colonialism, and settler colonialism, among other things" (108).

33. Saidiya V. Hartman, *Scenes of Subjection: Terror, Slavery, and Self-Making in Nineteenth-Century America* (New York: Oxford University Press, 1997), 115.

34. Frank B. Wilderson III, *Afropessimism* (Durham, NC: Duke University Press, 2020). Wilderson describes non-Black nonwhites as universal "junior partners" with the ambition of territorial recovery, unlike the Black ex-slave who is the sustained, in perpetuity, object of gratuitous violence to buttress the ontological capacity of the western subject, 94, 46.

35. Gary B. Nash, "The Hidden History of Mestizo America," *Journal of American History* 82, no. 3 (Dec. 1995): 945.

36. Patrick Wolfe, "Settler Colonialism and the Elimination of the Native," *Journal of Genocide Research* 8, no. 4 (Dec. 2006): 387–409, 388.

37. Sylvia Wynter has devoted a good portion of her work to addressing the revisions of the Western subject that might pivot around the powerful colonial framing embedded in Shakespeare's *The Tempest*. She follows George Lamming's 1960 naming of the condition in *Pleasures of Exile* as a node of slave and master dialectical articulation. "This is the beginning of an African's history as Caliban; and of [John] Hawkins's as Prospero. Both after that voyage had suffered a sea-change and had been transmuted into something terrible and strange" (27). She also notes that "Prospero creates a stereotype and sells this stereotype to himself, Miranda and Caliban" (29). See Sylvia Wynter, "We Must Learn to Sit Down Together and Talk about a Little Culture: Reflections on West Indian Writing & Criticism," pt. 1, *Jamaica Journal* 2, no. 4 (Dec. 1968): 23–32; and Sylvia Wynter, "1492: A New World View," in *Race, Discourse, and the Origin of the Americas: A New World View*, ed. Vera Lawrence Hyatt and Rex Nettleford (Washington, DC:

Smithsonian, 1995), 35: "It is at this conjuncture that the triadic model of what has been called the racial caste hierarchy of Latin America based on the ideal of *mestisaje* (Rodrigues 1991:24) was first laid down."

38. Quoted in Wayne Glausser, "Three Approaches to Locke and the Slave Trade," *Journal of the History of Ideas* 51 (April-June 1990): 208. On Locke as the Enlightenment thinker who paved the way for European property rights in the New World, see James Tully, "Rediscovering America: The *Two Treatises* and Aboriginal Rights," in *An Approach to Political Philosophy: Locke in Contexts* (Cambridge: Cambridge University Press, 1993), 137–76; and James Tully, "Aboriginal Property and Western Theory: Recovering a Middle Ground," *Social Philosophy and Policy* 11 (1994): 153–80. On the absence of money as evidence of inadequate self-government, see Bruce Buchan, "The Empire of Political Thought: Civilization, Savagery, and Perceptions of Indigenous Government," *History of Human Sciences* 18, no. 2 (2005): 5.

39. Maureen Konkle, "Indigenous Ownership and the Emergence of US Liberal Imperialism," *American Indian Quarterly* 32, no. 3 (Summer 2008): 304.

40. 21 US 543 Johnson v. McIntosh, March 10, 1823.

41. Wolfe, "Settler Colonialism," 391.

42. I am borrowing the framing from Stuart Hall, "The West and the Rest: Discourse and Power," in *Formations of Modernity: Understanding Modern Societies an Introduction Book I*, ed. Bram Gieben and Stuart Hall (Oxford: Polity, 1992), 185–227.

43. Abdul R. JanMohamed, "Negating the Negation as a Formation of Affirmation in Minority Discourse: The Construction of Richard Wright as a Subject," *Cultural Critique* 7 (Autumn 1987): 246–47.

44. "Fair, adj., and n.," *Oxford English Dictionary*, cognate with Old Saxon *fagar*: beautiful, pretty (www-oed-com.proxy1.library.jhu.edu/view/Entry/67704?rskey =xcuNTg&result=2&isAdvanced=false#eid).

45. Frank M. Snowden Jr., *Blacks in Antiquity: Ethiopians in the Greco-Roman Experience* (Cambridge, MA: Belknap Press of Harvard University, 1970): "the Greeks and Romans classified as Ethiopians several physical types of dark and black peoples inhabiting different parts of Africa. . . . To Greeks and Romans these people were *all* 'Ethiopians'" (vii).

46. Robert S. Davis, "Escape from Andersonville: A Study in Isolation and Imprisonment," *Journal of Military History* 67, no. 4 (Oct. 2003): 1067. The classic work on mortality at the prison is William Marvel, *Andersonville: The Last Depot* (Chapel Hill: University of North Carolina Press, 1994), but Marvel leaves aside questions of racial persecution. Studies suggest that Andersonville, a part of the emergence of the concentration camp system, was lethal because of mismanagement. A significant portion of twentieth-century scholarship was shaped by William Hesseltine, author of *Civil War Prisons: A Study in War Psychology* (Columbus: Ohio State University Press, 1930); Hesseltine suggested that a "triumph of war psychosis over reason" among Northern soldiers led to the view that Andersonville was the site of atrocities. See William Hesseltine, "Andersonville," *Georgia Review* 3, no. 1 (Spring 1949): 103–14, 114.

47. John David Smith, "Let Us All Be Grateful That We Have Colored Troops That Will Fight," in *Black Soldiers in Blue: African American Troops in the Civil War Era*, ed. John David Smith (Chapel Hill: University of North Carolina Press, 2002), 49.

48. See Katarzyna Naliwajek-Mazurek, "Music and Torture in Nazi Sites of Perse-

cution and Genocide in Occupied Poland, 1939–1945," *World of Music*, n.s., 2, no. 1 (2013): 31–50. Naliwajek-Mazurek suggests "entertainment" and "psychological torture" as the dual impetus for the forced performances (33).

49. William E. Connolly, *Neuropolitics: Thinking, Culture, Speed* (Minneapolis: University of Minnesota Press, 2002), quoted in Ruth Leys, "The Turn to Affect: A Critique," *Critical Inquiry* 37, no. 3 (Spring 2011): 436.

50. Nigel Thrift, "Intensities of Feeling: Towards a Spatial Politics of Affect," *Geografiska Annaler* 86 (2004): 68. My concern is with the importance of precognitive emotional corporal response although an important criticism of the position, that it is similar to the biological determinism model, is shaped by Leys, "The Turn to Affect," 436.

51. Jefferson, *Notes on the State of Virginia*, 187.

52. *The Oxford English Dictionary* notes that the early usage was in 1876 and roughly corresponded to robbery. In *A Familiar Strangeness: American Fiction and the Language of Photography, 1839–1945* (Athens: University of Georgia Press, 2008), 24, Stuart Burrows proposes that the 1898 short story by Stephen Crane, "The Five White Mice," a tale depicting an armed confrontation in Mexico City between Anglos the New York Kid, the Frisco Kid, and drunk Benson and street-corner Mexican gunmen as inaugurating the cliché. See Stephen Crane, *The Open Boat and Other Tales of Adventure* (New York: Doubleday and McClure, 1898), 303–36.

53. Kevin Bell, "Assuming the Position: Fugitivity and Futurity in the Work of Chester Himes," *Modern Fiction Studies* 51, no. 4 (Winter 2005): 850.

54. Loosely derived from Kant's *Critique of the Power of Judgement* 5:204–7, 217–18, 287, which is summarized in sec. 7.2: "The Purposiveness of Nature," at Michael Rohlf, "Immanuel Kant," ed. Edward N. Zalta, *Stanford Encyclopedia of Philosophy* (Fall 2020): https://plato.stanford.edu/archives/fall2020/entries/kant/.

55. Tobin Siebers, "Kant and the Politics of Beauty," *Philosophy and Literature* 22, no. 1 (April 1998): 31–50, 48. In other places, Kant writes that the judgment of taste presupposes a shared basis of "common sense."

56. Mark Seltzer, "Wound Culture: Trauma in the Pathological Sphere," *October* 80 (Spring 1997): 3–26, 4.

Chapter 3 • "That Damn War"

1. David McNaron, "From Iron to Dollars: The Currency of Clint Eastwood's Films," in *The Philosophy of the Western*, ed. Jennifer L. McMahon and B. Steve Csaki (Lexington: University Press of Kentucky, 2010), 149.

2. Daniel O'Brien, *Clint Eastwood: Film-Maker* (London: B. T. Batsford, 1996), 133; IMDb quotes $30 million.

3. Clint Eastwood, "Introduction by Clint Eastwood," *The Outlaw Josey Wales* (Burbank, CA: Warner Home Video, 2010), DVD.

4. Leone's 1968 western epic *Once upon a Time in the West* and 1973's *Duck, You Sucker* turned in more obvious directions as colonial critiques. Leone went on in 1973 to make the lighthearted western alluding to James Baldwin, *My Name Is Nobody*, and his collaborator, Franco Solinas, was also screenwriter for two of the 1960s' most radical films, *The Battle of Algiers* and *A Bullet for the General*. Christopher Duggan and Christopher Wagstaff, *Italy in the Cold War: Politics, Culture and Society, 1948–58* (Oxford: Berg, 1995); Austin Fisher, *Radical Frontiers in the Spaghetti Western: Politics, Violence*

and Popular Italian Cinema (London: I. B. Tauris, 2011); Pawel Goral, *Cold War Rivalry and the Perception of the American West* (Basingstoke, Hampshire: Palgrave Macmillan, 2014); Lee Broughton, *The Euro-western: Reframing Gender, Race and the "Other" in Film* (London: I. B. Tauris, 2016).

5. Hans Hansen, "Fallacies," *Stanford Encyclopedia of Philosophy*, ed. Edward N. Zalta (par. 2.1.4), https://plato.stanford.edu/entries/fallacies/#Ari.

6. David Hitchcock, "Reasoning by Analogy: A General Theory," in *On Reasoning and Argument: Essays in Informal Logic and on Critical Thinking* (Cham, Switzerland: Springer, 2017), 201–14.

7. The US Civil War and the American intervention in Southeast Asia known as the Vietnam War are structurally incommensurable military conflicts. The US Civil War did not involve foreign military intervention and had the internal issue of chattel slavery and the consolidation of the continental territory. The insertion of US ground forces in Vietnam following the defeat of France, and ostensibly as a side theater in the global drama of the Cold War waged against the USSR, was an act of nation-state imperialism. The hegemonic power in the Civil War, the North, eventually ground down its opponent by superior population size and industrial capacity. In Vietnam, despite the technological superiority and size of its military, the American secretary of defense, Robert McNamara, believed the war unwinnable by ground troops as early as November 1965, within nine months of the arrival of large numbers of American ground forces. George C. Herring, "The Strange 'Dissent' of Robert S. McNamara," in *The Vietnam War: Vietnamese and American Perspectives*, ed. Jayne Werner and Luu Doan Huynh (1993; New York: Routledge, 2015), 141–42; see also Andrew Alexander, *America and the Imperialism of Ignorance: US Foreign Policy since 1945* (Hull, UK: Biteback, 2011), 261; Christopher E. Goscha, *Vietnam: A New History* (New York: Basic Books, 2016); Henry Heller, *The Cold War and the New Imperialism: A Global History, 1945–2005* (New York: Monthly Review Press, 2006), 5; Ivan Eland, *The Empire Has No Clothes: U.S. Foreign Policy Exposed* (Oakland, CA: Independent Institute, 2004); Mansour Farhang, *U.S. Imperialism: The Spanish-American War to the Iranian Revolution* (Boston: South End Press, 1981); and David Harvey, *The New Imperialism* (Oxford: Oxford University Press, 2003).

For an argument that the ideological practices of the US South—oligarchic governance, violent labor exploitation, and severe resource extraction—were transferred to the West and symbolically imbue the cowboy archetype, see Heather Richardson, *How the South Won the Civil War: Oligarchy, Democracy, and the Continuing Fight for the Soul of America* (Oxford: Oxford University Press, 2020).

8. Michael Fellman, "'I Came Not to Bring Peace, but a Sword': The Christian War God and the War of All against All on the Kansas-Missouri Border," in *Bleeding Kansas, Bleeding Missouri: The Long Civil War on the Border*, ed. Jonathan Earle and Diane Mutti Burke (Lawrence: University Press of Kansas, 2013), 13.

9. James M. McPherson, "Out of War, a New Nation," *Prologue Magazine* 42, no. 1 (2010): 1. "The Civil War had greater impact on American society and the polity than any other event in the country's history."

10. What I am describing here might be akin to the Bourdieu-defined *habitus* or internalized "structures of perception and recognition" (64) of a social class swathe. See David Gartman, "Bourdieu and Adorno: Converging Theories of Culture and

Inequality," *Theory and Society* 41, no. 1 (Jan. 2012): 41–72. Eastwood is targeting the mass-market white American consumer, the lower populist end of the hierarchized American consumer society with his portrait. Drawing from the cultural-production argument of Pierre Bourdieu, we can see Eastwood innovating his film with contemporary political arguments to achieve a new set of attitudes within the traditional genre of the western, coincident with his own movement from member of the avant-garde to member of the efficient petit bourgeoisie. Pierre Bourdieu, *The Field of Cultural Production: Essays on Art and Literature*, edited and introduced by Randal Johnson (New York: Columbia University Press, 1993), 55–73.

11. Jacques Rancière, "The Paradoxes of Political Art," in *Dissensus: On Politics and Aesthetics*, ed. and trans. Steve Corcoran (London: Bloomsbury, 2010), 139.

12. Adolph Reed's "Black Particularity Reconsidered" is an excellent and very early analysis of the civil rights movement as a "talent search" for Black elites. See Adolph Reed, "Black Particularity Reconsidered" (1979), in *Is It Nation Time?*, ed. Eddie Glaude Jr. (Chicago: University of Chicago Press, 1997), 54. The line of argument that the legacy of the civil rights movement has been commandeered by conservative politicians appears in Jacquelyn Dowd Hall, "The Long Civil Rights Movement and the Political Uses of the Past," *Journal of American History* 91, no. 4 (March 2005): 1233–63.

13. Frank Wilderson, *Red, White and Black: Cinema and the Structure of U.S. Antagonisms* (Durham, NC: Duke University Press, 2010), 3.

14. Richard Slotkin, *Gunfighter Nation: The Myth of the Frontier in Twentieth-Century America* (New York: Harper, 1993), 347.

15. Robert Altman, director, *Buffalo Bill and the Indians, or Sitting Bull's History Lesson* (Dino DeLaurentis and United Artists, 1976).

16. Stanley Corkin, *Cowboys as Cold Warriors: The Western and U.S. History* (Philadelphia: Temple University Press, 2004), 2. The failure to win lavish studio support for *Outlaw* had telling impact on the film's special effects, very distant from the state-of-the-art renderings of onscreen violence pioneered in Sam Peckinpah's tour de force *The Wild Bunch* (1969) and taken further by Francis Ford Coppola in *The Godfather* (1972) and *The Godfather II* (1974). While costume, armament, and natural scenery were superlative throughout *Outlaw*, the special effects used to simulate bullet wounds, with the exception of the four corpses in Towash, were mediocre and characteristic of B films.

17. See Will Wright, *Six Guns and Society: A Structural Study of the Western* (Berkeley: University of California Press, 1975); Robert Rosenstone, *Visions of the Past: The Challenge of Film to Our Idea of History* (Cambridge, MA: Harvard University Press, 1995); Robert Burgoyne, *Film Nation: Hollywood Looks at U.S. History* (Minneapolis: University of Minnesota Press, 1997). There is also an argument that might be made regarding the western's most regular temporal location as being well after the metal cartridge technologies were widespread as a necessary element to support the considerable numbers of onscreen deaths, actuating the films' allegorical referents to the battlefields of Korea and Vietnam.

18. The explosion of Black images on the screen began with Sam Goldwyn acquiring the rights to the Chester Himes novel *Cotton Comes to Harlem* in 1967, leading to a film in 1970, followed by *Shaft* and *Superfly*, both directed by African Americans and starring Black actors, in 1971. The star power and sex appeal of the athlete Jim Brown

created the terms for the breakthrough portrait of a Black western lawman and interracial sex in the film *100 Rifles* (1969), followed by several serious attempts to produce Black westerns. *Buck and the Preacher* (1972), a vehicle of the production company of Sidney Poitier, Harry Belafonte, and Ruby Dee, is perhaps the best known and financially successful of the group and asserted a significantly less repentant Poitier hero.

Other valuable films include Fred Williamson's trilogy, beginning with *The Legend of Nigger Charley* (1972), and perhaps the most complex of the films, *Thomasine and Bushrod* (1974), starring Max Julien and Vonetta McGee (who starred alongside Eastwood in 1975) and directed by *Superfly* director Gordon Parks Jr. The later films insisted on a narrative of large-scale black flight from the slave South and into the West, as well as the genre's most progressive gender politics. While unheralded by western film historians, it seems that these portraits and the politics of the era influenced writers and directors. After revolutionizing the portrait of onscreen violence in *The Wild Bunch*, director Sam Peckinpah revisited the genre in 1973 with *Pat Garrett and Billy the Kid* and included a Black cowboy; the generic convention of the period demanded it.

19. Indeed, the presentation of postwar western cinematic film stars whose capacity to "go native," or their creation of new modes of existence as westerners, might be connected to their subsequent onscreen performances of interracial sex. In 1970, Johnny Cash, "the man in black," was introduced in newspaper accounts: "He is part Cherokee, was raised poor, has spent time in jail . . ." (Nan Robertson, "Cash and Country Music Take White House Stage," *New York Times*, April 18, 1970, 33). Cash, who starred as a Cherokee on the Trail of Tears in the television film *Death of a Nation* (1970), was the most significant postwar ballad singer in the country-and-western genre himself and was married to an African American woman during the era when he wrote his classic music, 1954–67.

20. Richard Thompson and Tim Hunter, "Clint Eastwood: Auteur," *Film Comment* 14, no. 1 (Jan./Feb. 1978), 26.

21. In terms of interracial romance, *The Eiger Sanction* follows in the footsteps of Charlton Heston and his African American costar Rosalind Cash in *The Omega Man* (1971), where the two kiss onscreen.

22. Forrest Carter, *Gone to Texas* (New York: Delacorte, 1975), rear jacket flap.

23. Carter, front jacket flap.

24. "Is Forrest Carter Really Asa Carter? Only Josey Wales May Know for Sure," *New York Times*, August 26, 1976, 39; Dan T. Carter, "Southern History, American Fiction: The Secret Life of Southwestern Novelist Forrest Carter," in *Rewriting the South: History and Fiction*, ed. Lothat Honnighausen and Valeria Gennaro Lerda (Tugingen: Francke, 1993), 286–304.

25. Martin Luther King Jr., *The Autobiography of Martin Luther King, Jr.* (New York: Grand Central, 2001), 172.

26. Joseph E. Lowndes, "Unstable Antistatism: The Left, the Right, and *The Outlaw Josey Wales*," *International Journal of Politics, Culture and Society* 16, no. 2 (Winter 2002): 246.

27. Gerald Horne's *The Counter-Revolution of 1776: Slave Resistance and the Origins of the United States of America* (New York: New York University Press, 2014) states in the most unflinching terms that the Declaration operated decisively as a countermeasure to Virginia governor John Murray, Fourth Earl of Dunmore's principally destabi-

lizing freedom proclamation, which claimed the attention of freedom-bound Black Americans.

28. Thomas Jefferson, *Notes on the State of Virginia* (1787), in *The Portable Thomas Jefferson*, ed. Merrill Peterson (New York: Penguin, 1977), 188, 98.

29. Thomas Jefferson, "Advice to Indian Chiefs: To Captain Hendrick, the Delawares, Mohicans and Munries," Washington, Dec. 21, 1808, in Gary B. Nash, "The Hidden History of Mestizo America," *Journal of American History* 82, no. 3 (Dec. 1995): 943.

30. Jefferson, *Notes on the State of Virginia*, 187, 188.

31. Vine Deloria Jr., *Custer Died for Your Sins: An Indian Manifesto* (1969; Norman: University of Oklahoma Press, 1988), 8.

32. Wallace Coffey, "Blessings and Welcome," *Wicazo Sa Review* 19, no. 2 (Autumn 2004): 138. For a fuller context, see Deloria's *Custer Died for Your Sins*, especially "The Red and the Black" (168–96). Describing his unwillingness to participate in the March on Washington in 1963 and his deep sympathy with the Black Power movement of the later 1960s, Deloria writes: "In our hearts and minds we could not believe that blacks wanted to be the same as whites. And we knew that even if they did want that, the whites would never allow it to happen. As far as we could determine, white culture, if it existed, depended primarily upon the exploitation of land, people, and life itself. It relied upon novelties and fads to provide an appearance of change but it was basically an economic Darwinism that destroyed rather than created" (180).

33. Lowndes, "Unstable Antistatism," 246.

34. See, e.g., Eduardo Bonilla-Silva, *Racism without Racists: Color-Blind Racism and the Persistence of Inequality in America* (Lanham, MD: Rowan and Littlefield, 2018).

35. Theodore W. Allen, *The Invention of the White Race: The Origin of Racial Oppression in Anglo-America*, vol. 2 (New York: Verson, 1997). I find compelling Allen's two-volume assessment of "the establishment of 'white' identity as a mark of social status" (562), consolidated in response to the likelihood of cross-racial militant attempts to overthrow English colonial governments in late seventeenth- and eighteenth-century Virginia.

36. Remarkably enough, the Dutch miscellany to Malory's *Morte d'Arthur* includes the portrait of Sir Morien, the African knight and son of Algloval, a sidelined portrait similar to sidelined portraits in *The Outlaw Josey Wales*.

37. See Bruce Nichols, *Guerilla Warfare in Civil War Missouri: September 1864–June 1865* (Jefferson, NC: McFarland, 2014), 109–10.

38. Henry M. Painter, *Brief Narrative of the War in Missouri and of the Personal Experience of One Who Has Suffered* (Boston: Press of the Daily Courier, 1863), 3.

39. *Kansas Raiders*, dir. Ray Enright (Universal International, 1950).

40. Elizabeth D. Leonard, *Men of Color to Arms! Black Soldiers, Indian Wars, and the Quest for Equality* (New York: Norton, 2010), 40–42.

41. Shawn Michelle Smith, *At the Edge of Sight: Photography and the Unseen* (Durham, NC: Duke University Press, 2014), 22.

42. Ralph Ellison, "The Shadow and the Act," in *Shadow and Act* (New York: Random House, 1964), 278, 277.

43. Ralph Ellison, "Twentieth Century Fiction and the Black Mask of Humanity," in *Shadow and Act* (New York: Random House, 1964), 36.

44. "Data Analysis: African Americans on the Eve of the Civil War," www.bowdoin.edu/~prael/lesson/tables.htm.

45. Harrison Anthony Trexler, "Slavery in Missouri, 1804–1865" (PhD diss., Johns Hopkins University, 1914); republished by CreateSpace Independent Publishing Platform (2015), 9.

46. Trexler, 12.

47. In the same way, many twenty-first-century films seeking to associate heroism and dramatic political change with deadly violence overstate the transformative possibilities available to violent enslaved men. Mel Gibson's *The Patriot* (2000), for example, basically refuses the very idea of historical fact, at all, suggesting that Blacks worked for wages in eighteenth-century South Carolina and that George Washington, not Lord Dunmore, offered freedom to Blacks willing to shoulder arms. Even films purporting divergent ideological paths, like Nate Parker's *Birth of a Nation* (2016), depict a completely successful Nat Turner–led slave revolt, only ended by the appearance of regular US troops at a fort.

48. For an argument that the "war of attrition" became a systematic war of massacring the Vietnamese in the countrysides, see Nick Turse, *Kill Anything That Moves: The Real American War in Vietnam* (New York: Picador, 2013).

49. "Affairs in the West: A Negro Regiment in Action—The Battle of Island Mounds—Desperate Bravery of the Negroes—Defeat of the Guerillas—An Attempted Fraud," *New York Times*, Nov. 19, 1862, 8.

50. There are multiple records of the event that do not reproduce the same numbers of dead. See "Report of Major General Samuel R. Curtis, U.S. Army, March 28, 1863—Guerilla Attack on Steamer *Sam Gaty*," in *The War of the Rebellion: A Compilation of the Official Records of the Union and Confederate Armies*, ser. 1, vol. 22, pt. 1, "Operations in Missouri, Arkansas, Kansas, the Indian Territory, and the Department of the Northwest, November 20, 1862–December 31, 1863," 245–46. "A band of guerillas took the steamer *Sam Gaty*, and murdered several soldiers and 9 contrabands." See also Benjamin Loan, Brigadier General Missouri State Militia, to Major General Samuel Curtis, March 29, 1863, vol. 22, pt. 2 "Correspondence": "Gaty robbed to-day by guerillas. Meyers and Henry of Company E killed; other escaped. Twenty negroes killed" (183); "The Army of the Frontier: Dispatches from Major-Gen. Curtis," *New York Times*, April 5, 1863, 1; "Bushwhacking on the Missouri: The *Sam Gaty* Boarded and Plundered-The Murder of Two White Men and Fifteen Negroes," *Junction City (KS) Smoky Hill and Republican Union*, April 4, 1863, 2; "Bushwhacking on the Missouri," *Emporia (KS) News*, April 4, 1863, 2; "Guerillas on the Missouri River," *White Cloud Kansas Chief*, April 2, 1863, 2. One Confederate account denies that the race massacre occurred. "Some wanted to kill the negroes. Cole Younger swore they should not be harmed, and Cole Younger's word was law even with the most desperate of the band." John N. Edwards, *Noted Guerillas, or the Warfare of the Border* (St. Louis: Bryan, Brand, 1877), 161.

51. "Report of Brigadier General Thomas Ewing Jr., August 31, 1863," in *The War of the Rebellion: A Compilation of the Official Records of the Union and Confederate Armies*, ser. 1, vol. 22, pt. 1, "Operations in Missouri, Arkansas, Kansas, the Indian Territory, and the Department of the Northwest, November 20, 1862–December 31, 1863," 583. Richard S. Brownlee put the number at seventeen. See Richard S. Brownlee, *Gray Ghosts of the Confederacy: Guerilla Warfare in the West, 1861–1865* (1958; Baton Rouge: Louisiana State University Press, 1984), 123.

52. "Report of Lieut. James B. Pond, Third Wisconsin Cavalry, October 7, 1863," in

The War of the Rebellion: A Compilation of the Official Records of the Union and Confederate Armies, ser. 1, vol. 22, pt. 1, "Operations in Missouri, Arkansas, Kansas, the Indian Territory, and the Department of the Northwest, November 20, 1862–December 31, 1863," 700.

53. Dudley Cornish, *The Sable Arm: Black Troops in the Union Army, 1861–1865* (1956; Lawrence: University Press of Kansas, 1987), 176.

54. John Cimprich, "The Fort Pillow Massacre: Assessing the Evidence," in *Black Soldiers in Blue: African American Troops in the Civil War Era*, ed. John David Smith (Chapel Hill: University of North Carolina Press, 2002), 155–56. Even Union soldiers from faraway Michigan serving in Tennessee had a noted tendency to foment or commit atrocities. See Travis Faustin, "They Are Free Men Now: Analyzing the Racial Perceptions of Michigan Civil War Soldiers" (master's thesis, Central Michigan University, 2020); and John Bebee to Nelson Bebee, Jan. 14, 1862, Nelson W. Bebee Correspondence, folder 4, box1, Clarke Historical Library, Central Michigan University. Bebee advised his brother to "kill every damn niger [sic]." George Ewing wrote his father that he "wished to shoot them when [he saw] them." George Ewing to his father, April 2, 1863, George and James Ewing, *The Ewing Family Civil War Letters*, ed. John T. Greene (East Lansing: Michigan State University Press, 1994), 54. Finally, Ira Gillaspie found an "oald [sic] negro den whare [sic] [they] kept whiskey to sell to the soldiers," and for sport he and a group of other men decided "to pull some of them up by the neck." Ira Gillaspie, *The Diary of Ira Gillaspie of the Eleventh Michigan Infantry*, ed. Daniel B. Webster (Mount Pleasant: Central Michigan University Press, 1965), 23.

55. Gregory J. W. Urwin, "Battle of Jenkins' Ferry," in *Encyclopedia of the American Civil War: A Political, Social and Military History*, ed. David S. Heidler and Jeanne T. Heidler (New York: Norton, 2000), 1068–69.

56. "Report of Lieut. Col. Bazel F. Lazear, First Missouri Cavalry, August 10, 1864," in *The War of the Rebellion: A Compilation of the Official Records of the Union and Confederate Armies*, ser. 1, vol. 41, pt. 1, "Operations in Louisiana and the Trans-Mississippi States and Territories, July 30–December 31, 1864," 220.

57. "Report of Capt. Edgar A. Barker, Second Kansas Cavalry, September 20, 1864," in *The War of the Rebellion: A Compilation of the Official Records of the Union and Confederate Armies*, ser. 1, vol. 41, pt. 1, "Operations in Louisiana and the Trans-Mississippi States and Territories, July 30–December 31, 1864," 771.

58. Carter, *Gone to Texas*, 55–56.

59. Forrest Carter, *Josey Wales: Two Westerns: Gone to Texas/The Vengeance Trail of Josey Wales* (Albuquerque: University of New Mexico Press, 1989), 64. Of course, this statement also has broader application to African Americans since according to the oral tradition passed down and recorded in WPA narratives by survivors of enslavement, Africans were beguiled aboard transatlantic slave ships by promises of red cloth. See Michael Gomez, *Exchanging Our Country Marks: The Transformation of African American Identities in the Colonial and Antebellum South* (Chapel Hill: University of North Carolina Press, 1998), 201–5.

60. Most critics, apparently in the attempt to recover Eastwood's liberal politics or situate him as a centrist, however, suggest that the screenwriters under Eastwood's guidance softened Carter's racist views. "Extras," *The Outlaw Josey Wales* (Burbank, CA: Warner Home Video, 2010), DVD.

61. Frank Cunningham, *General Stand Watie's Confederate Indians* (San Antonio, TX: Naylor, 1959), 153–54; Bruce S. Allardice, *Kentuckians in Gray: Confederate Generals and Field Officers of the Bluegrass State* (Lexington: University Press of Kentucky, 2008), 101.

62. Rather than regarding the cultural devices in film deployed by Eastwood as rearguard reactions, they are anticipating and preparing the stage for newly ascendant values. Weaver's essay, "Frontlash: Race and the Development of Punitive Crime Policy," *Studies in American Political Development* 21 (Fall 2007): 230–65, points to formations opposing the application of civil rights legislation so early as to introduce and champion a new issue, crime, and format and distort the eventual unfolding of the legislation and setting the stage for "Mass Incarceration." "Losers in a conflict become the architects of a new program, manipulating the issue space and altering the dimension of the conflict in an effort to regain their command of the agenda.... By maneuvering into a new issue space and carving a new niche to mobilize around, the disadvantaged/defeated group opens the possibility of reversing its fortunes without violating established norms" (236). I am arguing that *The Outlaw Josey Wales* incorporates a similar kind of "frontlash" strategy on the cultural front that is manifestly determined to identify and seal off Black representation.

Chapter 4 • *"Hold It Real Still"*

1. Joseph E. Lowndes, "Unstable Antistatism: The Left, the Right, and *The Outlaw Josey Wales*," *International Journal of Politics, Culture and Society* 16, no. 2 (Winter 2002): 249.

2. My observation of the Black portraits are the first, to my knowledge, and it occurred during close scrutiny of the film during the spring of 2017 in an African American Studies seminar on Race and the Western at Johns Hopkins that included extraordinary undergraduate students Aaron Lewis, Vanessa Richards, Steph Saxton, and Ian O'Connor-Giles.

3. Fredric Jameson, "Reflections in Conclusion," in *Aesthetics and Politics*, by Theodore Adorno, Walter Benjamin, Ernst Bloch, Bertolt Brecht, and Georg Lukács (London: Verso, 2007), 202.

4. John Lewis Gaddis, *Strategies of Containment: A Critical Appraisal of American National Security Policy during the Cold War* (1982; New York: Oxford University Press, 2005), 4. In a 1948 lecture Kennan described the logic of containment as one of creating a situation whereby the adversaries of the United States might "exhaust themselves in internecine conflict" and suffer their own "intolerance and violence and fanaticism" (28). The hard edge of the containment rationale in international relations had a particularly expansive and "long-term" domestic counterpart in the Counter Intelligence Program (COINTELPRO), run by the Federal Bureau of Investigation, "to expose, disrupt, misdirect, discredit or otherwise neutralize the activities of black nationalists, hate-type organizations and groups, their leadership, spokesmen, membership and supporters." J. Edgar Hoover, "Memorandum to Special Agent in Charge, Albany, New York," August 25, 1967, 1 (quoted in *Modern Black Nationalism: From Marcus Garvey to Louis Farrakhan*, ed. William L. Van Deburg [New York: New York University Press, 1997], 134). The FBI targeted the Student Nonviolent Coordinating Committee (SNCC), Southern Christian Leadership Conference (SCLC), Nation of Islam (NOI), and Congress of Racial Equality (CORE). See *FBI Files on Black Extremist Organizations, Part 1:*

COINTELPRO Files on Black Hate Groups and Investigation of the Deacons for Defense and Justice, 31 vols. (Bethesda, MD: University Publications of America, 2011).

5. By the end of the 1960s—with the 1956 works of historians like Kenneth Stampp (*The Peculiar Institution: Slavery and the Old South*) and John Hope Franklin (*The Militant South, 1800–1861*) already in place at the beginning of the decade—historians of US slavery had arrived at a paradigmatic consensus that slavery operated as a root cause for the war, embedded in the "modernization" thesis, which, as described by Frank Towers, "foregrounded slavery as the war's cause, situated within a global process of modernization," and worked to return "slavery to the forefront of causal arguments." Frank Towers, "Partisans, New History, and Modernization: The Historiography of the Civil War's Causes, 1861–2011," *Journal of the Civil War Era* 1, no. 2 (June 2011): 237–64, 239, 246.

6. The compounding of racist tropes absent from the novel but used to develop the film also included the song "Rose of Alabama," a minstrel song (like the Rebel anthem "Dixie" itself) from the 1840s. While later sung by Confederate troops, "Rose of Alabama" was originally circulated in Negro dialect form in an undated London broadsheet, a hymn to "Wenus," who "followed all the nigger boys" and whose "skin's as black as any sloe." Used to imply the innocent longing of the character Jamie for his family, "Rose of Alabama" was actually a courtship ditty between two Black people enslaved in Alabama. The lyric identifying "brown Rosey" of Alabama is symbolic, also figuratively the "sweet tobacco" cash crop bonanza of the nineteenth century. Nor does the signification circuit end there. Indeed, in the shrewd business calculations for which Eastwood is known, and his unique understanding of major niche markets and US mass-culture psychology, he crafted a film for precisely the audience that would have consumed the Lynyrd Skynyrd smash hit "Sweet Home Alabama." "Rose of Alabama" (E. Hodge, London: St. Andrew Street Seven Dials, n.d.), Kenneth Goldstein Collection, Special Collections, University of Mississippi. Several scores were generated, the earliest in 1830, though the earliest words seem to have appeared in 1846. See S. S. Steele, "The Rose of Alabama," arrangement and words (Boston: G. P. Reed, 1846); Théod von La Hache, "Fantasia and Variations on the Ethiopian Air 'The Rose of Alabama,' op. no. 2" (Philadelphia: A. Fiot, 1846); Silas Sexton Steele, "The Rose of Alabama," arrangement and words (New York: Henry De Marsan, 1859–60?); "Boatmen Dance: The Rose of Alabama" (Baltimore: W. C. Peters, 1830) [piano score]; A. B. Meek, "The Rose of Alabama: New Words" (New Orleans: W. T. Mayo's Music Store, 1847). In the 1860s the song appeared in the collection "Dime Negro Melodies: A Collection of all Negro Songs yet Published" (Philadelphia: A. Winch, 1865).

7. The habit of expectoration, a central trope of the Wales character, and the embedded range of race and Civil War narratives within the film allude to John Ford's *Judge Priest* (1934). In that film, which culminates in a courtroom finale, a Confederate veteran (Si Jenks Juror No. 10?) spits tobacco juice and phlegm with enough precision to round corners and still produce a ringing sound in a spittoon, to the delight of the court's jury, Confederate veterans anxious to leave the courthouse and to begin the Confederate Day parade. The men are shown to have a comic and nostalgic memory of the slaughter that has occurred during the fighting, until the horror of the fight is vividly depicted by Reverend Bran, a former artillery captain from Virginia, who refers to the conflict as fought for "the Southern Confederacy." After adjusting the easy heroism from

the veterans' nostalgic memories with a tale of the requisition of convicts to fight in 1864, Bran's testimony wins the freedom of the doomed man. The success is augmented by the character actor Lincoln Perry leading a band playing "Dixie" at the key moment of the jury's deliberation. The condemned man is also associated with the battlefield laborers, the post of southern African Americans, notwithstanding the eventual decision of the CSA to enlist Black soldiers in 1865. The film ends with Stepin Fetchit (Perry) leading the parade and wearing a raccoon coat with a bright white vest, the final act the Confederate veteran spitting a quid into the silk hat of the pompous state's attorney, who is himself not a veteran.

8. While not a scholarly work, filmmaker John Ridley's "The Manifesto of Ascendancy for the Modern American Nigger," *Esquire*, Dec. 2006, zeroed in on Rice's power and her use of the lethal state apparatus. See also Jodi Melamed, *Represent and Destroy: Rationalizing Violence in the New Racial Capitalism* (Minneapolis: University of Minnesota Press, 2011).

9. Dudley Cornish, *The Sable Arm: Black Troops in the Union Army, 1861–1865* (1956; Lawrence: University Press of Kansas, 1987), 240.

10. Herbert Aptheker, "Negro Casualties in the Civil War," *Journal of Negro History* 32, no. 1 (1947): 30, 29.

11. Cornish, *The Sable Arm*, 288.

12. David Blight, *Race and Reunion: The Civil War in American Memory* (Cambridge, MA: Harvard University Press, 2003), 38.

13. Elizabeth D. Leonard, *Men of Color to Arms! Black Soldiers, Indian Wars, and the Quest for Equality* (New York: Norton, 2010), 16–21.

14. Irit Rogoff, "Studying Visual Culture," in *The Visual Culture Reader*, ed. Nicholas Mirzoeff (New York: Routledge, 1998), 22.

15. Professor Mixon Robinson's "Between Stations" has been extremely helpful in alerting me to Railroad Bill reproductions. See Raleigh Mixon Robinson Jr., "Between Stations: American Liberty and Locomotion from Walden to Plessy" (PhD diss., Emory University, 2018). See also Pamela Haag, *The Gunning of America: Business and the Making of American Gun Culture* (New York: Basic Books, 2016); Jeannine Marie DeLombard, *In the Shadow of the Gallows: Race, Crime, and American Civic Identity* (Philadelphia: University of Pennsylvania Press, 2012); Burgin Mathews, "Looking for Railroad Bill: On the Trail of an Alabama Badman," *Southern Cultures* 9, no. 3 (Fall 2003): 66–88; Shawn Michelle Smith, *At the Edge of Sight: Photography and the Unseen* (Durham, NC: Duke University Press, 2013); Larry L. Massey, *The Life and Crimes of Railroad Bill: Legendary African American Desperado* (Gainesville: University Press of Florida, 2015). Lynching postcards constitute a genre that "Railroad Bill on the Cooling Board" roughly fits. See Amy Louise Wood, *Lynching and Spectacle: Witnessing Racial Violence in America, 1890–1940* (Chapel Hill: University of North Carolina Press, 2009). Wood argues that the "morbid popularity" of these cards "coincided with a larger postcard craze in the United States between the late 1890s and World War I. . . . Because many newspapers did not have the technology to print high-quality images until the 1920s, postcards . . . presented for the public a visual record of newsworthy events. Most Americans witnessed significant events, places, and people through the production and circulation of postcards" (107). Beyond this, they were "totemic relics that allowed the collector to feel an exclusive connection to the emotive power of the event" (76).

16. Jacqueline Dowd Hall, "The Long Civil Rights Movement and the Political Uses of the Past," *Journal of American History* 91 (March 2005): 1237.

17. Terry Eagleton, "Culture, Atheism and the War on Terror," *Field Day Review* 6 (2010): 169.

18. Evelyn A. Schlatter, *Aryan Cowboys: White Supremacists and the Search for a New Frontier, 1970–2000* (Austin: University of Texas Press, 2006), 3.

19. Melamed, *Represent and Destroy*, 1.

20. Melamed, 13.

21. Antoine Fuqua's 2016 remake of *The Magnificent Seven* is extraordinary for its willingness to embrace this convention. Fuqua, an African American, is more precise than simply featuring perhaps the most recognized Black actor of our times (Denzel Washington) in the starring role; he includes three Black male extras and one Black female child, but he eliminates Black women, completely, from the West.

22. Public Law 88-352-July 2, 1964, Title VI-Nondiscrimination in Federally Assisted Programs, sec. 601, at 252.

23. Jerome Karabel, "How Affirmative Action Took Hold at Harvard, Yale, and Princeton," *Journal of Blacks in Higher Education* 48 (Summer 2005): 58–77.

24. Lee Epstein and Jack Knight, "Piercing the Veil: William J. Brennan's Account of *Regents of the University of California v. Bakke*," *Yale Law and Policy Review* 19, no. 2 (2001): 341–79, 352.

25. University of California Regents v. Bakke, Opinion of Powell, J., 438 US, at 294.

26. Nikhil Pal Singh, *Race and America's Long War* (Oakland: University of California Press, 2017), 133.

27. United States v. Carolene Products Co., 304 US 144 (1938), Harlan Fiske Stone, opinion, at 152n4.

28. Eduardo Bonilla-Silva and David Dietrich, "The Sweet Enchantment of Color-Blind Racism in Obamerica," *Annals of the American Academy of Political and Social Science* 634 (2011): 190–206, 192.

29. Francis Bacon, "Of Friendship," *The Essays of Francis Bacon*, ed. Mary Augusta Scott (New York: Scribner's, 1908), 117.

Chapter 5 • "Their Slaves, If Any They Have, Are Hereby Declared Free Men"

1. Alexander H. Stephens, "Cornerstone Speech," March 21, 1861, www.battlefields.org/learn/primary-sources/cornerstone-speech.

2. James M. McPherson, *The Negro's Civil War* (1965; New York: Vintage, 1993), 27.

3. Charles H. Wesley, "The Employment of Negroes in the Confederate Army," *Journal of Negro History* 4 no. 3 (July 1919): 239–53, 247.

4. Wesley, 251.

5. See "Federal Troops Attacked by Armed Negroes," *Douglass' Monthly*, Feb. 1862, 598. Douglass reprinted a letter from a member of the Twentieth Indiana published in the *Indianapolis Journal* that claimed to record a battle in December 1861 near New Market Bridge in Newport News, Virginia, at which time seven hundred Black soldiers armed with muskets fired on General Mansfield's Twentieth New York Regiment, the German Rifles.

6. Although the debate over the participation of Black soldiers as armed combat-

ants for the Confederacy is not the subject of the chapter, the numbers of regular soldiers and even guerilla fighters was tiny—the attempts of freedmen in Virginia and Louisiana to join the Southern army at the beginning of the war and the Confederacy's eventual March 1865 law permitting Black enlistment, notwithstanding. For coverage of Black Confederate service during the war and the argument that the mythology of Black Confederate soldiers emerged in response to 1970s and 1980s popular historicist efforts to assert slavery as the prime cause of the Civil War and Black Union soldiers, see Kevin Levin, *Searching for Black Confederates: The Civil War's Most Persistent Myth* (Chapel Hill: University of North Carolina Press, 2019). Where research has been done on a state with a large enslaved population where significant warfare occurred, like Virginia, only three hundred people of African descent ever received pensions for Confederate war service. See Ervin L. Jordan Jr., *Black Confederates and Afro-Yankees in Civil War Virginia* (Charlottesville: University Press of Virginia, 1995), 198.

7. On John Noland's role among Quantrill's men, see Joseph M. Beilein Jr., *Bushwhackers: Guerila Warfare, Manhood, and the Household in Civil War Missouri* (Kent, OH: Kent State University Press, 2016), 49–51.

8. O. S. Barton, *Three Years with Quantrill: A True Story Told by His Scout John McCorkle* (New York: Buffalo Head Press, 1966), 92. Beilein believes that Noland was captured and never returned to Quantrill's force with information. See Beilein, *Bushwhackers*, 51.

9. Barton, 92.

10. Report of Colonel William Wood, Eleventh Missouri Cavalry, March 15, 1864, in *The War of the Rebellion: A Compilation of the Official Records of the Union and Confederate Armies*, ser. 1, vol. 34, pt. 1, "Operations in Louisiana and the Trans-Mississippi States and Territories, January 1–June 30, 1864," 154.

11. Michael K. Johnson, *Hoodoo Cowboys and Bronze Buckaroos: Conceptions of the African American West* (Jackson: University Press of Mississippi, 2014), 154–55. "Incident of the Buffalo Soldier" (dir. Ted Post) aired on Jan. 6, 1961, on CBS (*Rawhide*, season 3, episode 10); the episode featured Strode as the intractable Corporal Gabe Washington (www.imdb.com/title/tt0683045/?ref_=nm_flmg_act_59).

12. See Doug McAdams, *Political Process and the Development of Black Insurgency, 1930–1970* (Chicago: University of Chicago Press, 1982).

13. Despite the fact that the film featured a highly regarded Black actor in Jeffrey Wright and was not a clumsy intervention into the genre, not until it was rereleased on DVD in 2010 was its strong racial liberalist intervention a topic for the film's publicity.

14. Toni Morrison, "Talk of the Town: Comment," *New Yorker*, Oct. 5, 1998, 32.

15. Lester K. Spence, *Knocking the Hustle: Against the Neoliberal Turn in Black Politics* (Brooklyn, NY: Punctum, 2015), 33–39.

16. Simon Reid-Henry, *Empire of Democracy: The Remaking of the West since the Cold War* (New York: Simon and Schuster, 2019), 308.

17. Jeremy Scahill, *Blackwater: The Rise of the World's Most Powerful Mercenary Army* (New York: Nation Books, 2007), 376–77.

18. William Blum, *Killing Hope: U.S. Military and CIA Intervention since WWII* (Monroe, ME: Common Courage Press, 1995), 131.

19. Much of the original reporting was done by investigative journalist Seymour Hersh in the wake of 1974 CIA investigations for the overthrow of the Allende govern-

ment of Chile. Seymour M. Hersh, "Huge C.I.A. Operation Reported in U.S. against Antiwar Forces, Other Dissidents in Nixon Years," *New York Times*, Dec. 22, 1974, 1, 26, www.nytimes.com/1974/12/22/archives/huge-cia-operation-reported-in-u-s-against-antiwar-forces-other.html. For the increasing congressional oversight of the intelligence services in the 1970s (the Rockefeller Commission of 1975, the Church Committee of 1975, the Senate Select Committee on Intelligence of 1976, House Permanent Intelligence Committee of 1977, and the Foreign Intelligence Service Act of 1978) and the restriction of executive branch power (the Hughes-Ryan Act of 1974 and the Rockefeller Commission of 1975), see Brent Durbin, "Politicizing US Intelligence, 1973–1978," in *The CIA and the Politics of US Intelligence Reform* (Cambridge: Cambridge University Press, 2017), 130–60.

20. Durbin, "Politicizing US Intelligence," 214.

21. I do not have space for a full construction here, but the "conclusion" of the Reagan-Bush era culminates with two westerns that are actually much better understood as harbingers of the Clinton era: Kevin Costner's *Dances with Wolves* (1990) and Eastwood's *Unforgiven* (1992). These highly celebrated films revived the commercial feasibility and political import of the genre while simultaneously establishing new standards for historical accuracy in cinematic reproductions. The neoliberal achievement of the films was the *Bakke* decision logic that enabled them to embrace fully racial liberalist ideals of ethnic assimilation while utterly capturing the onscreen practices of nonwhite containment and erasure.

22. See, e.g., Nikhil Pal Singh, *Race and America's Long War* (Oakland: University of California Press, 2017). Citing the work of political theorist Naomi Murakawa, Singh finds that rather than encountering an upswing of crime in the 1960s that became racialized in the course of the decade, the nation-state instead responded to a racial problem with massive criminalization.

> The end of the 1960s marked the reactivation of an old reciprocity between acts of "legitimate" state violence and the "inhuman" worlds that become their object and rationale. In this mode of thought and social policy, violent state action and biopolitical security take precedence over any understanding of politics rooted in consensual democratic action—even if democratic consent is sought to ratify these agendas. . . . Violence becomes the figure and ground, the consequence and cause, of a categorically new social relation. . . .
>
> This may offer one approach to the vexing question of how racial differentiation persists and reconstitutes itself across profound changes in and to socio-legal, spatial, and racial disorders. . . . It can begin to explain the apparent contradiction between the simultaneous normalization of racial liberalism and intensification of racially inscribed domination. If racism is defined, following Ruth Wilson Gilmore, as state-sanctioned production of group-differentiated vulnerability to premature death, then acts of state violence take precedence over ideological discourses as differentiating practices. (132–33)

23. The political right wing of the academy—e.g., the philosopher Allan Bloom, *The Closing of the American Mind: How Higher Education Has Failed Democracy and Impoverished the Souls of Today's Students* (New York: Simon and Schuster, 1987); and the historian Niall Ferguson of the 2010s and 2020s, in books like *Civilization: The West*

and the Rest (New York: Penguin, 2011)—argue that "multiculturalism" and "identity politics," as signaled by something like the academic discipline of African American Studies, are communist and socialist attempts to splinter the economic consensus of unregulated corporate capital exchange markets hegemonically dominated by the European Economic Forum, which became the Global Economic Forum, the North Atlantic Treaty Organization, and the Bank of International Settlements.

24. "Audio Commentary: Frederick Elmes, A.S.C., Drew Kunin, and Mark Friedburg," *Ride with the Devil*, dir. Ang Lee (1999; Criterion Collection, 2010), DVD.

25. Susannah Radstone, "Cinema and Memory," in *Memory: Histories, Theories, Debates*, ed. Susannah Radstone and Bill Schwarz (New York: Fordham University Press, 2010), 330.

26. Woodrow Wilson, *A History of the American People: Volume Five* (New York: Harper, 1902), 49.

27. *The Birth of a Nation*, dir. D. W. Griffith (1915), intertitle, Internet Archive, https://archive.org/details/dw_griffith_birth_of_a_nation, 1:28:03.

28. US Census 1860, State of Missouri, Lafayette County, Table No. 1—Population by Age and Sex (274–83): 13,688 White; 36 Free Colored; 6,734 Enslaved, www2.census.gov/library/publications/decennial/1860/population/1860a-23.pdf.

29. Michael Fellman, *Inside War: The Guerilla Conflict in Missouri* (New York: Oxford University Press, 1990), 13–14.

30. Jennifer L. Morgan, "*Partus sequitur ventrem*: Law, Race, and Reproduction in Colonial Slavery," *Small Axe* 55 (March 2018): 1–17.

31. *Ride with the Devil* performed wretchedly with the audience that its producers and backers advertised it to, achieving a box-office success of less than $700,000. IMDB. https://www.imdb.com/title/tt0134154/characters/nm1722096?ref_=ttfc_fc_cl_t15

32. Daniel Woodrell, *Woe to Live On* (1987; New York: Pocket Books, 1998), 38.

33. Albert Boime, "Blacks in Shark Infested Waters: Visual Encodings of Racism in Copley and Homer," *Smithsonian Studies in American Art* 3, no. 1 (Winter 1989): 18–47, 36.

34. Fred Moten, *In the Break: The Aesthetics of the Black Radical Tradition* (Minneapolis: University of Minnesota Press, 2003), 26.

35. Woodrell, *Woe to Live On*, 38.

36. Boime, "Shark Infested Waters," 36.

37. Woodrell, *Woe to Live On*, 86.

38. Laws of the State of Missouri, Fourteenth General Assembly, Jefferson, Missouri, 1847, "Negroes and Mulattoes: An Act Respecting Slaves, Free Negroes, and Mulattoes," sec. 1, at 103.

39. Cited in Donald Gilmore, *Civil War on the Missouri-Kansas Border* (Gretna, LA: Pelican, 2006), 138.

40. Gilmore, 138–39.

41. There is a provocative echo in this moment of maternally invoked presence that enables subjective materiality in Fred Moten's musings on Hortense Spillers in Black commodity reproduction; Moten "attempt[s] to describe the material reproductivity of black performance and to claim for this reproductivity the status of an ontological condition." Moten, *In the Break*, 18.

42. Fellman, *Inside War*, 211, 301.

43. See Edward Leslie, *The Devil Knows How to Ride* (New York: Knopf, 1996), 194–95.

44. Woodrell, *Woe to Live On*, 167.

45. Leslie, *The Devil Knows How to Ride*, 202.

46. Richard Cordley, *A History of Lawrence Kansas from the First Settlement to the Close of the Rebellion* (Lawrence, KS: E. F. Caldwell, 1895), 206.

47. "The Lawrence Massacre: Atrocities That Make the Blood Run Cold," *New York Herald*, August 24, 1863, 8.

48. S. E., "The Tragedy of Lawrence: A Letter from a Citizen and Eye Witness," *Chicago Tribune*, August 29, 1863, 1.

49. Rev. Richard Cordley, *William Clarke Quantrill and the Civil War Raid on Lawrence, Kansas, August 21, 1863*, ed. Richard B. Sheridan (Lawrence: Kansas State Historical Society, 1999), 14.

50. S. E., "The Tragedy of Lawrence," 1.

51. Cordley, *A History*, 214.

52. Cordley, 225–26.

53. Woodrell, *Woe to Live On*, 168.

54. Harriet Beecher Stowe, *Uncle Tom's Cabin, or, Negro Life in America*, vol. 2 (Leipzig, 1852), 82.

55. The influential plays *The Dutchman* and *The Toilet*, written by Amiri Baraka, who was then known as Leroi Jones, both emphatically chart the pursuit of the white erotic object by the Black subject as the fulfillment of a death drive social psychology. An alert reading by Matthew Rebhorn suggests it records "the way the black man, if he is a black *man* indeed, yearns to be 'punished' by the agents of the white power structure" (797). Matthew Rebhorn, "Flaying Dutchman: Masochism, Minstrelsy, and the Gender Politics of Amiri Baraka's 'Dutchman,'" *Callaloo* 26, no. 3 (Summer 2003): 796–812.

56. Cordley, *A History*, 225.

57. Woodrell, *Woe to Live On*, 194.

58. David Harvey, *A Brief History of Neoliberalism* (Oxford: Oxford University Press, 2005), 2, 81–83.

59. Surprisingly, when the film was transferred to DVD for the Criterion Collection in 2010, the filmmaker decided to have an extended interview with Jeffrey Wright, arguably the finest Black Hollywood actor of his generation (he was born in 1965). Wright, of course, is not a historian, but because of the complexities of racial portraiture and his later stature as a serious actor against the other principals in the film, it was imagined somehow serious and uplifting to ask him a series of questions about his participation with the western genre. In other words, it was an attempt to deploy the Black actor to justify the choices and decisions of the filmmaker and to somehow stress the film as an attempt at civil rights. After the fact, the producers seemed to have requested the lone Black principal to advocate for the intellectual dimensions of the film, in itself a formidably racist convention, presuming that the white actors themselves were oblivious to or uninvolved in the same dynamic. Indeed, if the perspective of Lee and Schamus commenting on the film about eight or nine years later is any indication, they make an abject performance consciously innocent of race at crucial moments of the film.

Chapter 6 • "I Am That One in Ten Thousand"

1. Brian Knowlton, "Gore Camp Shaken as Voting Officials Abandon Recount in Biggest County of America's Acrimonious Election," *International Herald Tribune*, Nov. 23, 2000, 1, https://search-proquest-com.proxy1.library.jhu.edu/docview/319404536?accountid=11752 (by subscription).

2. For an account of widespread twenty-first-century voter suppression tactics, see Carol Anderson, *One Person, No Vote: How Voter Suppression Is Destroying Our Democracy* (New York: Bloomsbury, 2018).

3. John F. Harris, "Bush Rejects the Taliban Offer," *Washington Post*, Oct. 15, 2001.

4. Peter Jennings, "seen in command in a more vigorous way," 9/11—ABC News Live with Peter Jennings [Part 5]," video, 52:42, www.youtube.com/watch?v=AKoAnjCCiok; Peter Jennings, "Claire, where's Mr. Bush?," ABC News 9-11-2001 Live Coverage 12:00 p.m. E.T.–6:30 p.m. E.T., www.youtube.com/watch?v=Mm2DNn1Rw_o, 2:27:50."

5. Thomas E. Ricks, "Air Power to Team with Special Forces," *Washington Post*, Sept. 20, 2001, A1; Steven Mufson, "The Way Bush Sees the World," *Washington Post*, Feb. 17, 2002, B1; Dan Balz, "Bush Warns of Casualties of War; President Says Bin Laden Is Wanted 'Dead Or Alive,'" *Washington Post*, Sept. 18, 2001, A1.

6. Imputing the saying to Sheridan seems primarily symbolic. The phraseology shows up in a congressional debate on the "Indian Appropriations Bill" in 1868, spoken by James Cavanaugh of Montana, "I like an Indian better dead than living. I have never in my life seen a good Indian (and I have seen thousands) except when I have seen a dead Indian" (42). Wolfgang Mieder, "'The Only Good Indian Is a Dead Indian': History and Meaning of a Proverbial Stereotype," *Journal of American Folklore* 106, no. 419 (1993): 38–60.

7. Stephen W. Silliman, "The 'Old West' in the Middle East: U.S. Military Metaphors in Real and Imagined Indian Country," *American Anthropologist* 110, no. 2 (2008): 239–40.

8. Steve Coll, *Directorate S: The CIA and America's Secret Wars in Afghanistan and Pakistan* (New York: Penguin, 2018), 102.

9. Jeremy Scahill, *Blackwater: The Rise of the World's Most Powerful Mercenary Army* (New York: Nation Books, 2008), 189–92.

10. Macon Phillips, "President Barack Obama's Inaugural Address," Obama White House (blog), Jan. 21, 2009, https://obamawhitehouse.archives.gov/blog/2009/01/21/president-barack-obamas-inaugural-address.

11. President Barack Obama, "Remarks by the President at the Acceptance of the Nobel Peace Prize," Dec. 10, 2009, White House, Office of the Press Secretary, https://obamawhitehouse.archives.gov/the-press-office/remarks-president-acceptance-nobel-peace-prize.

12. See Samantha Power, *A Problem from Hell: America and the Age of Genocide* (New York: Basic Books, 2002).

13. "Barack Obama's Keynote Address at the 2004 Democratic National Convention," PBS News Hour, July 27, 2004, www.pbs.org/newshour/show/barack-obamas-keynote-address-at-the-2004-democratic-national-convention.

14. The subsequent 2016 election of Donald Trump, with gender and race again as lightning rods, showed that rather than the arrival of the end of anti-Blackness, some-

times confused with the "postracial" epoch, another condition had emerged—that is, the indistinguishability between the willingness to ignore racial identity and a willingness to ignore racist acts.

15. One survey, conducted among Louisiana Black voters, had 88 percent supporting Obama during the primary contest, and 64 percent of those supporting him because of his racial ancestry alone. Jas M. Sullivan and Melanie S. Johnson, "Race Is on My Mind: Explaining Black Voter's [sic] Political Attraction to Barack Obama," *Race, Gender & Class* 15, no. 3/4 (2008): 51–64, 58. An enduring feature of American news media coverage is to diminish or ignore the electoral power of the African American voting bloc. But in 2020, largely African Americans in South Carolina, led by Congressman Jim Clyburn, revived the moribund candidacy of Democratic presidential hopeful Joe Biden. Biden won the South Carolina 2020 Democratic primary with 60 percent of the vote after receiving Clyburn's endorsement. African Americans constitute 56 percent of the state's Democratic voters. Donna M. Owens, "Jim Clyburn Changed Everything for Joe Biden's Campaign," *Washington Post*, March 31, 2020.

16. In the immediate aftermath of the election the *Wall Street Journal* editorial page proposed that "we can put to rest the myth of racism as a barrier to achievement in this splendid country," and politicians like former New York City mayor Rudolph Giuliani claimed, "We've moved beyond . . . the whole idea of race and racial separation and unfairness." In Bettina L. Love and Brandelyn Tosolt, "Reality or Rhetoric? Barack Obama and Post-Racial America," *Race, Gender &Class* 17, no. 3–4 (2010): 20. See also Eduardo Bonilla-Silva and David Dietrich, "The Sweet Enchantment of Color-Blind Racism in Obamerica," *Annals of the American Academy of Political and Social Science* 634 (2011): 190–206, 191.

17. One of the most totalizing arguments delineating the incapacity for Africans to exist as human beings in the modern world, perpetually traded and accumulated in a cathedralized slavescape, and called into being as an antagonist in the modern world, is Frank B. Wilderson's *Red, White & Black: Cinema and the Structure of U.S. Antagonisms* (Durham, NC: Duke University Press, 2010). Wilderson proposes that the unspoken grammatical structure of political ethics and, indeed, western discourse always presents an irreconcilable and permanent antagonism in the feature of black subjectivity, "an ontological grammar, a structure of suffering" (5).

18. Lawrence D. Bobo et al., "The Real Record on Racial Attitudes," in *Social Trends in American Life: Findings from the General Social Survey since 1972*, ed. Peter V. Marsden (Princeton, NJ: Princeton University Press, 2012), 38–83, 65.

19. "Senator Barack Obama Delivers Remarks at Selma Voting Rights Commemoration," Political Transcript Wire, March 4, 2007; Barack Obama, *Dreams from My Father: A Story of Race and Inheritance* (New York: Three Rivers Press, 2004), 417–20; Cameron Duodu, "The British Tortured Obama's Grandfather," *New African*, Feb. 2009, 72–74.

20. Dana Milbank, "Obama Offers the Perfect Response to Confederate Flag Wavers," *Washington Post*, July 17, 2015,

21. Ryan Lizza, "The Consequentialist," *New Yorker*, May 2, 2011, 55.

22. "Django Unchained," IMDb, www.imdb.com/title/tt1853728/?ref_=nv_sr_srsg_0.

23. Henry Louis Gates Jr., "An Unfathomable Place," *Transition*, no. 112 (2013): 46–66; Lawrence D. Bobo, "Slavery on Film: Sanitized No More," *The Root*, Jan. 9, 2013, https://historynewsnetwork.org/article/150020. According to Bobo, "*Django [Un-*

chained] is the most cinematically and culturally important film dealing with race since Spike Lee's *Do the Right Thing*" (par. 2).

24. Contrary to an important reading by Adolph Reed Jr. about labor and work in the film, Candie, who appears also to be the proprietor of a functional cotton plantation, characterizes the shift from an agricultural and industrial mode of production to the form of speculative capital that exists currently, with spectacle entertainment as one of its nodes of accumulation. Adolph Reed Jr., "*Django Unchained*, or, *The Help*: How 'Cultural Politics' Is Worse Than No Politics at All, and Why," Nonsite.org, Feb. 25, 2013, https://nonsite.org/feature/django-unchained-or-the-help-how-cultural-politics-is-worse-than-no-politics-at-all-and-why. I am thinking of writers like Douglas Kellner, "Media Culture and the Triumph of the Spectacle," *Fast Capitalism* 1, no. 1 (2005): https://fastcapitalism.uta.edu/1_1/kellner.html.

25. Peter Suderman, "*Red Dead Redemption 2* Is True Art," *New York Times* (International Edition), Nov. 26, 2018.

26. Jean Baudrillard, *Simulacra and Simulation*, trans. Sheila Faria Glaser (Ann Arbor: University of Michigan Press, 1994), 1. For the argument that Obama's successful winning of the presidency was itself a moment of the precession of the simulacrum, delivering the symbolization of postracial America without changing the real conditions, see Max Paul Friedman, "Simulacrobama: The Mediated Election of 2008," *Journal of American Studies* 43, no. 2 (August 2009): 341–56.

27. Obama writes that the cabinet officers and military personnel moved from the designated seating of the Situation Room to a smaller conference room with a "live aerial view" and that he willingly took "a spot in a side chair" while brigadier general Bradd Webb manned the controls. Although the circumstance of this historic photograph is not unusual (the unplanned shift from one room to another), the fact that the photograph was released at all marks the influence of the larger system of representations under discussion in this book. Barack Obama, *A Promised Land* (New York: Crown, 2020), 694.

28. Frederick Douglass, *Narrative of the Life of Frederick Douglass*, in *The Classic Slave Narratives*, ed. Henry Louis Gates Jr. (New York: Mentor/Penguin, 1987), 266.

29. Donald E. Pease, "Negative Interpellations: From Oklahoma City to the Trilling-Matthiessen Transmission," *boundary 2* (Spring 1996): 1–33. Glossing Louis Althusser's term, Pease defines *interpellation* thus: "the State links individuals to a pervasive sense of representation, which is reproductive of imaginary relations to these individuals' real condition of existence . . . the quintessential point of transference whereon the Repressive State Apparatus (the army, the police, the courts, the prisons, the administration, etc.) disguises the violence whereby it conducts its functions through the secondary repression of that violence in the workings of the Ideological State Apparatuses (the family, the schools, the churches, the communications networks, the political system, the cultural apparatus, the labor unions, etc.)" (2–3).

30. The argument concerning the value of deadly force to overcome bondage has been a right-wing talking point among blacks since the early 1990s and the great wave of American militia cadres. See Abiola Sinclair, "Lenora Fulani, James Johnson Tap Militia Movement," *New York Amsterdam News*, June 10, 1995, 26. In 1995, when the federal government began the process of limiting access to assault weapons, in the midst of the Oklahoma City bombing, Waco, and Ruby Ridge, the circuit of public notoriety

included James Johnson of Ohio, who repeatedly said, "If our ancestors had been armed, they would not have been slaves."

31. Copeland and Struck point out that the romantics' (Coleridge et al.) distinction was actually a revival in favor of the earlier interpretation of Platonic allegories, symbol. See Rita Copeland and Peter T. Struck, introduction to *The Cambridge Companion to Allegory*, ed. Rita Copeland and Peter T. Struck (Cambridge: Cambridge University Press, 2010), 9.

32. Elda E. Tsou, "This Doesn't Mean What You'll Think": Native Speaker, Allegory, Race," *PMLA* 128, no. 3 (May 2013): 575–89, 583 (quoting Theresa Kelley, *Reinventing Allegory* [Cambridge: Cambridge University Press, 2010], 15); Maureen Quilligan, *The Language of Allegory: Defining the Genre* (Ithaca, NY: Cornell University Press, 1992).

33. Quoted in Leland de la Durantaye, "The Potential of Paradigms: *Homo Sacer: Sovereign Power and Bare Life*," in *Giorgio Agamben: A Critical Introduction* (Stanford, CA: Stanford University Press, 2009), 200–246, 212.

34. Vik Kanwar, "Review Essay: Giorgio Agamben, *State of Exception*," *International Journal of Constitutional Law* 4, no. 3 (July 2006): 580.

35. See Richard Allen, "Representation, Illusion, and the Cinema," *Cinema Journal* 32, no. 2 (1993): 21–48; Jean-Louis Baudry, "Ideological Effects of the Basic Cinematographic Apparatus," *Film Quarterly* 28, no. 2 (Winter 1974–75): 39–47. For Baudry, this jolt occurs as the result of "the disturbing effects which result during a projection from breakdowns in the recreation of movement, when the spectator is brought abruptly back to discontinuity—that is, to the body, to the technical apparatus which he had forgotten" (42).

36. Pioneered by Manning Marable in the 1970s, the logic of the slave world reproducing itself first under the segregationist regime between 1877 and 1968 and then around 1974 to the present as mass incarceration has been articulated again by people like the sociologist Loic Wacquant and legal scholar Michelle Alexander. The shortcomings to this *New Jim Crow* model, which tends to elide the contradictions among Black populations that ended segregation and made mass incarceration possible, are reflected on in James Foreman Jr., "Racial Critiques of Mass Incarceration: Beyond the New Jim Crow," *New York University Law Review* 87 (Feb. 26, 2012): 101–46. While audio existed of the killing of fifteen-year-old Martin by George Zimmerman, the video of three white vigilantes killing Ahmaud Arbery in Georgia in 2020 served as the rationale, along with the video killing of George Floyd in Minneapolis, for the global protest movement aligned roughly with Black Lives Matter, created in the wake of the 2014 killings of Michael Brown in Ferguson, Missouri, and Eric Garner in Staten Island, New York.

37. The *Scott* decision, quoted in James F. Simon, *Lincoln and Chief Justice Taney: Slavery, Secession, and the President's War Powers* (New York: Simon and Schuster, 2006), 122.

38. Simon, 122, and passim 122–26; Taney continued to explain the unpopular decision in his private writings. See Roger B. Taney, Diary, Box 9, Perine Family Papers, Maryland Historical Society, 4–5:

> The Supreme Court did not decide the case upon the ground that slavery of the Ancestor, afficsed [sic] a mark of inferiority upon the issue, which degraded them

below the rank of Citizens. It stated the enslaved condition of the whole negro race at the time when the Constitution was formed, as is well known historical fact, in order to show the meaning of the words used in that instrument. The argument in the opinion rests,—not upon the actual condition of the Ancestors of the plaintiff as to freedom or slavery, but is placed altogether on the condition of the race to which he belonged; and upon the opinion then entertained, by the white race universally in the civilized portions of Europe and in the Country, in relation to the powers and rights which they might justly and morally exercise over the African or Negro race."

39. Laws throughout the slave states prohibited firearm possession and firearm training from all the enslaved and often from free Blacks; Black capacity with the somewhat complicated and rapidly evolving firearms technology of the 1850s and 1860s broadly speaking was probably poor. Jake Roedel's line, "Well, a nigger with guns is a nervous thing to me," operates alongside this double front, that Blacks are a clandestine enemy and equally untrained and unreliable. At the Not Fucking Around Coalition rally to protest the death of an emergency medical technician named Breonna Taylor during a police raid on her home in Louisville, Kentucky, on July 25, 2020, the all-Black militia began to form, and during a "weapons-check," a round went off, injuring three people. Police did not file charges against the lawful assembly, but right-wing commentators quickly filled in the standing racist tropes about the unreliability of Blacks with guns.

40. Most Texas runaways headed to Mexico. See Kyle Ainsworth, "Advertising Maranda: Runaway Slaves in Texas, 1835–1865," in *Fugitive Slaves and Spaces of Freedom in North America*, ed. Damian Alan Pargas (Gainesville: University Press of Florida, 2018), 207. East of the Mississippi were multiple destinations, including the Virginia and North Carolina Dismal Swamp and St. Augustine and Pensacola, Florida. See Matthew J. Clavin, *Aiming for Pensacola: Fugitive Slaves on the Atlantic and Southern Frontiers* (Cambridge, MA: Harvard University Press, 2015); and Sylviane A. Diouf, *Slavery's Exiles: The Story of the American Maroons* (New York: New York University Press, 2014).

41. Researchers have noted 985 runaway notices in Texas papers between 1835 and 1865. See Ainsworth, "Advertising Maranda"; and Manisha Sinha, *The Slave's Cause: A History of Abolition* (New Haven, CT: Yale University Press, 2016), chap. 12, "Slave Resistance." For the far-reaching punishments of the enslaved in rebellion, see Douglas R. Egerton, *Gabriel's Rebellion: The Virginia Slave Conspiracies of 1800 and 1802* (Chapel Hill: University of North Carolina Press, 1993), 186–88; David F. Allmendinger Jr., *Nat Turner and the Rising in Southampton County* (Baltimore: Johns Hopkins University Press, 2014), 289–99; Winthrop Jordan, *Tumult and Silence at Second Creek: An Inquiry into a Civil War Slave Conspiracy* (Baton Rouge: Louisiana State Press, 1995); and Patrick Breen, *The Land Shall Be Deluged in Blood: A New History of the Nat Turner Revolt* (New York: Oxford University Press, 2015).

42. Philip Bobbitt, *The Shield of Achilles: War, Peace, and the Course of History* (New York: Knopf, 2002), 178–204. While Bobbitt glosses over the romantic component, he traces the evolution of the ethnic boundary state, with German unification as the key example, the welfare oriented "nation-state," where "governments existed to better the lot of national peoples" (179), distinguished from territorial states of the preceding epoch.

43. "B Movies" are typically identified on the basis of limited production value and small budgets, but the films also have a parallel history of developing new or breaking existing genre conventions, applying available elements of the detective story, the science fiction story, the horror grotesque story, and taboo violations into sex, violence, and race mixing. See Blair Davis, "Big B, Little B: A Case Study of Three Films," in *The Battle for the Bs: 1950s Hollywood and the Rebirth of Low-Budget Cinema* (New Brunswick, NJ: Rutgers University Press, 2012), 164–200. The internet databases and YouTube platform represent the capacity for a broad archive (and its recovery) of films and images that previously had been controlled by the commercial success or prestige of the film, the commercialization of internet and platform access notwithstanding.

44. See James Baldwin, "Everybody's Protest Novel," in *Notes of a Native Son* (1955; Boston: Beacon, 1984), 13–24; and Ralph Ellison, "The World and the Jug," in *Shadow and Act* (Random House: New York, 1964), 107–43.

45. The same reductionism operates in right-wing overtly totalitarian texts written in the spirit of Thomas Dixon Jr's *The Clansman* (1905) and continues to shape the tastes and ambitions of the white public and inspire them to action. Andrew McDonald's (the pen name of William Pierce) *The Turner Diaries* influenced US Army veteran Timothy McVeigh, who blew up a federal building in 1995, while more anaesthetized revisionist fantasies, like Harry Turtledove's novel *The Guns of the South*, circulate widely.

46. Jaap Kooijman, "Chapter 9. The Oprahfication of 9/11: September 11, the War in Iraq, and *The Oprah Winfrey Show*," in *Stories of Oprah*, ed. Tristan T. Cotten and Kimberly Springer (Jackson: University Press of Mississippi, 2010), 133.

47. Gates, "An Unfathomable Place," 52.

48. Wilderson, *Red, White & Black*, 38.

49. Stephen Ney, "Teleology and Secular Time in Armah and Ngũgĩ: Augustine, Manicheanism, and the African Novel," *Research in African Literatures* 48, no. 2 (2017): 40. See also Abdul Jan Mohammed, *Manichean Aesthetics: The Politics of Literature in Colonial Africa* (Amherst: University of Massachusetts Press, 1983); and Frantz Fanon, *The Wretched of the Earth* (New York: Grove, 1967): "Manicheanism ... generates such a powerful socio-political-ideological force field that neither colonial nor African literature is able to escape or transcend it" (93).

50. Tarantino is noteworthy for his agility in the portrait of Black and white interracial sexual desire, particularly his remarkable restraint from exploiting the sensational representations that B films and pornography notably deliver. For some ongoing observations about the fetish of Black male sexuality, see Ralph Ellison, "Beating That Boy," in *Shadow and Act* (New York: Random House, 1964), 100: "it is practically impossible for the white American to think of sex, of economics, his children or womenfolk, or of sweeping socio-political changes, without summoning into consciousness fear-flecked images of black men"; and Arthur Flannigan Saint-Aubin, "Testeria: The Diseases of Black Men in White Supremacist, Patriarchal Culture," *Callaloo* 17, no. 4 (Autumn 1994): 1057: "if popular culture can be said to speak at all, it talks incessantly about black sexuality and black male sexuality in particular."

51. Obama, *Dreams from My Father*, 115.

52. Tarantino's trope of Black rivalry is so successful it became incorporated into the most recent film chronicling the heroic slave experience, *Harriet* (2019), in the

form of a literal Black bogeyman, Bigger Long, played by *Django Unchained* bit player Omar Dorsey.

53. President Barack Obama, "Remarks by the President at Morehouse College Commencement Ceremony," May 19, 2013, Century Campus, Morehouse College, Atlanta, GA, Office of the Press Secretary, White House, https://obamawhitehouse.archives.gov/the-press-office/2013/05/19/remarks-President-Morehouse-College-Commencement-Ceremony.

54. Ta-Nehisi Coates, "How the Obama Administration Talks to Black America: Convenient Race Talk from a President Who Ought to Know Better," *The Atlantic*, May 20, 2013.

55. "No Excuse for Violence in Baltimore, Obama Says," NPR, Washington, DC, April 28, 2015, www.npr.org/2015/04/28/402856025/no-excuse-for-violence-in-baltimore-obama-says.

56. Daniel Desormeaux, lecture delivered at Sharp Street Methodist United Church, Baltimore, Dec. 2019. Richard S. Stowe, *Alexandre Dumas père* (Boston: G. K. Hall, 1976), 20. Stowe's account describes Dumas as "fair-skinned and blue-eyed, in contrast to his father, only his hair revealed that he was a quadroon."

57. Alexandre Dumas, *Georges* (1843), Project Gutenberg ebook; "Chapitre XIV—Philosophie négrière." I have used portions of Google translation here.

58. Gorgio Agamben, *The State of Exception*, trans. Kevin Attal (Chicago: University of Chicago Press, 2008), 11.

59. Siba Grovogui, "Looking Beyond Spring for a Season: An African Perspective on the World Order after the Arab Revolt," *Globalizations* 8, no. 5 (Oct. 2011): 567–72, 568.

Chapter 7 • *"Why Don't They Kill Us?"*

1. Michael Luo and Jeff Zeleny, "Reversing Stand, Obama Declines Public Financing," *New York Times*, June 20, 2008, A1.

2. *Young Guns* also included a scene with Fort Stanton's Black troops, occluded as were the Black troops in *The Outlaw Josey Wales*.

3. Eric Schmitt, David Sanger, and Charlie Savage, "Mining Terror Is Called Crucial to Fight Terror: Obama Sees Trade-Off," *New York Times*, June 8, 2013, A10.

4. *Oxford English Dictionary*, 3rd ed. (2010), s.v. "cowboy."

5. James Risen, *Pay Any Price: Greed, Power, and Endless War* (Boston: Houghton Mifflin Harcourt, 2014), xiii.

6. Mandy Smithberger and William Hartung, "Making Sense of the $1.25 Trillion National Security State Budget: A Dollar-by-Dollar Tour of the National Security State," Project on Government Oversight (May 7, 2019), www.pogo.org/analysis/2019/05/making-sense-of-the-1-25-trillion-national-security-state-budget/.

7. Barack Obama, "In His Own Words, Then and Now: Senator Barack Obama," *New York Times*, April 30, 2008, A17.

8. Quoted in Philip Bobbitt, *Terror and Consent: The Wars for the Twenty-First Century* (New York: Anchor, 2009), 433.

9. Bobbitt, 439.

10. Nikil Pal Singh, *Black Is a Country: Race and the Unfinished Struggle for Democracy* (Cambridge, MA: Harvard University Press, 2004), 44.

11. Booker T. Washington, *Up from Slavery: An Autobiography* (1901), in *Three Negro Classics* (New York: Avon, 1999), 35.

12. I depart from Homi Bhabha's reading of the mimicry by colonized populations of colonial cultural practices as a place for irony and mockery, menace and deformation, that discloses "the ambivalence of colonialist discourse and disrupts its authority" in two ways. First, the African enslaved is also a kidnapped prisoner, not being courted as a translator to assist with dominion abroad, and the performance of mimicry carries another series of affects, erasures, and displacements. Second, I posit a lower threshold for accomplishing the designs of the imperial regime, as well as a far larger range of mimic candidacies, particularly the failed or incomplete mimetic performances. See Homi Bhabha, "Of Mimicry and Man: The Ambivalence of Colonial Discourse," *October* 28 (Spring 1984): 125–33, 129.

13. Daniel Klaidman, *Kill or Capture: The War on Terror and the Soul of the American Presidency* (New York: Mariner, 2013), 118.

14. The film's release coincided with budding epigenetics arguments against racial social construct theory, based on the examination of DNA allele sequencing, that proposed not so much races but genetic clusters ("clinal groupings") would have some predictive capacity for fixed human traits like intelligence, disease susceptibility, and athleticism. See Jiannbin Lee Shiao, Thomas Bode, Amber Beyer, and Daniel Selvig, "The Genomic Challenge to the Social Construction of Race," *Sociological Theory* 30, no. 2 (June 2012): 67–88.

15. John White, "The Anchorless Postmodern Experience within an Ahistorical Filmic Space: *Django Unchained* (2012)," in *The Contemporary Western: An American Genre Post 9/11* (Edinburgh: Edinburgh University Press, 2019), 123.

16. William H. Rehnquist, Assistant Attorney General, March 9, 1971, "Hearings on Federal Data Banks, Computers, and the Bill of Rights," Senate Subcommittee on Constitutional Rights, 92nd Congress, 1st Session, Feb.–March 1971 (Washington, DC: US Government Printing Office, 1971), 602; see also Paul J. Scheips, *The Role of Federal Military Forces in Domestic Disorders* (Washington, DC: Center of Military History, 2012), 396–97.

17. US Department of Justice, "Memorandum for the Attorney General Re: Applicability of Federal Criminal Laws and the Constitution to Contemplated Lethal Operations against Shaykh Anwar al-Aulaqi," July 16, 2010, 33.

18. US Department of Justice, 40.

19. US Department of Justice, 41.

20. Jeff Houser, tribal chairman of the Fort Sill Apache (Geronimo, whose Native name was *Goyahkla*, is buried at Fort Sill), sought an apology from Obama and called the label applied to the operation "inappropriate." Jerry Wofford, "Tribe Resents Code Name 'Geronimo,'" *Tulsa News*, May 5, 2011, A3; Joe Singara, "Geronimo Name Deserves Respect," *East Brunswick (NJ) Home News Tribune*, May 11, 2001.

21. See Meghana V. Nayak and Christopher Malone, "American Orientalism and American Exceptionalism: A Critical Rethinking of US Hegemony," *International Studies Review* 11, no. 2 (June 2009): 257–60.

22. President Barack Obama, "Osama Bin Laden Dead," White House, Briefing Room Blog, May 2, 2011, https://obamawhitehouse.archives.gov/blog/2011/05/02/osama-bin-laden-dead.

23. Mark Mazzetti, Helene Cooper, and Peter Baker, "Behind the Hunt for Bin Laden: Clues Slowly Led to the Location of Qaeda Chief," *New York Times*, May 3, 2011, F3.

24. Peter Baker and Steven Lee Myers, "Bin Laden's Dramatic Demise," *International Herald Tribune*, May 3, 2011.

25. "Remarks by President Trump on the Death of ISIS Leader Abu Bakr al-Baghdadi," Oct. 27, 2019, www.trumpwhitehouse.gov/briefings-statements/remarks-president-trump-death-isis-leader-abu-bakr-al-baghdadi/.

26. Mazzetti, Cooper, and Baker, "Behind the Hunt for Bin Laden," F3.

27. Klaidman, *Kill or Capture*, 52.

28. Mazzetti, Cooper, and Baker, "Behind the Hunt for Bin Laden," F3; Phil Bronstein, "The Shooter," *Esquire*, March 2013, 132. In the 2013 *Esquire* article, written in response to the publication of Mark Owen's *No Easy Day: The Autobiography of a Navy Seal: The Firsthand Account of the Mission That Killed Osama bin Laden* (New York: Dutton, 2012), the alleged shooter described the event a year or so later as killing a man pushing his wife, Amal, forward with "a gun on the shelf right there, the short AK he's famous for": "I shot him, two time[s] in the forehead. Bap! Bap! The second time as he's going down. He crumpled onto [the] floor in front of his bed and I hit him again, Bap! . . . His forehead was gruesome. It was split open in the shape of a V."

29. Mark Landler and Helene Cooper, "New US Account in Bin Laden Raid: He Was Unarmed: Haste to Report to Public Led to Errors, in Confusion after Chaotic Scene," *New York Times*, May 4, 2011, A1.

30. Mark Landler and Mark Mazzetti, "Obama on Death Photo; New Raid Detail," *New York Times*, May 5, 2011, A1, A17.

31. Seymour M. Hersh, *The Killing of Osama bin Laden* (London: Verso, 2016), 25–51.

32. See Joseph B. Treaster, "Hit-and-Run Raids," *New York Times*, Dec. 23, 1989, 1.

33. Frank Bruni, "Bin Laden, Torture, and Hollywood," *New York Times*, Dec. 9, 2012, SR3; Matthew Kaminski, "The Weekend Interview with Mark Boal: The Art and Politics of 'Zero Dark Thirty,'" *Wall Street Journal*, Feb. 16, 2013, A11. While Boal "worked his sources" at the CIA, he found strong resistance from some Democratic senators, who wrote to Sony films criticizing the favorable portrait of torture in the film and lobbying against its release.

34. Craig Whitlock, "At War with the Truth: Confidential Documents Reveal U.S. Officials Failed to Tell the Truth about War in Afghanistan," *Washington Post*, Dec. 12, 2019, A14.

35. United Nations Security Council Resolution 1970 (2011), Feb. 26, 2011; United Nations Security Council Resolution 1973 (2011), March 17, 2011.

36. Horace Campbell, *Global NATO and the Catastrophic Failure in Libya* (New York: Monthly Review Press, 2013), 167–69.

37. Adrian Blomfield, "Assad Betrayed Gaddafi to Save His Syrian Regime," *Daily Telegraph* (London, England), Oct. 1, 2012, 14; Max Fisher, "Qaddafi Was Captured Alive—Who Killed Him?," *The Atlantic*, Oct. 21, 2011, www.theatlantic.com/international/archive/2011/10/qaddafi-was-captured-alive-who-killed-him/247113/.

38. Campbell, *Global NATO*, 211.

39. Parliament, United Kingdom, House of Commons, "Libya: Examination of Intervention and Collapse and UK's Future Policy Options" (2016), #38.

40. "Transcript: Clint Eastwood's Convention Remarks," National Public Radio, August 30, 2012; www.npr.org/2012/08/30/160358091/transcript-clint-eastwoods-convention-remarks.

41. David Kirkpatrick and Mona El-Naggar, "Qaddafi's Forces Strike with Fury as Unrest Grows," *New York Times*, Feb. 22, 2011, A10.

42. Joe Parkinson, "Libyans Protect Assets amid War," *Wall Street Journal*, June 11, 2011, B1.

43. Russell Gold, "Exxon Courts Libya for Oil Pacts; Scramble Is Seen over Huge Reserves; a Tent Meeting with Gadhafi," *Wall Street Journal*, March 8, 2007, A9.

44. Anthony Shadid, "Clashes in Libya Worsen as Army Crushes Dissent," *New York Times*, Feb. 19, 2011, A1.

45. Sheryl S. Gay and Brian M. Rosenthal, "White Nationalist Protest Leads to Deadly Violence," *New York Times*, August 13, 2017, A1.

46. Colin Campbell and Luke Broadwater, "'Safety and Security' Prompted Mayor: Pugh 'Enough Grandstanding,'" *Baltimore Sun*, August 17, 2017, A1; "The Last of the Segregation-Era Monuments Targeted for Removal by N.O. Mayor Mitch Landrieu Is Plucked from Its Spot Overlooking the City," *New Orleans Times-Picayune*, May 20, 2017, A01. Doug MacCash, "The Last Stand of Jeff Davis—With Protesters Looking On, Mid-City Statue Is Taken Down," *New Orleans Times-Picayune*, May 12, 2017, A01; Kevin Litten, "They'll All Fall Down—Last Barrier to Remove Confederate, White League Monuments Is Cleared," *New Orleans Times-Picayune*, March 10, 2017, A01.

47. Alan Blinder, "SEC Demands Mississippi Remove Confederate Emblem on State Flag," *New York Times*, June 19, 2020, B10; Rick Rojas, "Mississippi Lawmakers Vote to Retire State Flag Rooted in the Confederacy," *New York Times*, June 29, 2020, A19; Alan Blinder, "N.C.A.A. Pressures Mississippi on State Flag's Confederate Emblem," *New York Times*, June 20, 2020, B10.

48. Mary Elliott, "The 1619 Project," *New York Times*, August 18, 2019, MC4.

49. Andrew Cockburn, "No Joe! Joe Biden's Disastrous Legislative Legacy," *Harper's Magazine*, March 2019, 31.

50. Colin Freeman, "The Saharan Caravans of Cocaine That Fund al-Qaeda," *Sunday Telegraph*, Jan. 27, 2013.

Conclusion

1. Osama bin Laden and Ayman al-Zawahiri, a Saudi and an Egyptian, created Al Qaeda in specific response to the stationing of US troops in Saudi Arabia during the invasion of Kuwait and the Gulf War against Iraq with "Declaration of War against the Americans Occupying the Land of the Two Holy Places." For the argument that global jihadism is an underdog version of the "politics of control," see Faisal Devji, *Landscapes of the Jihad: Militancy, Morality, Modernity* (Ithaca, NY: Cornell University Press, 2005).

2. Robert Skidelsky avers in *Keynes: Return of the Master* that Western governments in general and the United States in particular readopted new Keynesian macroeconomic policies of vast government financial stimulus packages to reprime the economies in the midst of the Great Recession; however, my point here is that unlike the New Deal

programs of the Depression era in the United States, the financial stimulus packages of 2008 and 2020 were direct contributions made to private banks, who paid the money out in dividends and bonuses and unaccounted for spending. Even in the direct payments to out-of-work Americans in 2020, of the $3 trillion of federal money allocated, only 20 percent went directly to the unemployed, and virtually no money went into infrastructure. Joseph Stiglitz, "The Non-existent Hand," *London Review of Books* 32, no. 8 (April 2010): www.lrb.co.uk/the-paper/v32/n08/joseph-stiglitz/the-non-existent-hand.

3. Daniel T. Rodger, "Exceptionalism," in *Imagined Histories: American Historians Interpret the Past*, ed. Anthony Mohlo and Gordon S. Wood (Princeton, NJ: Princeton University Press, 1998), 25.

4. I am grateful to Jean-Marie Jackson for some recommendations here. See Mark Currie, "The Novel and the Moving Now," *NOVEL: A Forum on Fiction* 42, no. 2 (2009): 322. "It is easy to make the case that the contemporary world has enhanced a basic human faculty, the anticipation of retrospection, with an enormous technological apparatus of archiving machines, which contribute to a sense that the contemporary world increasingly experiences the present, both personally and collectively, as the object of a future memory."

5. James Baldwin, *The Fire Next Time* (1963; New York: Vintage, 1990), 100.

6. Mark Mazzetti, Nicholas Kulish, Christopher Drew, Serge F. Kovaleski, Sean D. Naylor, and John Ismay, "SEAL Team 6: A Secret History of Quiet Killings and Blurred Lines," *New York Times*, June 6, 2015, A1; Dave Philipps, "Navy SEAL Is Accused of Bloodthirsty Killings," *New York Times*, Nov. 16, 2018, A17.

7. Jack Healy, "Soldier Sentenced to Life without Parole for Killing 16 Afghans," *New York Times*, August 23, 2013, A1. The American soldiers like Michael Behenna and John Hatley sentenced to the Disciplinary Barracks at Ft. Leavenworth for murder tend to have been convicted of killing bound detainees. Robert Bales wandered alone into a village and slaughtered sixteen inhabitants.

8. R. H. Tawney, "Introduction," in Max Weber, *The Protestant Work Ethic and the Spirit of Capitalism* (1905; Lanham, MD: Start, 2012, ebook):"Labour is not merely an economic means; it is a spiritual end" (21).

9. The Coen brothers' film removes a relationship between Moss and a teenage hitchhiker that suggests statutory rape.

10. Cormac McCarthy, *No Country for Old Men* (New York: Vintage, 2005), 291, 56, 52.

INDEX

Page numbers in italics signify photographs.

affirmative action, 123–24, 167
Afghanistan, 176, 178, 224, 288n7
African Americans: in antebellum South, 96–97; *Birth of a Nation* depiction of, 29–30, 32, 132–33, 164; blackface portrayals of, 32, 133; changes to public image of, 13–14; criminalization of, 275n22; *Dirty Harry* depiction of, 14–18, 108, 117, 118–19; *Django Unchained* depiction of, 193–98, 201–2, 203–4, 210–16, 218–19, 283n52; Eastwood's imagining of, 77–78; explosion of on-screen characters, 86, 265–66n18; and fungibility, 54–55, 260n31; *The Good, the Bad and the Ugly* depiction of, 55–56, 61–63, 70–72, 73, 114; Great Migration of, 35; with guns, 196, 281n39; massacres of, 97–100, 161–66, 168, 177, 268n50; music of, 36–37; and Native Americans, 90–92, 97, 102, 112–13, 229, 267n32; Nixon's representation of, 13; *Outlaw Josey Wales* depiction of, 30, 96, 106–10, *111*, 113–17, 119, 133, 137, 236; police and racist killings of, 191, 225–26, 281n36; *Ride with the Devil* depiction of, 142–43, *145*–55, 161, 162–65, 166–70, *171*; stereotypical portraits of, 22–23, 25, 32, 35, 96, 163–64, 256n54. *See also* Black erasure; Black soldiers; racial liberalism; slavery
African American Studies, 136, 275–76n23
Agamben, Giorgio, 190, 206
Alamo, The (1960), 21, 23
Alexander, Michelle, 281n36
allegory, 189–90, 281n31

Alonso, Chelo, 52
Al Qaeda, 177–78, 179, 225, 234–35, 287n1
Althusser, Louis, 252n21
Altman, Robert, 84, 194
American Enterprise Institute, 176, 207
American Sniper (2014), 229, 230–37; conclusion of, 9; *Outlaw Josey Wales* allusion to, 221
Amistad (1997), 200
Anderson, William "Bloody Bill," 93–95, 115, 136, 161
Apocalypse Now (1979), 114, *115*
Arbery, Ahmaud, 281n36
Aristotle, 129
al-Awlaki, Anwar, 210, 217
Axelrod, David, 220

Bacon, Francis, 129
Baez, Joan, 34–35
al-Baghdadi, Abu Bakr, 219
Baker, Simon, 135, *145*, *166*
Bakke decision, 8, 123–24, 126, 136, 181
Baldwin, James, 199
Band, The, 6, 34, 38
Baraka, Amiri, 168, 277n55
Bardem, Javier, 237, 240, 241, *241*
Barron, David J., 217
Battle of Algiers, The (1966), 2, 43, 230, 263n4
Battle of Elderbush Gulch, The (1913), 31
Baudry, Jean-Louis, 281n35
Baxter Springs massacre, 131
Beckett, Katherine: *Making Crime Pay*, 14

Beguiled, The (1971), 105, 106, 108
Belafonte, Harry, 266n18
Bell, Kevin, 76
Berlant, Lauren, 252n20
Bhabha, Homi, 285n12
Biden, Joe, 279n15
Big Gundown, The (1966), 43, 44, 258n16
Billy the Kid, 69, 207
Bingham, George: *Field Order No. 11*, 106, *107*, 108, 142
bin Laden, Osama, 178, 210, 286n1; targeted killing of, 184, 218–22, 287n20
Bird (1988), 118
Birmingham, AL, 37
Birth of a Nation, The (1915), 2, 30, 36, 91, 103, 108, 172, 241; and Eastwood films, 6, 7, 15, 78, 230; historical sources for, 138; KKK depicted in, 31–32, 137; and Lost Cause narrative, 33; Native Americans depicted in, 31, 255n43; portrayal of Blacks in, 29–30, 32, 132–33, 164; racial liberalism of, 120; and *Ride with the Devil*, 135–36; textual insertions in, 172, *173*, 189; use of blackface in, 32, 133; and western film genre, 29–32, 237
Birth of a Nation, The (2016), 268n47
Black erasure, 6, 7, 35–36, 113, 249n3; in *Outlaw Josey Wales*, 30, 96, 106–10, 114–17, 137; in *Ride with the Devil*, 162–65, 171; in Western genre, 38–39
blackface, 32, 133
Black Power movement, 38
Black rivalry, 203–4, 282n52
Black Skin, White Masks (Fanon), 49
Black soldiers: in Civil War, 113, 273–74nn5–6; Confederate massacres of, 98–100, 161–66, 168; in fight against Native Americans, 90, 102, 112–13; *Outlaw Josey Wales* depiction of, 108, 109–10, 111, 113–17, 133, 236
Black violence, 210–16, 218–19
Blazing Saddles (1974), 105
Blight, David, 32; *Race and Reunion*, 113
Blight, Edward, 163
Bloom, Allan, 275n23
B movies, 199, 283n43
Boal, Mark, 286n33
Bobbitt, Philip, 209
Bobo, Lawrence, 183

Boime, Albert, 146
Bonilla-Silva, Eduardo, 125
Bonnie and Clyde (1967), 86
Bouaké, Côte d'Ivoire, 1–4
bounty hunters, 196–97, 258–59n20; in *Django Unchained*, 183, 187, 197, 211–12, 214, 216; in *The Good, the Bad and the Ugly*, 45–47, 52, 53, 55, 57, 69; in *Outlaw Josey Wales*, 87, 103, 117–18, 121
Bourdieu, Pierre, 264–65n10
Brandis, Jonathan, 137, *167*
Brecht, Bertolt, 109
Brennan, John, 220
Broderick, Matthew, 133
Broken Arrow (1950), 101
Brolin, Josh, 237
Bronco Billy (1980), 118
Bronson, Charles, 25, 44, 50, 66
Brown, Everett, 133
Brown, Jim, 25–26, 133, 265–66n18
Brown, Michael, 281n36
Brown, Sterling A., 256n54
Browne, Roscoe Lee, 28
Brown v. Topeka Board of Education, 123–24
Brynner, Yul, 50
Buck and the Preacher (1972), 133, 202, 266n18
Buffalo Bill and the Indians, or Sitting Bull's History Lesson (1976), 84
Buffalo Soldiers, 97, 112
Bullet for the General, A (1966), 43, 44, 258n16, 263n4
Bush, George H. W., 112
Bush, George W., 112, 181, 208, 219; as cowboy, 175, *177*; election of, 134, 176; use of US power abroad by, 134–35, 176–77, 209, 210, 218, 223, 230, 235
Butch Cassidy and the Sundance Kid (1969), 84, 194

Cameron, David, 223
Campbell, Horace, 224
Cantor, Eric, 207
capital regression, 38, 257n57
captivity narratives, 46, 187, 195–96, 258n17
Carpenter, Louis, 165
Carter, Asa (Forrest), 104–5, 111; *The Education of Little Tree*, 88, 91; *Gone to Texas*, 85, 88, 97,

99–100, 107, 127, 128, 171; Native American disguise by, 88–89, 90, 91
Casas, Antonio, 52
Cash, Johnny, 266n19
Cavanaugh, James, 277n6
Caviezel, James, 136
censorship, 22–23
Central Intelligence Agency (CIA), 135, 178, 217, 275n19
Chaffey, Don, 187
Chandler, Silas, 132
Charlie One-Eye (1973), 187
Chernus, Sonia, 88
Christianity, 74–75, 231
Chronic, The (Dr. Dre), 5
Church, Frank, 217
Cimino, Michael, 87, 88, 232
Civil Rights Acts, 78, 111, 123
civil rights movement, 7, 12, 37, 82, 83, 90, 123
Civil War, 23–24, 37, 64, 96; Ang Lee depiction of, 137–38, 165–66; Black troops fighting in, 113, 272nn5–6; and Confederate monuments, 225–26; *Django Unchained* depiction of, 189; Lawrence Massacre during, 98–99, 161–66, 168; *Outlaw Josey Wales* depiction of, 91–100; prison camps in, 71–72, 262n46; and slavery, 110, 157–59, 271n5; and Vietnam, 34–35, 80–82, 264n7; and westerns, 85
Clansman, The (Dixon), 29, 31–32, 91, 200, 283n45
Cleaver, Eldridge, 123
Clement, Archie, 137
Clinton, Bill, 134, 136, 181
Coates, Ta-Nehisi, 3
Cobb, Howell, 131
Coen, Joel and Ethan: *No Country for Old Men*, 9, 64, 237–44
Coffey, Wallace, 90
COINTELPRO (Counter Intelligence Program), 270n4
Cold War, 19; and "War on Terror," 227–28; and western genre, 18, 83–84, 96
Coleman, Gary, 183
Confederacy: Black inferiority as cornerstone of, 130–31; Black service for, 131, 132, 154, 274n6; Eastwood effort to redeem, 7–8, 38–40, 77, 137; Lost Cause mythology around, 32–33, 35, 38, 39, 40, 82, 131, 132–33, 164, 165; massacre of Black soldiers by, 98–100, 161–66, 168; requisition of convicts in, 269–70n7
Confederate monuments, 225–26
Confederate Veteran, 164
containment, 109, 270n4
Cooke, Sam: "Change Is Gonna Come," 36
Cooper, Bradley, 230, 232
Cooper, Gary, 25, 41, 138
Cooper, James Fenimore, 250n7; *The Last of the Mohicans*, 255n43
Copley, John Singleton: *Watson and the Shark*, 146, *147*, 148, 150, 171, 174
Coppola, Francis Ford, 114, *115*, 265n16
Corbin, Barry, 243
Corbucci, Sergio, 44, 45, 257n16; *Django*, 195–96, 198, 257n16; *The Great Silence*, 44, 86–87, 257n16
Cordley, Richard, 162–63
Corkin, Stanley, 38
Costner, Kevin, 237, 275n21; *Dances with Wolves*, 175, 227, 275n21
Côte d'Ivoire, 1–4
Cotton Comes to Harlem (1970), 13, 15, 265n18
Coulthard, Glen Sean, 261n32
Cowboys, The (1972), 28, 86
Crosby, Stills, and Nash, 36

Damiani, Damiano, 44, 45, 258n16
Dances with Wolves (1990), 175, 227, 275n21
Davis, Angela, 27, 123
Davis, Ossie, 15, 86
"Dead or Alive" language, 177, 278n6
Dee, Ruby, 202, 266n18
Deer Hunter, The (1975), 87, 232
Defiant Ones, The (1958), 24, 167, 235
Delacroix, Eugene: *The Sultan of Morocco and His Entourage*, 67
Deloria, Vine, 90, 267n32
DeMille, Cecil B., 36
Democratic Party, 39, 134
Dench, Ernest Alfred, 259n28
DiCaprio, Leonardo, 183, 184, 190
Dietrich, David, 125
Dirty Harry (1971), 14–17, 125, 137, 235; portrayal of Blacks in, 16, 108, 117, 118–19

Dirty Harry films, 11–12, 14–18; *Dirty Harry*, 14–17, 108, 117, 118–19, 125, 235; *The Gauntlet*, 14; *Magnum Force*, 14, 66; *Sudden Impact*, 12, 251n12

"Disco sucks," 37

Dixon, Thomas, Jr.: *The Clansman*, 29, 31–32, 91, 200, 283n45

Django (1966), 195–96, 198, 258n16

Django Unchained (2012), 8–9, 175–206, 207–26; artistic and commercial success of, 182, 183; Black rivalry in, 203–4, 283n52; Black violence and killing in, 210–16, 218–19; bounty hunters in, 183, 187, 197, 211–12, 214, 216; Civil War depiction in, 198; conclusion of, 205–6; Django-King Schultz relationship in, 184–87; gender incongruities in, 202–3; Manicheanism of, 198–201, 203, 204–5, 206, 210, 212–13; narrative gap in, 190–91; plot summary, 183; racial liberalism in, 197, 199, 236–37; reduction of Blacks in, 193–98, 201–2, 203; Skittles scene in, 189–90; slavery depiction in, 182, 186–87, 191–93; as western genre triumph, 182–88

Dorsey, Omar, *201*, 284n52

Douglass, Frederick, 131, 158, 186, 273n5

Dred Scott decision, 158–59, 160, 192, 193, 196–97, 281n38

drone killings, 216–18, 219, 224

Duck, You Sucker (1973), 45, 87, 263n4

Dumas, Alexander, 195, 203, 204–5, 206

D'Urville, Robert, 84

Eagleton, Terry, 119

Eastwood, Clint: and America's western narrative, 20, 39–40, 77, 119; Black erasure by, 6, 30, 96, 106–10, 114–17, 137; and Confederate mythology, 7–8, 38, 39, 40; description of *Outlaw Josey Wales* by, 79–80, 87; and Dirty Harry character, 14–18; dry humor of, 105; equivalency arguments of, 60–61, 229; ethically indefinable roles of, 45–46, 74, 87; *Fistful of Dollars* role of, 28, 45; gender politics of, 112; global recognition of, 5–6, 226; in *The Good, the Bad and the Ugly*, 8, 42, 47, 49–50, 52, 53–54, 55–57, 60–63, 66–70, 73, 74–76, 105, 192; and ideology, 19–20, 82–83, 252n20; "Make my day" line of, 11–12, 16–17, 251n12; and neoliberalism, 122, 124–25, 237, 275n21; New Right values of, 13, 83, 119–20; photos, *58, 67*; and racial liberalism, 17, 19, 119–20, 237; at Republican convention, 10–12, 224; rise of, 28–29, 42, 77; and Wayne, 86, 128; as western antihero, 42; western genre transformed by, 28–29, 38–40, 84–85, 128

Eastwood, Clint (films directed): *American Sniper*, 9, 229, 230–37; *Bird*, 118; *Bronco Billy*, 118; *Dirty Harry*, 14–17, 16, 108, 117, 118–19, 125, 137, 235; *The Eiger Sanction*, 86, 106–7; *The Gauntlet*, 14; *Gran Torino*, 105, 229–30, 250n20; *Heartbreak Ridge*, 118, 229; *High Plains Drifter*, 28, 29, 87; *Magnum Force*, 14, 86; *Play Misty for Me*, 86, 106; *Sudden Impact*, 12, 251n12; *Unforgiven*, 24–25, 116, 118, 133, 1667, 175, 193, 227, 275n21; *White Hunter, Black Heart*, 118. See also *Outlaw Josey Wales, The*

Easy Rider (1969), 87

Education of Little Tree, The (Carter), 88, 91

Ehrlichman, John, 13

Eichmann, Adolf, 72

Eiger Sanction, The (1975), 86, 106–7

Eisenhower, Dwight, 123

Elkins, Stanley, 200

Ellison, Ralph, 26, 96, 199, 254n25, 283n50

Enright, Ray, 94

Equal Protection Clause, 124

Esquire, 221, 286n28

Estevez, Emilio, 207

Ewing, Thomas, Jr., 106

Face to Face (1967), 258n16

Fanon, Frantz, 2–3, 49, 254n25, 283n49

Farrakhan, Louis, 209

Ferguson, Niall, 275n23

Fernandez-Kelley, Patricia, 38, 257n57

Field, Allyson, 254n25

Field Order No. 11 (Bingham), 106, *107*, 108, 142

Fistful of Dollars, A (1964), 28, 41, 45

Fitch, Edward P., 165

Flat Rock massacre, 102

Fleischer, Richard, 194, 202

Floyd, George, 281n36

Fonda, Henry, 44, 66, *66*

For a Few Dollars More (1965), 41, 45–47, 238; Eastwood role in, 28, 45–46, 52; Indio role in,

46, 47, 260n29; Monco-Indio duel in, 73–74; sexual violence in, 122
Ford, John, 7, 21, 85, 237; *Fort Apache*, 21, 229; *How the West Was Won*, 50; *The Man Who Shot Liberty Valance*, 21, 23, 24, 25, 86, 193; racial liberalism of, 21, 23–24, 119–20, 229, 232; *The Searchers*, 21, 22, 53, 86, 101, 128–29, 138, 193, 199, 240; *Sergeant Rutledge*, 23–24, 174; *Stagecoach*, 7, 21
Forrest, Nathan Bedford, 30, 69, 89, 99, 213
Fort Apache (1948), 21, 229
Fort Pillow massacre, 98, 99, 269n54
Foxx, Jamie: photos, *182, 185, 195, 215*; as *Django Unchained* star, 183, 184, 190
Franks, Tommy, 178
Frayling, Christopher, 49
Freeman, Morgan, 25, 133
Frémont, Charles, 158
Friedberg, Mark, 137–38
frontierism, 119–20
fungibility, 54–55, 57, 260n31
Fuqua, Antoine, 273n21

Gaddafi, Muammar, 210, 222–25
Gallagher, Eddie, 233
Gates, Henry Louis, Jr., 183, 194
Gauntlet, The (1977), 14
Gaye, Marvin: "Mercy, Mercy Me," 36
Gbagbo, Laurent, 3–4
George, Chief Dan, 91, 101, 102, *110*
Georges (Dumas), 205
Gibson, Mel, 268n47
Gish, Lillian, 32
Giuliani, Rudolph, 279n16
Glory (Zwick), 133, 139
"Go ahead, make my day" line, 11–12, 16–17, 251n12
Godfather, The (1972), 265n16
Godfather, The: Part II (1974), 265n16
Goethe, Johann Wolfgang von, 195, 198
Goldman, Martin, 198
Gondola, Didier, 247n2
Gone to Texas (Carter), 85, 88, 97, 99–100, 107, 127, 128, 171
Gone with the Wind (1939), 133, 138
Good, the Bad and the Ugly, The (1966), 2, 8, 41–78; Angel Eyes role in, 42, 48, 52–53, 62, 70–71, 73, 74; Black troops in, 70–72, 73, 114;
Blondie character in, 8, 42, 47, 49–50, 52, 53–54, 55–57, 60–63, 66–70, 73, 74–76, 105, 192; bounty hunters in, 45–47, 52, 53, 55, 57, 69; conclusion of, 73–77; and Confederate gold, 68–73; ethics of, 74, 210, 237; fungibility and race in, 50–58; Morricone's music for, 44, 51; Native American depictions in, 59–61, 66; *No Country for Old Men* homage to, 242; nonequivalent properties in, 58–63; racial collusion in, 55–56; racial designations in, 61–63; and slavery, 47–48, 57–59, 61, 62, 69, 72; summary of, 45–50; Tuco character in, 8, 47–48, 49–50, 51–52, 54, 55–57, 58–65, 66–70, 73, 74–77, 259n21, 260n29; and weapons technology, 63–66
Goodbye Africa (1966), 43, 257–58n8
Goodbye Uncle Tom (1971), 43, 257–58n8
Gottdiener, Mark, 252n21
Gran Torino (2007), 105, 229–30, 252n20
Great Silence, The (1968), 44, 86–87, 258n16
Green Berets, The (1968), 21, 26
Grenada, 222, 229
Griffith, D. W.: *The Battle of Elderbush Gulch*, 31; *The Massacre*, 30–31. See also *Birth of a Nation, The*
Guevara, Ché, 5
Guinier, Lani, 21
Guns of the South, The (Turtledove), 283n45

Hackman, Gene, 25
Hairston, Jester, 23
Haiti, 196
Hale, Dorothy, 50
Hang 'Em High (1968), 28
Harrelson, Woody, 239
Harriet (2019), 283n52
Harris, Joel Chandler, 163, 164, 186
Hartman, Saidiya, 54
Hateful Eight, The (2015), 26
Hawkes, Howard, 20
Heartbreak Ridge (1986), 118, 229
Heaven's Gate (1980), 87, 88
Helms, Levon, 6
Herder, Johann Gottfried, 198
Hersh, Seymour, 220, 275n19
Heston, Charlton, 15
High Noon (1952), 45, 51, 92
High Plains Drifter (1971), 28, 29, 87

Himes, Chester, 15
Hirst, Paul, 252n21
Hitler, Adolf, 200
Homeland Security Department, 208
Home of the Brave (1949), 23, 254n25
Hondo (1953), 22
Horne, Gerald, 266n27
Houphouët-Boigny, Félix, 3, 5
How the West Was Won (1962), 50

ideology, 19, 252n21
Immerman, Richard, 39
Inglorious Basterds (2009), 200
interpellation, 187, 280n29
interracial romance and sex, 26, 86, 152, 202, 266n19, 283n50
Intruder in the Dust (1949), 23
Iraq, 178, 218, 221, 223, 230–37
Italy, 42, 257n7

Jackie Brown (1997), 199
Jackson, Jesse, 184
Jackson, Michael, 5, 135
Jackson, Samuel L., 26, 184
Jacopetti, Gualtierro, 43
Jaji, Tsitsi, 249n2
James, Jesse and Frank, 69, 85, 93–94, 128, 146
Jameson, Fredric, 109, 138
Jayhawkers: in *Outlaw* Josey Wales, 91–92, 111–12, 125–26, 128; in *Ride with the Devil*, 141–44, 162
Jefferson, Thomas, 89–90, 195
Jennings, Peter, 176–77
Jesse James (1939), 85, 133
Johnson, Jack, 132
Johnson, Lyndon, 123, 175, 179
Jones, Tommy Lee, 237, 243
Jordan, Michael, 135
Joyce, James: *Ulysses*, 250n7
Judd, John, 141
Julien, Max, 86, 266n18

Kansas Raiders (1950), 94
Kaufman, Philip, 88
Kennan, George, 109, 270n4
Kennedy, John F., 179
Keynesianism, 228, 287n2

Khashoggi, Jamal, 216
King, Henry: *Jesse James*, 23
King, Martin Luther, Jr., 33–34, 36, 133, 179
King, Rodney, 135
Kinski, Klaus, 44, 87
Kissinger, Henry, 84
Klein, Melanie, 18
Kluge, Richard, 27
Konkle, Maureen, 60
Ku Klux Klan, 18, 30, 31, 33, 137, 213
Kurosawa, Akira, 45, 47

Ladd, Alan, 41
Laird v. Tatum, 217
Lane, Jim, 95
Lapoque, Pierre, 226
Lawrence massacre, 98–99, 161–66, 168
Lee, Ang, 8, 120, 133–34, 137; Civil War depiction by, 137–38; and Lost Cause mythology, 164, 165; racial liberalism of, 134, 135–37, 182, 183–84, 229, 236–37, 274n13. See also *Ride with the Devil*
Lee, William Henry, 148
Lee, William Mack, 132
Legend of Nigger Charley, The (1972), 198, 264n18
Leone, Sergio: *Duck, You Sucker*, 45, 87, 263n4; European skepticism of, 28–29; *A Fistful of Dollars*, 28, 41, 45; *Once upon a Time in the West*, 44, 64, 66, 73, 87, 150, 263n4; political message of, 41–42, 43–45, 80; *A Professional Gun*, 44; surface symbolism in, 49–50; and western genre, 41, 42–43, 44, 84. See also *For a Few Dollars More*; *Good, The Bad and the Ugly, The*
Leslie, Edward, 162; *The Devil Knows How to Ride*, 137
Libya, 210, 223–25
Lincoln (2012), 137
Lincoln, Abraham, 103, 158
literacy, 155–57
Little Big Man (1970), 84, 101
Locke, John, 59
Locke, Sondra, 92, 111, *111*
Logan, Ned, 116
Lost Boundaries (1949), 23
Lost Cause mythology, 32–33, 35, 131; and Ang Lee film, 164, 165; and *Birth of a Nation*, 33,

132–33; and Eastwood films, 38, 39, 40; and Vietnam, 39, 82
Lowndes, Joseph, 89, 107–8
Luce, Henry, 239
Lukács, Georg, 109
Lynch, Silas, 32
lynching, 74–75, 115

MacArthur, Douglas, 239
Magnificent Seven, The (1960), 50
Magnificent Seven, The (2016), 273n21
Magnum Force (1973), 14, 86
Maguire, Tobey, 137, *139, 140, 157, 161, 167, 172*; *Ride with the Devil* role of, 137, 144
Malcolm X, 209
Malory, Thomas: *Le Morte d'Arthur*, 92
Mandingo (1975), 194, 202
Manicheanism, 48–49, 198–201, 200, 283n49
Manifest Destiny, 18, 30, 45
Man Who Shot Liberty Valance, The (1962), 21, 23, 24, *25*, 86, 193
Marable, Manning, 281n36
Marcuse, Herbert, 123
Marley, Bob, 5
Marshall, John, 60
Martin, Trayvon, 191, 281n36
Massacre, The (1912), 30–31
Mbembe, Achille, 19
McCarthy, Cormac, 237, 238, 239
McCarthy, Kevin, 207
McCrea, Joel, 138
McDonald, Andrew, 283n45
McEachin, James, 26, 86
McGee, Vonetta, 86, 202, 266n18
McKinney, Bill, 92
McNaron, David, 79
McQueen, Steve, 50
Melamed, Jodi, 21, 119–20
Mercer, Mae, 105
Merrell, James, 255n43
Mexican Stand-Off, 74, 263n52
Mexico, 18–19, 43, 47–48, 196
Meyers, Jonathan Rhys, 136–37, *148*
militia movement, 189, 280n30
minstrelsy, 32, 35, 110, 271n6
Modleski, Tania, 252n20
Mohammed, Abdul Jan, 61–62
Mondo docudrama series, 43–44

Moral Majority, 14
More, Thomas: *Utopia*, 59
Morricone, Ennio, 44, 51, 87
Morrison, Toni, 26, 134
Moten, Fred, 149, 276n41
Muhammad, Elijah, 209
multiculturalism, 120, 276n23
Munier, Jacques, 205
Murphy, Audie, 94
My Lai massacre, 98, 177, 220, 238

NAACP (National Association for the Advancement of Colored People), 133
Nation of Islam, 209
Native Americans, 22, 24, 89–90, 97, 102; and African Americans, 90–92, 229, 267n32; and Asa Carter, 88–89, 90, 91, 104–5; Black troops fighting against, 90, 112–13; enslavement of, 55; erasure of, 50, 259–60n28; *For a Few Dollars More* depiction of, 46, 47; *The Good, the Bad and the Ugly* depiction of, 59–61, 66; Griffith depiction of, 31, 255n43; and landholding, 60; massacres of, 30–31, 120–21, 255n43; *No Country for Old Men* depiction of, 244; "only good Indian a dead Indian" language about, 177, 278n6; *Outlaw Josey Wales* depiction of, 100–106; rape of, 121–22; subjectivity of, 260–61n32
neoliberalism, 3–4, 123, 133, 134, 136; colorblind logic of, 145, 167, 232–33; and Eastwood films, 122, 124–25, 237, 275n21; false equivalencies in, 6; and Obama, 180, 232–33; and Tarantino, 120, 193–94, 197, 213
Nero, Franco, 195, 198
Newman, Paul, 84
New Testament, 33, 256n47
New York Times, 41
"Night They Drove Old Dixie Down, The," 6, 34–35, 36, 38
Nixon, Richard, 13, 14, 37–38, 39, 84, 232
Nkrumah, Kwame, 3, 210
No Country for Old Men (2007), 9, 64, 237–44; structure of, 237–38
No Country for Old Men (McCarthy), 237, 238, 239
Noland, John, 131, 132
Noriega, Manuel, 221, 222
Nyere, Julius, 210

Obama, Barack, 7, 8-9, 178-79, 189, 225; election of, 10, 180-81, 280n15; foreign policy of, 181-82; and Jeremiah Wright, 188, 204, 206, 208-9; and national security state, 208; and neoliberalism, 180, 232-33; and racial identity, 187-88, 203; and surveillance, 208; and targeted killings, 184, *185*, 209-10, 213, 218-22, 224, 280n27, 285n20
O'Brien, Edmond, *25*
Office of War Information board, 22-23
Once upon a Time in the West (1968), 44, 64, 66, 73, 87, 150, 263n4
100 Rifles (1968), 25-26, 133, 266n18
Outlaw Josey Wales, The (1976), 8, 79-105, 106-29; *American Sniper* allusion to, 221; Black erasure in, 30, 96, 106-10, 114-17, 119, 137; Black soldiers in, 108, 109-10, 111, 113-17, 133, 236; bounty hunters in, 87, 103, 117-18, 121; Civil War depicted in, 91-100; conclusion of, 128-29; Confederate and western mythology revived in, 7-8, 38, 40, 77, 128; and cultural shift, 82, 265n10; and *Dirty Harry*, 118; and *Django Unchained*, 215; Eastwood comments about, 79-80, 87; Eastwood decision to make, 7, 85, 86; expectoration in, 111, 150, 271n7; filming of, 87-88; historical evasions and distortions in, 97, 98; and historical realism, 138; ideological reduction in, 82-83; Jayhawkers in, 91-92, 111-12, 125-26, 128; Native American depictions in, 100-106; neoliberal ethics of, 124-27; New Right values in, 13, 119-20; and *No Country for Old Men*, 241, 242; praise for, 79; and *Ride with the Devil*, 174; slavery depicted in, 120-22; special effects in, 263n16; and Vietnam, 79-80, 128
Outtara, Alassane, 3

Panama, 221, 222
Parker, John, 130-31
Parker, Nate, 268n47
Parks, Gordon, Jr., 266n18
Pat Garrett and Billy the Kid (1973), 266n18
Patriot, The (2000), 268n47
Patriot Act, 19, 135, 208
Pease, Donald E., 280n29
Peckinpah, Sam, 210; *The Wild Bunch*, 78, 214, 232, 240, 265n16, 266n18
Penn, Arthur, 84, 86, 101

Perault, Charlemagne, 115
Perry, Felton, 86
Phillips, Kevin, 39
Phoenix Program, 134-35
Pinky (1949), 23
Play Misty for Me (1971), 86, 106
Poitier, Sidney, 24, 133, 166, 266n18
police dramas, 14, 251n10
police killings, 225-26
Pond, James, 99
Pontecorvo, Gilberto "Gillo," 43-44; *The Battle of Algiers*, 2, 43, 230, 263n4
Popwell, Albert, 16, 86, 117, 118
Pork Chop Hill (1959), 24
postmodernism, 189-90, 198-201
Powell, Colin, 112, 176, 177, 178
Powell, Louis F.: and Powell Manifesto, 83, 123-24, 126, 136, 176
Power, Tyrone, 23
Price, Sterling, 92
Professional Gun, A (1968), 44
Project for a New American Century, 235-36
Prosperi, Franco, 43
protest novels, 199
Pulp Fiction (1994), 199

Quade, John, 116
Quantrill, William Clarke, 94, 99, 131, 153, 165-66; and Lawrence Massacre, 161, 162

racial liberalism, 36, 275n22; of Ang Lee, 134, 135-37, 182, 183-84, 229, 236-37, 274n13; and Eastwood, 17, 19, 119-20, 237; of Ford, 21, 23-24, 119-20, 229, 232; of Griffith, 237; of Tarantino, 197, 199, 229, 236-37; as term, 21-22; of Wayne, 20-26, 27-28, 87, 119
Radstone, Susannah, 138
Railroad Bill, 115, 272n15
"Raindrops Keep Fallin' on My Head" (Thomas), 194
Raisin in the Sun, A (1960), 24
Rambo movies (Stallone), 229
Rancière, Jacques, 48-49
rape, 121-22, 160
Rawhide, 133
Rawls, John, 250n5
Reagan, Ronald, 7, 39, 124, 175, 179, 181, 208; "Make my day" invoked by, 12

"Real photo" picture postcards, 115, 272n15
Rebhorn, Matthew, 277n55
Reconstruction, 97–98, 138
Red River (1948), 20–21
"Redskins," 250n7
Reed, Adolph, Jr., 265n12, 280n24
Rehnquist, William H., 217
Republican Party, 39, 127, 134, 176; Eastwood speech at convention of, 10–12, 224
Reservoir Dogs (1992), 199
"reverse racism," 8, 126, 136
Rice, Condoleezza, 112, 135, 176
Rice, Susan, 181
Ride with the Devil (1999), 130–74; and *Birth of a Nation*, 135–36; Black erasure in, 162–65, 172; Black lead character in, 139; Black service depicted in, 145–55, 160, 166–70; Black-white relations in, 166–70; box-office failure of, 175; conclusion of, 170–74; and historical realism, 138; Jayhawkers in, 141–44, 162; Lawrence Massacre depicted in, 161–66, 168; North-South reconciliation theme of, 138–39; origin of, 133–34; race and literacy in, 155–60; racial liberalism of, 134, 135–37, 183–84, 236–37, 275n13; slavery depicted in, 139–41, 150, 154–55, 159–60
Ridley, John, 194
Rio Lobo (1970), 85
Risen, Jim (James), 38
Robertson, Robbie, 6
Robinson, Andrew, 137
Robinson, Cedric, 25
Rocky movies (Stallone), 229
Rogoff, Irit, 113
Romano, Sergio, 42
Romney, Mitt, 10, 208
"Rose of Alabama, The," 110, 271n6
Ross, Rick, 194
Rotibi, Sammi, 187, *201*, *202*
Roundtree, Richard, 187
Ruiz, Antonito, 52
Run, Man, Run (1968), 258n16
Ryan, Paul, 207–8

Saddam Hussein, 223
Salem, Peter, 148
Sand Creek massacre, 121
Sankara, Thomas, 5

Santa Fe Trail (1940), 85
Sarkozy, Nicolas, 223, 224
Savage, Archie, 25
Schamus, James, 133–34
Schindler's List (1993), 200
Searchers, The (1956), 21, 86, 101, 193, 199, 240; about, 22; Wayne role in, 53, 128–29, 138
September 11, 2001, attacks, 134, 176–77, 288
Sergeant Rutledge (1960), 23–24, 86, 133, 174
Sexton, Jared, 54, 261n32
Shaft (1971), 13, 265n18
Shakespeare, William: *The Tempest*, 57, 261n37
Shakur, Tupac, 194
Shaw, Robert Gould, 133
Sheen, Charlie, 207
Sheik, Sammy, 234
Shelby, Joseph, 47–48, 92, 169
Shelby, Thomas, 99
Sheridan, Philip, 177, 278n6
Shindler, Zeno, 103
Shuttlesworth, Fred, 217
Siebers, Tobin, 77
Siegel, Don, 15–16, 105
Silverheels, Jay, 260n28
Singh, Nikhil Pal, 275n22
Sissako, Abderrahmane, 249n2
skin color, 67, 126, 262n45
Skynyrd, Lynyrd: "Sweet Home Alabama," 37, 38
slavery: and armed slaves, 196, 281n39; and Civil War, 110, 157–59, 269n6; *Django Unchained* depiction of, 182, 186–87, 191–93; and Dred Scott decision, 158–59, 160, 192, 193, 196–97, 282n38; and *The Good, the Bad and the Ugly*, 47–48, 57–59, 61, 62, 69, 72; and literacy, 156–57; and Native Americans, 55; *Outlaw Josey Wales* depiction of, 120–22; *Ride with the Devil* depiction of, 139–41, 150, 154–55, 159–60; and slave narratives, 187, 195–96; and slave trade, 54–55, 269n59
Slotkin, Richard: *Gunfighter Nation*, 18, 128, 210
Smith, Shawn Michelle: *At the Edge of Sight*, 96
Snoop Dogg (Calvin Broadus), 5
Snowden, Frank M., Jr., 262n45
Solinas, Franco, 43, 87, 263n4
Sollima, Sergio, 45, 258n16
spaghetti westerns, 6, 42–43, 49, 249n2
Spielberg, Steven, 137, 199–200, 209

Stagecoach (1939), 7, 21
Stallone, Sylvester, 229
Steiger, Rod, 50
Stephens, Alexander H., 130
Sterling, Joseph Winston, 5
Stevens, Christopher, 224
Stewart, James, 24
St. Jacques, Raymond, 26
Stone, Harlan Fiske, 124
Stowe, Harriet Beecher, 164, 166
Strode, Woody, 7, 25, 26, 133, 150, 254n26; as Sergeant Rutledge, 23–24
Strong, Pauline Turner, 258n17
Sturges, John, 50
Sudden Impact (1983), 12, 251n12
Sul Te Wan, Madame, 32
Superfly (1972), 13, 265n18
Sutherland, Kiefer, 207

Taney, Roger B., 158, 192, 193, 281n38
Tarantino, Quentin, 8–9, 120; *The Hateful Eight*, 26; *Inglorious Basterds*, 200; *Jackie Brown*, 199; postmodernism of, 189–90, 198–201; *Pulp Fiction*, 199; and racial liberalism, 229; reduction of Blacks by, 193–98, 201–2, 203; *Reservoir Dogs*, 199. See also *Django Unchained*
targeted killings, 210, 216–25
Taylor, Charles Fletcher, 95
Tea Party, 10, 207
Tenet, George, 178
Theodore Roosevelt, 175
Thomas, B. J., 194
Thomas, Clarence, 112, 135
Thomasine and Bushrod (1974), 86, 202, 266n18
Three Musketeers, The (Dumas), 203, 204
Tiomkin, Dmitri, 51
Touré, Samory, 5
Towers, Constance, 24
Towers, Frank, 271n5
Trintignant, Jean-Louis, 87
True Grit (1969), 26, 86, 168
Trueman, Paula, *111*
Truman, Harry, 253n22
Trump, Donald, 134, 219, 225, 278n14
Turner, Frederick Jackson, 180–81
Turner Diaries, The (McDonald), 283n45
Turtledove, Harry, 283n45

Twain, Mark, 141, 166
12 Years a Slave (2013), 194, 249n3
Two Mules for Sister Sarah (1970), 19

Ulrich, Skeet, 135, *140*, 144
Uncle Remus, 163, 164–65, 186
Uncle Tom, 164, 166
Undefeated, The (1969), 26, 86
Unforgiven (1992), 24–25, 116, 118, 133, 166–67, 193, 275n21; success of, 175, 227
United States v. Carolene Products, 124
"Urban Contemporary" format, 37

Van Cleef, Lee: in *For a Few Dollars More*, 45–46; in *The Good, the Bad and the Ugly*, 42, 48, 52–53, 62, *70*, 70–71, 73, 74
Vera Cruz (1954), 25
Vernon, John, 95
Vietnam War, 27, 33–34, 39, 137, 232; and Civil War, 34–35, 80–82, 264n7; My Lai massacre during, 98, 177, 220, 238; and *Outlaw Josey Wales*, 79–80, 128; Phoenix Program in, 134–35
Virginian, The (Wister), 29, 138, 168
Volontè, Gian Maria, 46, 50, 260n29

Wacquant, Loïc, 17–18, 281n36
Wagner, Richard, 195, 198
Wallace, George, 37, 88, 89, 111
Wallach, Eli: background of, 50; in *The Good, the Bad and the Ugly*, 8, 47–48, 49–50, 51–52, 54, 55–57, 58–65, 66–70, 73, 74–77, 257n21, 258n29; photos of, *51*, *58*, *67*
Waltz, Christoph: *Django Unchained* role of, 183, 184, 190, 191; photos, *185*, *215*
Wanzo, Rebecca, 18
"War on Terror," 8, 19, 199, 210; and Cold War, 227–28
Washington, Booker T., 211
Washington, Denzel, 133
Washington, Kerry, 203
Washington Post, 221
Watergate, 37–38, 128
Watie, Stand, 102, 169
Watson and the Shark (Copley), 146, *147*, 148, 150, 170, 174
Wayne, John, 8, *25*, 86, 232, 253n22; *The Alamo* directed by, 21, 23; in *The Cowboys*, 28, 86;

cultural significance of, 20–21, 42; Eastwood compared to, 28, 29, 86, 128; *The Green Berets* directed by, 21, 26; in *Hondo*, 22; and racial liberalism, 20–26, 27–28, 87, 119; in *The Searchers*, 53, 128–29, 138; in *True Grit*, 26, 86, 168; *The Undefeated* directed by, 26, 86; and western genre, 21, 41, 237; white supremacist beliefs of, 26–27
Weaver, Vesla M., 105, 270n62
Weber, Max, 237
Welch, Raquel, 25–26
West, Cornel, 209
western film genre: and *Birth of a Nation*, 29–32, 237; Black erasure in, 38–39; civilizational clash in, 237; and Civil War, 85; and Cold War, 18, 83–84, 96; cultural significance of, 17–18, 42, 105, 177, 228–29; decline of by 1970s, 84, 85, 87; *Django Unchained* as triumph of, 182–88; Eastwood and transformation of, 28–29, 38–40, 84–85, 128; and imperial expansion, 9, 30, 45, 82, 175; and Leone, 41; and Lost Cause narrative, 32–34; racial liberalism in, 20–26, 27–28, 87, 119–20, 229, 232; revival of, 128, 175, 227; and slave narratives, 187; spaghetti westerns, 6, 42–43, 49, 249n2; and weapons technology, 85, 265n17; Zapata westerns, 42–43
White Hunter, Black Heart (1990), 118
Whitman, Ernest, 23, 133
Widmark, Richard, 23
Wild Bunch, The (1969), 78, 214, 232, 240, 265n16, 266n18

Wilderson, Frank, III, 54, 83, 200, 260n32, 261n34, 279n17
Willenberg, Samuel, 71
Williams, Bert, 32
Williamson, Fred, 198, 266n18
Wilson, Woodrow: *A History of the American People*, 138
Winfrey, Oprah, 199–200
Wister, Owen, 29, 138, 168
Wolfe, Patrick, 55
women's liberation movement, 83
Wonder, Stevie: "Living for the City," 36
Wood, Amy Louise, 270n15
Woodrell, Daniel: *Woe to Live On*, 134, 144, 162, 166, 170
Wright, Jeffrey: photos of, *145, 148, 149, 157, 161, 167, 172*; in *Ride with the Devil*, 8, 139, 144–55, 148; interview with, 277n59; on "redskins," 250n5
Wright, Jeremiah, 188, 204, 206, 208–9
Wynter, Sylvia, 261n37

Yellowstone, 237
Yojimbo (1961), 45, 47
Young, Neil, 37; "Southern Man," 36
Younger, Cole, 98, 268n50
Young Guns (1988), 207, 285n2

Zapata Westerns, 42–43
al-Zawahiri, Ayman, 219, 288n1
Zero Dark Thirty (2012), 221, 234, 286n33
Zwick, Edward, 133